SHAKESPEARE AND THE POWER OF PERFORMANCE

This study opens new horizons upon Shakespeare's achievement by redefining the relationship between language and performance in the early modern playhouse. In Shakespeare's theatre the growing authority of the text was not superimposed upon performance; rather, the Renaissance impulse of "mighty" eloquence accommodated – even collaborated with – a performance practice marked by self-sustained energies and appeals. Shakespeare foregrounds this power of performance in its boldest bodily delivery through his use of Vice descendants, clowns and fools, gendered disguise, and "secretly open" modes of role-playing. Throughout his career, Shakespeare's plays were therefore driven by a dynamic relationship between language and show. Meeting the challenge of Performance Studies, the authors effectively bridge the gulf between stage-centered and text-centered approaches. This book rewrites the history of a formative phase in Shakespeare's contribution to world theatre.

ROBERT WEIMANN is Professor Emeritus, Department of Drama, at the University of California, Irvine. His publications in English include *Shakespeare and the Popular Tradition in the Theater* (1978), *Authority and Representation in Early Modern Discourse* (1996), and *Author's Pen and Actor's Voice: Playing and Writing in Shakespeare's Theatre* (Cambridge, 2000).

DOUGLAS BRUSTER is Professor of English at the University of Texas at Austin. His books include *Drama and the Market in the Age of Shakespeare* (Cambridge, 1992), *Quoting Shakespeare* (2000), and *Prologues to Shakespeare's Theatre* (with Robert Weimann, 2004).

SHAKESPEARE AND THE POWER OF PERFORMANCE

Stage and Page in the Elizabethan Theatre

ROBERT WEIMANN

AND

DOUGLAS BRUSTER

CAMBRIDGE
UNIVERSITY PRESS

CAMBRIDGE UNIVERSITY PRESS
Cambridge, New York, Melbourne, Madrid, Cape Town, Singapore,
São Paulo, Delhi, Dubai, Tokyo, Mexico City

Cambridge University Press
The Edinburgh Building, Cambridge CB2 8RU, UK

Published in the United States of America by Cambridge University Press, New York

www.cambridge.org
Information on this title: www.cambridge.org/9780521182836

First published 2008
First paperback edition 2010

A catalogue record for this publication is available from the British Library

ISBN 978-0-521-89532-3 Hardback
ISBN 978-0-521-18283-6 Paperback

This book is dedicated to two younger colleagues
David Hillman and William West
who gave their best at earlier stages, and to our good friend
Friederike Riese
whose very special support helped complete the project.

Contents

Acknowledgments

Robert Weimann would like to acknowledge his first and largest debt to his co-author, without whose contribution this study would not have been possible. My gratitude to him is scarcely lessened by an overlapping indebtedness to two younger colleagues and friends whose names – given in the dedication – are connected with those chapters that were conceived, drafted, and mostly published in versions reaching back to the 1990s. Altogether and throughout that decade, my thinking and writing much benefited from stimulating discussions with my students in the English and Drama departments of the University of California, Irvine. In fact, this study has been in the making for so long because it concludes a larger project, with several preparatory book-length studies such as those on authority and representation in Reformation discourse and Renaissance fiction (1996), on the sociology and dramaturgy of the Elizabethan theatre (2000), and, with Douglas Bruster, about prologues on early modern stages (2004). Since these studies in their turn were preceded by even earlier work in German reaching back as far as 1983, it is impossible for me in retrospect to do more than thank all those who directly or indirectly helped and contributed to the evolution (which is also a devolution) of the project at large. If the present volume may be granted an exception, I would gratefully acknowledge that several of its chapters were read and most helpfully commented on by colleagues and friends, among them Catherine Belsey (Cambridge), William Dodd (Siena), Nora Johnson (Swarthmore College), Ludwig Pfeiffer (Siegen), William West (Northwestern) and Wolfgang Wicht (Potsdam). In no way responsible for what flaws remain, they graciously gave their acumen and perspicacity to improve my contribution to the present study and thereby foster a better book. Last but not least I owe a very special, personal gratitude to family members of the younger generation, particularly Jochen and Robbi, and to the unfailing support and forbearance of Maja, my wife. Finally, I was blessed to be able to rely on the invaluable, ever generous help of a good friend and former colleague, whose name is gratefully inscribed in the dedication.

At the same time, I wish to thank editors and journals for permission to incorporate and/or adapt previously published texts and materials. Our opening on the moral play was in its original version published under "'Moralize Two Meanings' in One Play: Divided Authority on the Morality Stage," *Mediaevalia* 18 (1995), 427–50. Considerable parts of the present study of *Richard III* were first published as "Performance-Game and Representation in *Richard III*," in Edward Pechter, ed., *Textual and Theatrical Shakespeare: Questions of Evidence* (University of Iowa Press, 1996), 66–85. The essay on *King John* was (in a somewhat different form) first printed under the title "Mingling Vice and 'Worthiness' in *King John*," in *Shakespeare Studies* 27 (1999), 109–33. The argument and some important material in the present study of cross-dressing and disguise (chapter 6) first appeared as "Textual Authority and Performative Agency: The Uses of Disguise in Shakespeare's Theater," *New Literary History* 25 (1994), 789–808. While the "secretly open" mode of personation (chapter 7) was (in radically different form) first presented at the SAA Convention in Miami (2001), it benefited considerably from the more focused treatment contained in a recent contribution to the collection *Shakespeare and Character*, edited by Paul Yachnin and Jessica Slights (Palgrave, 2008). This contribution was as much adapted as was, in chapter 9, the much earlier essay on "Society and the Individual in Shakespeare's Conception of Character," published in *Shakespeare Survey* 34 (1981), 23–31. Finally, the socio-semiotic reading of the conflict in *King Lear*, though here crucially integrated in the much-augmented context of chapter 10, goes back to a German-language contribution to the Festschrift for B.A. Sørensen, "Autorität der Zeichen versus Zeichen der Autorität: Status und Repräsentationsproblematik in *King Lear*," in *Orbis Litterarum* 42 (1987), 221–35.

Douglas Bruster would like to express sincere gratitude to his wife, Elizabeth Scala, and their two daughters, Madeleine and Claire, for patiently supporting his scholarly endeavors. Thanks go as well to two extremely encouraging Department Chairs, James D. Garrison and Elizabeth Cullingford, for helping make this research and writing possible, and to Phoebe Francis, for her help with the Index. A final acknowledgment must go to this volume's brilliant and generous co-author, without whom this book – and so much of our knowledge concerning the agency of early modern performance – would not exist.

In conclusion, both authors cannot do better than join words and sentiments in appreciation of their medium, Cambridge University Press, and all those whose performance made this book possible. In particular, there is good reason to be grateful to both our distinguished general editor, Sarah Stanton, sensitive and supportive throughout, and Rebecca Jones, our gracious editor who had so much insight, understanding, and more.

Introduction

This book concludes a larger project on authority and representation in early modern discourse and theatre. Having previously discussed the conjuncture of playing and writing on Elizabethan stages, and in prologues delivered on them, we now shift focus to Shakespeare's plays themselves. Here we approach them through the confederation and dissension of the two media, dramatic language and performing bodies. Just as language in Shakespeare's theatre was used in myriad ways, so also did performing assume and extend multiple modes, styles, and functions – especially in the apparently impromptu range of its interaction with language. Still, there remained a gap even in the interdependence of the two media. Drawing on two different forms of cultural production, the plays in performance sought to overcome and yet allude to and use the rift between them. Shakespeare's achievement cannot be separated from his astonishing readiness not only to acknowledge but also to play with the difference between the meaning of words and the practice of their delivery. The gap between language and the body afforded the playwright a new reach, cogency, and mobility in the uses of embodied signs.

This gap and the ways to accommodate and exploit it were marked by highly particular circumstances. The latter arose as the late Renaissance culture of literacy and the new technology of print began to affect and to intermingle with traditional ways of delivering oral or nonverbal feats and skills. As far as they had entered the marketplace and were entrenched in commercially run theatres, these practices showed considerable resilience. They continued to assert their own rights of display even after theatrical shows began to be indebted to new uses of dramatic language. At this juncture, the theatre – against all kinds of learned precept and pious prejudice – could lay claim to a certain "sovereign grace" (*The Comedy of Errors*, 3.2.160).[1] The stage flourished at the very point where two socially and culturally different practices came to be conjoined in a workable alliance. It was precisely the joint transaction, the joint appeal of the two

1

different media, that allowed for a situation in which the authority of the text could be either affirmed or intercepted by the rights of performance. Either way, the alliance between the two cultural practices derived from and sanctioned a purely pragmatic, unwritten contract of mutual entertainment (in both senses of the word) between the institution and its audience. In the sixteenth century this bifold mode of cultural production, even when formally hedged by courtly interest, patronage, or censorship, was unprecedented, its workings largely untried. Yet this theatre was powerful enough *in its own right* to speak to thousands. It was free to show unknown locations and unexplored circumstances without the slightest reluctance to display, rather than conceal, the work of its performing tools and agents.

The combined potency of diverging arts and media was not, and cannot be grasped as, a purely technical or formal matter. The hybrid mode of communication, now drawing on both expanding literacy and print, proved of the highest consequence, especially in its accessibility for a considerable mass of people. The Chorus to *Henry V* went out of his way to offer his service to both those who knew and "those who have not read the story" (*Henry V*, 5.0.1). The conditions under which "the story" and the "unworthy scaffold" (Pro. 10) came together were largely self-fashioned by those who played there and in turn fashioned "the scene" (Pro. 4; 20–34, 42; 3.0.1; 4.0.48) by presenting their roles on it. Comprising "our performance" (3.0.35), "our stage" (Epi. 13) and the "brightest heaven of invention" (Pro. 2) and representation, the conjunctural work of the theatre was very much a matter of time and place. Historically, this conjuncture was shaped by: (1) the economic needs and opportunities of a commercially based cultural institution; (2) the social and historical momentum of a situation marked by rapid change, transition, and "mingle-mangle"; (3) and, following the Reformation and the growing impact of the printing press, an increasingly practiced literacy. Finally, these new forces of economic, social, cultural, and religious change met with, and were affected by, (4) still strong premodern culture. Even while this traditional component was being widely exposed to an expanding market for cultural goods, some of its habitual forms and functions continued to be taken for granted on London's public stages.

In these circumstances, the "swelling," double-coded "scene" was spacious enough for a quickening moment of interactive give-and-take not only between material bodies and imaginary uses of language but also, in the audience, among sensory faculties – in particular "th' attest of eyes and ears" (*Troilus and Cressida*, 5.2.122). The "heaven of invention" could project a "story" of the past over its enactment in the present, right there. Between the representation of something past or absent and its delivery in the present,

Shakespeare's theatre offered astonishing links and yet revealed incalculable gaps in time and space. In the Prologue cited, the distance between who and what was representing the play and who and what was represented in it was foregrounded rather than concealed. While the former was a matter of "our performance" here and now, the latter, as outlined in "story" and history, was altogether different in its lofty and purely imaginary shape.

In our context, it is crucial to understand how the theatre used the gap between "So great an object" (Pro. 11) of representation and such mode of its presentation "as may unworthiness define" (4.0.46). The spatial extension of this "distance" clearly had important social and temporal dimensions. Pulsating at the heart of relations between page and stage, the mediation between then and now, there and here, high and low required a dramaturgy largely unknown to the all-encompassing sense of presence in the mystery cycles and even in some of the older morality plays. For Shakespeare, who both performed and wrote, it must have been a supreme challenge to scan and interrelate these different, newly disposable spaces. As his Prologue phrased it, the playwright was prepared to work with the use as well as with "Th' abuse of distance" when it came to "force a play" (2.0.32).

THE ARGUMENT

The articulation of three general goals may help signpost the direction of this project. These include, first, a redefining of early modern performances as a miscellaneous assemblage of contingent, formally and culturally variegated practices. If on Elizabethan stages relations between the practice of perform-ance and the authority of writing were as yet rather unsettled, the most consequential reason was this extraordinary diversification among perform-ance practices. The latter were divided at the very point at which they were and were not consonant with the demands of verbally prescribed utterances. While this difference is potentially given in any performed instance of language use, it was especially pronounced on early modern stages.

As this first aspect suggests, we propose to address stage/page relations through the issue of difference – that is, from how in the theatre the specific form and force of each medium defines, and is defined by, the other. The same principle informs our second goal: redefining an approach to the symbolic order of representation. The act of performance is primarily, though not exclusively, anchored in bodily practice. Representation, in particular its world-picturing function, is primarily, though again not exclusively, indebted to scriptural uses of language. It is in and through written discourses that a remote, absent, complex world can be represented. Apparently disconnected circumstances, hidden motivations, anachronistic sequences, rugged spaces, abstruse happenings – all these can be captured in images of dramatic speech and action.

The achieved relationship of performance and text in Shakespeare's theatre has usually been approached from ontological premises. While indebted to more recent anthropological and performance studies, we seek to shift emphasis to sociological bearings and a focus on socio-cultural history. Far from wishing to foreground large or overriding narratives, then, our third aim is to contextualize the relationship of performance and text *in concreto*, that is, as a changeful ensemble, in Shakespeare's theatre, of socially and formally different cultural productions. Along these lines, our approach will provide us with important clues to the history and genealogy of Shakespeare's own works in the theatre, unlocking hidden connections, rarely perceived trends and formations in the dramatist's oeuvre. As several significant configurations emerge from his plays, these shed new light on what is distinctly his own peculiar position in the history of the Elizabethan stage. As goes without saying, neither the historical dimension in the stage/ page relationship nor the uses of performing and writing can be exhaustively traced here throughout the dramatist's entire oeuvre.

As the arrangement of our material suggests, we have focused on the most prominent lines of interaction between the powers of performance and the shaping faculties of dramatic composition. The encounter between the two has a genealogy that attests to a premodern impulse in the "contrariety" that Philip Sidney had associated with "our comedians." Their contrarious impulse is documented in our first chapter, a reading of *The Tide Tarrieth No Man*. This mid-Elizabethan moral play is teeming with performing energies, with the scheming, cunning, diversionary élan of showmanship. As an unbound force of indifference and self-willed inversion, Courage the Vice practices mischief, moving within the allegorical order of transcendent morality the better to defy this very order.

The project of his evil fortitude is followed up in the next two chapters by Shakespeare's highly varied adaptations of a Vice protagonist in, respectively, Richard Gloucester (chapter 2) and Philip Faulconbridge (chapter 3) – both, incidentally, as intrepid as the undaunted Iago and Edmund. We have chosen *Richard III* and *King John* because the royal villain in the former play can, even while publicly exhibiting the nasty arts of his counterfeiting, profit from the semi-tragic compensation of his disability. Alternatively, the witty, quipping, conniving Bastard in the early scenes of *King John* is himself "amaz'd," and fears "I . . . lose my way" when the "vast confusion" (*King John*, 4.3.140, 152) happens to be already there, in the surrounding world of the play itself.

Because further inversion of this perverted state of affairs is self-forbidding, contrariety itself is inflected by a given, circumstantial politics of commodity in the tugging and the scrambling for "The unowed interest of proud swelling state" (147). In both plays, then, a thick performative is jostling side by side with representations of personal and sometimes national plight.

On an entirely different plane, these engagements between textual direction and performative prowess also inspired a doubly encoded clowning. As we suggest in chapters 4 and 5, this bifold structure in the agency of clowning tends to preclude clear and fixed lines between the live actor and his imaginary role. The line between them is liable to swerve in directions marked by either author's pen or actor's voice. There results an extremely volatile dramaturgy by which the representational can be slanted toward presentation, and the presentational toward some kind of meaningful representation.

This dramaturgy provides a largely unacknowledged clue to the fashioning of imaginary personhood on Shakespeare's stage. Even while the culture of print and literacy helped produce configurations marked by a more complex sense of identity, Shakespeare twirled agency itself around for scrutiny in the mirror of character. As we show in chapter 6, the strongest and most consequential attestation of the actor's presence comes in the image of Shakespeare's cross-dressed heroines. The alluring presentation of gendered disguise was one way of accrediting the skills of playing itself. The boy actor gracefully representing a young woman presenting herself as page or trusted servant steered the figuration back to what in life embodied a double-gendered representation.

But Shakespeare the actor also accredited the zest and gusto, the sheer energy in the presentational *gestus* of his fellow players elsewhere, especially in the twinkling eye of counterfeiting role delivery (chapter 7). We call this practice personation, the "secretly open" exposure of the actor behind the dramatic role and its persona. Personation privileges the *making of* the mask, the *skill* and the *show* of playing the role of another. As a presentational practice, it falls back on the dramaturgy of "A juggling trick – to be secretly open." Thersites's phrase here (*Troilus and Cressida*, 5.2.24), in its use of a "juggling trick," betrays predramatic origins, even physical skills in a marketplace type of entertainment. In the drama of this personation, the personator is not entirely lost in the personated. Rather, the dramatist is prepared to foreground and thereby to honour the actor's presence in the delivery of the text. So the text makes allowance for a representational practice that suggests vital links with, and inspirations from, a wider world of performance action and behavior. Here, as elsewhere, this practice reveals what bifold authority could also be about: an acknowledgment of mutually concerted action.

The double-encoded force of personation in Shakespeare's theatre coexisted with (rather than being replaced by) the "deep" characterization typically associated with his middle and later plays. As chapter 8 seeks to demonstrate, the agency in personation often appears at precisely those moments when selfhood and subjectivity are most meaningfully at issue. As presented upon the boards of the Elizabethan stage no less than in the pages of contemporary playbooks, the grammar of personal identity found itself advanced in the first person singular of "secretly open" speakers. Laboring at their craft with the assistance of a strong performative, these actor/characters project, in the form of a presentation, an apparently self-sustained image of dramatic selfhood. For Viola to declare, "I am not what I am" (*Twelfth Night*, 3.1.141) is to deliver an open, playful inflection, with change in pitch and tone, of the actor's body, gender, and identity.

Such inflection, we observe in chapter 9, frequently comes at dramatic moments in which characters' relationships to issues of agency and identity are considered through, and with the assistance of, written materials. As far as any dramatic subjectivity echoed within the assertive "I," it was often indebted to images of dramatic composition that surface regularly in Shakespeare's plays. These representations speak not only to the economy of part and role in the professional acting repertoire of the day, but also to the imaginary, wide-ranging shapes of print outside the playhouse. In the publishing of dramatic playbooks especially after the watershed year of 1594, the "imaginary puissance" (*Henry V*, Pro. 25) in the dramatist's composition itself must have affected the dynamic, pivotal role of character. These representations of dramatic character were inflamed not simply by his literary leanings; they must also have been fuelled by prospects of a wider circulation and, potentially even more important, in response to the resources of a structural transformation of print during the late Elizabethan era.

As this summary suggests, we have chosen performance to serve as our gate of entry in this study, on the grounds that it is the more recently discerned, controversial component in the alliance of writing and staging. With those multiple modes and styles of delivery in mind, we will pursue an approach that seeks critically to integrate, rather than uncritically subscribe to, recent performance studies. From these we will borrow what, transcending J. L. Austin's primarily linguistic terms, may be called the "performative" in early modern cultural practices. With this broader extradramatic field before us, it seems difficult to deny that, in William Worthen's phrase, performance should not critically be reduced to a "merely interpretive mode of production." The purpose of performing is not exhausted by a histrionic practice which "recaptures or restates the authority of the text."[2] Here, obviously, important issues are at stake. In particular, this new, broadly anthropological understanding of performance constitutes a far-reaching challenge to what, in Michael Bristol's formulation, is the centuries-old "ministerial" approach to the actor's practice as subservient to the playwright's text.[3]

However, at this point questions arise which so far have not received satisfying answers. What kind of practice, what type of staged action and delivery do we actually mean when talking about performance in its own right – that is, as an independent, even sovereign force in Shakespeare's theatre? True, in certain ancient ritual ceremonies, just as in the latest displays of today's performance artists, performance can do very well without verbal language. But if, as Worthen goes on to note, "performance has no intrinsic relation to texts," the question is: what sustains the relationship when, in the early modern theatre, the two media have come close to interactive conjunction? Here Simon Palfrey and Tiffany Stern have drawn attention to the mediating force of the individual "part" as "at once a physical artefact, and an actor's vocation" bearing "both text and context in its own right." If the part "never ceases to be a creative catalyst" for Shakespeare and, simultaneously, is identified by the actor "as the vital thing to be opened-up and expanded," a more complex mode of give-and-take would inform the relationship over and beyond any purely ministerial pattern.[4]

To acknowledge the importance of the text on the actor's scroll is not, therefore, to minimize the nonministerial dimensions of performance in Shakespeare's theatre. On the contrary, it sharpens the contours of the problem. For performers on Elizabethan stages to "open and expand" their parts may or may not exhaust the frontiers of interpretation. But if it is one thing to postulate an "opened-up and expanded" mediation of the text, it is an entirely different matter to demonstrate the ways by which and the degrees to which the uses of performance transcend the mediating purpose of interpretation. For an answer, the actor's own voice and em*bodi*ment, the circumstantial space and purpose of his/her action must be a crucial point of departure.

As against a purely and exclusively interpretive practice, we shall look for and locate in Shakespeare's plays conditions of a surplus type of performance action. Are there any specific sites and situations demanding or witnessing to what Michael Goldman called the "terrific" energy of the actor? Or, in Bernard Beckerman's phrase, where and when can the performer be traced "as his own inventor," as a "*self-generative*" agency whose

presence in presentation is marked by "spontaneity and uncertainty"?[5] Even
to raise those questions in reference to Goldman and Beckerman is to
submit an important qualification. The present inquiry into the "power"
of nonministerial performance practices confines itself to those particularly
enabling conditions, situations, and figurations in Shakespeare's plays that
can best circumscribe the springs, forms, and functions of self-sustained
acting.

Our response to Worthen's and other critics' challenging propositions, in
fact, is to show how the performed interpretation goes hand in hand with
something larger than itself. So we need to ask: how, when, and in which
context can the staged mediation of Shakespeare's text be informed by some
more independent, self-sustained activity on the part of the performer? In
other words, from where and by what means does the actor's practice reach
beyond the ministerial delivery of the text? These questions point to the
exceptional difficulties in fixing what is, in fact, a radically fleeting borderline between textually sanctioned interpretation and what is more than such
interpretation. Rather than offering a phenomenal, but ultimately unwork-
able definition, then, this study seeks to historicize the issue in its socio-
cultural context. This, of course, takes into account the *terra incognita* of
mid-Elizabethan theatre history, where as early as 1567, with the opening
of the Red Lion playhouse near Stepney, we are confronted with a startling
disparity between the existence of large-scale theatre and the absence of
dramatic texts. The story of discontinuity between (early) theatre history
and a history of extant dramatic texts beginning only two decades later is
by now well known.[6] This discontinuity can serve as important, though
not fully accountable, grounds on which to posit, in the London area, a
tradition of performance for which the uses of language were either secondary or merely incidental.

In reference to frequent Elizabethan allusions to a multitude of unlicensed entertainers and practices, not to mention recent studies by Philip
Butterworth and of course the rich mines excavated in the REED series, we
propose to distinguish two major trends in contemporary performance
practices.[7] Each of these is marked by a different social background and a
different cultural genealogy. Relations between them, and the diversity in
the aims and poetics of their performance practices, can best be grasped in
those differential terms by which the respective force and form of each trend
help define, and are defined by, the other.

In its roughest outline, one of these modes of performance was in touch
with the work of the schools, their supreme concern with the teaching of
language and the neoclassical memory of humanists comprising certain

echoes of ancient Greek and plenty of Roman and contemporary Italian stageplays produced for "the better sort." Performance deriving from these premises had no difficulties with role-playing. On the contrary, what mattered was the mimetic endeavor to counterfeit an other, to assume a persona so as to wear the mask of an imaginary identity.

While this mimetic side of the actor's task was in itself representational, the second trend and direction in performance practices sought to bypass the mirror of representation. As against neo-Aristotelian precepts, these performing entertainers more than anything displayed the strength and appeal of their presence on stage; that is, the show of their performative zest, their poignant, pungent delivery, the anonymous wit and repartee in their jesting, their adroit bodies, and nimble movement.[8] Such "self-resembled show" had its roots in predramatic ritual, rural ceremonial, or a marketplace experience ripe with the physicality of jugglers, dancers, tumblers, fencers, or even those who exhibited animal tricks and baitings next door. In our context, this nonrepresentational dimension of playing will be of special import when it comes to tracing a performance practice that was self-sustained (though not of course unmediated) and beyond the politics of any textual regime.

Shakespeare's stage was spacious enough to comprehend, but also to qualify both these traditions. The altogether unequal degree of qualification in either of these modes of performance meant that, intriguingly, boundaries between the verbal signs of language and the visible signs of the body became as porous as they were contingent. For Shakespeare, therefore, the familiar opposition of "performance versus text" (or vice versa) would be entirely unhelpful. The pressure of such opposition would have been punctured in the heat of the battle over the following question: how can a performer exert authority, let alone sovereignty in his own right, when the dramatist's language itself has already assimilated the player's *gestus*, speech rhythm, and kinetic thrust prior to any subsequent embodiment? Verbal and visible signs come together in the literary as well as the material production, but also in the audiovisual response of auditors-spectators. All three are conjoined in a dramatic discourse that is an object of, as well as an agency in, the staging of the play. The performative dimension of Shakespeare's language has generally been recognized since the days of Rudolf Stamm and has continued to receive distinguished attention by David Bevington and others.[9] We must content ourselves here with one exemplification of how language in the composition of a stage play proceeds by itself to assist in rendering, even directing the "swelling scene."

Returning to *Henry V*, we are struck by how the kinetic energies required in the material process of its production are either intercepted by, or in their turn unleashed in, the speeches of the Prologue/Chorus. As he sets forth "our swift scene" (*Henry V*, 3.0.1–3), events proceed "With winged heels" (2.0.7); the audience, summoned to "Play with [their] fancies" (3.0.7), must follow suit. Urged "upon your winged thoughts" with "So swift a pace" (5.0.8, 15) to follow the play, onlookers are implored from moment to moment, "Work, work your thoughts" and in their "minds" to "Grapple" (3.0.25, 18) with the difference between "royal face" or "majesty" (4.0.35, 40) and what on so imperfect a scaffold "may unworthiness define" (4.0.46). The task of the audience, then, is for themselves to be swift in their own border-crossing activity between what presents and what is represented on the platform stage. The challenge is to bridge or simply make the most of the "distance" we have noted. In this operation there is a point at which the language, the staging, and the watching coincide with the grand design, of import to both players and spectators: "And make imaginary puissance" (Pro. 25).

Here the power of performance and the puissance of imagined meanings become finally indivisible. In the language of *Hamlet*, "scene" and "poem" are conjoined, as linked by a mere "or" in the phrase, "scene individable, or poem unlimited" (*Hamlet*, 2.2.399–400). Paradoxically, the symbolic order of represented meaning is most wanted when the performed play's demands upon cooperating audiences become quite irresistible. This happens because many circumstantial forces in Shakespeare's theatre do not derive from literary, rhetorical, or compositional sources. These forces operate between the written text and its reception in the playhouse. Their broadest common denominator can perhaps best be defined as "presentational practice" – the process of transaction that in its own turn is accompanied by responsive action in the yard and from the galleries. As these are aroused, the Chorus adopts the grammar of an imperative form: there is something compelling for and in "your imaginary forces." What is called for is sheer meaning-making, as suggested by "Suppose . . ."; "Think . . ."; "For 'tis your thoughts that now must deck our kings" (Pro. 18–28). The clarion call is for the signifier and, with it, the signified, and for those "imaginary forces" that make them both work and interact.

This brings us to our second area of concern: the symbolic order of representation. The more immediate point of departure is that the culture of literacy and print contributed to the rendering of purely imaginary replications of things and passions. However, the rise, in this context, of world-picturing and self-picturing modes of postallegorical dramatic speech and action is a larger issue that raises the timely question of early modern representation.[10] Just as the move, in the sixteenth century, from allegorical to early modern drama was entirely nonlinear, so was the emergence of a secular, highly particularized mode of representation a drawn-out process in which a new *auctoritas* of signs could engage the signs of *potestas*.[11] In briefly hinting at these political uses of representation, we propose to challenge persistent critical objections to representation. According to its earlier poststructuralist critique, representation bridges difference, removes rupture, constitutes closure. Under certain circumstances, these may indeed serve as harmonizing functions, attuned to a poetics of empathy and indifference. However, representation in early modern drama cannot be reduced to healing the breach between language and the world.

Far from constituting a space exclusively of unity and homogeneity, the Elizabethan theatre brought forth varieties of representation that tended to defy closure and plenitude. True enough, the world-picturing, world-appropriating mode of representational speech did not and could not presume direct access to the world. The latter was "always already" textually inscribed – which is not to say that these uses of language could be free from a touch of the real. As David Schalkwyk poignantly observes, "representation is not a purging of the world from the sign . . . but the essential contamination of the sign by the real."[12] Indeed, in the words of Louis Montrose, representations "are engaged in shaping the modalities" of social living; they help accommodate "their writers, performers, readers, and audiences to multiple and shifting subject positions with the world that they themselves both constitute and inhabit."[13] These worldly representations, as Catherine Belsey puts it, are "exchanged, negotiated and, indeed, contested in a society." Whether or not they "coincide with existing practices," they may "determine or legitimate them; or alternatively, they may challenge them."[14]

In other words, dramatic meanings can be inflected, even adapted by performance practices, just as these practices are not indifferent to signification. Rather, they can participate in or help bring forth life circumstances predisposing signifiers in their potency and direction. Shakespeare, as Pauline Kiernan notes, "throughout his work is preoccupied with the relations between insubstantial image and corporeal substance." Although the dramatist distrusts "the disembodied language of rhetoric . . . and all forms of de-materializing representation" (for instance, those in which symbol appears congruent with meaning), his concern is "with the process by which life is turned into a representation."[15] Thus theatrical representation, unthinkable without the writing of dramatic texts, thrived in conjunction with the mode and institution of their transaction, that is, as language embodied by agents, their voices, their faces, their limbs. Nor was this conjunction necessarily marked by perfect consonance. True enough, the impact of performance upon representation was rarely in the nature of an onslaught coming from without, as some external molestation. Rather, the performative impulse should be seen to affect the staged action from within, yielding a double-encoded, contrarious force. Such force implicates dramatic representation in what Mikhail Bakhtin calls "a critical interanimation of languages." What Shakespeare's performed representations can convey is indeed "a concrete heteroglot conception of the world," often enough "a special type of double-voiced discourse."[16]

CRITICAL RETRENCHMENTS: STAGE-CENTERED *VS.* PAGE-CENTERED APPROACHES?

There is as yet, unfortunately, no substantial critical effort to reexamine the grounds in history and theory on which it could be possible today to demonstrate, as Lukas Erne suggests, that "the stage and the printed page did not necessarily present two rival forms of publication" and that the dramatist "could afford to write plays for the stage *and* the page."[17] Here Erne's study of *Shakespeare as Literary Dramatist*, while arguably the most discriminating, offers one voice among the many that have addressed the resonance of the printed dramatic page. Patrick Cheney joins him in contesting what he calls the "critical preoccupation with Shakespeare as a man of the theatre."[18] Cheney instead foregrounds the poet's standing as an early modern writer firmly anchored in what, in the later sixteenth century, emerges as very much a national institution of authorship. Similarly, Douglas Brooks, Alan Farmer, and Zachary Lesser, to name only three, have underlined a critical trajectory which, while it by no means overlooks the theatre, finds its consummation in the production and circulation of printed texts.[19]

That this renewed emphasis on page over and against the stage is not limited to the aforementioned studies or critics can be seen in the rising consideration of literary form and intertextuality as they pertain to the drama of the period. No doubt such work extends, while it does not duplicate, an enduring focus on the language of Shakespeare's plays. Indeed, a much more conspicuous separation from the playhouse can be discerned in Frank Kermode's well-received study, *Shakespeare's Language*. Suggesting that Shakespeare may have intended to become a poet "not of the theater but of the page," Kermode examines the complexities of Shakespeare's verse largely in abstraction from its delivery in the playhouse.[20] And although his portrait of this complexity by no means precludes theatrical pleasure, one reviewer of his book has noted that "These essays are the opposite of, say, Granville Barker's analyses of Shakespearean staging; rather, they treat the plays as if they were poems by Mallarmé, unique – and uniquely – structures of words."[21] Likewise if, in her influential monograph, *The Theatre of the Book*, Julie Stone Peters sees drama as more than printed "structures of words," her deft sketch of the many connections between stage and printed page in the Gutenberg era nonetheless challenges a performance-centered approach to drama in arguing that the institution of print functioned as a powerful engine behind "the late fifteenth- and sixteenth-century theatrical revival."[22] Along these lines, even some of the finest text-centered work in our own day continues to insist on what Graham Holderness in his *Textual Shakespeare* acknowledges as the "substantial gap between theatrical writing and theatrical practice in the theatre of Shakespeare's day."[23]

These studies reveal a swing of the critical pendulum. Their renewed stress on the page dissents from the claim that it is "in performance that the plays lived and had their being," and that "the proper focus of academic attention should, therefore, be performance-based."[24] Indeed, David Scott Kastan, who raises this issue in *Shakespeare and the Book*, does not conceal his doubts about performance criticism. According to Kastan, there is "much to be said for such a focus, and much – too much . . . – has been said for it."[25] Indeed, there are perfectly plausible grounds that make "the commitment to stage-centered approaches to Shakespeare suspect." From a scholar's sense of what, historically, the words of the text stood for, it is evident that in various contemporary Shakespearean productions "performance yields too easily to our desire" or at least to a design of directorial originality imposed only with great strain. While the postmodern theatre increasingly blurs the line between interpretation and adaptation, the word on the page earns endorsement through "its greater resistance to appropriation."[26]

Among its more immediate aims, then, this study seeks to address a renewed or, as many would say, growing rift between page and stage in Shakespeare studies. Two or three decades ago, the rift in question seemed almost closed when, in the work of such critics as Michael Goldman, Inga-Stina Ewbank, Robert Hapgood and others, Shakespeare was viewed as a "poet in the theatre."[27] Weighing the rule of "textual imperialism" against "the tyranny of the School of Performance,"[28] these critics sought a middle ground in the "choice between a literary and a theatrical Shakespeare."[29] They could indeed do so as long as language in the drama was taken to be "the grammar of the dramatic situation" and the text was read as, *tout court*, "a design for performance."[30] The balance, in fact, was such that Hapgood in *Shakespeare the Theatre-Poet* could submit that dramatic language actually "served as the best guide a performer could have," the perfect "guide to enactment."[31]

In the long and consequential wake of 1968, however, the claims of a newly energized array of performance studies were the first to upset the precarious poise that temporarily obtained, in critical discourse, between writing and playing. This invigorated approach to performance challenged much more than the authority traditionally invested in an institution of authorship. What various critics sought to establish (at least as far as they did not dismiss the traditional theatre as hopelessly outdated) was, in the words of Erika Fischer-Lichte, a "reversal of the hierarchy between text and performance."[32] Henceforth the relationship in question had ceased for many to be thinkable except in terms of conflict or, as Eugenio Barba puts it, in the form of a "clash": "In western theater, the actor is – or should be – a creator. His clash with the text, through his own sensibility and his own historical perspective opens up a unique and personal universe to his audience."[33]

It is precisely at this point that the present study seeks to reconstruct, in Shakespeare's theatre, a dramaturgy of "bifold authority" which, bridging and yet exploiting the gap between language and performance, does not permit an order of "hierarchy" between them. In critical terms, we propose to insist that there is an alternative to either the reaffirmation of a purely literary, page-centered study of the dramatist or an approach exclusively through performance and the social and technical circumstances of his theatre. Now, such an alternative cannot aim at *die radikale Mitte* or, simply, be content to have it both ways. If we propose not to minimize the weight and relevance of recent preferences for, respectively, a literary or a performative Shakespeare, we do so because each of these approaches finds a set of correlatives in Shakespeare's plays themselves.

Our point is that stage and page do more than coexist. Rather, they submit to those competing sources of authorization which in *Troilus and Cressida* are alluded to as "author's pen" and "actor's voice" (from the prologue). Both pen and voice stand for communicative media or tools of cultural production derived from diverse sources, traditions, or experiences; their relations are marked not by continuity or concurrence but by difference. Ultimately, the difference is that which exists between two socially anchored modes of sensation and perception, *habitus* and impact. Even while pen and voice appear to complement one another in staging, they remain in fact incommensurable in that, as Kastan poignantly notes, "(n)either is the effect of the other; neither reproduces, or draws upon (except rhetorically) the other's claim to authenticity."[34] The difference, in short, is not simply cultural or aesthetic in any general sense; it points to two versions of epistemology, two modes of communication and, in the early modern contexts, two ways of appropriating, comprehending, and achieving diversion in the circumstantial world.

Yet nonidentity in the relations of "pen" and "voice" cannot be the last word. If the difference in question is such that it can be played with on the "scene individable" (*Hamlet*, 2.2.399), then an intriguingly interactive relationship of text and performance advances itself. Probing further into this interactive moment, we come to the junction where neither the perception of discontinuity nor the emphasis on concurrence and continuity provides an adequate point of departure. In the early 1590s metropolitan playing and secular writing were only beginning to come to grips with an emergent need, in the theatre, for fluidity and adaptability. In light of this untried alliance, and in the absence of any traditionally fixed or given hierarchy between text and performance, therefore, it is helpful neither to overemphasize divisions and contestations of authority in the relations of these two media nor to postulate any given pattern of concurrence and complementarity between them. Instead, we propose to explore the extent to which (in the familiar shorthand terminology) "actor's voice" is in "author's pen," but also, and with increasing weight, the ways and ends to which "author's pen" is in "actor's voice."

We invoke the reversible order deliberately, but also tentatively, in search of a historical sequence. By historical sequence we do not mean only, or even primarily, a chronological one. Once the differences between pen and voice – as well as the ways and means to use or even suspend them – are being traced in the circumstantial world of social and theatre history, "bifold authority" will be seen as far from static or unchangeable. Relations between the two cultural media cannot be determined ontologically or according to any one discipline – be that aesthetics or anthropology.[35] Rather, an element of contingency precludes any facile or fixed order in the confederation of pen and voice. Hence, from the early to the late plays, Shakespeare's theatre reveals a kind of movement which, often enough, goes two ways.

To illustrate the degree of liquidity in relations between text and performance, let us return to their widest spectrum. This spectrum is marked on one end by uses of the text and on the other by uses of performance.

Between these, we have shifting degrees of strength and preeminence on either side, no doubt with a preponderance of the text. Even so, these mutable relations must be viewed as *inter*relations wherever Shakespeare's dramatic text engages, or enters into dialogue with, bodily signification, and vice versa. As Simon Shepherd notes, the two media establish a vital "dialectic": we have a staging of both "body material or/and meaning" *and* "body constructions or/and representation."[36]

We turn first to a conjuncture in which the impetus of performance is particularly strong. In terms of our imagined spectrum, some more or less self-sustained positions of performance practice would be informed by ties to certain extradramatic, inversionary ceremonies, to our knowledge first called "topsyturvydom" by R. J. E. Tiddy.[37] This preliterary figure of performance can amply be traced in its dramatic assimilations to late medieval and early modern stages, even while its matrix in more ancient Saturnalian and more recent carnivalesque ceremonies can scarcely be doubted. In sixteenth-century England certain seasonal festivities such as sword-play, maying, and misrule survive into Shakespeare's lifetime. Most of these predramatic practices constitute or help effect an inversion which – thoroughly performative – finds astonishing analogies or at least correlatives in late medieval drama. As the morality play adapts some of these analogues, the historian is tempted to speak almost of performative accretions. In one instance only we pursue this inversionary type of performative on the pre-Shakespearean stage. There we examine Mischief's nonsense patter in *Mankind* and the figure of "contrariety" in the doings and sayings of Courage, the Vice in *The Tide Tarrieth No Man*.

These and related figures of inversionary practice possess remarkable continuity; they appear throughout Shakespeare's plays, and come up in his adaptation of the Vice tradition in *Richard III* and its more hybrid form in *King John*. Related practices can be traced in Edward Gloucester and other figures in *King Lear*. There the same figure of the topsy-turvy, upside-down world inspires the Fool's prophecy (*King Lear*, 3.2.80–94) and infests the mind and language of the tragic protagonist. As far as Lear's insanity is staged as an inversion of blind reason into prophetic madness, his language, in assimilating the very figure of "handy-dandy" (another word for "topsy-turvy"), illustrates how an inversionary figure can bring forth meaning rich with social connotation.

However, if such dominant *gestus* of inversionary performance appears to require a stage-centred approach here, it would be entirely wrong to over-look that, in most cases, traditional forms of a performative sleight-of-hand are assimilated by the symbolic order of representation.[38] For a moment, the phrase "and handy-dandy, which is the justice, which is the thief?" (*King Lear*, 4.6.153–4) may refer us back to the staging of some pretextual legerdemain. As Butterworth documents, certain types of juggling and tumbling thrived in prominent companies like the Admiral's and Lord Strange's Men well into the late 1580s.[39] But while, as Robert Langham notes, in the 1590s "such feats of agilittee" were "not expressible by pen or speech," in Shakespeare's plays they were – as when the show of this upside-down gesture is, in its "handy" connotation, subsumed under an overriding representation.

This bifold, two-directional move is not in the order of a binary opposition. The give-and-take between imaginary, world-picturing representation and the presence of material, bodily delivery in presentation is incommensurable, especially when seen (as in chapters 7 and 8) in Émile Benveniste's distinction between the subject uttering and the subject in the utterance. This is no less the case when and where performative practice is transformed and potentially revitalized on the level of dramatic action – that is, as a figure in the plot itself. Shakespeare's plays feature a broad spectrum of topsy-turvy figurations which comprise all sorts of transformations and confusions, from the politically radical comic inversion in *2 Henry VI* to the handy-dandy powers of Prospero and his Ariel. Next to the inversionary might of the witches, "Fair is foul, and foul is fair" (*Macbeth*, 1.1.11), in tragedy, we have in comedy a strong staple of no less incisive inversion. There is, for instance, the handy-dandy treatment of gender, especially in the sexual inversion and disguise of Shakespeare's boy-heroines: the strong, alluring presence of the young performer merges with the enchanting image of the performed. What proud loveliness and irony results in feminine appearance bears witness to a remarkable complementarity between the verbal and the performative components in characterization. On an altogether different plane, we have the enactment of a social and marital jumble in *The Taming of the Shrew*, with Sly as an outrageously used vehicle of topsyturvydom. We also encounter the "disfigurement" of Bottom and the erotic confusion among two pairs of lovers in *A Midsummer Night's Dream* performed and happily healed, events that contrast greatly with the consequence, in a profound tragedy, of Iago's vicious contrariety.

In all these instances, the performing powers of contrariety and confusion affect Shakespeare's uses of language in a manner to which, strictly speaking, no stage-centered approach can do justice. Indeed, any retrenched opposition of the two approaches appears self-forbidding, even self-defeating, where Shakespeare's language itself serves as both the basic means and the principal object of a handy-dandy confusion. That is the case where the dramatist, in the fashion of his clowns, can "mistake the word" (*The Two Gentlemen of Verona*, 3.1.284) – that is, play upon its meaning by turning it upside-down. In Dr. Johnson's phrase, "some malignant power" is at work in this topsy-turvy phrasing; but if "its fascinations are irresistible" to the dramatist, the incentive to pun is largely a performative one, certainly at odds with a representation marked by "reason, propriety and truth."[40] Often enough such wordplay is not designed to represent – that is, to render or stand for the nimble wit of its speaker. Rather, it has the force of impertinence – of the recklessly not pertinent – and as such it was likely to transmit a provocative zest in the player's speech, a winking eye and a tingling tongue. These in their turn may have coaxed spectators pleasurably to taste the phrase and, handy-dandy, to decode the unsettling upheaval of meaning. Here it is tempting to adapt Johnson's famous phrase about Shakespeare's "fatal Cleopatra": if for "a quibble" our playwright "lost the world, and was content to lose it," he also and simultaneously lost (and was content to lose) a measure of cogency in characterization. The quibble was "malignant" in that its performative power put up some resistance to the discipline and control a verisimilar type of representation required in the fashioning of character.

All these topsy-turvy elements point to a performance practice that refused to fall in with what was reasonable, cogent, and appropriate to the "necessary question of the play" (*Hamlet*, 3.2.42–3). There must have been a potent linkage between the handy-dandy arts exhibited in the marketplace and the staged counterfeiting of the role-playing actor. As Pascale Drouet argues, such a link between the counterfeiting of the cony-catcher or the displaced and needy and that of travelling players may well have been much stronger than can today be realized.[41] From its very inception, double-dealing elements of guile and wile are wrought into what is transformative in dramatic performance. Here we can recall only in passing the staggering extent to which transfiguration is the starting point of any performing actor, and the basis of any performance. The elementary task is to be what one is not. The handy-dandy force of transfiguration resides within the staged act of counterfeiting itself. In this sense, the actor's being on stage is in itself a confusion, a bringing together of, perplexingly, more than one *gestus* or identity.

Our first model of performance, then, envisions a histrionic practice in which the player – far from being lost in the text – possesses actorly authority to invent, to bring forth something "self-generative." This author-ity derives from a commission and competence in his craft which, on the brink of transformation into a fiction, retains a trace of a purpose and identity larger than personal talent. As far as this purpose can overrule an exclusively textual faith and guidance, it is informed by association with a theatre whose ultimate vocation is to offer pastime, public game, and entertainment. Still, on Shakespeare's stage, these continue to flourish in conjunction with a more recent modern dedication to empathy, insight, and judgment vis-à-vis dramatic representations. Even in these rhetorically refined productions, the spectrum of relations in Shakespeare's theatre between language and the body remained exceedingly wide. In terms of the language used in a study preparatory to this book, here the actor's voice would resonate in author's pen, even as the latter pointed in new and newly meaningful directions.

However, in view of the all-important activity of Shakespeare as poet and playwright, this emphasis on the self-generative strength of performance needs to be balanced – to a certain extent even intercepted – by relations of language and the body somewhere on the other end of our imagined spectrum. For that, we propose to look anew at the dramatist's modes of characterization. For centuries celebrated as his most distinctive achievement, Shakespeare's unique gallery of artificial persons has justifiably been understood as crucially indebted to the arts of writing and dramatic composition. In our convenient phrase, rather than having the author's pen inspired by player's voices, we should expect to find the author's pen guiding, inspiring, disciplining, and fashioning an excellent actor's voice and body into character.

Clearly such neat juxtapositions (here designed, again, as a summary introduction) can be dangerous as soon as they threaten to obscure the full range of engagements between dramatic language and histrionic bodies. But to do justice to these engagements, we propose to approach them at the intersection of historicity and anthropology. Let us glance, then, at the state of things whereby an "excellent actor" appears to be altogether lost in the image of his or her role. Here performance practice, following the prescribed text of the other medium, submits to the symbolic order of representation. For many spectators, this order would conceal the histrionic talent and action proper and suspend the transformative act of counterfeiting in the counterfeit image of character. Foregrounded is the semblance of a person whereby the simulated image of a particularized human being can be perceived under the illusion of just being there, speaking, moving in this moment. To characterize the modes and aims of such histrionic transfiguration, we could say that the representation of character is shown in the product, no longer through the process, of transfiguration. The process is, as it were, displaced, made invisible to the extent that the living personator seems to disappear in the image of an imaginary personated. Now the stage is dominated by a poetics of "reflection" whose major figures are resemblance and verisimilitude. To hold the mirror up to nature is first of all to suit the action of performance to the word in the text; to achieve *immediate* visual and auditory contact with a pictured product seems to require no mediation, no mediator. Vanishing in the eyes of those spellbound by what is displayed on it, the stage to a greater part surrenders its authority to what is artfully composed and verbally articulated. Intriguingly, this mimetic concept of reflection *qua* imitation parallels that psychology of "reflection" to which Ulysses refers directly in *Troilus and Cressida*.

To be sure, such empathy is not unknown in Shakespeare's theatre – we need only recall mention of the tears shed over "brave Talbot" in the early 1590s or, in 1610, for Desdemona. Without anticipating our reading of Ulysses's important speech in *Troilus*, we can stress that such socially saturated "reflection" helps constitute the semblance of self-willed characters equipped with a within. Such semblance derives not simply from language use but from a verbal, dialogic interaction *in the course of which* various agencies apparently produce an identity open to change and development. As William Dodd has shown in a brilliant reading of Isabella's first interview with Angelo (*Measure for Measure*, 2.2), this fluid encounter of two imaginary selves proceeds through mutual interpellations; the "dramatist's simulation of the *contingency* of reciprocal negotiations of personhood" is achieved by an ongoing performance of "affective preference" and response.[42] By implication at least, this reading provides the "missing link between character in its aspects of agency and character as an arena of discourses, utterances, or voices."[43]

Here, then, is a rare conjunction where the dramatist's writing has been celebrated for its unequalled genius. Empathy in the reception of such near-symbiosis between actor and character has long been the touchstone of dramatic excellence and pleasure. Yet dramatic "character in its aspects of agency" requires an approach to where inscription meets embodiment. Even at their closest contiguity and near-identity, actor and character are not the same. To understand their conjuncture, it seems safest to follow those historians and theoreticians of the theatre who, like Jean Alter in his *Sociosemiotic Theory of Theatre* and Marvin Carlson in his *Theatre Semiotics: Signs of Life*, have incisively addressed "the inherent duality of theatrical activity."[44] On the one hand, we have the "performant function" as serving "the technical skill and achievement of the performer, the visual display of dazzling costume, or scenic effects" of various kinds.[45] Clearly, this function of performance draws attention from the story space to the stage space. On the other hand, we have a spatial move in the opposite direction. In a verisimilar representation of characters and events, the "referential function" (Alter's phrase) would be in aid of a different effect. Serving empathy and recognition, such representation propels attention from the stage as stage to the stage as story space, that is, as symbolic site localized as town, garden, court, battlefield, and so forth.

Since the two, ostensibly antipodal, points on the Shakespearean spectrum constantly overlap and thereby engage one another, the actor-character conjoins two different types of interest, *habitus*, and identity. As a consequence, the staged usage of dramatic language is bound doubly to encode, even when privileging the represented character. As has been shown elsewhere, such division in codes and interests informs, and derives from some "bifold authority" affecting both text and institution as well as their relationship.[46] Therefore, it is not sufficient when "duality" is posited simply in terms of the "actor-character," or viewed on the level of a "dual consciousness" (William Archer's term). Unfortunately, even the most penetrating, highly perspicacious soundings of this doubleness tend to abstract from its socio-cultural matrix and isolate the tension in characterization from what enables it in the first place.

This is not to say that the duality in question has gone unobserved. On the contrary; if, for instance, we look at Michael Shapiro's focus on the "playful complicity in games of illusion-making" the conjuncture in question is persuasively argued as an important site of "theatrical vibrancy."[47] Anthony Dawson goes one step further when he notes that in the work of the boys' companies "the discrepancy between actor and character" was deliberately foregrounded, when the "very disjunction between the actor's body and what it represents" allows "for the evocation onstage of interiorized personhood."[48] While it is certainly helpful, in the words of Lesley Wade Soule, to accord "the actor" certain "important non-representational functions" and to underscore "tensions between performer and role,"[49] the question we shall raise in the present study points in a different direction: how to account for the resilience of self-generating performance on a stage where the act of histrionic enunciation maintains its force in the midst of superb, preeminent, often enough preponderant poetic utterances?

Again, a stage-centered approach is scarcely qualified for probing more deeply into the *énoncé/énonciation* relations in question, even when ultimately bifold authority wants to have a verbal correlative in the theatre itself. For that, let us resort one more time to the Prologue to *Henry V* and draw attention to a phrase that, in terms of dramaturgy, provides us with a remarkable clue to scenes and words as interlinking. The phrase is that of the "swelling scene" (*Henry V*, Pro. 4). Far from humbly downplaying – as in the case of the scaffold shelf – any stagings, "swelling" here comprises space and word in an imaginative expansion beyond the original "object" (11). Even the signs of power are intercepted, as it were, by the power of a signifier which can "make imaginary puissance" (25) in and through its performance.[50] The inherent dimension of a "swelling" *mise-en-scène* witnesses here as elsewhere in the plays a distending force effecting an enlargement from within. This particular meaning of "swelling" returns, for instance, in those "happy prologues to the swelling act / Of the imperial theme" (*Macbeth*, 1.3.128–9). It is also confirmed in "the unseen grief / That swells with silence in the tortur'd soul" (*Richard II*, 4.1.297–8), and echoed in Prospero's "Their understanding / Begins to swell" (*The Tempest*, 5.1.79–80).

The "swelling scene" remains a crucial trope for our argument because Shakespearean relations of page and stage more often than not tend to enlarge one another. Over and beyond their difference, this comprises the capacity for performance to bring down to earth the lofty flight of rhetoric without belittling the pathos of passion, or the (hitherto) unknown languages of what was strange, remote from everyday experience.

HISTORICITY IN RELATIONS OF PAGE AND STAGE

Concluding this overview of the book's aims and methods and their critical contexts, we turn to our final emphasis: historicity. In a conjunctural understanding of history, with plenty of links and gaps between past significance and present meaning, the question of what is present then and present now looms large. As Terence Hawkes and Hugh Grady have recently reminded us, there is a lot to be said for Shakespeare in the present – even more so when intertwined with an awareness of historicity in Elizabethan performance practices.[51] To inquire into the latter needs no justification, when in performance studies critics again and again have called for historicizing the subject. To date, as the recent *Companion to Shakespeare and Performance* reconfirms, historically oriented students of performance have achieved their finest insight in the study of individual plays. However, the question needs to be raised whether such perfectly legitimate study is sufficiently qualified to deal with the larger spectrum of variegated purposes of playing. In other words, there is some doubt whether a "project of theatre historiography" is sufficient when conceived as "the historiography of Shakespeare in performance."[52] For us, the point is to understand what and how performance, in Barbara Hodgdon's words, can be marked by "labor, work, play" – activities not fully accessible to a "reading relationship."[53] To do full justice to the impact of the actor's work, to what labor is invested in the act of presentation, we shall proceed to envision Elizabethan socio-cultural history as a rapidly changing context affecting, especially in the 1580s, and after, basic modes of communication and entertainment. The idea is so to study the link between the process of presentation and the different modes of performance that we learn more about different histories at work in a fluid dramaturgy.

Ultimately the text/performance relationship must be seen as a crucial, even constitutive element in the genealogy of the Elizabethan theatre. Once the diversification of performance practices is acknowledged, these practices can be viewed as part of that "swelling scene" right at Shakespeare's own doorstep. While we cannot, of course, here historicize the media and practices which went into the making of the Elizabethan theatre, let us at least offer an illustration of how page and stage are involved in the contingency of their relationship. Our text is Thomas Heywood's *Apology for Actors* (probably written in 1607/8, published in 1612). While the treatise has generally been considered as the most balanced account among Shakespeare's contemporaries, closer scrutiny reveals an unsuspected partisanship: Heywood takes a problematic position on the diversification of histrionic practices. In fact, he follows, as William West has poignantly shown, the late Renaissance "imaginary theatre and the encyclopedia in attempting to regulate the actor," that is, to reduce the actor's part to a purely reflective one vis-à-vis "some authorized text."[54] On the one hand, Heywood unambiguously disapproves of those players who "are condemned for their licentiousness" (E3ʳ). In his censure he is quite outspoken against "any lascivious shewes, scurrilous jests, or scandalous invectives," even prepared to "banish them from my patronage" (F4ʳ). As against these, Heywood's advice is "to curb and limit" performance practices "within the bands of discretion and government" (E3ʳ).

Here the use of "discretion" is coupled with the call not only for "sober" and "temperate carriages" but, more significantly, for restraint in "this presumed liberty." There is good reason to suspect that such "liberty" was supposed to stamp licentious players who felt independent enough to disregard any consistently ministerial dealings with the text. At this point, we may recall that Hamlet speaks of "discretion" in his advice to the players, immediately before he recommends first of all to "Suit the action to the word." Although, of course, this is closely coupled with a reverse endorsement of suiting "the word to the action," the weight and direction of the former clause are fairly unambiguous in the light of protracted strictures on those "players" who "strutted and bellow'd" and spoke "more than is set down for them" (3.2.17–18, 32–3, 39–40). Here Shakespeare's protagonist voices a demand for continuity between word and action – a demand held out against a situation marked by discontinuity between what the author wrote and what in fact these comedians were wont to do. In line with the emergence of new textual parameters of response to well-reasoned performance, an innovative terminology comes to the fore. At the turn of the century and shortly after, terms such as "judgment" and the "judicious" begin to be used by both Heywood and, again, Shakespeare in *Hamlet* in ways which indicate shifting modes of response and expectation on the part of audiences rather than spectators. These shifts testify by themselves to a considerable amount of reshuffling in relations between pages and stages.[55]

Such new accents must not be read as refracting purely intrinsic, quasi-autonomous changes within the genre of drama. On the contrary, the prominence of more nearly "sober" and "temperate" standards of production and audience appeal lag behind the changing cultural scene of late Elizabethan England. They follow upon but also begin to coincide with what social historians have called a "second reformation," a "cultural revolution," a "moral and cultural watershed" – terms we find in the work of Peter Burke, Keith Wrightson, Patrick Collinson, Mervyn James, and others.[56] In the 1580s "a deep social change of a new kind" (Collinson's phrase) gained considerable momentum. One of its most consequential results was a cultural divide between the "middling sort" and the rest of the population. These transformations affected basic ways of living, working, and spending, including reading, writing, and playing in late Elizabethan England.[57]

Marked by social divisions, withdrawals, and new alliances, interactions between verbal language and bodily performance were affected though not of course suspended. Nor was the important dialectic, foregrounded in Huston Diehl's study, effective enough to amount to anything more than a halfway house between staging certain results of reform and reforming the stage to a certain degree.[58] As long as the engagement between scriptural and bodily forces allowed the performer to be "self-generative" (Beckerman's phrase) in terms of spontaneous and unpredictable leanings toward the text, the dissonance between the media itself could be vitalizing. Even under rapidly changing circumstances, bodies in performance continued to profit from whatever dynamic the engagement harboured.

While results such as these are ephemeral as well as imponderable, we have unquestionable evidence at least of the stimulating effect of printed language on the performance of Shakespeare's plays. As Barbara Mowat has reminded us, it was possible for a group of provincial players such as Sir Richard Cholmeley's Men to perform for the 1609 Christmas season in Gothwaite, Yorkshire, from the quite recently printed quartos of *King Lear* and *Pericles*.[59]

Once we take into account not only itinerant professionals like these, but amateur practices shown in household revels or, as Suzanne Westfall proposed, "household theater," multiple lines of transmission and reception of printed plays come into the picture. The least we can say is that, in Mowat's words, "relationships among performance, playscript, and printed text are . . . more fluid, more disturbed, than scholars have tended to imagine and describe them."[60] While the technology of print undoubtedly increased the "dependence of early modern theatre on literary culture,"[61] the print form tended to multiply all sorts of performance options – gestural, verbal, semantic, characterizing – and thereby could enhance the performer's range of "self-generative" action between scriptural statement and oral utterance.

As long as the range of such histrionic action remained vital, a Marlowe, Shakespeare, Webster and their like could produce, and in turn see produced, magnificent plays in which the script and the show mutually engaged and intensified one another. If this study focuses on their glorious scene, our caveat is that it was short-lived. The throbbing, pulsating space of this "swelling scene" was destined to be blocked off from what was creative in the clash between material boards and bodies *and* the imaginary pictures and illusions obtained through puissant playing. Gradually the *platea* was destined to shrink into some picturing locality; the bifold springs of action and perception tended to run dry under the proscenium arch. To the degree that, in Margreta de Grazia's words, "this enframed space is voided of properties of its own," the "*scene* blurs into the homonymic *seen*."[62] Engulfed by an imaginary, world-picturing scene, actors were more and more divested of aims and equipments of their own making. They were expected to submit to purely "reflective" uses of the text (William West's phrase) so as to serve the ideal of an enlightened, educational theatre that was to come of age in the eighteenth century. In these circumstances, the power of performance would be sapped until, in the twentieth-century theatre, the absence of that other space was perceived in its disturbing consequences.

CHAPTER I

"Moralize two meanings" in one play: contrariety on the Tudor stage

The "memory" that held "a seat / In this distracted globe" (*Hamlet*, 1.5.96–7) clearly included the recollection of the Morality stage. For one thing, Shakespeare's plays remembered the morality tradition through the latter's most theatrical figuration: the "old Vice" (*Twelfth Night*, 4.2.124). As highly performative equivocator, the Vice drew on two divergent modes of authorizing the uses of dramatic language and theatrical space. Central to this divergence in discursive practice was a formal incongruity between the serious and the comic which, though deeply embedded in the earlier history of medieval drama, continued to provide a semantic underside to the morality context. Combining sinfulness and sport, the Vice – a strange gallimaufry of types and roles – appealed to a divided authority in signification. Through the performative thrust of his own lop-sided inclination, this farcical agent pointedly upset symmetries in the allegorical order of things. Disturbing the homiletic bifurcations between good and evil, the Vice championed all sorts of confusions between serious sinfulness and comic theatricality.[1]

In English Renaissance drama the Vice is perhaps best remembered in the traces he left, via Richard Tarlton and Will Kemp, in the Shakespearean clown. More broadly, his legacy helped Renaissance dramatists straddle the divide between the comic and the tragic, and gave them a powerful model for, among other "playwright" figures in dramatic texts, the darkly humorous plotters of revenge tragedy.[2] Grotesquely celebrating the space for (in)congruity between comedy and tragedy, the descendants of the Vice, from the title character of *Richard III* to Edmund in *King Lear* and Vindice in *The Revenger's Tragedy*, continued to excel in the vigor of histrionic showmanship by equivocating in the representation of a sinful role. What Richard Gloucester or, in the early parts of *King John*, Faulconbridge displayed was a sense of contrariety in the production and authorization of theatrical meaning. As Richard confides to spectators, such characters (including himself) can "moralize two meanings in one word" (*King John*, 3.1.83). In a self-reflexive stance,

Richard compares himself to "the formal Vice, Iniquity" (82), recalling his own genealogy in the medieval theatre.

These ambidextrous uses of language imply a remarkable awareness not simply of what is performed as a fiction, but of how such performing may be done and from where its artifice derives. A surplus of double-voiced signification blurs the all too obvious outcome of the struggle between piety and sinfulness; with a savage element of grotesque comedy, the moralizing transaction could not bypass the here and now. The yawning gap between texts and bodies, between allegorical representations and their material delivery, constituted a site where "two meanings" were confounded in one dramatic action. This site was marked by deep divisions in the conjuncture of two media, two cultures, two ways of cultural production and consumption. The eloquent art and rhetoric of serious representations encountered the irreverent demands of performative practice. The former were again and again exposed to an alien *habitus* of transaction, to a performance that made self-display inseparable from a gamesome type of counterfeiting practice. The resulting mélange comprised but also made porous the borderline between rule and misrule, morality and theatricality.

To illustrate this mélange in its bodily as well as verbal connotations, we will call upon the figure of *gestus*, as first developed explicitly in the Brechtian poetics of the theatre. Pointing beyond its original context, Patrice Pavis notes, "*Gestus* radically cleaves the performance into two blocks: the shown (the said) and the showing (the saying) . . . *Gestus* thus displaces the dialectic between ideas and actions; the dialectic no longer operates within the system of these ideas and actions, but at the point of intersection of the enunciating gesture and the enunciated discourse."[3] At this point of intersection, contrariety comes to the fore as soon as the nonidentity of (written) statement and (oral) utterance is recognized as offering a crucially important space for *gestus*. As enacted on stage, the site of this nonidentity offers the performer a "terrific" moment for those "self-generative" transactions which, as noted above (pp. 7–8), Michael Goldman and Bernard Beckerman have anticipated as a source of the actor's self-sustained, unpredictable spontaneity.

In the speech and action of the Tudor Vice, such contrariety, therefore, informs the vibrant use of *gestus* where scripted language and performing body intersect. Beneath the discourse of role-playing, the élan and buoyancy, the sheer resilience and presence of visible, audible performers shine through. Their unyielding physicality and unconcealed earthiness exude a "power and corrigible authority" (*Othello*, 1.3.325–6) that can seep into the texture of the play. The phrase, revealingly, is said by Iago, who, as a descendant of the Vice, foregrounds the act of counterfeiting in honest reference to "the blood and baseness of our natures" (328). No moral representation is compatible with his lust for "sport and profit" (386) which, precisely, are two articles the theatre can give and take. There must be contrariety where Iago's "double knavery" (394) comes in: "Virtue? a fig!" (319).

Such "contrarious" meaning performed on the threshold of a "secretly open" honesty and a "secret close" knavery strangely overlaps with a different version of contrariety in Renaissance thought and writing, given to the recognition of opposites within the same topic or domain. This philosophical version of contrariety indeed appears as an important trope in a number of discourses of the period, from religious controversy to Petrarchan verse and satire. In his study of Shakespeare's "mighty opposites," Robert Grudin has explored the role of contrariety in the Paracelsian tradition as it unfolds in the works of Giordano Bruno, Montaigne, and even Castiglione.[4] To Grudin, though such figures differ greatly in style and subject, they are united in the belief "that contrariety can be a positive and regenerative principle, and that the only coherent response to experience, in theory or practice, lies in the acceptance of contrariety and the application of its special power."[5]

To a rhetorically trained culture, this mode of contrariety was a familiar, ready way to enfigure the experience of forceful contradiction. Abraham Fraunce in *Lawyer's Logic* (1588) defines contrarieties as "such opposites" in which "the one is so opposed to the other, as yet there may bee in other respects a mutuall consent and reciprocall relation between them."[6] John Hoskins, in his *Directions for Speech and Style* (1599), would call "Comparison of contraries" the "most flourishing way of comparison."[7] Thomas Wilson also praised contrariety's rhetorical advantages: "By contraries set together, things oftentimes appear greater."[8] Not surprisingly, modern critics have explored manifestations of this phenomenon using various terms, among which we could include Rosalie Colie's focus on paradox through *coincidentia oppositorum*, Joel Altman's *argumentum ab utramque partem*, and, not to forget, the workings of "amphibology" that Steven Mullaney has highlighted in *Macbeth* and in Renaissance discourse generally.[9] Indeed, contrariety in its various modes could be thought of as what Debora Shuger has termed a contemporary "habit of thought."[10] As Michael Neill reminds us, when Guarini, in his *Compendium of Tragicomic Poetry* (1601), "presented his experiments in generic paradox as a proper response to the heteroclite world," he appealed "to the commonplace occurrence of mixed forms in the other arts, in the realm of politics, and in the order of nature itself" when asking, rhetorically, "'Are not these contraries? yet they join in a single mixed form.'"[11]

Our use of the term in this study acknowledges the widespread discourse of the contrarious during this period, but is based on the observation that in its staging, the language of "contrariety" suffers a *transport* (in both senses of the word) in which its bodily medium turns the verbal statement into a more complex, arresting and potentially more commensurate utterance. For an illustration, we propose to study the language and action of Courage, the Vice in George Wapull's *The Tide Tarrieth No Man* (published in 1576). As main agent on stage, Courage aptly, and with an appropriate doubleness, styles himself as "contrarious" and "contrary." Yet his uses of the phrase are quite different from any of the literary versions of "contrariety" examined above nor, for that matter, are they identical to those strange and intense "antinomies" that critics have repeatedly noticed in medieval drama.[12] For what Courage does goes beyond – even when it comes close to – doing what the Vice in Thomas Lupton's *All for Money* (published in 1578), is supposed to do: as a stage direction informs us, "Here the vice shall turn the proclamation to some contrary sense at every time all for money hath read it."[13]

The peculiar strength of this "contrarious" element in *The Tide* derives from a set of marked cultural differences in the uses of social, verbal, and spatial conventions in a particular theatrical context.[14] As in *All for Money*, the agent of contrariety is apt to speak an unscripted text; here is an extemporal agency of *inversion* – a practice rooted in preliterate culture. Since the explicit language of contrariety occurs in a mid-Elizabethan play, it is just possible that it provided a cue for Sir Philip Sidney's use of the same word in his *Defence of Poesy* (composed *c.* 1580–5). The well-known critical context is Sidney's complaint that contemporary popular plays "match hornpipes and funerals":

So falleth it out that, having indeed no right comedy, in that comical part of our tragedy we have nothing but scurrility, unworthy of any chaste ears, or some extreme show of doltishness, indeed fit to lift up a loud laughter, and nothing else: where the whole tract of a comedy should be full of delight, as the tragedy should be still maintained in a well-raised admiration. But our comedians think there is no delight without laughter; which is very wrong, for though laughter may come with delight, yet cometh it not of delight, as though delight should be the cause of laughter; but well may one thing breed both together. Nay, rather in themselves they have, as it were, a kind of contrariety . . .[15]

The concept is prominently lodged at a veritable juncture of confusion, at the heart of what John Lyly, still under the impact of humanist disapproval, called the "Hodge-podge" or "mingle-mangle" by which "Time has confounded our minds, our minds the matter."[16] In other words, contrariety appears centrally implicated in the unsanctioned practice of a much to be deplored gulf between the dramatic text's poetic diction and the common player's delivery on vulgar scaffolds. Sidney is very emphatic and quite unambiguous in relegating the figure to what he believes is an abusing kind of performance practice. The trouble is not with what imaginary roles represent but with what performing agents have "in themselves" to molest or corrupt them. Along these lines, "our comedians" are branded for their "scurrility," "doltishness," and "loud laughter." No question, Sidney's understanding of "contrariety" is derived from certain performance practices of the time. As far as Shakespeare adapted or assimilated the language of contrariety, it was a case of actor's voice, even his *gestus*, in author's pen.

This is not to suggest any clean bifurcation between the performer's act of *énonciation* and what was staged as *énoncé* but, rather, a mutually uneven engagement between the two. It is the point where "in one line two crafts directly meet" (*Hamlet*, 3.4.210). As against Hamlet's own humanist poetics, "the purpose of playing" is suffused by double-dealing strategies. Thus in *A Midsummer Night's Dream* it is perfectly possible to figure forth a world of elves, courtship, and festivity and yet in their midst to "disfigure, or to present" (3.1.60–1) an action through the underside of its unworthy performance. Nor is such double-dealing purpose of playing confined to Shakespearean comedy. In a tragedy like *Macbeth* or *Antony and Cleopatra*, to name only two, contrariety thrives at the greatest moment of tragic action and suspense, as when the Porter's performance brings forth an uncanny confusion of heaven and hell, or the "rural fellow" (5.2.233) in the latter play amid laughter and terror wishes "all joy of the worm" (260): contrariety in the obscene, equivocating act of enunciation itself. In view of such tragic versions of polyvalence or, as Mikhail Bakhtin phrased it, "heteroglossia,"[17] the question proves even more daunting: who is speaking through a contrariety thriving, it appears, between represented text and (re)presenting performers?

With this question in mind, we can study the enunciations of Courage more searchingly, especially when his position in the play at large is taken into account. In its main theme and direction, *The Tide Tarrieth No Man* responds to a growing sense (well documented in mid-sixteenth-century historiography) that the transcendent aims of pious living are being surrendered to secular ambition, material acquisition, and sensual fulfillment. It is a situation offering newfound space for a free-wheeling allegory of evil "to negotiate the discursive vacuum produced by the withdrawal of the divine Word."[18] In his animal energy, willful blindness, and reckless appetite, Courage boldly seeks to appropriate the proverbial message of the play, the message from which it takes its title. The proverb was no doubt far from unambiguous in its interpretation. Too close to the Latin *tempus fugit*, the scale of meaning stretched from its orthodox reading in *Everyman* earlier in the century through a number of variations in the works of John Heywood, Nicholas Udall, Anthony Munday, and John Lyly (to name only these). But in the morality context, the pious, sanctioned reading of the proverb dominated; it urged an awareness of life's brevity as an impetus to prepare one's soul for eternity. In the words of Wapull's Prologue, "There is time to ask grace . . . / For that tide most certain will tarry no man."[19] As against this orthodox text, Courage enters as frivolous agent of contrariety in signification; he inverts the eschatological emphasis into the more earthy advice of *carpe diem*, urging, through his blandishments, several of the characters to make hay while the sun shines.

By both appropriating and corrupting the play's central metaphor, the Vice moralizes two meanings in one title. In doing so he physically disturbs, invades, and finally blurs altogether the borderline between the allegorical site of orthodox doctrine and an unsanctioned space for bringing forth quite another meaning. What results is, over and beyond a blending of discourses, a mutual interrogation of two radically different sources of authority – one idealistic, orthodox, and religious; the other materialistic, irreverent, and empirical. Only in the last quarter of the play (ll. 1440–879) is the role of Courage reduced until overcome by Authority and Correction to be led away for execution (1822–7). Even so, the two meanings in one proverb linger on and cannot be dispensed with equal ease.

For one thing, the Vice and his three henchmen (Hurtful Help, Painted Profit, and Feigned Furtherance) can mobilize their own semantic authority by reference to secular wisdom and common experience. Courage's stark message is especially effective (and grim) when delivered to an audience whose members as a matter of course were confronted with the prospect of dying young: "Take time while time is, / Lest that you do miss, / Tide tarrieth no man" (144–6). As assimilated here, the proverbial lesson, in addition to its downright hedonism, offers a strange mixture of fear and defiance. Through almost two thousand lines of largely uninspired verse, the alliterative phrase achieves an almost formulaic quality; its distinctively oral and proverbial emphasis provides a signature in rhythm and semantics more insistent, even, than Iago's Vice-like, oft-repeated "put money in thy purse" (*Othello*, 1.3.339 ff.).

Joined to the weight of this other, secular reading, in most instances (such as ll. 62, 146, 172, 372, 476, 584, 650, 853, 902, 913, 1234, 1270) the rhetoric of repetition is couched in what Greediness calls "contrary talk"

(376) – amphibology or doublespeak. In the language of Neighbourhood (who cancels part of his full allegorical name, which should read "No Good Neighbourhood"), Courage himself could have said, "Because of my name men should stand in doubt" (441). In other words, the language, the entire configuration of Courage is semiotically unreliable. Addressing the audience directly, he says:

> Now may you see how Courage can work,
> And how he can encourage, both to good and bad:
> The Merchant is encouraged, in greediness to lurk,
> And the Courtier to win worship, by Courage is glad.
> The one is good, no man will deny,
> I mean courage to win worship and fame:
> So that the other is ill, all men will say. (698–704)

Although the Vice's instigations must be almost entirely read as encouragements to sin and evil, Courage resists such a univocally oppositional interpretation when he enters in the colors of semantic ambivalence. Note how "Courage the Vice entereth":

> Courage contagious,
> Or courage contrarious,
> That is my name:
> To which that I will,
> My mind to fulfill,
> My manners I frame.
>
> Courage contagious,
> When I am outrageous,
> In working of ill:
> And Courage contrary,
> When that I do vary,
> To compass my will.
>
> For as in the Bee,
> For certain we see,
> Sweet honey and sting:
> So I in my mind,
> The better to blind,
> Two courages bring. (93–110)

As in many other moral plays, there is in the early parts of the play a traditional piece of self-introduction, through which the Vice *qua* leading player establishes a doubly encoded sort of identity. Courage's speech is noteworthy in that his role, far from showing any univocal self, reveals a penchant for moralizing two dispositions in one role. Clearly, such disposition cannot be made from within a self-contained play or character. Rather, it is a double-speak by which the leader of the troupe intervenes with a word of his own, as authorized by the playwright. No doubt, here we have "the self-exposing tendencies of self-speaking rhetoric" (the phrase here is Richard Hillman's)[20] – a "self," however, shrouded in ambivalence. Again, multiple subjectivities emerge out of a deliberately enframed gap between Courage speaking his "mind" and Courage "framing" his "manners." His variations on the theme of an unstable identity add up to a somewhat facile division between inside and outside (or between "mind" and "manners," language and gesture or costume). What is at issue is not the question of impersonation, but that of his persona in the form of a variation itself: as "Courage contrary, / When that I do vary / To compass my will." In more than one sense, then, the Vice is denied a "meaning" as a representation of character. Instead, his talk of "Two courages" is to moralize two meanings in one name.

The strategy of self-introduction here tends to go beyond the "secretly open" reasoning which Courage offers as an explanation ("The better to blind . . ."; "To color my guile," 109, 118). What in fact is foregrounded is the person behind the persona explaining the tools of a trickster. Ultimately there is a residue which cannot (and should not) be explained away. As Courage notes, with tongue in cheek, he is able to deliver "very clean / And not be understood" (121–2). Clarity in the figure's speech and delivery appears deceptive. Similarly, it is difficult to decide whether or to what degree Courage's "Sweet honey and sting" has, in its contrariety, a representational underside, or whether his "When that I do vary" is a meaningful (rather than technical or material) extension of a contrarious potential in personation. As things stand, the signifying process in such discursive figuration as Courage can best be described as postallegorical in his unfixed "mind," his unstable shape, and unpreordained movement.

In Shakespeare such indeterminate movement will come to be used purposively, as a pattern in the codification of madness. For instance, "clean" conveyance and semantic confusion are deliberately brought together as some form of "matter and impertinency mix'd! Reason in madness!" (*King Lear*, 4.6.174–5). What is impertinent in Courage's phrase is the pun in "conveyance" – on "stealing," another type of confusion between mine and thine. In Shakespeare's more stringently representational context, the most incisive "contrary" figure was indeed the theme of madness in a tragic context; on the purely verbal level, it was, most profusely, the use of wordplay.

Did Sidney's reference to the "kind of contrariety" he found in Tudor comedians embrace such punning? We do not know, but it can be traced on the lips of the amoral Vice for at least a hundred years, back to presumably the oldest of the itinerant moral plays extant. In *Mankind* (*c.* 1471) it can be seen to dominate the play's prologue-like opening, when Mercy, spokesman of clerical orthodoxy, is rudely interrupted by Mischief, the main Vice in the play. Again, the site of punning is marked by a proverbial saying:

Mercy.   Prick not your felicities in things transitory!

        . . .

        For, sickerly, there shall be a strait examination.
        "The corn shall be saved, the chaff shall be brent" –
        I beseech you heartily, have this premeditation.
        [*Enter* MISCHIEF]
Mis.   I beseech you heartily, leave your calcation,
        Leave your chaff, leave your corn, leave your daliation;
        Your wit is little, your head is mickle; ye are full of predication.
        But, sir, I pray you this question to clarify:
        Mish-mash, driff-draff,
        Some was corn and some was chaff.
        My dame said my name was Raff.
        Unshut your lock and take an ha'penny!
Mercy.   Why come ye hither, brother? Ye were not desired.
Mis.   For a winter-corn thresher, sir, I have been hired.
        And ye said the corn should be saved and the chaff should be fired.
        And he proveth nay, as it sheweth by this verse:
        'Corn *servit bredibus*, chaff *horsibus*, straw *firibusque*' . . .
        This is as much to say, to your lewd understanding,
        As: the corn shall serve to bread at the next baking;
        – 'Chaff *horsibus, et reliqua*' –
        The chaff to horse shall be good provent;
        When a man is forcold the straw may be brent;
        And so forth, *et cetera*.
Mercy.   Avoid, good brother; ye ben culpable
        To interrupt thus my talking delectable.
Mis.   Sir, I have neither horse nor saddle;
        Therefore I may not ride.
Mercy.   Hie you forth on foot, brother, in God's name!
Mis.   I say, sir, I am come hither to make you game.[21]

Of course, the theme is "the Last Judgment," and Mercy's mentioning of it has homiletic urgency. His language, with its obtrusive Latinisms, is in a strict sense moralizing, its purpose hortatory, its order of discourse symbolic.

But although Mercy's central metaphor has ample biblical authority ("The corn shall be saved, the chaff shall be brent"; cf. Matthew 3:12; Luke 3:17), the Vice in his brazen onslaught seizes upon it so as to "moralize" another meaning in the same image.

Thus between Mercy and Mischief the same shared metaphor ("corn"/ "chaff") is being double-voiced or, we might say, doubly encoded. The social and cultural difference between the two characters literally fuels what contrariety implodes in the opening "dialogue." We give this word quotation marks here because, instead of the representation of dialogic exchange, we have more nearly an encounter between two radically differing modes of authorizing discourse: on the one hand, the discursive location of authority is marked by uses of language as institutionalized in the office of a cleric, with his barely concealed Latin education; on the other, there is a seemingly naïve common understanding of language, which is impervious to both pious exhortation and the perception of any metaphysical tenor in the biblical metaphor. In its place Mischief substitutes a playfully ingenuous reading of its vehicle, connecting a distrust of transcendent symbolism with an insistent awareness of rural experience. It is the empirical horizon of a "winter-corn thresher" which resonates in the language of alliterative wordplay, nonsense rhyme and dog-Latin, together with an unmistakable allusion to the most widespread, and certainly most traditional, formula of the Mummers' Play, "Your wit is little, your head is mickle" (47).[22]

This is not the place to provide more than a brief reminder of the deeper roots of this type of double-voiced language in medieval drama. Suffice it to say that the actual engagement between contrary modes of discursive practice must not be minimized, either by relegating the Vice's impertinent intervention to the status of comic relief, or by shrugging off Mercy's position in the play as a ludicrous butt of popular abuse. What must be emphasized is the antinomy between the two cultural codes and the strength of their collision, in the course of which some related type of "Courage contrary" and encouragement "contrarious" thrives long before Sidney could have noticed it. For although Mercy's voice is the recognized and authoritative source of clerical moralization and literacy, it is Mischief who, by radically and purposefully "misunderstanding" the former's code, provides the more effective – or, as Courage puts it, "contagious" – counterpoint. In both cases, the language of the Vice, far remote from any bookish language (let alone a Latinized idiom), is largely marked by oral patterns of discourse.

The opening scene of *Mankind* may well be said to be dramatically kindled by a clash between page and stage. There is on one hand the literate culture of writing, reading, and preaching marked by a symbolic order of transcendence, a capacity for abstraction and cognizance. On the other hand, there is a culture of ordinary living and oral utterance, with a more sensory type of perception and a knowledge marked by immediacy. As far as the antinomy between the two is rooted in contrarious ways of living and seeing, it embraces variegated ways and media of communication – ways which in their confrontation flare up in strange, but thoroughly comic, patterns of misreading and misunderstanding.

When viewed against the clash (here sketched in its roughest outlines only) between these two different cultures, the uses and abuses of symbolization in *The Tide Tarrieth No Man* and in *Mankind* are in many ways similar. Both plays provide "contrary" meanings to an orthodox reading of biblical doctrine. These meanings foreground material interests and immediately available experience, though the later play, disdaining "the chaffy treasure of the world" (l. 1480), does not go to the length of rehearsing the "corn" and "chaff" and "straw" as nonallegorical "good provent." In both plays the doubly encoded uses of language embrace images of specific, well-known, material patterns of living in the present – sensory patterns that may accurately be described as "contagious," in the sense of "communicable by direct contact." And yet, as against these patterns, the written texts of the plays were designed to accept and balance, but finally to reduce the over-whelming presence of a farcical performative. The concluding part in each case reassesses the basic division in social, educational, and clerical matters. What so far had appeared as self-assured uses of game and sport, pleasure and profit is itself exposed to a more searching and imperious kind of scrutiny. The temporary aperture of moral and political disorder gives way in the end to a representation of reasserted clerical and secular authority.

The moral play moves, then, toward a vision of "order" in which the equivocal energy of the Vice is contained through the allegorical representation of Christian and civil authority. Order is restored, and the figure called Christianity can flourish, "when all malefactors are duly thus punished" (1828). Here one recalls Angus Fletcher's phrase that he "suspects the mode [of allegory] of lending itself too readily to a restriction of freedom."[23] The allegorical *modus dicendi*, precisely because it says one thing and means another, presupposes certitude, if not necessarily fixture, in the given correspondence between utterance and statement, between what is said and what is meant. Relying on a comparable pattern of correspondences between detail and generality, the senses and the spirit, this type of allegory may well be said to defy any order with two equivocal meanings in its signs. As Stephen Greenblatt suggests, such allegory often arises in response to "periods of loss, periods in which a once powerful theological, political, or familial authority is threatened with effacement."[24]

In response to some such feeling of threat and "loss," the ending of *The Tide Tarrieth No Man* attempts a symbolic recuperation of social order through the representation of its violent enforcement. The space for contrariety is radically reduced when its near-obliteration is achieved through the performed action of the very medium that seemed to challenge it. Now two entirely unambiguous representations of authority backed by force make their appearance, Correction and Authority himself. While Courage is *"reasoning with himself"* (1760 S.D.) about the death of immortal "Greediness," Authority enters to have the Vice, with the help of Correction, arrested and punished: "Draw near Correction and thine office do, / Take here this caitiff unto the Jail" (1813 ff.). Quite unambiguously, the language of Authority is articulated as in alliance with some "office" to be delegated in pursuit of justice and correction. At this point, Authority partially surrenders his function as the personification of an abstract quality in favor of a particular association with an officially sanctioned power to enforce things by "commandment" (1815), by "this power," and by "force of the same" (1860–1). Even before Authority enters, one of the virtuous figures of allegory is shown in search of him: "I marvel where Authority is . . . / His absence greatly disquieteth my mind, / I will not cease seeking, until him I do find" (1746, 1750–1). In other words, Authority (and, by implication, the culture marked by law and literacy) never ceased to be operative. He needs only to be *found* in order to have his regime ensured. But then the disquieting state of Authority's "absence" is conveyed theatrically as the actor of Authority, through his physical absence from the stage, is made to signify the "absence" of his own allegorical meaning. In other words, the emplotment of symbolic order itself assumes a figure of deferment. In fact, its retrieval will eventually be able to take care of what turns out to be merely the temporary supremacy of Courage and his ilk.

There is, then, an unresolved, almost grotesque paradox in what happens to the figure called Vice, especially marked at the point where script and delivery part company. Verbally and symbolically condemned to die or to be locked away, these figures can rekindle on the strength of their performance what is inert or stale. On stage they serve as vehicles of vibrant growth and movement; their impact on the play at large is as quickening as it is provocative. As David Bevington has shown, their stage presence is near-overwhelming: Courage, like Inclination, for three-quarters of the play's duration; others for five-sixths, even nine-tenths of the play.[25] True enough, a Vice like Courage is presented as a morally abhorrent figure, an ugly tool of seduction and aberrance. But even when outrageously straying from the path of rectitude, the figure is resilient and full of infectious buoyancy. "Courage contrary" is more than a symbol of negation when its images of reckless release, though admittedly irresponsible, are as "contagious" as the desire to live life to the fullest of its possibilities. Something similar can be said about other figures of Vice for whom, as in the case of Mischief ("I am come hither to make you game"), a preoccupation with playfulness and sport can constitute a level of performance practice impervious to moralizing standards of representation. This performative energy, with its ultimate roots in a communally sanctioned world of game and self-assured release, enlivens the morality Vice even as it goes under.[26] It is most alive and intriguing where it refuses to submit to the psychomachian order of such oppositions as normally prescribe the representation of meaning in the orthodox part of the morality. For instance, in his provocative self-introduction in *The Trial of Treasure*, Inclination explains that "The mighty on the earth I will subdue":

> Forsooth, I am called Natural Inclination . . .
> I make the stoutest to bow and bend:
> Again, when I lust, I make men stand upright;
> From the lowest to the highest I do ascend,
> Drawing them to things of natural might.[27]

The popular praise of folly celebrates those unsanctioned "things of natural might" that unhinge the coordinates of good and evil. Like Mischief and Courage, Inclination here transcends the homiletic uses of allegorical fiction and significantly eludes the all too predictable representation of an opposition between sinful and virtuous standards of behavior.

In these plays the discourse of the figure called Vice has an appeal, even – in terms of the agency of its performance – a kind of authority of its own. Following the Vice as the leading player who combined the offices of the troupe's principal and its director, these "comedians," in Sidney's phrase, had it "in themselves" with taunts to fleer and gird at the entire mode of allegorical symmetry and indirection. For them, the allegorical veil itself, the obliquity of personified universals, might well have run counter to a penchant marked, in Courage's phrase, by "catching and snatching," "running and riding," and "Coming and going." This language of nimble corporeality flanks not simply an absent image of questionable release but, in the staged figuration of the Vice, affects the performed as well as the performing. Such cleavage in performance between the imaginary product of mimesis and the actual process of miming provides the elementary grounds of "contrariety."

Even when reinscribed in the frivolous *gestus* of Mischief or Courage, such language could not of course hope to serve as an adequate counterpoise to the more awesome fixed authority of Christianity, sanctioned by the written text of the Bible and firmly anchored and institutionalized in ecclesiastical doctrine. But despite his subsequent defeat and punishment, the Vice's part in the play constitutes a countervailing force of remarkable energy. Take, for example, the desperate and rather stubborn determination as conveyed by Courage in his self-introduction:

> Now sir to show,
> Whether we do go,
> Will do very well,
> We mean to prevail,
> And therefore we sail,
> To the Devil of hell. (123–8)

The defiant "We mean to prevail" recalls the even stronger note of defiance in the language of Inclination, who is never subdued by the forces of order: "Well, yet I will rebel, yea, and rebel again, / And though a thousand times you shouldest me restrain."[28] The springs of this rebellion derive from something scarcely representable in terms of the discourse of allegory. Transgressing the dichotomous order of allegorical good and evil, the visceral strength of it can best be conceived in terms of the incommensurate, vitalizing force in the self-generative performance of madness and folly.

Such transgression must not be thought of as constituting an exclusively discursive, argumentative gesture of nonconformity. To say this is not to question the peculiar strength, rooted in performance practice, of the Vice's defiance. In fact, the matrix of his contrarious forays into the nonrepresentable and the nonfictional is inseparable from the flexible uses of open theatrical space, which (following medieval precedent) continues to be referred to as "place."[29] Once the Vice character enters to address the audience directly, he tends to assume a *platea*-like position from which he never quite withdraws in the course of the play.[30] This spatial positioning offers him a unique, double-voiced range of reference to both allegorical figurations and unworthy circumstances. From these contrariously played-out positions of reference, Courage can easily negotiate proverbial wisdom, lead off into a song, or address individual spectators in the audience ("But hush sirs I say, no moe words but

mum" [340]; "How say you good wives, is it not so?" [718] and *passim*).
His part is inseparable from a sustained sense of sharing the same ground
with everybody present on the occasion, "within this place": "I think there
is no man, within this place, / But he would gladly such neighbors
embrace" (570–1).

Similarly, Nichol Newfangle, the Vice in *Like Will to Like* (published in
1587), strikes up with "*a gittern or some other instrument*" so that jolly knaves
"*must dance about the place*" after his "trim singing." Alone on the stage,
Nichol, snorting "Ha, ha, ha, ha, ha, ha, ha!," sings, "*Though they be gone, I
am in place.*" These theatrical uses of "place" can scarcely be subsumed
under any allegorical regime of representation. In fact, they provide a space
for the performer and his body to cross the frontiers of representation,
moving, dancing, laughing himself right across the limen between real
"sport" and allegorical fiction. Although the script attempts to textualize
his vicious laughter in its sevenfold iteration of "ha!", it cannot capture the
unrepresentable delivery of what this laughter stands for, let alone the
performer's explosive breath, the airstream's vibrations in his vocal cords,
or the membranes in his glottis. Whether such laughter, as Bakhtin postulated, served as a shield of resistance, it does betray a sense of momentary
triumph in its remarkable blend of release and resilience.

On another festive occasion, the Vice joins the revelers "as they go out
from the place." Finally, a complete stage direction reads:

Here entereth in NICHOL NEWFANGLE, *and bringeth in with him a bag, a staff,
a bottle, and two halters, going about the place, showing it unto the audience, and
singeth thus*:
　　Trim mer- chandise, trim trim: trim mer- chandise, trim trim.
　　[*He may sing this as oft as he thinketh good.*][31]

Such showmanship goes hand in hand with a display of both vocal competence and commodities comprising material objects rather than icons or
signs of these objects. Here a strong "performant function" obliterates
boundaries between players and petty chapmen. Although Nichol
Newfangle is a fictive name, the sign of a role, the signified relocates his
newfangledness in the traditional proximity of players and tradesmen.
Thus, since his ties to dramatic fiction are quite tenuous, the player
performs extempore with his voice in "the place" as a site, contrariously
used, for both unprescribed performance and indeterminate reception. An
awareness of this *platea*-like position, then, makes it possible for the Vice to
straddle the worlds of both dramatic fiction and theatrical business.
Crossing again and again the threshold between representation and the

circumstantial world of actual performance, he partially unsettles relations of expectation and demand, communication and entertainment.

Courage's restive, intractable desire for "ebbing and flowing / Coming and going" connects with parameters of instability, unsettled meanings, and inconclusive trajectories. Moving between readings and perceptions as yet unsanctioned by (and largely unrecorded in) the dominant types of judicial, moral, and religious discourse, Courage links his own reading of the play's moral with a distinctly modern sense that temporality and mobility constitute restless articles in a rudderless "Barge of sin":

> Take time while time is,
> Lest that you do miss,
> Tide tarrieth no man.
>
> With catching and snatching,
> Waking and watching,
> Running and riding:
> Let no time escape,
> That for you doth make,
> For Tide hath no biding.
>
> But ebbing and flowing,
> Coming and going,
> It never doth rest:
> Therefore when you may,
> Make no delay,
> For that is the best. (137, 144–58)

Courage and other Vices such as Nichol Newfangle (who sets out for "a journey into Spain") or Hickscorner ("Sirs, I have been in many a country")[32] show an extraordinary penchant for traveling. This movement relates to the character's wayward and erratic disposition, which goes hand in hand with, but ultimately transcends, the agility of his own body. This nimbleness affects language itself, unfixing given patterns of meaning and understanding. Thus, closely allied with images of kinetic energy and spatial motion, there is an element of unpredictable and often impertinent movement informing the process of signification itself. If anywhere in the Morality uses of language are marked by an active and playful expansion of discursive norms, it is the speech associated with the Vice, especially in its forward-looking response to the gestural, vocal, communicative, and scenic conditions of stage delivery. Here was a veritable fountainhead, an invaluable source for late Elizabethan players and playwrights alike.

CHAPTER 2

Performance, game, and representation
in Richard III

To move from a late moral play to Shakespeare's first tetralogy is to encounter a puzzling hiatus. This hiatus divides the moral interludes and related dramatic medleys of the 1560s and 1570s from the new and startling impetus coming from Kyd and Marlowe in the second half of the 1580s. Never sufficiently accounted for, the space between these types of plays, and between their dates of composition, bears significantly on the emergent Elizabethan relations of page and stage. Grappling with the *terra incognita* of these years, theatre historians, particularly in the wake of Janet Loengard's work on the Red Lion theatre, have encountered a marked "disparity between theatrical activity and printed texts," where the extremely small number of extant texts sits uneasily with widespread flourishing of performance practices.[1] As we know, regular stagings of amphitheatrical shows for large audiences occurred not only after the opening of the Theatre (1576) and the Curtain (1577) but even a decade earlier, with the setting up of the Red Lion (1567). Recent work in theatre history has given us a cultural landscape that, even when tantalizingly obscured, prompts new and pertinent questions.

Up to a certain time, the history of dramatic literature (the work of such authors as, for example, Nicholas Udall, Richard Edwards, George Whetstone, and George Gascoigne) was largely discontinuous with itinerant and nonacademic shows. These shows clearly proliferated prior to the Shakespearean stage. The late 1570s, for instance, sponsored more than thirty identifiable playing companies. On the basis of such numbers, William Ingram has calculated a potential need for about a hundred different play scripts each year. Since their nonexistence can hardly be accounted for by loss, Ingram's conclusion appears sound: "as long as our focus is on dramatic texts, we are likely to view this early period as a desert."[2] We need to dispense, therefore, with the idea that dramatic composition was the primary impulse behind early modern theatre.

Before Marlowe, Kyd, Greene, Nashe, and Shakespeare began to write for the Elizabethan stage, playing was largely self-sustained. Performance enjoyed a measure of self-sufficiency as a sovereign craft among all sorts and conditions of nonverbal and preverbal practices. Keeping these practices in mind helps us understand the contemporary process of differentiating common players from a host of what David Bradley calls "fencers, musicians, rope-dancers, acrobats, tumblers, mountebanks, puppeteers, and exhibitors of all kinds of marvels and grotesques."[3] Bradley defines these as "amateur groups, as well as random collections of unemployed persons who might temporarily have found some kind of limited protection as players." As Robert Weimann noted years ago, many of these "unemployed persons," in want of both "protection" and sheer sustenance, must have been uprooted by large-scale enclosures. Condemned to vagabondage, they confronted a fiercely repressive regime – of which the Cade/Iden episode (*2 Henry VI*, 4.10) recalls a highly partial trace. This episode is unlike that of the "Poor naked wretches" in *King Lear* (3.4.28) with their "houseless heads" and "unfed sides" (30), or the same play's Poor Tom, chased from "tithing to tithing" (134). This background is of more than sociological significance. If they were driven away from their rural holdings, members of those "amateur groups" must have been in close touch with many postritual and predramatic village ceremonies, customs and practices – some of them potentially useful in terms of their performative proficiencies.[4]

Such performance practices must have appeared almost impervious to any verbal or textual appropriation. In fact, from Shakespeare's first tetralogy to the otherwise inexplicable departure of Will Kemp from the Lord Chamberlain's Men almost a decade later, we encounter traces of resistance to prescribed language use.[5] One of the earliest plays in the tetralogy offers circumstantial evidence of this in Jack Cade's bloody Saturnalia. The entire scene (*2 Henry VI*, 4.2) is inspired by a performative *gestus* par excellence. Two players, [George] Bevis and John Holland (in the Folio text listed under their own names) enter with a clownish word on their lips, recalling the Vice's token of identity: "Come and get thee a sword, though made of a lath" (1), to be followed up by Holland's "it was never merry world in England since gentlemen came up" (8–9). Appropriately, the scene concludes on a strong note of contrariety, with Cade exclaiming, "But then are we in order when we are most out of order. Come, march forward" [*Exeunt*.] (189–90). This wayward performance of topsyturvydom is especially significant when it culminates in furious hostility against literacy. Such literacy is at stake when the clerk of Chartham, a Kentish town, is brought in and charged: "He can write and read and cast accompt" (85–6). Upon his confession, "I can write my name," the verdict is, "Away with him, I say! Hang him with his pen and inkhorn about his neck" (106, 109–10).

At this early stage in his career, Shakespeare the writer continued to face the gaps between bodily-centered mass entertainment and the socially and culturally different matrix of rhetoric and composition. While the broad popular attraction of oratorical delivery should not be underestimated, the unruly body in performance almost invariably veered in the direction of the popular. Whatever the vexed chronology of the three opening plays in the first tetralogy, Shakespeare's uses of language there were largely formal and rhetorically conventional save for in the Cade scenes.

The difference we see between these alternating sequences of elite and more common performance would tellingly punctuate a single, and otherwise calm, conversation between Prince Edward and Buckingham in *Richard III*, the explosive new play which rounded out Shakespeare's tetralogy. Hearing that Julius Caesar built the Tower of London, the Prince inquires how this fact came to be preserved: "Is it upon record, or else reported / Successively from age to age, he built it?" (3.1.72–3). Placing "record" – what we could associate with the chronicle tradition from which the play draws – over and against that which is "reported," Edward goes on to assert that if

> it were not regist'red,
> Methinks the truth should live from age to age,
> As 'twere retail'd to all posterity,
> Even to the general all-ending day. (75–8)

What makes this speech so compelling is not only its quiet meditation on the nature of historical knowledge, a meditation that values the oral and popular alongside if not indeed over the "regist'red" page, but how this almost academic question is diverted by Edward's malevolent uncle. Just before analogizing himself to the most powerful figure on the pre-Shakespearean stage, Richard complicates any simple notion of what is orally "retail'd" when he utters, in a menacing aside, a piece of folk wisdom that he will use to justify his high Machiavellian design: "So wise so young, they say do never live long" (79). Challenged to explain his first aside, Richard does so, only to share triumphantly with the audience another: "Thus, like the formal Vice, Iniquity, / I moralize two meanings in one word" (82–3).

Evident in these arch asides, and in the play of *Richard III* itself, is a new, mutually demanding kind of interplay between speech and performance. Not only do the arts of dramatic discourse and the arts of performance interact, but performance begins to infiltrate the very composition of character itself. In other words, the former disparity of "performance" and "character" gives way to a mutually effective penetration. In thought and action, protagonists absorb what is most performative in the craft and craftiness of counterfeiting. Performance now saw its radius doubled: even as it remained the actor's task, performance was also and simultaneously assimilated within the actor's (and the writer's) projection of a character's thinking and doing.

This development itself made possible a new phase in the culture of the theatre and its dramaturgy. On its most general level, the challenge was to meet, in Cornelius Castoriadis's phrase, the need for an "ensemblizing" potential, an ensemble practice in the theatre which did not suppress difference and disparity but, on the contrary, was prepared to work with them.[6] More specifically, the demand was for a multiplication of dramatically effective perspectives on difference, on what Ruth Lunney has called a "framing rhetoric" bringing together on stage and among spectators a new amplitude as well as immediacy in seeing and connecting signs and meanings.[7]

Perhaps the best way to grapple with this scenario of radical change is to scrutinize how the "disparity" in question is addressed, suspended, intercepted, and – partially at least – resolved in popular Renaissance plays in the decade after 1585. Focusing on Shakespeare, we propose to study the after-effects of this disparity and its suspension in terms of a continuing difference between institutionalized performance and dramatically inscribed representation. As these points of reference suggest, the new ensemble quality in the workings of the theatre accompanies not only the rise of new, postallegorical types of representation but also new modes of theatrical *mise-en-scène* and reception. The relationship of stage and page is crucially at issue in this process, for it lent momentum in several ways to the genealogy of the early modern theatre.

This emerging capacity – on stage and off stage – for understanding, using, and connecting signs and meanings differently remained distinct from allegory, with its conventional antitheses between good and evil. As against the calculated consequences for any of the (limited) choices on the part of *humanum genus*, the new dramatic mode of representation radically reduces moments of predictability. The medieval scheme of trial and exemplification is replaced by exposure to horizons of contingency against which grief can lead to joy just as "joy grieves, on slender accident" (*Hamlet*, 3.2.199). Concomitantly, there are relatively open choices for hearing, viewing, and understanding signs and signals contextually, according to a moment-to-moment perception of an evolving, specific situation.

But variability in the representational structure of the scene – variability enabled by the domination of the text – is not everything. In place of the earlier "disparity," the textually given dialogue continues to leave room for a "duality," a bifold structure in the actor-character's personation. In accordance with the performer's presence in what is performed (further traced in chapters 6 and 7), the so-called "performant function" (Jean Alter's term) can serve a broad spectrum of practices. These range from a referential verisimilitude in mimesis to a self-sustained display of the competence and appeal it takes to put the show across.[8] To different purposes and degrees, then, performance maintains an independent element of self-sufficiency, a show value in its own right. At the same time, spectators are invited to judge and, after the play is ended, to respond to and discuss both the story and its performance. Occasionally, they are invited directly to participate in the game, to be privileged in their awareness of a "secret close intent" (*Richard III*, 1.1.158), even admitted to a semi-directorial foresight of what is about to happen on stage.[9]

Along these lines, disparity between the two media metamorphosed into a convergence of their differences. In the process the space for histrionic presentation and self-display either shrank radically or was, in its apartness, isolated from the play proper. The *locus classicus* of such apartness is Christopher Marlowe's *Tamburlaine*, where the "fond and frivolous jestures" of clowning mother-wits served as almost an appendix or a mere digression, "unmeet" for the "matter of worthiness"[10] in the serious substance of the play. In Shakespeare's early *First Part of the Contention* (cited above as *2 Henry VI*), the rebellion headed by Jack Cade provided space for a politically significant Saturnalia of outrageous clowning, already with ties (however fragile) to the serious matter of history.[11] Not unlike the strong presence of clowning in the early comedy *The Two Gentlemen of Verona*, Shakespeare set out (one must assume deliberately) to accommodate, if not fully to integrate, uses of carnivalesque sport, game, and the playful punning mother-wit of seeming folly.

Yet at this juncture Shakespeare – himself an actor – went one step further, beyond the strategy of adding or inserting specimens of the surrounding world of performance practices. In *The Taming of the Shrew*, the transformation of the divergence between the two media into a convergence of their differences resulted in not only the framework of the Induction but the agency of that framework, an agency through which the social, cultural, and linguistic differences between the two media were brought to bear on the play at large. In other words, the disparities between writing for and playing on large public stages were intercepted from without and within the play. Since the setting of the comedy proper is "fair Padua, nursery of arts" (1.1.2), its divergence from the Induction's *platea*-world accommodating a hearty if hapless English plebeian appears in the present context highly significant. When the latter in his popular pride says, "Look in the chronicles; we came in with Richard Conqueror" (Ind.1.4–5), we hear a phrase that could just as well have been on the lips of Jack Cade and his men.

Not until *The Tragedy of Richard III* would Shakespeare assimilate the full thrust and surplus of performance to the semi-tragic shape of a Renaissance protagonist. Adapting a horrible-laughable, grotesque legacy from late medieval drama, the playwright thereby incorporated mixed cultural origins within the representational contours of a leading dramatic character. He does so by turning the play's compound of serious representation and sinister sport into the duplicity of the treacherous "Richard Conqueror," a figure of farce and tragedy.

The traditional role most apt to provide bodily form and intellectual conflict to this differential space between the two cultural formations was the Vice.[12] More than any other dramatist, Shakespeare seized early on the old-fashioned convention and adapted the traditional timelessness of ritual and eccentricity to a new sense of temporality and particularity. Revitalizing the exuberant stage presence, the performative buoyancy of this figure thus involved a reauthorization and a reorientation of language and sport on the stage. It was in fact the contrarious bearing of the Vice figure between these two media that enabled the production of entirely multifarious meanings. No other figure could, with its strong performative heritage, lend itself to such an altogether bewildering range of adaptations in Shakespeare's plays. These adaptations would comprise both clownish comedy and villainous trickery. Part of the heritage of the Vice could be sequestered for sheer comedy, living on in Launce's "old vice still" (3.1.284). Stretching from clown to Duke, this chequered gallery of figurations ultimately shared one spatial dimension: an open stage on which to bring home to spectators a duplicity in the *gestus* of both language and action. Such images of apartness can be traced in several other adaptations of the Vice, but especially in those where their isolation was complemented by *platea*-like uses of a privileged type of performance space, available even for a momentary "aside," with its surplus of awareness and audience rapport.[13]

As the descendants of the Vice enter to raid the world of history and representation, they accord well with an air of showmanship, allowing not only the conspiratorial *gestus* of alliance with a gaping audience, but serving a directorial *travail théâtral* which, as we have seen in the preceding chapter, was incompatible with the constraints of either too much doubling or too consistent a form of characterization. The leading player/character was in charge of overseeing and directing the play; within the play itself, such direction involved providing explanations whenever necessary, and filling in necessary intervals between other characters' changes of dress and appearances.[14] Ambidextrously serving both impersonation in a fiction and the existentially needful requirements for entertainment in person, the Vice could turn his directorial function itself into some kind of entertainment: with a twinkling eye to display his own work in staging the play, to offer his acts of go-between and manipulation as some kind of game, which the audience was more than once invited to see through, and thus participate in.[15]

Here, then, was a highly transgressive master of ceremonies, an agent of theatricality who easily crossed the boundary between plot and complot, emplotment and manipulation. Constantly drawing and crossing the line between representation and showmanship, this entertainer must have displayed his consummate grasp of the arts of performance as a great game, blending even in the symbolism of his role a mixture of appropriation and dispossession, of selfish ambition and good fellowship turning sour. Small wonder when the bifold order in this potent agent of liminality lived on, to be remembered and uniquely inscribed in Shakespeare's plays, but especially so in the early history of *Richard III*.

As an illustration, let us look at Richard's wooing of Lady Anne. The scene is turned into a game of performance out of which the popular Renaissance stage can "force" a representation of astonishing density. In Act 1, scene 2 of *Richard III*, the threshold between game and representation is crossed twice; flanking the scene there is, of sorts, a prologue (1.1.145–62) as well as an epilogue (1.2.227–63), both spoken by Gloucester alone on stage. His language (blank verse in direct address) is forthright but conspiratorial in the sense that, in sinister comedy, he draws the audience into his "secret close intent" (1.1.158):

> For then I'll marry Warwick's youngest daughter.
> What though I killed her husband and her father?
> The readiest way to make the wench amends
> Is to become her husband and her father:
> The which will I . . . (1.1.153–7)

This is a *platea* occasion, with its correlative in Gloucester's uses of language. The scheming player/character forgets about decorum and illusion and falls in with the common idiom of the day when he refers to the daughter of the Earl of Warwick, wife to the late Prince of Wales, as "the wench." The vulgar language of petty tradesmen is cited for proverbial wisdom when he notes, "But yet I run before my horse to market" (160), and reassesses his own politic accounts by "count[ing] my gains" (162). Anachronism, too, may appear when he predicts that "George be packed with post-horse up to heaven" (146).[16] Richard's language here addresses not the past of a stately history; it draws on a horizon of ordinary understanding in the present to encode its signs and images, even its syntax, in a grim kind of *sermo humilis*, breaching courtly illusions by mingling laughter with terror.[17]

Such discursive practice finds authority in neither the chronicles nor Thomas More's portrait of the ferocious witty tyrant. But in Shakespeare the ordinary idiom of tradesmen is followed by the poignant wit and stichomythic rhetoric of courtship and persuasion as Gloucester makes good his "secret close intent" and displays "the readiest way" to win the wench (1.2.33–212). After Lady Anne's fierce hatred has melted in the heat of his violent play of wooing, Gloucester, again alone on stage, congratulates himself, not so much upon the represented action as upon the outcome of his performance:

> Was ever woman in this humour woo'd?
> Was ever woman in this humour won?
> I'll have her, but I will not keep her long.
> What? I that kill'd her husband and his father,
> To take her in her heart's extremest hate,
> With curses in her mouth, tears in her eyes,
> The bleeding witness of my hatred by,
> Having God, her conscience, and these bars against me,
> And I no friends to back my suit at all
> But the plain devil and dissembling looks –
> And yet to win her! All the world to nothing! Hah! (227–37)

Appealing to the authority of the act of performing, not of what is performed, the player/character stands back and looks at his own part in the preceding scene. But rather than replaying the aggressive strategy of his impudent courtship, he proceeds to relish the virtuoso quality of his "dissembling looks." The opening question posed (227–8) is "frivolous" enough; its repetition urges the audience (and grants them time) to respond.

The outgoing bravura is that of a self-congratulating entertainer who rejoices over an uncommon feat, success against formidable odds. What the performer (rather than the performed suitor) reviews is the high degree of his professional competence. The sheer pleasure at the outcome of the game finds its climax in the sardonic "Hah!" – the Vice's oft-recurring interjection, here a grunt of gratification. This is indeed a moment of supreme triumph, when the full extent of "contrariety" through execration emerges. It is a moment that seems to justify C. L. Barber's characterization of the Vice as a "recognized anarchist."[18] The exultation at the achieved equivocation is offered to and shared with the audience who, right up to the actor's exit, are involved on a level where the arts of representation and the playing of the game, never quite the same, come to complement each other.

This conjuncture reveals a fine balance between the language of representation and the show of a performance shining in its own right. Here two locations of authority engage one another: the authority of what is represented collapses in, or at least comes to terms with, the authority of what is performing. The fictitious representation of Gloucester's role as suitor jostles with the histrionic competence required to counterfeit it. There is neither complete rupture nor perfect continuity between what was represented in a fiction and what (or who) was doing the performing. Instead, "contrariety" balances strangely between the icon of representation and the craft of performance.

If, then, the player/character of Gloucester is both the performing agent and the performed object of a dramatic transaction, duality in dramaturgy and duplicity in characterization are virtually predetermined. The ambidextrous engagement between the two dimensions has the use and "abuse of distance" at its center.[19] At the threshold of representation and being, the two levels of authority combine. The signs and symbols of the character's isolation ("And I no friends to back my suit withal") stimulate the virtuoso quality of the performance. The measure of Gloucester's success in courtship is that he has nothing but "the plain devil and dissembling looks" at his disposal. This could with equal poignancy be said of the common player who confronts "So great an object" of performance (*Henry V*, Pro. 11) as (in the guise of the evil Duke) having to court the Prince of Wales's widow.

The game of the scene draws on the sheer distance between the still and serene image of "that brave prince . . . no doubt right royal" (1.2.239, 244) and the "dissembling," performing Duke of Gloucester, almost an outsider dispossessed of the luminous pleasures of the court. In his own bustling ambition and mobility, Gloucester finds the language ("But first I'll turn yon fellow in his grave" [260]) for the audience in horror and laughter to go along with the disadvantaged hunchback ("and am misshapen thus?" [250]). At the same time, the actor in the character appears to rouse his "dissembling looks" from a lower ground so as to confront the difficulty (well described in the language of the Prologue to *Henry V*) of a "crooked figure" (Pro. 15) – a veritable zero, a social nil – to "make imaginary puissance" (25) and come to terms with the performed character's ambition.

This reading of the wooing scene cannot of course do justice to the complex role of Richard Gloucester, who is simultaneously the most Marlovian of Shakespeare's heroes, a Machiavellian intellect of ruthless self-aggrandizement, minister as well as scourge of a corrupt and murderous world, and "one of the most historically self-conscious characters ever presented onstage."[20] Here we must content ourselves with acknowledging that *Richard III*, not unlike Marlowe's treatment of Tamburlaine, is in fact so "stately a history" that it is also indebted to, among other things, a Renaissance discourse of political biography and historiography.[21] The point is not to minimize the importance of this discourse in Shakespeare's text but to underline the degree of difference even from Marlowe's image of the mighty upstart. In *Richard III* the representation of greatness is redefined. Gloucester's angle of vision comprehends an unexpectedly large area of social confusion: upward mobility, blandly practiced, is widely to be observed. As he complains to Elizabeth, "Since every Jack became a gentleman, / There's many a gentle person made a Jack" (1.3.71–2). Again, these lines can be read as celebrating two meanings in one conceit. They suggest the upward exchange of roles in the world of both society and the theatre. The dark dialectic of appropriation and self-projection is at work in a performance practice where almost every ordinary player in this history does, and therefore undoes, "a gentle person." Absorbing both the professional role of the lowly actor and the elevated role of the ambitious courtier, the Protean mimicry, especially in the Vice in the Duke, may well have touched off notions of vertical mobility.

Whether that was so, the play must have brought across a supreme lesson in role-playing. Note the facility with which Richard can assume an ordinary person's voice of indignation: "Cannot a plain man live and think no harm?" (51). Along these lines, he is honest Gloucester, contemptuous of false, "apish courtesy" (1.3.49). Within this role-playing (which anticipates the "honest," forthright manner of Iago), we perceive a comedian so cheeky, frank, and enthusiastic in his counterfeiting that a more faithful rendering seems impoverishingly *comme il faut* and unpardonably dreary.

Such outspoken "frankness" in his showmanship is part and parcel of a larger duplicity of meaning. On a rather obvious level, Gloucester is free to play with hosts of moral and political choices because, unlike Margaret, Elizabeth, or Edward, he does not recognize any authority except that of his own appetite and self-interest. As is suggested in his reflection that "I have no brother, . . . I am myself alone" (*3 Henry VI*, 5.6.80, 83), he is not bound by norms of either family affection or loyalty to lineage. But on a subtler and hardly less consequential level, the game he performs is that of a player in front of a looking-glass, an actor who counterfeits the socially counterfeiting, who "descants" on the shadow of his "deformity": "Shine out, fair sun, till I have bought a glass, / That I may see my shadow as I pass" (1.2.262–3). The rhymed couplet gathers in a nutshell the doubly encoded actor/character. For the latter it conveys a sardonic glee over a triumph against all odds; for the former the flourish reflects skillful delivery, the fact of bringing across the mimesis of mimesis. The "glass" in question is an insubstantial icon; instead of Tamburlaine's stately progress in representation, the "shadow" in the mirror reveals the performer in self-reflexive effigy.

Similarly, the touchstone of successfully "dissembling looks" in the world of *Richard III* is the shadow of a shadow; not – as in Marlowe's Prologue – a represented "picture in this tragick glass" but a dissembling character's image in the player's mirror of "the deep tragedian":

> Tut, I can counterfeit the deep tragedian,
> Speak and look back, and pry on every side,
> Tremble and start at wagging of a straw;
> Intending deep suspicion, ghastly looks
> Are at my service, like enforced smiles . . . (3.5.5–9)

These, of course, are Buckingham's words, as he is baited by Gloucester to perform his part well in the bloody farce (the murder of Lord Hastings) staged before the eyes of the Lord Mayor and those who could "Misconster" (61) the results of the deed. A "tragedian," as defined in the *OED* (under 2), is of course a "stage-player who performs in tragedy." Again, performance provides a figure of authority in that it gives directions, and quite specifically so, of how the representation of ill repute can be precluded once the murderous commissioners are exposed to "the censures of the carping world" (68). The act of performance becomes inseparable from representation itself. Over and beyond its function as a means of transaction, performative practice secures an agency in the production of meaning. This practice is so prominent, not to say powerful, that it invades the text just as the writing of the text promotes the medium to a figuration of meaning. Stage and page regroup their relations on the level of perfect interplay and interaction.

In this context, the enhanced role of performance may be not at all fortuitous. As elsewhere, there is evidence (take only the post-Reformation antitheatrical pamphlets) that the liberty of performance and its role in productions is strongest where secular or ecclesiastical authorities are most in question. Performers are apt to authorize their own nonconformity, where their license can sound or echo elements of a vacuum, be that in powerful policy or controlling ideas and beliefs. Performance is most powerfully self-sustained, the player most self-authorized and, accordingly, least constrained by prescribed language where doctrine, form, and meaning are unsettled. As Ritchie Kendall notes in *The Drama of Dissent*, "in all nonconformist acting, the player is never totally subsumed by his persona."[22]

As the Reformation upheaval combines with the decline of allegory, the scene is set for the Vice-world of thick performance to unfold its destructive potential. Now "demonic playing" can uncover its own performative grounds, proving itself, even in 1587, in the printer Richard Jones's words, "far unmeet for" any official reading of "the matter" of church doctrine or political history. Gloucester, precisely because power is his sole aim and point of departure, utterly discredits the authority of power *qua* sheer *potestas*. Remarkably, the performer's readiness to waive social norms combines with a reference to the quite different self-authorizing practice in the Protestant mode of legitimation. As far as the play explores the links and gaps between the uses of secular power and the abuses of Protestant conscience, two massive locations of authority are exposed in their intriguing complicity.

Richard playfully, and with more than usual duplicity, falls back on a discourse of "conscience." He thereby betrays the embarrassing extent to which private conscience proves to work with public ideology. Thus, in his ambidextrous posturing, he can be shown to straddle the juxtaposition, even the conflict between the two, by exempting himself from both demands. But to eject both locations of authority is to establish a non-committal site, unbound by most of their norms and where power and conscience can engage one another in uncommon corruption. To achieve powerful room at the top, Gloucester is free again, like Buckingham, to "play the orator" (95) and to "clothe" his murderous ambition by appeal to divine authority:

> But then I sigh, and with a piece of scripture,
> Tell them that God bids us do good for evil:
> And thus I clothe my naked villainy
> With odd old ends, stol'n forth of holy writ,
> And seem a saint, when most I play the devil. (1.3.333–7)

Here Gloucester falls back on the uses of contrariety that seem to have obtained widely among Tudor players. As Edmund Grindal, then Bishop of

London, wrote to Sir William Cecil on February 23, 1564, there were infamous "*Histriones*, common players" who so practiced their craft "that God's word by their impure mouths is prophaned and turned into scoffs."[23] Grindal only echoed what dozens of other commentators kept complaining about and of what Gloucester, exhibiting his histrionic skill, provided an example: the discourse of scripture, the unique authority of the Bible, was profaned through the sheer force of a counterfeiting voice in irreverent action.[24]

The performer behind the character displays, even foregrounds, the act of counterfeiting itself. To do so is, surely, bad policy and poor motivation if the issue were to represent the image of a murderous magnate by the standards of his own interests and language. But since the representation of such a character is suspended in foregrounding a skillful show of mimicry, the performer behind the role gains the upper hand. What Richard stages is not so much an act of hypocrisy or a representation of falsehood, but an assay of the quality and value of the performer's craft and craftiness. It is another instance of delivering the act of delivery itself. Here we have a recurring context, where staged performance in the power of its "swelling scene" is as interactive with as it is equal to the force of the text. The metatheatrical finds its fullest and, we suspect, originary function: metatheatricality not just as a formal artifice but as engine of the most intense engagement of page and stage and what socio-cultural correlatives were involved.

As the Duke literally rehearses a "sigh" and openly "clothes" his true intent, as he professes to know his "seems," he reveals the trademark of the player whose authority is radically "unmeet" to the real text of devotion. As the Protestant meaning gleaned from "holy writ" is (de)moralized into a devilish travesty, scripture provides a mock authority, good enough for a farcical exercise in contrariety. Vice and virtue are turned upside-down. The specific role that Richard plays herein, the sinister design behind his parody of biblical authority, is rooted in the topsy-turvy world of a bottomless mimesis. Again, this role is inseparable from his unbounded capacity for performing, and thus for appropriating, interpretations in order to upset any order of continuity between textual signs and their sanctioned reading and application.

The underlying clash of two authorities – one secular, one spiritual, suspending one another – is further developed in the following scene, with horror and laughter constituting another, possibly even more stunning, game of contrariety. While the two Murderers contemplate Clarence, their victim, the question of their "warrant" is foregrounded:

Second Murderer.	What, shall I stab him as he sleeps?
First Murderer.	No, he'll say 'twas done cowardly when he wakes.
Second Murderer.	Why, he shall never wake until the great Judgement Day.
First Murderer.	Why, then he'll say we stabbed him sleeping.
Second Murderer.	The urging of that word 'judgement' hath bred a kind of remorse in me.
First Murderer.	What? art thou afraid?
Second Murderer.	Not to kill him, having a warrant, but to be damn'd for killing him, from the which no warrant can defend me. (1.4.100–12)

Moralizing two meanings into the language of the Last Judgment – a topos central to the Vice's performance in *Mankind*, and in *The Tide Tarrieth No Man* – makes for a grim kind of comedy. The written authority (the "warrant" for murder) relieves the Second Murderer of any sense of guilt, but it cannot cancel out apprehensions of the "judgement" as an external agency of punishment and damnation.

Here "Judgement Day" is invoked to demonstrate the limits of any "warrant" from secular power and its "little brief authority" (*Measure for Measure*, 2.2.118). For this murderous clown, the ruling power and the heavenly vision are at loggerheads. Hence his "passionate humour" (118) – his "holy humor," according to the Quarto – is thrown back at another, even more questionable authority, his "conscience" (121). Although the Second Murderer can easily, and at considerable length (134–44), borrow from the Book of Common Prayer (in particular, the commination service, where the workings of conscience are spelt out)[25], his own resort to it is in the manner of "courage contrarious." Conscience is treated as a most volatile site of authority; if it does reside "in the Duke of Gloucester's purse" (128), it is "a dangerous thing" (142). Small wonder when "every man that means to live well endeavors to trust to himself, and live without it" (142–4); that is, without conscience. Thus a foremost source of Protestant authority is exposed to, and inverted in, the "fond and frivolous jestures" of the theatre. More than just two meanings are moralized in the uses of "conscience," which finally, handy-dandy, is made synonymous with "the devil" (147). At issue is the Protestant mode of self-authorization, when "to trust to himself" turns out to be the opposite of listening to one's "conscience" as a valid court of appeal.

The murderers' scene serves as a grotesque variation on what happens to Gloucester when, having ascended the throne and sloughed off the accoutrements of the Vice, he is fully drawn into the nongrotesque world of history and representation. In his gravest moment, in his dream on the eve of battle and shortly after, "conscience" is on his lips no less than four times. The vision is once again that of the Last Judgment, when his "sins . . . / Throng to the bar, crying all, 'Guilty, guilty!'" (5.3.198 ff.). As in the earlier scene, where, according to the Second Murderer, conscience "makes a man a coward" (1.4.134–5), "coward conscience" (5.3.179) returns as a troubling instance, finally to be dispensed with on the grounds that "Conscience is but a word that cowards use" (309). Here it is again transferred to a site of material power; this site cannot, of course, be "the Duke of Gloucester's purse," but – in a noteworthy parallel – "Our strong arms be our conscience, swords our law!" (311). Their performance is so much more crucial than anything words can do. In other words, even when the farcical-grotesque guise of the Vice is shed, Richard continues to champion material delivery over textual expression. "Conscience" – like "honour" for Falstaff – is but a word; the symbolic order of language is not nearly as vital as one's limbs, such as "a leg? . . . Or an arm?" (*1 Henry IV*, 5.1.131–2).

In both the most comic and the tragic scenes in *Richard III*, then, the external authority of sheer might, physical or economic, is shown to engage (and to be engaged by) the self-authorized workings of an inner voice. This voice represents "conscience" as a site of instability. Its semantic underside is deeply divided, marked by the absence of any univocal center of meaning: "My conscience hath a thousand several tongues" (*Richard III*, 5.3.193). Its language, at least for Richard, is untrustworthy, even as he confronts the ghastly images of his vicious doings as a premonition of his own undoing. What these altogether different scenes have in common is a structure marked by a comically/tragically rendered conflict. At the heart of the clash, the two media, the language of conscience and the body in action, the symbolic and the material, engage one another. The outcome is such that, with these clownish and Vice-derived agents, the symbolic mode of rendering an inward guidance has no choice but to surrender to both the performance and the representation of material action and interest.

As spectators listen to Richard's "moralizing" of two meanings in one word, as they follow his frivolous gestures, read in his twinkling eye, they literally profit from what he (in both senses of the word) betrays. It is his duplicity which, willy-nilly, invites complicity. But then, as if to affirm contrariety on every level, Richard, in sharing his superior awareness, can snare the audience's sympathy – only to betray their trust. Having ascended to the throne and consummated his ambition, he forgets about the vicious alacrity of a mounting spirit. What remains, after the play with "conscience" is over, is the picture, much in the glass of worthy narrative, of a ferocious feudal magnate, shouting and dying, unhorsed and immovable, in the self-enclosed armor of his caste.

CHAPTER 3

Mingling vice and "worthiness" in King John

When Shakespeare began to write for the London stage, Marlowe's plays were sharply redefining the aims of representation in the Elizabethan theatre. As the prologues to *Tamburlaine* suggested, the dramatist felt authorized to "lead" the theatre to a new horizon of legitimation, one against which the hero could more nearly be viewed as a self-coherent "picture." This at least is how the prologue to *The Second Part of Tamburlaine the Great* projected innovative uses of "this tragic glass" from the earlier play's introduction:

> But what became of fair Zenocrate,
> And with how many cities' sacrifice
> He [Tamburlaine] celebrated her sad funeral,
> Himself in presence shall unfold at large.[1]

Such processing of page and stage, the intricate conjuncture of verbal and visual signs, drew on and transformed – even confounded – traditional modes of response. The cultural impact of print helped the protagonist "unfold," for readers and audience members beholding the scene "at large," various new shifting, wavering meanings from dramatic fiction.

So it was with good reason that the play's printer, Richard Jones, assumed in his preface to the Octavo and Quarto editions of 1590 that these "tragical discourses" would appeal "To the Gentlemen Readers and others that take pleasure in reading Histories." Moving from pen to stage and then back to printed page for privileged "reading," these eminently perusable representations recommended themselves in terms of what "worthiness" the "eloquence of the author" could profitably deliver to a gentle preoccupation with "serious affairs and studies." Authority now seemed to flow not simply from text to performance, but – in an even closer circuit – from the dramatic writing, via print, into the studies of those familiar with "reading Histories."

Jones's partisan position gives context to stage and page before 1594. To different degrees and effects, the orally shaped performance tradition of comic, irreverent, physically accentuated "jestures" was mingled with, or otherwise related to, the "worthiness of the matter itself." In Marlowe's early plays the confederation of bodily delivery and verbal artifice was fraught with great liabilities. Thus it was possible, at least in print, to consider serious literary matter incompatible with the "graced deformities" of performative practices. The latter were clearly alien to, even ostracized from, a formally written and then printed text. Participating in the countermanding flow of authority, the printer, apparently without intervention on the part of the dramatist, saw fit radically to cancel out the most gaped-at traces of performance. Since common players were obviously viewed as having no authority of their own, the tragical discourse was not to be contaminated by "some fond and frivolous" treatment; these needed to be refined out of existence from "so honorable and stately a history."

Shakespeare, himself a player, may well have taken a different position on what in the early 1590s continued to be a crucial issue in the formative period of early modern drama. He never belittled the difficulties in question, not even when, toward the end of the decade, he confronted the relation of page and stage pragmatically, in terms of an achieved cooperation. But even then, social and cultural divergences of the interactive media appeared to linger. We have Shakespeare's own word for it that the difference between "so great an object" in the writing of history and the "unworthy" scaffold of its performance was perceived, and that it loomed large, in the theatre of the Lord Chamberlain's Men. The Prologue to *Henry V* was designed both to expose and to appropriate the gap between noble matter and its common staging, to "digest" the use and the "abuse of distance." This distance was geographical and spatial, surely, but also temporal and social. As such, it remained of great consequence; in Leeds Barroll's phrase, things must have been so "turbulently new" in the late 1580s and early 1590s that "no comfortable conceptual models were yet available."[2] There is little doubt that this "distance" must have affected as well as reflected the enabling conditions under which the playwrights and their companies mingled the deformities of the Vice and the forms and figures of "worthiness." Shakespeare grapples with this cultural divide in his own way, much closer to the matrix in which the stamp of his own life and work was cast.

The theatre of Marlowe helps throw into relief how, on the "unworthy scaffold" of both *Richard III* and *King John*, it was possible for the greater dramatist to assimilate, modify, or undo the difference between two generic conventions, two types of poetics and epistemology and, finally, two modes of cultural production and reception. To do so was possible in and through an unfixed space for (dis)continuity between dramatic text and performance practice.[3] Introducing the performative energy of the old Vice into the "tragic glass" of history and subjectivity, the dramatist's idea was *not* to eliminate these "graced deformities" and these "fond and frivolous jestures" from the realm of "serious affairs and studies." Instead, it was to digest the distance between them. Shakespeare set out to use, rather than abuse, the socio-cultural divide in question. His project was not to accept but to transgress and so reform the humanist-sanctioned boundary between form and deformity. Mingling vulgar Vice and worthy history, the protagonist of *Richard III*, as we have seen, absorbed significant "deformity" in the very image of the tragic hero. Reducing any unnecessary "digressing" in purely presentational practice, this vicious, grimly frivolous protagonist was (to use Marlowe's terms) "himself in presence" designed to "unfold at large" the play in question.

The opening of *King John* takes an entirely different direction. Faulconbridge enters with an impertinency on his lips, revealing a rather boorish but also boyish exuberance. He is distinctly in the Vice tradition, but not a fully-fledged villain; in fact it is only in the course of the opening scene (1.1.157 ff.) that his bastardy is pronounced. In sheer contrariety, this bastardy turns out to be not a stigma but rather a means of advancement. Young Faulconbridge is knighted as Sir Richard, bastard to Richard Plantagenet. The mad, "unreverend boy" (227) with "country manners" (156), once he becomes King Richard's son, is made a gentleman. His use of language is thoroughly indecorous, marked by an inordinate amount of colloquialism ("a pops me out / At least from fair five hundred pound a year" [68–9]). His impertinence first emerges in relation to Queen Elinor, in his refusal to respond to the "necessary question" of the scene – that is, her points and questions in dialogue. His reply to the Queen's gracious invitation to familiarity is remarkably far from the purpose of *her* playing and meaning:

> *Elinor.* The very spirit of Plantagenet!
> I am thy grandame, Richard, call me so.
> *Bastard.* Madam, by chance, but not by truth; what though?
> Something about, a little from the right,
> In at the window, or else o'er the hatch.
> Who dares not stir by day must walk by night,
> And have is have, however men do catch.
> Near or far off, well won is still well shot,
> And I am I, howe'er I was begot. (167–75)

With this response "quite athwart / Goes all decorum" (*Measure for Measure*, 1.3.30–1). Like Mischief in *Mankind*, who assumes the role of an impertinent "winter-corn thresher,"[4] the Bastard is at pains to underline the rusticity of his language and imagery. As a "good blunt fellow" (1.1.71), his idiom is – in confronting the court – as proverbial as it is indiscreet.

Answering the Queen, he reproduces a series of homely allusions and commonplaces that defy representation in a scene at court. His reply is, in both senses of the word, impertinent: in its impudence it refuses to acknowledge pertinent – that is, referential – uses of dramatic dialogue. His words preclude the illusion of dialogue as a representation of meaningfully construed exchange and communication. But although his reply is, in the full senses of these words, scandalous and offensive, none of the courtly characters seems to mind. It is spoken, as it were, out of hearing, as if spatially remote from the *locus* of courtly manners and "worthiness." No less strange is his persistence in thoroughly irrelevant sexual innuendo, as when in eight lines (140–7) he manages to convey a good many obscenities, among them "heir" for "whore," "case" for "vagina." If anything, these quibbles serve to sustain his distance from the language of dramatic verisimilitude and courtly etiquette. Highly performative, these uses of language presuppose a verbal, social, and spatial apartness from the sites of courtly deportment and authority customarily represented in the dominant discourse of princely conduct.

If these apparently nonsensical eccentricities jeopardize representational form, they do so not to undo but to counter and alter the play's dominant representations. In fact, the Bastard stands for a remarkable freedom to moralize meanings in the play's thematic concern with social mobility, sexual propriety, and primogeniture. Unashamedly punning, he freely celebrates his own bastardy: "Now blessed be the hour by night or day, / When I was got . . ." (165–6). He is prepared to "thank" his mother "for my father:" "And they shall say, when Richard me begot, / If thou hadst said him nay, it had been sin. / Who says it was, he lies, I say 'twas not" (270, 274–6). Denial of "sin" here is part of a complex figure of inversion. The difference between vice and virtue, strictly implemented in allegorical uses of language, is suspended: the traditional meaning of "sin" (in relation to its contemporary referent) is de-moralized.

Faulconbridge therefore serves as a theatrically effective vehicle for demoralizing and remoralizing meanings in one word. His language is full of those "frivolous jestures, digressing and . . . far unmeet for the matter" which Marlowe's printer saw fit to omit. If, fortunately, these were not obliterated in the textual history of *King John*, the main reason is that Shakespeare so wrote these "graced deformities" into the discourse of historiography as to affect its direction from within. Faulconbridge does not need to "speak more than is set down" for him – the play itself provides space and idiom for a textually inscribed (and sanctioned) type of contrariety. Over and beyond what the dramatist found in his sources (including Raphael Holinshed's *Chronicles,* John Foxe's *Actes and Monuments,* and Matthew Paris's *Historia Maior*), he absorbed a perfectly eccentric potential for a performative *gestus.* This potential helped shape and qualify representational form in the play.

Remarkably, Shakespeare did not and could not find this peculiar potential of contrariety and performativity in his one important dramatic source, the play published anonymously in 1591 under the title *The Troublesome Raigne of King John.* Since Shakespeare could not have composed his *King John* before this date, the dramatist's deliberate reversion to the Vice as a supreme vessel of performative energy and liminality appears even more significant. In the Quarto Faulconbridge already appears as a bastard; in the words of his half-brother, he is "Base born, and base begot ... nor yet legitimate" (120, 126).[5] However, in a revealing phrase combining self-disdain and chivalric ambition, the Bastard's self-perceived "gross attaint ... tilteth in my thoughts" (329) until the "landless Boy" (413) is assured of his royal descent. While he shows a comparable vigor in his lust for status and glory, his response in the Quarto takes a significantly different direction.[6] He craves deeds of chivalry, and his first exploit is to chase and recover his royal father's lionskin, using "his knightly valor" to win "this hide to wear a Lady's favour" (584–5). Shakespeare not only omits the Bastard's hankering for the royal token, but disregards his wooing of Blanche for very good reasons. He eschews knightly ambition and also Senecan pathos, such as the latter's neoclassical invocations of an *Alecto,* a *Morpheus, Mors* (perhaps Mars), and *Hector* (561, 658, 660, 669).

To understand these obvious differences, it is helpful, though not sufficient, to note that the 1591 Quarto was published in two parts, with prefaces "TO THE GENTLEMEN READERS." In Part One the preface opens with an allusion to "the Scythian Tamburlaine" whose drama had also appeared in a two-part edition the same year, with an even more explicit preface for "Gentleman Readers." Small wonder then that the print version of *The Troublesome Raigne* carefully italicized (as in our citation above) references to classical antiquity. Much more important, the early scenes in the Quarto text introduce a Bastard eloquently intent on displaying the arts of rhetoric, including two or three set speeches (566–79, 656–69, 1044–56). It is at this point, actually on some of these quite specific occasions, that Shakespeare sets aside the neoclassically tinged representation in his source. The rhetorical role of the Bastard in the Quarto is superceded by radically different functions serving, in fact privileging, the Bastard's performative presence on stage. Shakespeare does this without in the least reducing the

Bastard's represented role as an intriguing character in theatrical action or on the reader's page. These new functions are marked by liminality and perform-ativity as well as by a strategically meaningful complicity with the story and the image of the world of history in the play. The two different func-tions pay tribute to, and mutually use to the utmost, the two modes of cultural production – playing and writing – that coalesce in the theatre. In Shakespeare's case, the Bastard is to double business bound. This has perhaps best been brought out by A. R. Braunmuller, who notes that the Bastard was informed by "the dramatist's response to the chaos of motivation" in his sources. With the kings and their followers "so inconsistent, so unprin-cipled," the Bastard – "Shakespeare's response to the problem of interpreting history" – "is both a reader of the text of history and part of that text."[7]

Shakespeare's Bastard exemplifies a dramatic strategy of combining, in one figure, presentational and representational modes of rendering. As a "reader of the text of history," he embodies, on the threshold of dramatic action proper, the roles of commentator or chorus. He performs – intran-sitively, as it were – predominantly on the strength of his performant function. At the same time, the actor behind the Bastard also performs transitively; that is, he represents a certain character called Philip Faulconbridge. In partially collapsing these two roles, what in the play is imaginatively performed and what or who is actually doing the performing, the Bastard achieves a "bifold authority" of a sort. In other words, his strength is not simply derived from what imaginary text the author has penned for this role. Over and beyond his profound debt to his author's pen, the figure is also thrown back upon the voice and body of an actor. In his delivery this actor is engaged in the real but difficult act of presenting a reading of the play and of his own fictitious part in it.

Even with his "calf-skin" theme (recalling the Vice's signature tune) churned out a reverberating five times in Act 3, scene 1 not to mention his epilogue, the Bastard maintains the stance of a double dramaturgy right into the center of the play. Up to this point, he retains his capacity for playing with the difference, in dramaturgy, between stage-centered presentation and the representation of character. As his own master of ceremonies, he can assimilate a *platea*-type of space in which to exercise his remarkable skill for a delivery of more than one role. What he does may not exactly be classified as "some necessary question of the play." But it remains both an enter-taining display of histrionic competence *and* an exquisite, meaningful making of images that participate in the staging of his own recently achieved social status:

> Well, now can I make any Joan a lady.
> "Good den, Sir Richard!" "God-a-mercy, fellow!"
> And if his name be George, I'll call him Peter;
> For new-made honor doth forget men's names;
> 'Tis too respective and too sociable
> For your conversion. Now your traveller,
> He and his toothpick at my worship's mess;
> And when my knightly stomach is suffic'd,
> Why then I suck my teeth, and catechize
> My picked man of countries. "My dear sir,"
> Thus, leaning on mine elbow, I begin,
> "I shall beseech you" – that is question now;
> And then comes answer like an Absey book:
> "O sir," says answer, "at your best command,
> At your employment, at your service, sir."
> "No sir," says question, "I, sweet sir, at yours";
> And so, ere answer knows what question would,
> Saving in dialogue of compliment,
> And talking of the Alps and Apennines,
> The Pyrenean and the river Po,
> It draws toward supper in conclusion so.
> But this is worshipful society,
> And fits the mounting spirit like myself . . . (1.1.184–206)

This is indeed an excellent game. An actor/character goes out of his way to stage a one-man show, using as his dialogic agents Question and Answer to catechize (as in an "Absey book" on social difference) the elementary principles of upward mobility and haughty condescension. Surely this satirical image of upstart behavior reflects the extraordinary late Elizabethan welter of classes and values. At the same time, though, it is not exactly a representation of his own character. Although himself an upstart, there is no implication that this is, in any reliable sense of the word, in character with, or a characterization of, Philip Faulconbridge.

Even as he says, "now can I make any Joan a lady," the purpose of playing behind this speech is more impertinent than this: "A foot of honor better than I was, / But many a many foot of land the worse" (182–3). With these quibbles (which immediately precede the longer speech in question), the Bastard plays himself out of the constraint of a purely self-referential application of meaning. Conflating the "foot" of his status or degree with the "foot" of simple measurement of material space, he conveys the limits of "honor" through its complicity with "land" and its capacity for commodification. Thereby, the play upon the signifier signals an awareness of and betrays a distance from the purpose of his own play-acting, the mimicry of a self-conceited upstart.

Throughout the first part of this speech, then, Faulconbridge serves less as one represented than as one who is doing the representing. The speaker does not so much map his own potential course of action but, more provocatively, mimics the abject arrogance of the *nouveaux riches* or, even, those that make up "worshipful society" (205). Again, the twist of the word "worshipful" displays a strongly performative gesture of impudence. Exuberance marks what the performer behind the Bastard performs. An irresistible gusto of play-acting invites spectators to attend to the "Now" (189) and the taunting, cutting "Thus" (194). Note the dazzling quality of performed action, the affably maintained relish of superiority, a stance best expressed in the subtext of the French analogue *suffisant* when his "knightly stomach is *suffic'd*" and "Thus, leaning on mine elbow, I begin . . . " The gloating here is that of the performer more than that of the performed. All this adds up to an act of stunning theatricality, by which the speech is zestfully turned into a histrionic display of the first order. Far from identifying with what he represents, the player can knowingly exhibit in miniature the skill, competence, and high spirits that go into the playing of this play.

Authority in Shakespeare's playhouse comes full circle in this remarkable interplay between "author's pen" and "actor's voice." By appropriating the scenario of a display of the player's skill, the playwright so adapts it to his larger theme and representation that, at the height of histrionic virtuosity, the focus remains on the "necessary question of the play." The "Law of writ" is clearly in evidence; its controlling instance here is more sustained than, by comparison, in the performant function in Q1 *Hamlet*. But while authorial authority effectively prevents these "frivolous jestures" from being "unmeet for the matter," the playwright follows rather than dictates the player's craftsmanship. Far from seeking to displace the player's appeal, the script actually helps mediate the performer's authority and competence. His calculated presence is not administered by or, simply, superimposed on the writing. The player's act of presentation is just there – an enabling, formative condition of how play-acting before us is inscribed into the text. While the "author's pen" throughout is in the "actor's voice," that voice finally helps find, and decides upon, the form, the genre, and the scenario of what we have before us.

Thus in *King John* the mingling of Vice and "worthiness" achieves a bewildering new turn, one that in the assimilation of contrariety is potentially even more experimental and, from a providential point of view, much less reassuring than *Richard III* and the entire first tetralogy. *King John* does project, through the stamp of a nonvicious protagonist, the frivolous figuration to the point of its containment: Faulconbridge faithfully rehearses most of the attributes of the Vice, only to go beyond them. In doing so he reaches out, with a remarkable twist, for something new. He seeks to redeem the unbridled energy of the valiant performer on behalf of his arduous task in the building of an anachronistic but forward-looking image of the nation-state. Along these lines Faulconbridge anticipates the more highly differentiated appropriation of the Vice figure in *Hamlet,* where Shakespeare infuses certain memories of this figure into an antic, mad version of "graced deformities" – one motivated by a desire to scourge the world and "set it right."[8] In the tragedy the gap between madness and "matter," frivolity and "worthiness," was projected as part of a composite structure, in its own way constituting "two meanings" in one play. Whether in the wake of this operation the tragic glass of Renaissance subjectivity cracked and the "unmatched form and feature" of Renaissance "youth" was "Blasted with ecstasy" (*Hamlet,* 3.1.159–60), or, as in Richard Gloucester's case, "curtail'd of this fair proportion" (*Richard III,* 1.1.18), the result was as unprecedented as it was paradoxical. Decorum, discretion, and the kind of authority postulated in the worthy discourse of princely conduct was confronted with what Marlowe's printer had called its own "great disgrace," as that was folding out performing "ecstasy" from *within* "so honourable and stately a history."

The strategy of integration between, on one hand, the uses of rhetoric, eloquence, and representation in writing and, on the other, the inscription therein of an excessive and "ecstatic" type of performance practice was not confined to such history plays as *2 Henry VI, Richard III,* or the two parts of *Henry IV.* But in *King John* – in the mingling of a bastardly deformed Vice-descendant with virtue, bravery, and patriotism – the aim was not to abandon "worthiness" in the discourse of history. Rather, the nonhumanist tradition, with its mad, frivolous performative, was effectively inserted into these literate images of high Renaissance endeavor. In the language of Marlowe's prologues to *Tamburlaine,* the self-contained "glass" of representation, the unfolding "presence" of the hero's own "picture," the *locus* of his "stately tent" and station – these were churned by an uncannily alien energy, a leavening of kinetic force and otherness unknown to neoclassical poetics and rhetoric. If the Bastard did not share Hamlet's "ecstasy," his position in *King John* certainly was ex-static, wildly driven off course, moved quickly to leave the familiar bifurcation behind.

The playhouses' assimilation of an eccentric source of performative energy turned the matter of representation itself into a vehicle of cultural contrariety. To have, as in *Richard III*, a martial hero, but to have him "rudely stamp'd" (*Richard III*, 1.1.16) allowed the stage to amplify and, theatrically, to enliven the worthy discourse of history from within the act of performance in *King John*. The distance in social station and language use between the mirror of warlike fortitude and the cultural echo of Elizabethan players yielded a quite peculiar site for "Bifold authority" (*Troilus and Cressida*, 5.2.144) in the matter of representation. Such mingle-mangle made it impossible to have things as Renaissance decorum suggested they should be. To have the "mould of form," the mettle, and the leadership of a worthy hero emerge out of frivolous bastardy implicated the disruption of "stasis" when the latter is defined as a "state of motionless or unchanging equilibrium" (*OED* 1b).

Decorum and discretion were undermined in the hodge-podge quality of fashioning so frivolous a hero. This frivolity was directly indebted to the legacy of the Vice, which, as Alan Dessen has shown, was well remembered, at least up to 1610, in the Elizabethan theatre.[9] So Faulconbridge's course in the play is such that the performative zest of his departure might well be summed up in Leontes's words:

> I ne'er heard yet
> That any of these bolder vices wanted
> Less impudence to gainsay what they did
> Than to perform it first. (*The Winter's Tale*, 3.2.54–7)

As G. Blakemore Evans annotates the passage, "Less" here stands "where a modern ear expects 'More,'" intensifying the word "wanted." The element of "impudence" (going, as im-pertinence or nonpertinence, against the grain of the "necessary question" in representation) must have been close to that "performant function," in Jean Alter's sense, which obtained in juggling.[10] Thus, as late as in Ben Jonson's *The Staple of News*, "the old way" of the Vice is remembered "when *Iniquity* came in like *Hokos Pokos*, in a Juggler's jerkin, with false skirts."[11] Here as elsewhere, memories of the Vice are closely related to a presentational practice in which performance is displayed in its own right.

Compounded as it is with "worthiness," though, how can Faulconbridge's residue of jesting, verbal juggling, and direct address serve as a lever for a theatrical treatment of history? His attributes of "impudence," bastardy, dispossession, and opportunism were symptomatic of how the nonhumanist world of cultural "deformities," always already "unmeet for the matter," could actually be made integral to it. His Protean figuration reveals a determination to assimilate on stage the "distance" between the well-composed Renaissance mirror of nobility and the highly nonstatic site of kinetic energies in performance. The idea was to explore and exploit the frivolous, fond, deforming, and unsettling contours of this site from within an expansive affirmation of "this tragic glass".

Going further, in the diversification of his dramatic functions, than any other adaptation of the Vice in Tudor drama, Faulconbridge ends up suspending, though not exactly revoking, his initial dispossession and apartness. In *King John* the process of adaptation is not marked by the absence, in a Renaissance figure of nobility, of "this fair proportion." There is no ungentle disfigurement irrevocably conveying a "misshapen" (*Richard III*, 1.2.250) character's sense of being socially apart. But while in Richard's case this apartness is given, at least up to his self-directed coronation, Faulconbridge determines not to stand apart but to meet the madness of the world, the rule of commodity itself. Henceforth the Vice in him cannot serve the alien energy of otherness, when "there is no vice but beggary" (2.1.597). In this "worshipful society" time-serving is the watchword: "For he is but a bastard to the time / That doth not smack of observation –" (1.1.207–8). At the same time, "observation" as a servile, sycophantic complaisance is strangely compatible with an altogether different "inward motion" or inclination "to deliver" a purgation or at least some "poison for the age's tooth" (212–13). The grounds of apartness are finally surrendered thereby when the "inward" impulse is to be, rather than "a bastard to the time," its true child as well as its corrective agent.

At this point, contours of a character emerge. Faulconbridge begins to be viewed as standing for something personal and worldly. He represents, and his "inward" action pictures, what happens when a person observes, accommodates to, a rise in the world. On stage the footsteps of this "mounting spirit" (206) now largely lead away from what was the material correlative in theatrical space, the *platea*-function, of Faulconbridge's initial position in the play. The force of this "inward motion" continues to be at least partially intercepted by his lingering resistance to closure, extending into the epilogue-function of his concluding speech. Yet the absorption of the Bastard by the elevated discourse of historiography seems quite undeniable.

The peculiar figuration of the Bastard best reveals his hybrid profile when compared with related adaptations of the Vice. In most cases, the images of isolation or apartness are accompanied by (and hence interact with) the allotment of a material, unenclosed downstage area for performance. In this decentered space "aside" from the central action, a surplus of awareness and audience rapport would redeem, or at least set off, self-isolating illegitimacy. It was also an area in which all kinds of social, lineal, racial, and economic apartness could be interrogated. In this way Aaron, in *Titus Andronicus*, tends to "speak aside" (3.1.188–91, 202–5; 4.2.6, 25–31). His position of difference is borne out by a site symbolically open to – as well as encoded by – his "slavish," "servile" memories and his blackness. There he reveals his fierce desire for liberation: "Away with slavish weeds and servile thoughts! / I will be bright, and shine in pearl and gold" (2.1.18–19). In Iago the sense of being underprivileged, even dispossessed and cheated, dramatically affirms (and, to a degree, motivates) stringent apartness in his plans for evil manipulation. His sardonic signature tune, "Put money in thy purse" (*Othello*, 1.3.339–43, 345–6, and *passim*), effectively recalls the choruslike refrain of the old Vice. At the same time, this phrase symbolically associates the absence of material means, an awareness of the hardness of things, with the instrumental need for making ends meet.[12]

In an altogether different vein, Edmund, the illegitimate son of the Earl of Gloucester, more brutally a "whoreson" (*King Lear*, 1.1.24), feels "branded" in his relation to the legitimate Edgar: "Why brand they us / With base? with baseness? bastardy? base, base?" (1.2.9–10). Such iteration resounds with a sarcastic crescendo of exuberant energy and inversion when affirming the "lusty stealth of nature" and other sources of "fierce quality" (11–12). Thus the enforced apartness of the underprivileged is turned into a resilient site of aggressive mobility where vice and virtue are never mingled as with Faulconbridge. While the latter never *presents* himself as overcharged by something deeply anomalous, Aaron, Gloucester, Iago, and Edmund excessively pursue designs marked by furtive and evil gaming. There is a need for all these characters, Iago especially, to be sarcastic as well as double-faced. Such sarcasm inspires, even seems to nourish, an unlimited art of counterfeiting. Delivered as the mimesis of mimesis, such self-relishing feigning thrives, even culminates, in a great density and mobility – an ecstasy, as it were, of performative practice. In all these figurations the sheer delivery of evil exceeds rational or socially responsible motivation to the extent that it verges on a motiveless malignity unaccountable for in terms of any mirrored *locus* of verisimilar action and consistency.

As against the allegory of evil, the Bastard Faulconbridge has a far more checkered genealogy and serves a new hybridity of functions.[13] The thoroughly experimental note in his amalgamation of Vice and worthiness emerges when his deliberate time-serving turns out to be seriously "honest" in that it does not seem furtive feigning but, rather, a brash, brusque way of forthrightness. At the same time, the complicity of scourge and minister was so adapted that the performative surplus of vicious speech and "jesture" could in the course of the play be domesticated and at least partially harnessed to the representation of bravado and virility in the service of the nation-state. Without altogether surrendering the boisterous quality of his early irreverence, Faulconbridge, once turned into a represented agent of courageous patriotism, ends up bastardizing his hybrid extraction.

Thus the conflation of Vice and worthiness is turned into a potent site where the strong performative of popular playing and the Renaissance discourse of Machiavellian politics interact. This interaction culminates in the celebrated speech on "commodity." Here the mingle-mangle in the staging of the Bastard – presentational and representational – suggests an uneasy conjunction between the unveiling language of the commentator and the complicity of the participant. The speech is significant because Shakespeare projects this conjunction into both the theme and its ironic treatment when Faulconbridge addresses

> that same purpose-changer, that sly devil,
> That broker that still breaks the pate of faith,
> That daily break-vow, he that wins of all,
> Of kings, of beggars, old men, young men, maids,
> Who having no external thing to lose
> But the word "maid," cheats the poor maid of that,
> That smooth-fac'd gentleman, tickling commodity,
> Commodity, the bias of the world –
> The world, who of itself is peized well,
> Made to run even upon even ground,
> Till this advantage, this vile-drawing bias,
> This sway of motion, this commodity,
> Makes it take head from all indifferency,
> From all direction, purpose, course, intent –
> And this same bias, this commodity,
> This bawd, this broker, this all-changing world . . . (2.1.565–80)

Here the Bastard, alone on stage, face to face with the audience, provides a sample of that "abundance of superfluous breath" (148) which is part of his presentational stance, his choruslike positioning in an almost extradramatic space. Simultaneously, this extravagant harangue serves the "disorderly motion" in the play's imagery and its representation of what "vast confusion" results from the attempt "To tug and scamble, and to part by th' teeth / The unowed interest of proud swelling state" (4.3.152, 146–7).

In addressing both the feudal magnates in their historically dated, ruthless tugging and scrambling for landed power, and the more modern or contemporaneous political economy of "interest" and self-interest, he achieves an almost blatant anachronism in figuration. The bastard is both a person in medieval history and a child of the time of his conception. The "abuse of distance" on a temporal plane is very much part of what divides his dramaturgy between *locus* and *platea* functions. Such division enhances the disturbing "motion" which follows up and exceeds the unique and "surprising commitment," in Holinshed's *Chronicles*, "to the underprivileged, the demotic, the untitled," of which Annabel Patterson has written so persuasively.[14] But in Shakespeare's play the perspective of the untitled reaches further still in that it allows us to perceive some of the vulgar, materially motivated springs of this "motion." Strikingly, the medium that affords such unofficial insight is the stage.

Earlier in the play, the Bastard, viewing "the battlements" of Angiers "As in a theatre," invokes "industrious scenes and acts of death" (2.1.375–6). For him to recall the performing medium is to broaden the scenario into a crowded picture in commotion, "Of kings, of beggars, old men, young men, maids" (570), propelled by an "all-changing" force of gain and interest. To speak of such "commodity" as "the bias of the world" is to invoke yet another image of play: covetous self-interest is defined in terms of a slanting game of bowls where the "off-centered weight" of "a wooden ball," thanks to a piece of lead – the "bias" – "Makes it take head," or rush from, a straightforward trajectory toward a curved course.[15] The Bastard's version of "how this world goes" (*King Lear*, 4.6.147–8) maps an oblique path, a hidden motivation, a direction; these are visualized as the image of a decentered motion in the world as pictured. As against "all direction, purpose, course, intent," this "sly devil," "this vile-drawing bias" offers a remarkable clue to what meaning is behind the motion. Turned into transitive/intransitive language, "commodity" sways and is swayed by a movement beyond all measure and "indifferency."

Since Faulconbridge is a self-styled "devil" (or at least "One that will play the devil" – 2.1.135), he fully participates in the rush from "indifferency," from settled meanings and balanced purposes. Disordered motion is shared between his own sense of "Legitimation, name, and all is gone" (1.1.248) and what contingency the world of the play at large contains. By recognizing the world as a place of disorder ("Mad world, mad kings, mad composition!" [2.1.561]), the Bastard's eccentricities seek to comply with the absence of "direction, purpose, course, intent." Here his mad, illegitimate make-up can fully participate, even achieve a representative function where the moral, social, and literary esteem of "worthiness" turns out to be unfounded. The "Mad world" is an environment the Bastard shares in, is representative of, albeit from a critical distance. In other words, Faulconbridge again stands as "scourge and minister," as a castigating medium of critical revelation and a source of complicity vis-à-vis the ambivalence of "worthiness," power, and ambition in the matter of history.[16]

In exploiting the instability of his own (re)presentational position, Faulconbridge is free to quibble himself out of having to make a choice: the "sway of" motion is such that, playfully, his open hand is stretched out "When his fair angels would salute my palm" (590). The currency of commodity conflates heavenly bliss and possession of metal coins called "angels."[17] "And why do I rail on this commodity?" The answer provided marks the point where, in his own complicity, the Bastard taunts the audience, inviting them to share a "tickling" disillusionment about the "mad composition" of things. Here and elsewhere the sarcastic descendant of the Vice can easily perforate closure. Serving as a liminal medium, his eccentric position – one not at all confined to the *locus* of historical narrative – conveys more knowledge about the playworld than the play's own representations can be made to contain. Faulconbridge, through his presentational dash, his sheer drive in delivery, is instrumental in shaping an awareness that helps penetrate the surface of the Elizabethan language of decorum and degree.

Yet the self-sustained, semi-independent type of performance in *King John* has its limits. Even before the text provides a cue for the performer to withdraw behind the character's persona, the remarkable élan in this playing with a difference subsides into the "dialogue of compliment." Thereafter, the descendant of the Vice – so far, close enough to the "old Vice" – appears to maintain his credentials strenuously through a proverbial reference to travel and traffic. Faulconbridge recalls the old Vice's penchant for boundless movements, as when (in one case among many) Hickscorner, in his nonsensical travelogue, listing no less than thirty places, claims to "have been in many a country."[18] But except for the impudent rhymed couplet (citing "the river Po, / . . . in conclusion so" [1.1.203–4]), the reference to a self-fashioning "mounting spirit" with a Renaissance sense of "myself" (206) remains a somewhat questionable, lame transition to the stirring verse of

> For he is but a bastard to the time
> That doth not smack of observation –
> And so am I, whether I smack or no;
> And not alone in habit and device,
> Exterior form, outward accoutrement,
> But from the inward motion to deliver

Sweet, sweet, sweet poison for the age's tooth,
Which though I will not practice to deceive,
Yet to avoid deceit, I mean to learn;
For it shall strew the footsteps of my rising. (207–16)

As Faulconbridge's rise and service in the play attest, the status of "bastard" (207) does not preclude "a little brief authority." So the question is raised here as to what – after "Legitimation, name, and all is gone" – in fact constitutes legitimacy or, in modern parlance, authenticity. The answer, despite its cynical overtones, points in a direction that Francis Bacon first attempted to formulate: "And with regard to authority, it shows a feeble mind to grant so much to authors and yet deny time his rights, who is the author of authors, nay, rather of all authority. For rightly is truth called the daughter of time, not of authority."[19] Bacon asks us to consider authority's subordination to "time." Hence Faulconbridge's resolution "to deliver / . . . poison for the age's tooth" becomes a double-edged weapon. Its twofold function neatly divides between vicious time-serving (unprincipled, like the old Vice) and virtuous service to one's time, place, and country. For the Bastard is prepared, with Bacon, not to "deny time his rights"; not, that is, to serve authority as perennially given but to follow a better criterion of "truth," one that is the "daughter of time." Nor will he himself "practice to deceive"; rather, he will "learn" to "avoid it," even though, as a true child of the age, he will not desist to feed the appetite for "observation" or obsequious flattery.

Even in this agenda for practical self-aid in response to the fashion of the times, the Bastard does not quite slough off the "sweet poison" of vicious ambivalence. As "mounting spirit," he is prepared to "smack of observation," that is, to go through the motions of flattery and tolerate obsequious practice. However, having affirmed a highly precarious identity, he is at once ready to juggle with what provocative "meaning" his own status of "bastard" has so far projected. Now "a bastard to the time" is used disparagingly; he plays with the natural and the metaphorical uses of the word. Similarly, the connotations of "smack" (to have a taste or trace of something) are promptly exploited with punning on "smoke" (the spellings were not yet distinguished). Paradoxically, though not perhaps fortuitously, this "mounting spirit" can, in one line, relish a licentious release of his first person singular; as Honigmann reads it, "And so am I, whether I smoke or no."[20]

The punning ("smack"/"smoke") and the ambiguous use of "observation" in each case, though with different senses, invoke vital awareness of the play. They also establish a gamesome pattern of instability between signifier and signified. Representation is paltered with, meaning remains elusive or is encoded ambiguously, when the alternative to *not* being a "bastard to the time" can, in Braunmuller's edition, be rephrased positively as "a legitimate or successful participant in current affairs."[21] Here, if anywhere, is a half-hidden clue to how the new sources of authority – those that, in Bacon's phrase, do *not* "deny time his rights" – are vulnerably exposed. The distinction is at best relative between time-serving and service to one's time and place in a contingent world. The Bastard might have read his Machiavelli, yet his vulnerability anticipates the great predicament of modern and even postmodern political expediency.

The Bastard's speech reveals the full dynamic, but also the impromptu nature, of Shakespeare's transmutation of the Vice. Up to a point, the figure constitutes a thoroughly performative force disrupting closure and decorum, an unprincipled agency of duplicity, neatly derived from a hybrid ancestry conflating allegory and farce. But in this popular Renaissance adaptation, a new commingling of worthiness and Vice, a new hodgepodge of ideology and skepticism, supersedes the older conflation with its binary order of vice and virtue. Through a new, duplicitous perspective on legitimacy and authority, as through the different uses of "bastard" itself, Shakespeare domesticates the "fond and frivolous jestures" of the irreverent juggler in recurring representations of the unruly self in "worshipful society."

This departure rehearses and yet leaves far behind the anti-allegorical potential of vicious action in the Morality play. As we have seen in *The Tide Tarrieth No Man*, the early modern loosening of fixture in the allegorical psychomachia underwrote new "contrarious" openings in the strategy of dramatic representation between the performing, uttering body and its function and position in the symbolic order of their meanings. In the early modern context, a largely immutable gap (an "abyss," as Walter Benjamin called it)[22] in allegory between figurality and meaning gave way to a dynamic, often ironic, nondualistic relationship between signifier and signified.

The current of innovations was from page to stage. As Weimann has shown elsewhere, in Erasmus, Rabelais, Sidney, and Nashe the gap between statement and utterance began to be filled by a dancelike movement between closure and rupture.[23] In medieval drama the structure of allegorical personifications had remained fixed in its dualism as long as the psychomachia was strong enough to marshal a moral universe for a consistent order of fixed values. But then the performative energy of the Vice by itself tended to transform and empty out from within the alleged element of correspondence between discourse and meaning. Shakespeare, already taking for granted various standards of "poor validity" between "passion" and "purpose" (*Hamlet*, 3.2.194, 195), uses a thoroughly secularized, recrudescent version of the Vice to expand the gap between what was said and what was meant.

In *King John* he projects this gap not only into a strangely groping, troublesome representation of the world and the self, but also into one of a self in its relation to the world. In its opportunistic, ambivalent response to "commodity," for instance, the emerging, self-conscious "I" is fairly remote from the high Renaissance image of man and the idealizing postulate of a consortium of speaking and doing. An illegitimate offspring of and anomalous commentator on an unprincipled society, the Bastard stands between criticism and commodity. Serving as an unadulterated vessel of both contrariety and opportunity, he is deeply torn between serving the times as well as his country *and* playing the game of "I am I" (1.1.175), as these times go.

Against this larger constellation, the emergent first person singular thrives in a context marked by reckless self-reliance, bodily energy, nonsensical speech, and a cultural semiotics of unsettling instability in relations of words, deeds, and meanings. Here we recall Richard Gloucester's "I am myself alone" (*3 Henry VI*, 5.6.83), and related uses of an "I," to which we shall return at greater length in the context of personation and character in chapters 7 and 8. What is noteworthy here is that the punctured allegory of evil yields a newly unstable perspective on a "forlorn" relationship between the world and the self. This power is best adumbrated where "deformity" (even in the shape of "commodity") works, contradictorily, as both source and outcome of untold dramatic energies. Thus "deformity" can "mock," invert, and help "To disproportion me in every part, / Like to a chaos, or an unlick'd bear-whelp / That carries no impression like the dam" (3.2.160–2). An unshaped, "bastard" quality in Faulconbridge's unstable make-up has a formlessness similar to those bear-whelps that, in Elizabethan lore, were believed to be born as formless lumps, only later to be licked into some shape. As Stephen Gosson put it in his address to the Reader before *The Ephemerides of Phialo* (1579), "Gentlemen & others I could wish it, that I had that virtue in my pen, which the Bear hath in her tongue, to lick out my whelps in some proportion, when I have cast them in a rude lump."[24]

Although the Bastard is exceptional in that – unlike Richard and the rest – he makes good, his point of departure is not unlike that of the latter in *3 Henry VI*:

> And I – like one lost in a thorny wood,
> That rents the thorns, and is rent with the thorns,

> Seeking a way, and straying from the way,
> Not knowing how to find the open air,
> But toiling desperately to find it out – (174–8)

Unlike Gosson, the dramatist *is* able to lick out his "whelps in some proportion" to the world, rupturing the safer allegorical linkage between "purpose" and "passion," their "thought" and their "ends." In the process both Faulconbridge and Gloucester exemplify a strenuous need to perform, "toiling desperately" to play a role, "to find it out," and, for better or worse, to take up arms against a thorny world. Both share a moment of "vast confusion," as in the Bastard's anguished outcry: "I am amaz'd, methinks, and lose my way / Among the thorns and dangers of this world" (4.3.152, 140–1). As an image, losing one's way among thorns is hardly unprecedented, but the sentiment points to a new, intense, and mutually painful interaction between the self and the social. This culminates in an aggressive endeavor that "rents the thorn" even while the intervening medium is itself "rent" by "thorny" circumstances that tear and split whatever identity or agency is at work.

This sense of being "lost" in a role-playing game of apartness attests to highly experimental uses of selfhood. In *King John*, as E. A. J. Honigmann has shown in his edition of the play, "the pronoun I is used fifty-eight times, fifty-one times by Faulconbridge" (6). These uses seem connected to his insecurity in the wake of his release from lineage ties and bonds of family and fealty when, bastardized, "Legitimation, name, and all is gone." Such loss and lostness accompany a free-wheeling license for self-definition, especially where a lusty spirit – Richard and Edmund no less than Faulconbridge – tentatively seeks to realign "Exterior form" and "inward motion." Hence the Bastard's impertinent "And so am I, whether I smack or no" points in a direction where the stubborn sense of an unrelenting, pushing self outrageously asks to be admitted to the ranks of "worshipful society." It is as if "degree, priority, and place," together with "proportion, season, form" (*Troilus and Cressida*, 1.3.86–7), and of course discretion and decorum need to be discarded before the new self with its "appetite . . . doubly seconded by will and power" (121–2) can take over.

Amid verbal, moral, sexual, and social disruption, then, the conjuncture of lostness and licence spawns a reckless type of subjectivity: "And have is have, however men do catch. / Near or far off, well won is still well shot, / And I am I, how'er I was begot" (*King John*, 1.1.173–5). The complicity between age-old topsyturvydom and threefold iteration of the first person singular in one line is remarkable. Unleashing the ties to the preordained meaning of his one-time iniquity, the descendant of the Vice turns his sardonic sense of sublunary relations to (in another pun) the sexually charged praise for an accurate shot. As is the case with Edmund, the private "stealth of nature" and the social cast of contingency are lusty bedfellows, especially when it comes to populating the world with "rising spirits." Somewhere between "outward accoutrement" and "inward motion," but certainly along the complex cultural semiotics residing in the site of their interaction, the early modern dramatic self emerges – snatching for itself, against "the plague of custom," status, and privilege.

CHAPTER 4

Clowning: agencies between voice and pen

The Tudor Vice was not, of course, the only inherited agent through which the Elizabethan theatre adapted "matter of worthiness" to public performance. Next to the Renaissance descendant of the allegory of evil, and certainly related to him, stood the clown and, at a further remove, the fool. Despite their obvious dissimilarities, an element of kinship joined these sinister and comic agents of contrariety. They shared the open, playhouse-conscious, and quickening space of the early modern stage, especially when addressing the spectators, anticipating their responses, and insinuating their complicity. Far from contenting themselves with representing verbally prescribed meanings, they could both play upon and "mistake the word." Such was indeed their "old vice still" (*The Two Gentlemen of Verona*, 3.1.284). Given this punning on topsy-turvy verbal action, Elizabethans must have recognized the similar play on words when Thomas Nashe referred to Will Kemp as "jest-monger and Vice-gerent general to the ghost of Dick Tarlton."[1] No doubt the kinship of Clown and Vice was marked by much flux and instability. We need only recall *The Book of Sir Thomas More* and the manner by which speech headings for Inclination – the Vice and leading player in the drama's interlude – were transformed into, simply, "clo." for Clown.[2]

Owing to its complexity, the "Clown's ancestry in the Tudor 'Vice'" cannot be addressed here in anything like the manner it deserves.[3] Yet we would draw attention to the way these figures' existing ties reveal elements of a common dramaturgy. In particular, both figures embodied varying portions of a traditional performance practice that antedated the formation of character as a self-consistent image of subjectivity. In their different ways and degrees of delivery, they retained, even from within textually prescribed roles, a partially sovereign stage presence. In view of the abiding strength of their interplay even in Shakespeare's late plays (as in Autolycus in *The Winter's Tale* or the clowning in *The Tempest*), the confluence between absent literary source and event-centered matrix of performance practice deserves closer study. These performers could defy the time, place, and propriety of any strictly circumscribed image of character.

However, even though their performance practice maintained strong and lasting ties to a world of extemporal entertainment, staged clowns and fools did have literary sources and correlatives. We shall return to some of these literary antecedents in the Erasmian *The Praise of Folly* and also in the classical figure of Silenus. What at this stage seems noteworthy is the need for us to approach even the most stringently self-sustained forces in performance against a network of mutually enmeshed pages and stages, as when Erasmus in his turn acknowledged folly as performed on, or even derived from, popular stages.

In the present context, these literary parallels underline what in performance practice informed considerable differences between the sinister and the comic modes of delivery. Shakespearean descendants of the Vice, for instance, tend to observe the order of imaginary fictions much more effectively than do clowns. These Vice figures at least go through the motions when, as Iago in *Othello* or Aaron in *Titus Andronicus*, they receive a hasty cue for motivating evil action. In the partial and rather stolid response to this cue we see the relative extent to which these artificial persons submit to standards of verisimilitude. Thus the regime of representation is far more compelling in the Vice tradition where the postallegorical villain can usurp serious positions of apparent "worthiness" in the play – including the throne, the sites of courtship, marriage, primogeniture and so forth – and proceed maliciously to use or upset their sanctioned functions.

In contrast, Shakespeare's clowns and fools never insinuate themselves into the *locus* of love and friendship in comedy, nor into that of heroic action in tragedy. They may wittily deflate the dominant representations in either genre, but their role in the dramatic formation of "worthy matter" remains marginal. Rather than intruding into and thereby exposing the space for privilege, possession, and power, they reveal its laughable underside. Even though they may verbally penetrate the delusions of love and the impositions of rule, their comic orbit of performance holds them aloof not only from any decisive dramatic action but also from such representations as render the image of subjectivity or the conflict of the passions.

Any reconsideration of clowning must acknowledge the breathtaking strength of its nonverbal performance. A glance at various types of clowning in the period reveals that Richard Tarlton, Will Kemp, and to a certain extent Robert Armin did much more than serve dramatic role-playing. Both Tarlton and Armin disposed of and drew upon the art of singing as a performant function *sui generis*. Like Tarlton's, Kemp's prehistrionic career as dancer, jester, and "instrumentalist" prepared the grounds on which he, already a celebrity, was to join a theatre company. As his biographer notes, his move "from solo comedian to regular company member" (of Lord Strange's Men) was an important step and, incidentally, a transition from patronage to commercial theatre. In defiance of this transition, it was the jig and "the persona of the Lord of Misrule to which Kemp always aspire[d]," even though the space for jig was surrendered or deferred until after the scripted play was over.[4] Nevertheless, clownish uses of contrariety continued to draw on a postritual fund of performative practice, despite the predictable, neat allegorical symmetry of rule and misrule having given way, as in *Henry IV*, to mutually contestatory views and pictures of the world.

The jester's quasi self-sufficient store of facial mimicry and vulgar bodily *gestus* defies any purely literary mode of representation. Yet – unlike the modern circus clown – the Shakespearean adaptation in its complexity complements the physical by a strong vein of textual artifice. As a result, the clown and, in part, the singing fool turns into a Janus-faced figuration which looks both ways: at a traditional culture of orality marked by thick performance and at a more modern culture unthinkable without writing and the arts of rhetoric. In his russet or patched coat, straddling a motley scene, the early modern comedian embraces and revealingly conjoins two different media, two different modes of cultural production. He brings together both orally inspired, visible acts of unscripted bodily performance and textually mediated signs and meanings conducive to a slanting type of imaginary representation.

Clowning can be studied, then, as an exceptionally revealing ground on which language and the body, representation and presentation, confront and engage one another in highly vulnerable ways marked throughout by contingency. Before we proceed to examine this protean equipment more closely, we will seek to offer a historical perspective on what changes affected clowning in the 1570s and 1580s. To understand its peculiar, almost unique role in mid-Elizabethan culture and society, we would do well to recall the pre-Shakespearean situation in the theatre with the astonishing "disparity between theatrical activity and printed text" in the years from 1567 (when the Red Lion opened) to 1587.[5] This disparity is in several ways highly significant, not to say symptomatic of the circumstances under which clowning began to thrive on public stages. With his extemporal practice, the clown must have been able to meet the demands of large-scale audiences without having at his disposal any rich supply of authorially fixed texts. In the absence of any dramatic literature worth mentioning, it seems difficult to resist John Astington's suggestion "that one of the simplest and most portable elements of performance, that of the individual actor giving a taste of his quality," might well have constituted sufficient public attraction, at least as long as the performer's arts of comic delivery were valued more highly than the quality of any dramatic dialogue.[6]

The appeal of such "performant function" (to invoke Jean Alter's term once more) must have been especially welcome at a time when there seemed no market for the printing, buying, and reading of the "long" Elizabethan play. To this lack we can add the absence, for any of the companies, of an abiding association with a securely established venue in London or beyond the City walls. Further, such absence may well have been interconnected, causally or as a consequence, with the paramount role which provincial touring played. For playing in the provinces, no repertory system was called for; itinerancy clearly reduced the demands as well as the opportunities for innovative composition and authorship. As Andrew Gurr notes, "One play could serve twenty towns."[7]

For illustration of this context, we are indebted not only to the new historiography of Elizabethan theatre companies but also to the invaluable work that, in the REED volumes and beyond, has considerably refashioned our notions of the range and role of itinerant playing: "travelling was the Tudor norm" at least in the pre-1594 period. As a brief glance at Leicester's Men reveals, this most prominent company of the 1570s, with its amply documented long history of provincial playing, appears not to have developed "any concept of a single settled place to play in."[8]

The preference for touring seems especially significant, since one of the company's leading players, James Burbage, after setting up the Theatre in 1576, did so most likely as a free-wheeling impresario without expecting "to provide Leicester's Men or any other company with a permanent home."[9] Under these circumstances, two interdependent themes in the history of this important company stand out. One is the prominent role of clowning performers, as when Robert Wilson, famous for his "quicke, delicate, refined, extemporal wit," was made to rejoin the company on their trip to the Netherlands, even though the no less famous Kemp was already with them in Utrecht in March 1586.[10] Such prominence of clowning underscores the other salient theme here: the remarkable paucity of textual traces relating to this most spectacular and certainly most famous of mid-Elizabethan companies. Its most recent historian records "the absence of any reliable texts or even titles for the plays they performed."[11] Such dearth is strange indeed, yet in giving us pause it affords us a direction for inquiry.

By the time we come to the even more prominent company of the Queen's Men, founded in 1583, we are on much safer ground for dramatic scripts. As Scott McMillin and Sally-Beth MacLean have shown in their groundbreaking study, nine published plays acknowledge performance by the Queen's. We are well advised, though, to assume "that print-culture and the Queen's Men were not a good match."[12] For one thing, the company abounded in clowning talent, with famous Dick Tarlton, Robert Wilson, John Adams, John Singer, and probably jig-dancing George Attewell in their midst. So if clowning was "at the centre" of this company, we can be fairly certain "that much of their knock-about improvisation was never recorded or lost its point in translation to the medium of print."[13] Whether "knock-about" or as sophisticated as its staging by Tarlton-Dericke in *The Famous Victories*, clowning contained a nonsensical ingredient that not only precluded representational meaning but could not easily be reproduced on page (if, in fact, it were able to be so reproduced at all). It was difficult offstage to reconceive of its ephemeral, moment-to-moment surplus of laughable energy, which by definition defied logic, above all the logic of verisimilitude. Meant to be perceived, clowning could not be perused. Part of a predominantly emblematic, visually oriented dramaturgy, its center of gravity was not semantic but close to a showmanship for which language served gesture and the body, often enough the needs of the belly. At this stage, a pre-Shakespearean antinomy between clowning and writing loomed large. Peerless Tarlton, the Queen's Men's greatest player, wrestled with and exemplified this contradiction in a telling paradox. Himself an author or even dramatist, he did not wish to write down, or was unable to pen, the way he clowned.[14]

The Queen's Men were a large company, open to nonverbal performers; numerous enough on occasion to divide, or, as Philip Henslowe phrased it, "they brock and went into the countrey to playe."[15] While this may reflect a noteworthy flexibility it also, ten years after their foundation (Henslowe's entry is dated 8 May, 1593), indicates a continuing proximity of dramatic actors to all sorts and conditions of performed entertainment. As David Bradley suggests, while one of these companies primarily consisted of "fiddlers and rope-dancers," there was also "a Turkish rope dancer" who belonged to one or other of the two companies "and possibly at times to either."[16]

As a backdrop to clowning, even perhaps as a formative environment teeming with preliterary performance practices, it would not be difficult to multiply contemporary evidence of jugglers, tumblers, dancers, swordsmen, minstrels and all sorts of mountebanks and exhibitors. These continued to rub shoulders with dramatic actors. Even greater proximity was enjoyed by the bear wardens, who regularly changed and shared places with actors in amphitheatrical arenas on the Bankside. As Terence Hawkes has shown in reference to John Norden's map of London, for "The Beare howse" to be a close neighbor of, even "almost indistinguishable" from, "The Play howse" implied more than just physical vicinity. Rather, "the two kinds of 'play', drama and bear-baiting, occupied the same frame of reference on the Bankside."[17] While the complexities in the concept of such "playing" might have helped confuse the captions in Wenceslas Hollar's "long view" of London, this comprehensive notion of "play" also made it possible through and in performance deliberately to solicit the "unruly uncontrollable range of 'here and now' or 'real world' experience."[18]

Recalling the longstanding contiguity, in early modern culture, of histrionic and nonmimetic agents of play draws attention to a larger and intriguingly mixed matrix. Against this matrix we can the better understand the medley quality in clownish practices. Once integrated into performed drama, clowns would as a matter of course modify their habitual penchant for solo performance. Even so, there remain strong traces of it, reflected in the "presentism" of a speech saturated with the *gestus* of deliberate, lively delivery from person to person(s). Whether these comedians articulate their awareness of the "here and now," the language of Launce, Bottom, Dogberry, the gravediggers, and the Porter betrays a sense of real-world experience that can deliberately inform an effectively anachronistic pattern of speech and behavior. Take only the castle's Porter in a remote corner of feudal Scotland, who appears extremely well versed in topical news about the trial of the Gun Powder Plot conspirators in 1606. This recalls as well the second gravedigger in *Hamlet* who, in the Folio version, is sent to "Yaughan" – possibly a Bankside alehouse-keeper – to fetch his fellow "a stoup of liquor" (*Hamlet*, 5.1.60; TLN 3249).[19] Such anachronism, to return to Hawkes's reading, can pique or quicken "a kind of eruption"; the play "explodes with 'presentist' energy into the here-and-now material life of its spectators," thereby "provoking, engaging with, moulding, constructing and modifying inchoate experience."[20]

The play in performance thereby achieves undeniable immediacy. The audience is caught up with its own immediate (that is, unmediated by character and story) experience and recollection of well-known, communally shared events and locations. The resulting shock of recognition, the turmoil of desire, anxiety, or relaxation is inseparable from the felt commotion of fact and fiction, whereby the "audience's response thus becomes part of the play."[21] As far as this response exceeds the audience's own conventional role, the participation of spectators is mobilised on the existential plane of their ongoing, nervous, moment-to-moment engagement with what is staged in front of them. For that, their own primary frame of reference is provoked and enhanced by the "'presentist' energy" of the comedian. The audience's sense of immediacy derives not from an absent, purely imaginary character but from a visible, audible performer right in front of them. With clowning, as distinct from the representation of purely imaginary persons, such engagement in the audience connects almost exclusively with the performant function, what Meredith Anne Skura calls "the performance dimension of acting."[22] What primarily matters for spectators is Tarlton's or Kemp's mode of delivery, not what figurations they represent in the world of the story.

The clown's "here-and-now" position and the ways agency is displayed in clowning shared strong, supportive links. While such agency, even in the case of Tarlton, Kemp, and Armin, was almost always busy in the self-made fleering, flouting dispersal of its own identity, it constituted, as Nora Johnson notes, "an extraordinary form of performance authority that fully rivals that of a playwright."[23] At the same time, such privileged power obtained because of the clown's readiness to undo wholesome closure in any autonomous sense of self, and thereby to taunt the assumed independence of a purely personal subjectivity. As Robert Weimann has shown in a study of *The Two Gentlemen of Verona*, Kemp-Launce can become both the clowning object and the laughing subject of his own mirth and that of the spectators.[24] The clown's own laughter is *with* the audience and therefore *at* his own comic representation. Such temporary divorce between Kemp's collective role as well-known laughing jester and the lame, highly vulnerable fiction of poor, leave-taking Launce testifies to the vulnerability but also to a self-secure strength in the achievement of a complex identity. The dazzling split in comic performance shows the composite admixture of the dramatically charged clown who is made to submit increasingly to an emerging regime of what we will call "doubly encoded" representation.

Without anticipating our reading of this doubly encoded performance practice in the following chapter, it seems important to point out the circumstances in which early forms of clowning engaged, even comically celebrated the gap between performing agency and performed meaning. In the formative years of the 1580s and early 1590s, the two components and the two different media continue to exist side by side: the clownish actor's here-and-now life agency and his imaginary role-playing in the story still entered into various forms of confederation. We need only consider Tarlton/Dericke in *The Famous Victories of Henry V* (before mid-1587) to trace the Janus-faced performer hilariously displaying so much comic dispersal and incongruity in the space of his own staged subjectivity.[25] To illustrate, the play offers several scenes in which agency itself is staged as a bewildering site of dramatic/extra-dramatic confusion. Dericke/Tarlton enters with an exclamation, repeated nearly half a dozen times, to attract attention: "Who, who there, who there?"[26] While these lines (at least by implication) articulate some persistent need for identification, Robin in his response volleys back a provocative answer:

Robin.   Why I see thou art a plaine Clowne.
Dericke.   Am I a Clowne? sownes, maisters, do Clownes go in silke apparell? I am
           sure all we gentlemen Clownes in *Kent* scant go so well: Sownes, you
           know clownes very well. (131–5)[27]

As Dericke asks "Am I a Clowne?," he is prepared to exhibit and examine the breach between his given comic performance practice and the lightly assumed imaginary identity in the playing of a role. This comic version of a highly unstable, comic type of bifold authority is pursued to the point ("we gentlemen Clownes") where the social identity of the performer is further confounded as well as compounded with, laughably, a counterfeit status. The comic agency at stake remains unanswerable from within the world of the play. The answer stems all too obviously from the circumstances of playing in the world. As Andrew Gurr notes, the comedy "depends largely on the audience knowing Tarlton as himself."[28]

Tarlton died in 1588, but the agency and authority of clowning continued well into the 1590s. Almost like Tarlton's, Kemp's celebrity could be taken for granted throughout and even beyond London. In the printed version of *A Knack to Know A Knave* (1594), the comedian's name was magnetic enough for the play to be advertised as containing "Kemp's applauded merriments of the men of Gotham." In this play, as in the next few years, Kemp's part appears designed as either a comic insertion or some clownish supplement in which role-playing serves at best as a threadbare guise of the performer's biographical agency. Kemp was obviously free to act as a perfectly self-sustained entertainer who, in David Wiles's phrase, preferred not to cope "with the tyranny of a script"; as such, he remains more or less aloof from any ministerial function in the text of the play.[29] As Thomas Nashe, who had greeted Kemp as "jest-monger" in the tradition of "Dick Tarlton" (his dedication to *Almond for a Parrot*, 1590), confirms in *Strange News* (1592), such disengagement must have been endemic in this early period.[30] Hence Wiles is on fairly safe grounds when in his biographical sketch he shows Kemp's career as "rooted in minstrelsy."[31] Most, if not all, mentions of him from the mid-1580s acknowledge either the status of a court jester (in the Earl of Leicester's glamorous entourage in the

Netherlands, 1585/6) or that of participant in a small group of "instrumentalists and tumblers" (on the mission to Denmark, to proceed to Saxony, later in 1586), along with his athletic prowess as dancer. It was only during Kemp's association with Lord Strange's Men that his performance practices underwent "a transition – from solo comedian to regular company member, from patronage to commercial theatre."[32]

In view of his rich and celebrated career as comedian of almost all seasons, it is unlikely that this transition was abrupt or conclusive. For one thing, Kemp continued to serve as famous dancer of jigs; in this, echoes reverberated of the Misrule and/or the fool in the morris tradition. Under these circumstances, it would appear altogether plausible that in the structure of Shakespeare's early comedy *The Two Gentlemen of Verona*, Kemp's performances (with one exception) are all, as Clifford Leech notes, "easily detachable from the text." As the play's editor speculates, they may well have been inserted as "additions."[33]

If the clown's part henceforth would be attached to a previously authored script, we have in the pre-1594 period at least one intriguing parallel in the collaborative additions to *The Book of Sir Thomas More*. Despite its different auspices, the parallel proves of exceptional interest because here we have a clownish agency recorded as speaking his own part in the play as an addition or supplement to an existing script. Such *self-authorized* clowning reveals most of the traditional divisions between voice and pen in a state of flux. While the date of these additions is a matter of debate, we follow the early dating of the Revels Plays editors, last not least in the light of Eric Rasmussen's groundbreaking research on Hand B in the manuscript of *The Book of Sir Thomas More* (Harley 7368 in the British Library).[34]

Challenging the traditional assumption that we have no evidence that an actor's interpolated lines were inserted into dramatic manuscripts, Rasmussen offers the example of Hand B's additional passages, which add more than a dozen utterances for the play's "Clown." What was the provenance of these utterances? Rasmussen argues that Hand B recorded lines that an actor-clown had improvised during a performance or performances of *Sir Thomas More* during the early 1590s. Where previous critics had ascribed the hand and additions to Thomas Heywood, Rasmussen builds his case for their performative origin by noting the speeches' "improvised rather than . . . scripted quality." On top of their resemblance to "the sort of improvisations in verse for which Elizabethan clowns were famous," these formal elements include repetition of brief phrases, gags, and "short interjections, heavily laden with double rhymes."[35]

Admitting that "there is no way of distinguishing what may be an actor's improvisations from what might be merely the work of an inferior playwright," Rasmussen nonetheless offers up a confirming piece of evidence for his hypothesis. The fact that several of the clown's lines appear to be misplaced in the manuscript suggests that "Hand B was not creating the role of the Clown, but simply writing down in the promptbook lines that an actor had improvised on stage."[36] In the years 1593/4, this transcription may have had a special urgency; after 1590, once the printing of plays was rapidly gaining ground and helped boost the authority of the playwright, the practice of improvisation met with increasing obstacles. In the circumstances, as Rasmussen suggests, it must have been tempting in writing to preserve the comic patter of a talented, improvising actor's voice. If the play, as Scott McMillin offers in a closely researched context, "was originally written for Strange's men between the summer of 1592 and the summer of 1593," further questions are raised by the written additions, at a later date, to this script.[37] While several of these do not admit of any conclusive answer, what the writing of this early play unquestionably witnesses to is the original "playwright's lack of control over his own compositions." As G. E. Bentley further notes, this state of affairs points to "a time when the social status of the playwright was low," which for us is one more reason to date the additions fairly early in the 1590s.[38]

Even later in the decade, the relative balance between playing and writing continued to assert itself. Whatever resilience there was in the semi-sovereign stage presence of the comedian, for instance, gradually gave way until the relative triumph of an "author's theatre" (Richard Helgerson's term) appeared to be confirmed by the exclusion of the rustic clown and, equally foreboding, the jig from the new Globe on Bankside.[39] The lines of confrontation and confederation were shifting. Clownage was more and more relegated to northern places like the Red Bull. In Shakespeare's Globe, too, things certainly changed in favor of textually more controlled clowning and fooling – even while the all-important interdependence between the literary and the performative continued unbroken. The ensuing transition in the person of the leading comedian was highly significant but, as Johnson has persuasively argued, the advent of Armin certainly did not mark an end to clowning in the Globe. Once the theatre is understood as at the heart of a vast social and cultural "mingle-mangle," therefore, we must be prepared to see the overlapping, even interpenetration, between both the strongly entrenched, persisting workings of a performance-centered "players' theatre" and a more forcefully text-centered "author's theatre."

A good deal of evidence, in fact, underlines continuity in the midst of important transformations. The traditional view, that the move is "from a robust, coarse-grained performer to a lyrical, introspective one," is certainly not the last word on this question, especially when Armin is depicted as, exclusively, "a sophisticated and versatile character actor."[40] While Alexander Leggatt's remarkable attempt to qualify the traditional view envisions Kemp's separation from the company as, perceptively, the disengagement from the practice of "an old-fashioned clown trading on a single personality," the suggested replacement of clownish agency by a "character actor" is less than the whole truth. In the first place, Kemp already (especially if in his later years he played Falstaff) must have coped with the assimilation of strong, textually preconceived images of characteristic temper and *habitus*. Whatever else Armin's arrival stood for, the new comedian, as Leggatt himself notes, would have been charged with taking over some of Kemp's older parts. Even more crucial, he presumably would have been invited to do "coarse-grained" figurations, such as those of Thersites, Pompey, and Apemantus, not to mention inveterate, albeit textually prescribed clowns like the gravediggers in *Hamlet* or the Porter in *Macbeth* (whose penned speeches were too good to be tampered with).

Yet Armin's own performance practice was far more deeply rooted in the tradition of clownish agencies and direct address than has commonly been assumed. His work, even when indeed it departed from the traditional clown's "trading on a single personality," did not altogether surrender the jester's personality as an identifiable source of appeal. As Johnson has documented, Armin's own position as newly versatile comedian was complemented by the authority (and celebrity) of penmanship. An actor-author, he cashed in on his own performed wit and the wittiness of others in the expanding market of the printing press and, as can be assumed, vice versa. In this process, which may be circumscribed as trading on his own peculiar version of "bifold authority," the performer projects his quipping stage presence onto the pages of jestbooks and pamphlets. Thus, as Johnson notes, Armin not only participates in and further develops "rich connections between the craft of acting and the business of authorship"; even while he explores and exploits unsuspected sites of intersection between stage and page, he conceives of an author-function "as something other," something that eludes analogies with functions of individual property or political sovereignty.[41]

What actually informed Armin's writing, then? Was it his own scriptural practice in terms of a theatre-derived "power to license and to guarantee pleasure?"[42] Did this practice rehearse a lingering, imaginary circuit from stage to page? Or did the jest in the writing recapture a revitalized practice of quipping, a continuing, communal give-and-take among actor and spectators? In the former case, the merry jests on page might record just those delightful memories of an old-fashioned game when words flew like apples between pit and scaffold. Johnson, however, provides us with good (and tempting) reasons to choose the latter of these several options, even when the evidence is not perhaps finally conclusive. To paraphrase her argument, Armin must have been able to reconcile, after the play or even perhaps in its course, a high degree of textual discipline with a traditional type of witty intercourse between player and spectator – amounting to an "agreement to make comedy together."[43]

The conjuncture of playing and writing that we find in the work of Armin (and that of actor-playwrights such as Robert Wilson, Nathan Field, Anthony Munday, William Rowley, and partially at least Thomas Heywood) can here serve as an important pointer and foil to how Shakespeare adapts and transforms traditional clowning.[44] In his mature comedies Armin as fool delivers a vista of worldly folly, which intricately conjoins his performance practice with a new and rhetorically artful dimension of literary discourse. The underlying changes in the relations of page and stage are such that they affect all manner of clowning and fooling. While the rural clown proper is destined to drift, like the shepherd's son in *The Winter's Tale* or Stephano and Trinculo in *The Tempest*, toward the degrading stage of one-dimensional simplicity or corruption, the metamorphosis of the jester into a figuration of wise folly is no less symptomatic of far-reaching cultural change.

This transformation endows the jester with the saving grace and the dangling freedom of a literary impulse prodding the figure into, socially, a melancholy nowhere. The change in question reflects and is propelled by shifting valuations and affiliations of the two media. While in this context we cannot recapitulate the sociologies of writing and playing, we may perhaps recur to the conceptual formula in the title of the present chapter; the clown in the 1580s and early 1590s is marked by the ways an actor's voice animates an author's pen.[45] At the same time, a counter-movement gathers momentum in the later 1590s, by which the author's pen more and more modulates actor's voice. This formula cannot do justice to what motion, friction, and contingency propel a highly untried and unstable conjuncture. It should not come as a surprise, then, that under the growing authority of dramatic authorship the strength and self-sufficiency of the comedian's solo delivery are sapped. Even so, there remains an element of hybridity wherever the two media, the nimble body and the witty pen, jostle side by side. A clownish grain, even in the late plays, continues to be doubly encoded; Apemantus, Autolycus, even Cloten in his delightful crassness preserve memories of a bifold stamp, a vocation to double business bound.

Notwithstanding the potential resilience in Armin's traditional audience address, and the radical self-dispersal of his own performative agency, the shifting grounds on which henceforth the wise fool can thrive are unmistakable. This shift coincided with, if it was not conditioned by, a growing authority and weight behind textual matters. To a certain extent, Shakespeare's major representations of folly, such as Feste, Touchstone, and Lear's nameless Fool, continued to share important portions of *platea* space and dramaturgy with Launce and all the other clowns. This traditional matrix was large enough to allow for a comic kind of surplus action, constant wordplay, and audience rapport. Yet, for all this continuing strength in their performative *gestus*, Shakespeare's dramatic figurations of folly demand a critical treatment prepared to honor the literary component that sustains them. Thus, in revisiting the staging of folly in Shakespeare's theatre, we are well advised, in the words of Lukas Erne, to situate them at the very "intersection of theatricality and literariness" on the basis, conclusively established by the same critic, "that the stage and the printed page did not necessarily represent two rival forms of publication."[46]

Nor is such rivalry necessarily given when we compare dramatic versions of folly with literary treatments of the same subject. Without in the least minimizing generic differences, we find an unsuspected range of parallels between theatrical and literary languages of folly. It is of course true that the bifold authority of stage clowns and fools has no equivalent in literature wherever (as in the following chapter) the staggering intricacies in double-encoded performance come into the picture. Obviously, there cannot be a bodily clownage in fiction involving a live personator and imaginary personated. However, as soon as we look at the verbal enunciations as such, there emerges a more than ordinary gulf, in both forms, between the *énonciation* and the *énoncé* – that is, between utterance and statement, the saying and the meaning. In both genres this gulf is used deliberately, often enough as a mask. As Mikhail Bakhtin notes about "the images of the clown and of the fool" in prose fiction, these masks "grant the right *not* to understand, the right to confuse, to tease, to hyperbolize life; the right to parody others while talking, . . . the right to act life as a comedy and to treat others as actors, the right to rip off masks."[47] As this allusion to the *theatrum mundi* topos suggests, the gulf in question can in both drama and fiction be amplified by a socio-semantic difference between the educated person rendering and the common folk rendered in this language. Thus we have in drama just as in prose fiction what Bakhtin calls "a special kind of *double-voiced discourse*."[48]

As is well known, the representation of fools and folly was an important part of late medieval and early modern literature. In the Renaissance alone, a considerable range marked the available literature of folly, comprising (to name only two) the orthodoxy in the late medieval catalogue of Sebastian Brant's *Ship of Fools*, available in two different English translations (1497 and 1507) and the Erasmian *Moriae Encomium* (1509) with Chaloner's translation into English (1549). In contrast to Brant's orthodox treatment, Erasmus must have appealed especially to all those intent on unfixing those static abstractions in the late moral and interlude plays, with their allegorical versions of disorder, sin, and vice. In fact, even though the learned Erasmus was steeped in classical texts such as the Lucianic genre of paradoxical encomium, in a long letter to Marten Dorp he went out of his way to claim for his own image of folly "the same freedom which the uneducated allow in popular comedies."[49] Accordingly, the Erasmian figure of Folly not only projected the deep irony of carnivalesque inversions and contrarieties; she also invoked expectations associated with stages in the marketplace, as when ostensibly she adopted "an extemporaneous speech" in, deliberately, the language of "pitchmen, low comedians, and jokesters."[50]

For the literary masquerade of folly ironically harboring wisdom, however, Shakespeare did not have to consult the foremost humanist's disquisition on the subject when, in 1593, he could turn to Charles Estienne's treatise just published in a second edition under the title *The Defence of Contraries. Paradoxes against Common Opinion*, translated "out of French by A.M. [i.e., Anthony Munday] one of the messengers of her Majesties Chamber." Herein was offered a remarkably broad concept of "things contrary to most mens present opinions," whereby "opposed truth might appear more clear and apparent" in its search for "sound reasons, proofs, authorities, histories, and very darke or hidden memories."[51] These words, taken from the work's English preface, point to a specifically literary fascination with "things contrary," developed with an eye on its classical sources. As the reader learns, "to live securely in this world, they [i.e., 'ancient Philosophers'] thought it best to use the counterfeit shadowe of a fool." Next, we turn to him who would "cunningly disguise himselfe with the masque of folly," or who, like Shakespeare's fool, is free to expose the arts of preluding and yet precluding duel after insult.[52] Even when the catalogue of "things contrary" is all too often reduced to contrastive patterns of reasoning, the final triumph of these "Paradoxes" is "to confound and overthrow the wisdome of this world."[53]

In drama we have a comparable context of folly and contrariety only a few years later, in Shakespeare's *A Midsummer Night's Dream*. This comedy, with its well-known arsenal of theriomorphic props and signs, could lead the reader to conclude that Bottom's "ass's head" (Folio's stage direction [3.1.202/203]) derives from, exclusively, a theatrical source. However, although this attribute has a theatre history reaching back to the preclassical *mimus*, we also have several literary sources in places where theatre historians content themselves with recourse to performance practice only.[54] If we take Bottom's dream with its inspired confusion in the perception of the senses, it is almost certain that Shakespeare borrowed material from the ending of *The Praise of Folly* – unless of course the dramatist grafted contrariety on the biblical "Eye has not seen, nor ear heard" (1 Corinthians, 2:9). Erasmus, who refers to the words of the prophet, does so with a remarkable twist when he links the promised state of blessing "for those who love [God]" with "Folly's part." Those few who have the ecstatic experience of "things unseen, beyond what can be seen" are led to "something very like madness: they talk incoherently, not in a human fashion, making sounds without sense." While this already anticipates Bottom's inability (or is it refusal?) to "expound this dream" (*Dream*, 4.1.207) and its meaning, the Erasmian rendering of such ecstasy appears even more suggestive:

For this undoubtedly is even the very guerdon that the Prophet promiseth, Saying, *what never man's eye saw, nor ear heard, nor thought of heart yet compassed, what, and how great felicity God hath prepared unto such as do love him* ... they are subject to a certain passion much like unto madness or witraving, when ravished so in the spirit, or being in a trance, they do speak certain things not hanging one with another, ... remembering also as little, either what they heard, saw, said, or did then, saving as it were through a cloud, or by a dream: but this they know certainly, that whiles their minds so roved and wandered, they were most happy and blissful.

Erasmus had to defend himself from such staggering audacity. Yet Shakespeare's treatment adds a further piece of contrariety by confounding, at least by implication, the supreme spiritual state of blessedness with the bottomless bliss of sensual rapture. All this is experienced under the pre-Christian mask of the ass's head.

Another purely literary infusion into the staging of clowning folly may well have occurred through Erasmian, or otherwise mediated, versions of Silenus. Since we have evidence of Shakespeare's contact with the Erasmian *Colloquia*, and, perhaps, the *Adagia*, recent critics seem more than justified in pointing to important links between the Silenus trope and dramatic versions of fools and folly.[55] These links go far beyond any purely verbal form of parallelism, and are remarkable, in our context, as forming a highly consequential site of conjuncture. In fact, the Erasmian invocations of Silenus are far-reaching in that they help prepare the ground for a startling frame of reference in *The Praise of Folly*.[56] There they affirm and enhance performative premises on which Silenus, emerging Falstaff-like in the shape of a "white-haired wooer," is shown as he "dances a *frisky jig*" (literally, a *cordax*, i.e., a vulgar or obscene comic dance). It was in some such shape that, traditionally, Silenus was likened to "a person whose looks and dress do not correspond at all to what he conceals in his soul."[57] But now in *The Praise of Folly* "the Sileni of Alcibiades" leave behind their Platonic reference to Socrates and turn out to epitomize the workings of contrariety itself: "notoriety will become fame; learning will be ignorance; strength, weakness; noble birth will be ignoble; joy will become sadness; success, failure; friendship, enmity." But we "find everything suddenly reversed if [we] open the Silenus." It is the stage that exemplifies what "all this [is] leading up to":

If someone should try to strip away the costumes and makeup from the actors performing a play on the stage and to display them to the spectators in their own natural appearance, wouldn't he ruin the whole play? ... Everything would suddenly look different: the actor just now playing a woman would be seen to be a man; ... the man who played the king only a moment ago would become a pauper; the actor who played god would be revealed as a wretched human being.[58]

The extraordinary parallelism which Erasmus elaborates is that of the gulf, in Silenus, between the inside/outside and the gap, on stage, between performed persona and performing person. The analogy is so unsuspected and far-reaching because the principle of inversion or contrariety (inherent in the classical *topos*: "you will find everything suddenly reversed if you open the Silenus") is made to highlight the metamorphosis resulting from the performing actor's mimesis. And vice versa: the Janus face of acting, the discrepancy between the persona in the world of the play and the person acting in the play of the world crucially prepares the ground for grasping the *totus mundus* perspective on worldly affairs. The gap in Silenus between his "looks and dress" and what he "conceals in his soul" is compellingly suggestive. This gap propels the composition of a figure whose folly is wisdom as against a wisdom that is foolish. Those that wear motley and bear wisdom within can best embody the "glassy essence" of mundane ambitions: "Now the whole life of mortal men, what is it but a sort of play, in which various persons make their entrances in various costumes, and each one plays his own part until the director gives him his cue to leave the stage?"[59] Here the interplay of stage and page comes full circle. It is on stages that players enact a worldly model, revealing insight into "the whole life of mortal men" as they come and go. These our actors practice a "deception" in that their "disguise" performs a circuit of actions that leaves us wondering which is the seeming, which is the "life" itself. This knowledge, offered on stages, is symbolically enacted even when conveyed through performance practice. Therefore, the legendary motto for the Globe theatre, *totus mundus agit histrionem*, stands for an awareness that is represented, not for the delivery of bodily action. In short, the motto requires thinking and the language in which to develop further thought, a scanning forward and backward. Additive constructions, paratactic connections, let alone formulaic expressions, as we have them in oral discourse, would not do where a highly variable symbolic order requires us to discern hidden connections and analogies.

For all that, it is the role-playing performer who, in the arch pattern of acting, provokes the insight expressed in the *totus mundus* topos. As Johnson notes, "performance and print build the significance of the fool in ways that are different but become so layered over each other that the printed text mirrors the staged performance and vice versa."[60] The ironic insight into the "whole life of mortal men" may call for a textual rendering in symbolic terms; but the achieved image of how this insight works and what it yields is derived from the province of performance. This rich compendium of relations between the idea of *totus mundus* and the performance of staged action radiates from the nub of the matter, which is the interface of page and stage.

In other words, what the image of folly owes to the mutual interplay of stages and pages is that each submits to and draws on something larger than itself. The largeness in question derives from the awareness of an unfathomed link between play *in* life and the play *of* life. Such unsanctioned awareness embraces both the natural space for growth and aging but also the social space for interpersonal contact, in which people meet, relate, and respond to one another. As an acute observer notes:

The attributes of a performer and the attributes of a [performed] character are of a different order, quite basically so, yet both sets have their meaning in terms of the show that must go on . . . the successful staging of either of these types of false figures [i.e., the theatrical actor and the "confidence man"] involves use of *real* techniques – the same techniques by which everyday persons sustain their real social situations.[61]

But is, then, the "real technique" in representation (as in relation-building) something in itself representable? The question points forward to what the following chapter refers to as "the frontiers of representation." In greatly different ways the sixteenth-century humanist and the twentieth-century anthropologist in their writings share a need to have recourse to nonliterary practices of staging and performance. While Erasmus in his approach to folly uses irony artfully, as a deliberate strategy, he does thereby confront what in the theatre is both a working practice and a working principle. Erving Goffman hints at this principle when he underlines the discontinuity between the staging of "false" fictions and the reality of the means used therein. On stages there is not too much space for the irony involved in this basic theatrical discrepancy. Yet to study the Erasmian dimension of a similar irony is to view this discontinuity in a broader perspective that illuminates early modern discourse in both literature and the theatre.

Important links between dramatic and prosaic representations of folly attest to the formidable extent of mutually operative entanglements between early modern writing and playing. What is especially remarkable in the unfolding relations of page and stage is the rapid growth of the literary component in even the most laughable stage presence of fools and folly in Shakespeare's theatre. As distinct from the clown proper, the rhetoric of the fool was neither dominated nor confined by the mother-wit peculiar to types of russet comedy. Rather, a fool like Touchstone in *As You Like It* resonated with memories of courtly arrogance, conduct, and discourse. True enough, there remained plenty of clownish life blood: "It is meat and drink to me to see a clown" (*As You Like It*, 5.1.10); but then, a mere thirty lines later, his verbal effusion can scarcely conceal the rhetoric of *copia*, fueled by the arrogance that goes with social rivalry and a readiness to lecture from above. He says to rural William:

Then learn this of me: to have, is to have. For it is a figure in rhetoric that drink, being pour'd out of a cup into a glass, by filling the one doth empty the other. For all your writers do consent that *ipse* is he: now, you are not *ipse*, for I am he.
. . .
He, sir, that must marry this woman. Therefore, you clown, abandon – which is in the vulgar leave – the society – which in the boorish is company – of this female – which in the common is woman; which together is, abandon the society of this female, or, clown, thou perishest; or to thy better understanding, diest; or (to wit) I kill thee, make thee away, translate thy life into death, thy liberty into bondage. (40–54)

Touchstone invokes "all your writers" as from a distance so as to justify a comic logic in his own use of language for which already, in a preceding sentence, he had adduced "a figure of rhetoric" as authority. Not unlike the mocking subtext in *The Praise of Folly*, this authority is a mock authority, the logic a mock logic, his own use of "rhetoric" a travesty of both grammar and logic.

But since, again, the mockingly inverted standards of literacy come close to being a foolish reversal of both logic and authority, Touchstone offers his audience an extremely canny indeterminacy. The fool addresses "all *your* writers" out there; he invokes a literary culture, which is not his own, only to abuse the medium for a celebration of its laughable abuses. In doing so he lifts a clownish strategy of contrariety and, to a certain extent, revives a strange kind of "consent" by smiling with his audience rather than offering himself as laughingstock. In other words, it is with a twinkling eye on his audience that he exhibits the madness in his crafty uses of language addressed, of all people, to a rural type of clown. The latter's shrewdness, his traditional versions of juggling wit and jostling exuberance, have been expropriated by a far more sophisticated (and arrogant) culture of literacy. Thus William, Audrey's friend and country fellow, is in this brief scene twice relegated to the status of a "clown" (10, 47). When Touchstone, after having arrogated to his lust William's Audrey, exposes the "clown" to his bravado threats, all the clownish simpleton can do is depart with a "God rest you merry, sir" (59).

As far as this scene may be said to crystallize highly ambivalent assimilations of rhetorically informed writing to comic performance, it does, despite their obvious difference, convey a sense of what Johnson has called the "strong continuities between performance and print." The scene documents what the same author has conclusively, we think, shown about the performer behind Touchstone. In Armin's case, "stage performance and print authorship went together," even to the degree that success in one medium is linked to his public prominence in the other. Rather than pitting the Elizabethan clown or fool in his embodiments against an "author's theatre," we do well to follow Johnson in her suggestion "to take seriously the authorial potential in comic performance." In fact, to do so corroborates an "alternative to the very actor/author split" on whose premises relations of performance and text cannot simultaneously be reconstructed in both their friction and their collaboration.[62]

Textually conceived representations depicting a new degree of individual isolation and self-centeredness proved especially congenial to highly performative descendants of the Vice.[63] A comparable, reverse movement from stage to page can be documented in sixteenth-century literature. This has been convincingly traced by David Schalkwyk in his study *Speech and Performance in Shakespeare's Sonnets and Plays* but it also, and especially in comic writing, informs some of the most impressive work of early modern prose fiction.[64] As an illustration, let us in conclusion glance at François Rabelais's *Gargantua and Pantagruel*, arguably the most innovative and incommensurable piece of sixteenth-century prose fiction. In our context, it seems particularly striking that a strong performative invades the uses of fictional language and reappropriates the postallegorical abyss between saying and meaning for representational aims and ends. The paradox is that, again, the writing of prose assimilates a highly stage-centered experience in the unfolding poetics of its representations, even before dramatic writing is able to adapt this poetics in its own, potentially even more compelling, ways.

Following Erasmus, Rabelaisian writing was able to mobilize the allegorical fixations and in its representational strategies to anticipate a paradigm change comparable to what we have in Elizabethan drama. The kinetic energy and the new elements of mobility and contingency in the relationship between the *énoncé* and *énonciation* connects with the reception of Janus-faced Silenus. The classically sanctioned figure once more proves to be a crucial catalyst in the authorization of semiotic indeterminacy between sign and meaning. At the same time, this move unleashes a pictorial force and world-appropriating plasticity that provide a unique space in which literature and prose fiction in particular initiate a newly symbolic mode of modern representation. Again, Renaissance authors were spurred on to what had long been associated with the Silenus figure in both classical prose and drama. As early as the fifth century BC, for instance, Silenus appears to have taken a central role (that of coryphaeus, or leader) in the ritualized chorus of tragedies and that of a lesser, subcoryphaeus for the ensuing satyr play.[65]

Fittingly, then, in his "Prologue de l'auteur" to the First Book, Rabelais invokes the exemplum of Silenus not simply as used in the Socratic context of Plato's *Symposium* but as the touchstone, even epitome, of a new broken chain among signs, signifier, and signified. Again pointing to the radical discrepancy in Silenus between the inside and the outside – the latter adorned with such gay comical figures as "harpies, satyrs, bridled geese, horned hares" – Rabelais proceeds to apply the ruptured nexus to the mode of his own writing. For that, "Silenus himself, the master of good old Bacchus," serves as an unpredictable, enigmatic figuration in which the grotesque, comic impulse of seeming folly brings forth the "symbolic" mode and the poetic potential of "another taste," with a deeper insight and awareness of both the sacred and the horrible.[66] Herein, then, is a "darker doctrine," one more profound and liquid, that helps reveal secrets "concerning our religion, but also the political state and the economic life."[67]

Mock-heroic overtones notwithstanding, the treatment of Silenus is part of a thoroughly earnest quest culminating in the solving of the mystery of

the Holy Bottle. On its way we have Bacchus's attack and victory led by
Silenus riding an "ass" in the midst of a wild company of rural, naked satyrs.
As Rabelais tells us, "They were all naked, sang continuously, and danced
the cordax" ("*tous nuds, tousjours chantans et dansans les cordaces*").[68]
Altogether, this stupendous treatment of folly, addressed to "my good
disciples and other leisured fools," seriously substantiates the author's
would-be facetious "doctrine."[69] It provides ample proof "that the subjects
here treated are not so foolish" as apparent outsides such "as the title on the
cover" may suggest. Rabelais does not at all disparage the literary rendering
of what by rhetorical standards is low and foolish, particularizing detail;
rather, he readily admits "that in the literal meanings you find jolly enough
nonsense." By implication Rabelais here distinguishes between the symbolic and "the literal meanings" – thereby preparing for a more intricate,
more highly interactive relationship between the particular and the general.
Rather than looking for an abstract or allegorical equivalence between image
and idea, he encourages readers to "interpret in a more sublime sense" (the
French has "*à plus hault sens interpreter*"), while dismissing those "allegories"
which used to be "squeezed out" of literary works in the past. Instead,
readers are (in the preface as in solving the Holy Bottle's mystery) urged to
consult their own experience and judgment: "You must be your own
interpreters in this matter."[70] Thus there are new and different demands
which readers must meet when immersing themselves in this new mode of
gathering meaning, "that is to say the meaning which I intend to convey by
these Pythagorean symbols" ("*c'est à dire ce que j'entend par ces symboles
pythagoriques*").[71]

It is surely not fortuitous, then, that the move out of allegorical forms
toward early modern representation is propelled by an unorthodox discourse of clowning and folly offering on the surface of things "nothing but
mockery, fooling, and pleasant fictions" (Pro. 37). As background to the
genealogy of secular dramatic representation, clowning must here be subsumed under these fooling fictions. Excepting a few harbingers of dramatic
clowning, from the early *Cambises* to *George a Greene* and *The Famous
Victories* in the 1580s, Elizabethan dramatists adapt and begin dramatically
to integrate clownish agencies only in the early 1590s.

Shakespeare's clowns and fools, far from offering any one particular
mode of mirth, are shifting in their cultural and comic demarcations.
They are either demarcated in their equipment, profession, and education
(as is Dogberry in *Much Ado About Nothing* or Pompey in *Measure for
Measure*) or moved upward in status, indulging in courtly memories
(Touchstone) or in the service of a noble Lady (Feste). The rural underside

so prominent in the Tarlton tradition is surrendered to a pastoral or country house environment in which courtly standards are simultaneously taunted and emulated. In the process there emerges a supercilious pose laughably and critically used in distancing rural folk as clownish and naïve. While this first appears in *As You Like It*, in the late plays the clown enters as a naïve or wretched simpleton, as for instance the Shepherd's son in *The Winter's Tale* and Stephano and Trinculo in *The Tempest*. As the interests of court, city, and country increasingly diverged over the early seventeenth century, the already tenuous Elizabethan compromise was less and less able to ensure mutual respect for or even understanding of various socially inflected attitudes and positions.

On the other hand, the emerging particularity of clownish figures indicates and goes with their growing ties to the playworld and its representational framework. In line with their role-playing, they can develop, as Bertram says about Parolles (whose *nomen* is *omen*), into a "counterfeit module" serving as "a double-meaning" (*All's Well That Ends Well*, 4.3.99–100) instance of awareness and representation. Even when their embeddedness in a nonveri-similar dramaturgy of audience address lingers, the wider field of cultural differentiation, figural particularity, and integration into the play's story is markedly indebted to the endeavors of art in writing. As we have seen in the *theatrum mundi* metaphor in Erasmus, the entire conglomerate comprising the world as a stage and the stage in the world is not derived from perform-ance practice pure and simple. While the *topos* indicates a closely experienced awareness of things theatrical, it is predicated on altogether specific and highly flexible notions of personation. These notions hedge at the attempt to embody or not to embody the issue of difference in role-playing: to be or not to be ready to conceal the actual agency in personation. As long as personators do not conceal their presence in the persona, the exhibited difference between being and acting can serve as fertile grounds on which to plant ideas of *theatrum mundi*. At the same time, the increasingly accessible suspension of agency may demand a kind of judgment of the world as something absent, out there. In other words, the *theatrum mundi* image is a *topos* crystallizing a representational notion; implicating a certain purpose of playing, it offers, in Heidegger's sense of the word, a world picture, even one with an epistemological dimension.

CHAPTER 5

Clowning at the frontiers of representation

In the preceding chapter we explored how the conjuncture of bodily performance and literary language helped constitute the agencies of clowns and fools. We now move from the study of doubly encoded agencies to the comically delivered forms and functions of clownish performance in both presentation and representation. For the preeminence of a presentational purpose, we will turn to what arguably is the most articulate jester in the Elizabethan period, the non-Shakespearean player/clown in Thomas Nashe's *Summers Last Will and Testament* (1592). Along with the more (re)presentational Launce in *The Two Gentlemen of Verona*, we shall then glance at the shape and purpose of several role-playing clowns in Shakespeare's plays after the watershed year of 1594.

The entirely pragmatic distinction made here between clowns and fools bypasses their complex genealogy. Reaching back to late ritual practices such as the men's ceremonial, "fool" actually antedates modern theatrical forms of clowning. As far as their etymology provides a clue, the word "clown" is, according to the *OED*, "of later introduction" and retains a rural connotation, such as a "mere rustic, a boor," or "a clout," with only a late sixteenth-century theatrical adaptation. In contrast, "fool" derives from Old French via Middle English sources. In Shakespeare's theatre the transition from clowning to fooling is not as clear-cut as the departure of clownish Will Kemp and the subsequent playing and singing of Robert Armin have led some critics to assume. Between them, the overlap is especially obvious where it was Armin who (in the absence of Kemp) was most likely to do the part of clowns in revivals of older plays. In any case, if there are considerable links between, say, Bottom and Feste, there is also a remarkable amount of difference. This difference reflects a rapidly changing socio-cultural landscape for the work of the company renamed, only a decade later, the King's Men.

As clowns are admonished to follow what Hamlet recommends as "some necessary question of the play" (*Hamlet*, 3.2.42–3), their dramatic function becomes more integral. Eventually they tend to join in the general task of all other players to serve as "the abstract and brief chronicles of the time" (2.2.524–5). However, even as they approach what in their previous solo entertainments was a fairly unknown province – that is, the purely imaginary space of representation – clowns retain much of their openness, anachronism, and zest in performance. While they are never transformed into well-contoured figurations in fiction, they can – as the gravediggers in *Hamlet* demonstrate – approach textually administered assignments very closely.

The Prince of Denmark's view of what is "necessary" is too much that of a courtly humanist for him to be more balanced in his censure. Vital audience rapport ensures a presentational dimension in clowning. It requires comedians to go beyond the fiction of role-playing to display some more existential being in flesh and blood, their body, their pain, and their own laughter. When Hamlet goes out of his way to warn the First Player not to "let those that play your clowns" stray from what "is set down for them," the Prince holds most abusive the direct, extratextual bond between comedians and spectators. So he singles out those "that will *themselves* laugh to set on some quantity of barren spectators to laugh too" (3.2.38–42; our italics). This is precisely what Joseph Hall's satire *Virgidemiarum* (1597) aims at when it scourges the clown's "laughter at his self-resembled show" – a passage to which we shall return.

At issue here are both a collision and, as we shall see, a collusion of pages and stages over the matter of representation. For clowns to laugh in this way is for "themselves" to authorize, not closure but disclosure, the "secretly open" manner of rendering speech and action. These comedians are predisposed to pursue a way of entertaining that elicits the visible pleasure of onlookers and confirms the player in his pains. What counts, for him, is to have the audience with him, participating and involved in the fun of the game, in a kind of release through contrariety. As Robert Weimann has shown in *Shakespeare and the Popular Tradition*, the clown has reason enough to laugh when his own merriment joins up with or leads to a "laughing with the audience." Such laughter rings with a late communal sense of gratification and relief at being one of them and yet having the wit and the skill to cater for an occasion that pays. This is precisely the moment when the performance of self-sufficient sport and game challenges the "necessary" regime of representation, its world-picturing, world-appropriating order of things.[1]

The symbolic order of figuration does not and cannot condone a fracturing of the achieved picture, when each image, each figure in the mirror cries out its need for an ultimate correlation. Such need calls not for unity but a sense of integration which structures the play and the relationship of its parts in terms of an effective, crisscrossing interplay of the media. Through a verbal web of mutually sustained correspondence and difference, the language of the play provided the clue to what questions were asked. From the humanist point of view, as we have seen, the "purpose of playing" was, in Hamlet's own words, first and foremost to "Suit the action to the word" (*Hamlet*, 3.2.17). The "word" came first. Its authority, in line with the author's endeavors of art and rhetoric, was preeminent. What pleasure and value derived from the here-and-now of stage experience, from an awareness of the player's voice and *gestus* – certainly not unimportant – was secondary.

Clowning, therefore, can best be studied on the enabling grounds of its difference from the language of representation – grounds which, paradoxically, a jester's dramatic use of the stage as stage presupposed. Even as clowns continue to present at least some of their comic action in its own right, their clowning does not come pure. Rather, on Elizabethan stages it is from verge to verge directed toward, though never by, what it is not. In other words, as this chapter's title hints, clowning *relates* to representation, seeks to inhabit and disturb its boundaries. Clowning is not representation's opposite but part of a bifold authority inspiring Shakespeare's theatre, shaping its tension from within. Clowns invade but also adjust certain modes of representation. As in *Hamlet*, to hold the mirror up to nature can reprehend the clown even while clowning in the play can vitalize what meaning is represented. For these reasons, we must not envision the onslaught of clownish performance upon representation as, so to speak, a raid or some other external molestation. Rather, the impulse affects the performed drama of representation from its core, as a contrarious force strong enough to question the values and validity claimed in representation. The jester's inroads upon symbolic meaning can infringe the representational principle of *quid pro quo* in that, as we shall see in Launce's case, the tenuous, if not entirely arbitrary quality of the links between the *quid* and the *quo* are exposed.

For illustrations, we are thinking of Shakespeare's mature figurations of clownage and folly. Take, for instance, Bottom in *A Midsummer Night's Dream*, the clownish marriage of Vice and Lord of Misrule in Falstaff, the no less significant Launcelot Gobbo in *The Merchant of Venice*, the unrivalled Porter in *Macbeth*, such exquisite embodiments of folly as Touchstone in *As You Like It* and Feste in *Twelfth Night*, or the nameless Fool in *King Lear*. However, we propose first to look closely at two pre-1594 figurations, among which Nashe's *Summers Last Will and Testament* takes pride of place. Unrivaled by any other Elizabethan clown, Summers is a (re)presentational figuration, brimming with abhorrence over the outrageous uses of "Inke and paper," even literacy itself:

Will Summers: Out vpon it, who would be a Scholler? Not I, I promise you: my minde alwayes gaue me this learning was such a filthy thing, which made me hate it so as I did: when I should haue beene at schoole, construing *Batte, mi fili, mi fili, mi Batte*, I was close vnder a hedge, or vnder a barne wall, playing at spanne Counter or Iacke in a boxe: my master beat me, my father beat me, my mother gaue me bread and butter, yet all this would not make me a squitter-booke ... Here, before all this companie, I professe my selfe an open enemy to Inke and paper. Ile make it good vpon the Accidence body, that In speech is the diuels Pater noster: Nownes and Pronounes, I pronounce you as traitors to boyes buttocks: ... Hang copies; flye out, phrase books; let pennes be turnd to picktooths: bowles, cards, & dice, you are the true liberal sciences; Ile ne're be Goosequil, gentlemen, while I liue.[2]

Right from the outset, we are led to ask: is the speaker a reembodiment of Will Summers (one-time fool to Henry VIII), or rather the clownish player who, having opened the play to a socially superior banqueting audience, enters half-dressed? He enters, significantly, in a liminal shape which accentuates the bifold space between the clownish role and the actual agent behind it ("for what with turmoyle of getting my fooles apparell, and care of being perfit"). Here the focus is not on the question of agency except as far as it translates into either the mode of representation or the function of presentation. The difficulty, as we shall see in a moment, is that the dramaturgy, including the practical *mise en scène*, precludes an "either/or" answer.

Foregrounding the act of presenting the play in the world of "gentlemen," the comedian readily displays and betrays, rather than simply enacts, the clownish role of Will Summers. Yet all the time the player knows "*Will Summers Ghost I should be* [latter italics added], come to present you with *Summers Last Will and Testament*" (233). In fact, he draws on both what presence and what absence there is on the threshold between presentation and representation. In his liminal stance the player reproves "the Idiot our Playmaker" (233), censuring the "scuruy *Prologue*" (234) just as he does the use of allegory in the "old vayne of similitudes" (234). Continuing, he holds up for scorn the boredom (as if "at a Sermon") where spectators "heare a filthy beggerly Oration" from "a beggerly Poet that writ it" (244). From his objections to literacy, the clown proceeds to object to those readers "that wrest a neuer meant meaning out of euery thing ... for here are no quips in Characters" (235). Finally, he levels reservations at the "deepe streame" (235) of textualized meaning itself. He repudiates a textually prescribed role in favor of an allegedly unrehearsed, slipshod type of oral extempore: "I care not what I say now, for I play no more then you heare; & some of that you heard to (by your leaue) was extempore" (235–6).

However, both Summers's impromptu note in distancing his own repre- sented role and his diatribe on "Inke and paper" are inscribed in the dramatist's text. In view of this inscription, the invective against writing and "learning" is either ironic or highly ambivalent. The paradox emerges when Summers's seemingly oral intervention finds itself in a kind of mimetic complicity with one of the major themes in the poetic representation of Winter. The clown paraphrases a sentiment that Winter conveys in his rather savage attack on "loytring contemplation": "there is no vice, / Which learning and vilde knowledge brought not in" (277). The learned and the literate, "these damned snares" (279), are denounced as among the "freshe-start-up" professions. These embrace "Grammarians," "Historiographers," "orators," and of course "Lawyers": "Vaine boasters, lyers, make-shifts, they are all" (277). Here Winter's argument falls in with the representation of a *disputatio*[3] even when it prepares the ground for another attack on "Schoolemasters" (279) – a word that provides a cue for Summers's abuse of the same profession.

Because the clown maintains a strong liminal stance in the play, his position is to a large extent extradramatic. His appeal, in prose, to a common type of experience (from "Horne-books" to "boyes buttocks") is not overheard by the leading *dramatis personae*, those allegorical figurations of the seasons that speak in verse. Thus Summers can, as from a threshold, comment on but also commend the "great labour" of the boy actors. Addressing the audience, he can freely lend his support and encouragement to those "poor fellows." Almost in conclusion, he asks spectators to "[S]it still a little and hear him [the boy actor] say his lesson without book. It is a good boy; be not afraid; turn thy face to my lord. Thou and I will play at pouch tomorrow morning for a breakfast. Come and sit on my knee . . ." (293). Note the way he swiftly moves from audience address to reassure not an actor-character but the boy actor all too prone to suffer from stagefright. Abetting the poor trembling lad not from within but from without the latter's role, Summers again defies the world of representation. Impervious to the impact of allegorical symbolism, he is amusingly unable to read Harvest, another allegorical personification, except to address the person- ator (rather than the personated) as "thou bundle of straw" (263).

Nashe's piece, as far as we know, was not produced in the public theatre. While the circumstances of its original performance (almost certainly Archbishop Whitgift's country palace at Croydon) are exceptional, the underlying dramaturgy is not. Certainly indebted to John Lyly's secular uses of allegory as well as to the rhetoric of the humanist *disputatio*, Nashe's allegorical framework is boisterously punctured by the way its performance is presented. Significantly, the resistance to the symbolic mode is confined to the process of its staging and the temporal level of what is presented now. Even here, the clown's merriment and his sadness are subtly interwoven with the season's theme of becoming and passing, which in its turn adumbrates the 1592 plague's fury; the awareness of both living and dying seems to be deep in the throat behind the clown's laughter.

To move from Will Summers to the near-contemporaneous Launce in *The Two Gentlemen of Verona* exemplifies the astonishing range of even the early clown's forms and functions. Launce's is worlds apart from the task of a presenter. His discourse has no axe to grind, no argument to set forth. Yet, as we shall see, an unprecedented, cunning kind of comedy marks his contrariety. It is as if his version of the gulf between the symbolic order of dramatic language and the visible, audible presence of headstrong bodies is itself turned into undisguised entertainment.

If we follow Clifford Leech's reading in his Arden edition of the play, the entire part of Launce may well have been inserted later into the fairly conventional stage adaptation of Italianate sources, dealing with Renaissance courtship, love, friendship, and betrayal. According to Leech, this was almost certainly done to accommodate the playing of Kemp, famous comedian, dancer, and "*Iestmonger* in the spirit of Dick Tarlton." But although Kemp's intervention in Act 2, scene 3 may well be read as a "one-man play-within-a-play,"[4] the solo quality of the clown's entertainment is at least partially intercepted by the verve and density in the clown's counterpointing purpose of playing. Elsewhere in the play, the clowning is made to deform as well as supplement upper-class or courtly sentiment in its high-flown use of language. However, the performative thrust in Act 2, scene 3 takes aim at the symbolic order of representation itself.

Launce enters upon the leave-taking scene of Proteus and Julia. As the gentle couple exchange their tokens and "seal the bargain with a holy kiss," Julia's "tide of tears" precipitates her exit in silence. Whereupon Proteus remarks, "What, gone without a word? / Ay, so true love should do: it cannot speak, / For truth hath better deeds than words to grace it" (*The Two Gentlemen of Verona*, 2.2.16–18). Here the false, inconstant representation of "true love," even "truth," through the use of "words" rather than "deeds," provides a cue for the clown to expose the "manner of it." Launce enters "weeping," only to offer his own inversionary flaunting of romantic tears and vows. What Launce renders in his tale – a whole family "weeping," "wailing," "crying," "howling" – is familiar enough. What has not been noticed or explored is how Launce proceeds, hilariously and obscenely, to reexamine the mode of representation itself. What he delivers is of course a travesty of it, but one which discloses those relations of "truth" and "deeds" and "words" set forth in the drama of romantic love and courtship:

why, my grandam, having no eyes, look you, wept herself blind at my parting. Nay, I'll show you the manner of it. This shoe is my father; no, this left shoe is my father; no, no, this left shoe is my mother; nay, that cannot be so neither; yes, it is so, it is so – it hath the worser sole. This shoe, with the hole in it, is my mother, and this my father – a vengeance on't! there 'tis. Now, sir, this staff is my sister, for, look you, she is as white as a lily and as small as a wand. This hat is Nan, our maid. I am the dog – no, the dog is himself, and I am the dog – O! the dog is me, and I am myself; ay, so, so. Now come I to my father: "Father, your blessing." Now should not the shoe speak a word for weeping; now should I kiss my father; well, he weeps on. Now come I to my mother. O that she could speak now like a wood woman! Well, I kiss her; why, there 'tis; here's my mother's breath up and down. Now come I to my sister; mark the moan she makes. Now the dog all this while sheds not a tear, nor speaks a word; but see how I lay the dust with my tears. (2.3.12–32)

While Launce's speech is grounded in yet another burlesque of romantic tears and gentle vows, it is not enough to say that the comedy remains on the level of mere parody. While reenacting his own clownish version of weeping, the performer displaces the fiction of leave-taking and invites spectators to look beyond the boundaries of its representation. Standing alone, on a *platea*-like space, the clown interrogates the presentation of the signs of the signs of parting. What this witty interrogation reveals is that someone who, like Julia, has no eyes to see can weep "herself blind" at parting.

To reveal "the manner of it," the clown shows up the tenuous relation between what is ideally represented and what is materially performing in all their arbitrariness. The "shoe," which serves as a sign, "is my father. No, this left shoe is my father; no, no, this left shoe is my mother; nay, that cannot be so neither." What "this shoe" signifies, then, is quite unstable. In fact, the staged process of representation is so unsettling and, as it were, so destabilizing, that the symbolic order of signs and their arbitrary meanings is turned upside-down no fewer than five times. Launce stubbornly continues to harass representational practice in its arbitrariness, until there results a thoroughly comic, grotesque version of it, culminating in the odor of what shoe personates his mother.

Throughout his speech, the symbolic mode of representation is found wanting on several levels. There is first of all the assumption led *ad absurdum* that any material object, once it is staged, would have its signified meaning in dramatic performance. Even the actor's outfit, the most elementary garment, may not serve as *quid pro quo*. In short, the ordinary article in its humble materiality (such as shoe, staff, hat) can defy symbolic mediation.

If the smelly shoe, like the wear and tear of ordinary living, resists synecdoche as the representational figure par excellence, what about the living animal? The dog enters the stage as Launce's companion. Featured dramatically, as a comedian's pet in staged action, the animal serves ill under the new regime of dramatic representation: it cannot be controlled. Significantly, its most visceral function (the dog's bladder) seems at fault. While the comedian is at pains to cope with the resulting embarassment, its hilarious entertainment value has a deeper meaning for the making of the play and its dramaturgy.

The poignant cue comes from Launce himself. After we have learned from him what the "shoe," the "staff," the "hat" stand for, the immediately following question (as translated in our language of theory) is "What does the dog represent?" This question is absolutely crucial since it connects with the first person singular, that is, the question of "What do I stand for?": "This hat is Nan, our maid. I am the dog – no, the dog is himself, and I am the dog – O! the dog is me, and I am myself; ay, so, so." The confusion does not simply repeat itself. In defiance of the entire regime of dramatic representation, the text comically grants Kemp his own self-sustained, self-authorized rights of performance. Under the threadbare guise of playing the role of Launce, he is entitled to renounce the unstable, alien figuration altogether, so as to assert: "I am myself."

Yet the exhibited process of role-playing and role-changing takes one more perplexing turn when the animal comes in. There are, now, two breathing bodies on stage. For a fraction of a second they may mutually change places and identities. But since both are as well known as their shapes are irreducible, "the dog is himself," too. So the boundary slips between bodies and what they embody. Launce needs to correct himself when this slippage affects even the most elementary question of status – the question for the actor to be or not to be an artificial person.

At this point, the existential underside itself ceases to be of a piece. The dog is pure flesh and blood, an animal that *is* itself rather than having any (controllable) body to play with, that is, to use for role-playing. The dog Crab "is a stone, a very pibble stone" (2.3.10). If "the dog is himself" (22), he is unable either to represent or properly to be turned into a representation. Crab's stage presence has a contiguity of a sort with the clowning Kemp, which Launce playfully points at: "I am the dog – no, the dog is himself, and I am the dog – O! The dog is me, and I am myself; ay, so, so." Here a basic distinction is made, one which – with rare exceptions – most students of the body in performance tend to ignore. The dog's body is all of a piece, its uncontrollable, unrepresentable physicality is visceral throughout – like the bear or the cock in Bankside next door. Now there is one side of the clown's body that resembles what with the dog is just flesh and blood, and as such nonrepresentable. As Launce/Kemp puts it in a seeming non sequitur, "the dog is me, and I am myself." What is on stage, then, is the clown's two bodies: on the one hand, the low-status signs of clowning can be read to represent the role of a dog, or should we say, an underdog. On the other, the audience beholds, through and beyond his threadbare guise, not the persona but the person of the famous entertainer. This of course is not to say the person is unmediated. Far from it; even the dog, once it is staged as Launce's pet, is at least partly mediated. Even so, as far as the jester is concerned, the distinction we pursue informs the histrionic body in the clown's double-dealing function, for which there is some fairly conclusive evidence.

Let us only recall the anecdote recorded about Tarlton's appearance at the Bull as Dericke in *The Famous Victories*. Since the player doing the "Judge" (to be resurrected as Lord Chief Justice in Shakespeare's *2 Henry IV*) was absent, "Tarlton himselfe (ever forward to please) tooke it upon him to play the same Judge, besides his owne part of the Clowne." In this said performance, "Knell then playing Henry the fift, hit Tarlton a sound boxe indeed, which made the people laugh the more, because it was he."[5] Here the person who was hit was not the "Judge" or any other persona; it was Tarlton the man, the jesting entertainer, and onlookers laughed the more "because it was he."

Read in conjunction with Kemp's solo presentation in Act 2, scene 3, the distinction we wish to make is not simply that of the clown's two bodies. Next to (1) the character Launce and (2) the "self-resembling" comedian Kemp, we have (3) yet another body or part of a body that is contiguous with the animal Crab. When Kemp/Launce says, paradoxically, "the dog is me, and I am myself," he may point to that third dimension, which is the flesh and blood of "myself." This is as much to say that apart (and yet inseparable) from the stoutness of the well-built entertainer Kemp there is a visceral, existential form of being. It is his flesh and blood that is given, the *Leib* (to which we shall return), the body in its labor, in its pain, in its products, and its shame.[6]

In early modern writings the clown's physiology has of course socially tinged connotations (take only Hall's version of the jester's teeth "in double rotten row"). Remarkably, Elizabethan "physiological discourse intersects with the major forms of social representation." As Gail Kern Paster further notes, "the vessels of the early modern body" can be endowed with a "symbolic centrality"[7] – at least in anatomical classifications. However, as soon as we compare physiological treatises with the uses of vessels, entrails, or "guts" in the drama, the perspective is more skeptical. As David Hillman observes in his essay on "Visceral Knowledge," there is, especially in *Troilus and Cressida*, *Hamlet*, and *The Winter's Tale*, a "distrust of the connection between language and the body."[8] This distrust witnesses to a number of antipodal relations between bodily defiance of representation in staged plays and a view of the visceral interior as a site of subjectivity.

In Elizabethan clowning, especially, we find, in Paster's phrase, "that vocabulary of gesture that enacts the richly nuanced performativity" but does not serve as a clue to the comprehension of subjectivity. In popular comedy, as in relations between Launce and Crab, the matter of physiology is marked by the difference between *Körper-Haben* and *Leib-Sein*, as developed by the German anthropologist Helmuth Plessner. It is the difference between the visible, controllable parts and functions of the body we *have* and the uncontrollable, visceral flesh and blood that *is*.[9] This distinction is incisive when we recall that, well into Carlo Goldoni's plays, the jester's preoccupation is with one part of his body – the belly and the stratagems to get it filled, even while the empty stomach and the visceral sensation of hunger and pain cannot equally be represented.

To allude to the etymology of *Leib*, it might be said that Crab is just "loafing about" the stage. Historically, Kemp's animal companion is on the threshold of a transition from predramatic to dramatic entertainment. To view for a moment Crab's presence on stage as a hilarious episode in theatre history, let us remember that just an exit away, almost contiguous with the site of world-picturing representations, animals – baited or tamed – continued to be used for sport and game. The dog was, like the tamed bear in the hands of *his* warden, a well-known article for artful display among traveling performers and exhibitors. With the tricks of a performing animal, the traditional entertainer exhibits his own skill, which is not subsumed under any textual regime, let alone a representational, as for him alien, logic. Instead, in the same amphitheatrical buildings, bears and bulls were baited savagely. Now spectators beheld a dog on stage and then, by contrariety, saw the animal not baited but spoilt and sympathized with. For its comic presence in the play, the dog was an event, one close to those "complex messy occasions" which Terence Hawkes has described so persuasively. The animal is associated with those "moments of performance when an apparently ungovernable and unruly uncontrollable range of … 'real world' experience seems suddenly to be deliberately solicited, sought out and provoked from within the 'play world' of the text."[10]

However, in the dramatic context of a comedy, the animal's performance in its traditional function as an exhibit is out of place. Crab's failure to shed a tear or even for "a pissing-while" (4.4.19) to control its bladder, may be read as a comic reminder, that the traditionally offered feat won't work in the new dramatic context. As an oblique paraphrase of misplaced expectations, the underlying discrepancy is between the dramatic need for representation and the animal's inability to meet it. The trouble with Crab is that the "cur cannot keep himself in all companies"; as Launce would have it, Crab should "be a dog indeed, to be, as it were, a dog at all things" (10–13).

While the dog remains uneasily on the threshold, both dramatist and player manage the crossing from traditional sport to innovative comedy. In fact, either of them knows how to poke glorious fun out of the discrepancy itself. The discrepancy attested to a "species boundary" (Andreas Höfele's phrase) between real animal and a dramatist's image of it. This boundary was crossed by playing upon it. The solo performer with a great reputation already is turned into a comic actor not by having to forget about his past cultural practice but by clowning it out at the frontiers of representation. Nor does Kemp have to surrender the self-sustained quality of his previous performance. The laughable denseness he delivers is not his own but just an article of skillful presentation. Hence the audience feels free to identify with the player and *laugh with him*, rather than *at his role* and whatever vulgarity its representation might have entailed.

So to identify the actor's (and the animal's) aggressive relation to the symbolic order of representation is not of course to consider it the play's last word on the subject. True enough, the comedian projects a highly significant counterpoise to any symbolic *locus* on stage. In doing so he finds himself partly at least in consonance with the play's wayward topography among uncertain locations such as Verona, Milan, and Padua. Even so, Kemp/Launce and their bifold authority tend to qualify, but do not deform representational action in a Renaissance comedy. Right through the play, we hear echoes of pastoral, novelistic, and earlier dramatic discourses, mainly of love and friendship in rivalry. Even the comic figuration of Launce has its own margin of complicity with at least one represented character: Julia. It is true that, for reasons we shall discuss in the following chapter, Julia in her disguise positively shares in the kind of dramaturgy that admits the rights of performance and, so to speak, can enfranchise the performer from any strictly observed regime of verisimilitude. But altogether, Renaissance narrative and dramatic sources from Jorge de Montemayor and, probably, Jacques d'Yver to Richard Edwards and John Lyly establish a somewhat disconcerting pattern of postallegorical representations.

As we move beyond the early comedy and the year 1594, we should at least throw a glance in the direction of social and cultural changes culminating about the turn of the century. In a suggestive reading of the social lexicon of *As You Like It*, most likely written and performed in 1599, Mary Thomas Crane has argued that this play "marked a pivotal moment in the status negotiations of the Chamberlain's Men," for it "links the exclusion of the rustic clown and jig from the Globe to the social mechanisms that helped justify the exclusion of lower-class persons from the limited upward mobility then becoming possible in the culture as a whole."[11] Crane sees *As You Like It* as displaying

an increase in authorial control and agency coupled with various kinds of upward mobility – for the author himself, for the theatrical company, and, indirectly, for the audience. Along with its ambition, however, the play seems to manifest an awareness of and a sense of regret about what it must exclude to achieve its ambition, including the incipient rejection of the theater's festive roots and established tradition of collaborative work.[12]

A symptom, if not cause, of this pattern of changes, in Crane's reading, was the move south, by the Chamberlain's Men, to the Bankside and the Globe playhouse in the year *As You Like It* was performed. Other developments, related more closely to the page than the stage, could be adduced as well. For instance, changes in the field of print culture had led to the rise of esteem for certain "best-selling" authors, authors whose engagements with the world often involved an appropriation of others' bodies and identities for their printed works. The resulting transformation of print did not bypass the text in the theatre in that the "legitimation" of the printed playbook during this period, persuasively described by Lukas Erne,[13] was part of a move toward what another perceptive critic, Richard Helgerson, has called an "author's theatre."[14]

However, while the general direction of these changes can scarcely be doubted, a good deal of the evidence appears more ambiguous than has usually been recognized. What cannot and must not be disputed are important transformations in the post-1594 gallery of Shakespeare's clowns and fools. Their comic and grotesque contributions continued to be prominent even when, at the turn of the century, traditional forms of clownage no doubt lost in public favor (at least in those quarters articulate enough to bring forth arguments against it). Here we can only briefly look back at some of the best-known evidence, including Hamlet's strictures on clowns "that will themselves laugh to set on some quantity of barren spectators to laugh too" (3.2.40–2). What has rarely if ever been pointed out so far is the double-edged quality of the testimony: in the very strength of its protests, it bears witness to a prevailing vitality in self-sustained, even self-authorized types of performance practice.

The same double-edged quality can be traced in what, after Sir Philip Sidney's reference in his earlier *Defence of Poesy* (see above, p. 29), is certainly the most highly suggestive polemic against Elizabethan clowning that we have: Hall's satiric harangue of 1597. It deserves to be cited at some length:

> Now, lest such frightful shows of Fortune's fall,
> And bloody tyrant's rage, should chance appal
> The dead-struck audience, midst the silent rout,
> Comes leaping in a self-misformed lout,
> And laughs, and grins, and frames his mimic face,
> And justles straight into the prince's place:
> Then doth the theatre echo all aloud
> With gladsome noise of that applauding crowd.
> A goodly hotch-potch! when vile russetings
> Are matched with monarchs and with mighty kings.
> A goodly grace to sober Tragic Muse,
> When each base clown his clumsy fist doth bruise,
> And show his teeth in double rotten row,
> For laughter at his self-resembled show.[15]

An aggressive, first-hand observer speaks on behalf of a learned literary culture. Significantly, he takes aim at what seems to thrive beyond the control of writing: the strong, unfettered performative, the presence on stage of flesh and blood, with "fist" and "teeth," and of course the textually unsanctioned rights of "laughter." What he holds up for scorn is the "self-misformed lout," who enters with an uncouth élan, "leaping in," laughing, grinning, making faces, with great physical dexterity and not a little rudeness. To "justle," as the now obsolete meaning of the word suggests, referred to a deliberate act of violence, as in "to joust or tilt" in a tournament (*OED*). Hence to jostle "straight into the prince's place" connotes an unceremonious physical advance; as the *OED* has it, "to come into rough collision with, to knock or push against; to elbow, hustle." The satirist, ever anxious to be up to date, delineates a lively picture that is remarkable for more than one reason. He first of all observes an extraordinary vigor, an unrelenting, continuing zest in his aggressive version of contrariety. The surcharged, overbidding energy in this performance practice is delivered by a "self-misformed" body, a player staging his own "self-resembled show." In other words, the jester takes the liberty of projecting his self-chosen and, as we say, self-sustained mode of action. Here, indeed, the self-directed clown presents, if anything, performance in its own right; a willful pushing and thrusting that resists the order of the text.

Hall shares some of the arrogance of literati such as John Marston and, partially at least, Ben Jonson. The latter refused to grant the actors any authority whatsoever, considering them, as in fact Robert Greene had called them, mere "puppets."[16] With his particularly acrimonious stance in what David Mann refers to as "the practice of common player disparagement,"[17] Hall cannot, of course, speak for Shakespeare, whose response to clownage, if we judge by the dazzling Porter in *Macbeth*, was not at all disdainful. Nor did the dramatist subscribe, as Hall did, to the poetics of that "sober Tragic Muse" which, in its neoclassical derivation, precluded "A goodly hotch-potch." Even so, Shakespeare must have been involved in the circumstances that led to Kemp's separation from the Lord Chamberlain's Men. While we must content ourselves with referring to David Wiles's account of it in his biography, there is space for one near-contemporary perspective on the rivalry between performers and writers. Here Kemp is remembered as one of the culprits, at least as Richard Brome recalled "the days of Tarlton and Kemp." Addressing the old clown, he noted:

> But you, sir, are incorrigible, and
> Take licence to yourself to add unto
> Your parts your own free fancy, and sometimes
> To alter or diminish what the writer
> With care and skill compos'd; and when you are
> To speak to your coactors in the scene,
> You hold interlocutions with the audients … (2.2.39–45)[18]

To "alter" and "diminish" the text was to challenge the authority not only of writing but of the poetics informing the *mise-en-scène*. The resulting departure from the author's text clearly demonstrates a release from textual discipline on behalf of the performer's self-determined practice, as authorized by a semi-contractual relationship with "the audients." So to flaunt the rights of comic performance may well have led to recurring tensions between the arts of oral entertainment and those of written authorship. Nor did such tensions cease in Shakespeare's late plays. As Douglas Bruster has argued, there is even reason to see, as late as Shakespeare's portrait of the emplotting "artist" in Prospero and that character's dysfunctional relationship to the folkish Caliban, a recollected version of the dramatist's relationship to the unruly Kemp.[19]

Ultimately, these tensions cannot be accounted for simply in terms of a discrepancy between the two media. They are more deeply informed by social differences in cultural *habitus* and language use. In these terms, there was a differential gap between "so great an object" (*Henry V*, Pro. 11) of representation and the ordinary tools of performance in the hands of common players. Take, as just one example, the gravediggers in *Hamlet* arguing about the act of Ophelia's drowning:

First Clown.   . . . an act hath three branches – it is to act, to do, and to perform . . .

Second Clown.   Nay, but hear you, goodman delver –

First Clown.   Give me leave. Here lies the water; good. Here stands the man; good. If the man go to this water and drown himself, it is, will he, nill he, he goes, mark you that. But if the water come to him and drown him, he drowns not himself; argal, he that is not guilty of his own death shortens not his own life. (*Hamlet*, 5.1.11–20)

Whether this scene involves an indecorous release of the First Clown's "self-resembled" water, it is another example of the clown's travesty through performance of a bifold matter of representation. The first topic is an anachronistic piece of parody that mimics the chopped logic of the argument in the case Hales *v.* Pettit (1560–2) over the alleged suicide of Sir James Hales.[20] The second matter, that of Ophelia's drowning, is a comically restaged representation of the supreme passage from the "grosser name" of sexuality to the image of death "in the weeping brook" (5.7.170, 175). The high-flown, emblematically rich rendering of unambiguous innocence among "fantastic garlands," "dead men's fingers," and "her melodious lay" is outrageously rephrased in the language of quibbling ignorance. The Clown, speaking in the order of brazen contrariety, substitutes "salvation" for "damnation," and "*se offendendo*" for "*se defendendo*" (5.1.2, 9). No question, the difference in language use is that between the educated "better sort" and the common, illiterate person.

Not unlike Launce's response to the lofty sentiments of "true love," the clowns in *Hamlet*, through their physicality and "plenty of old England's mother words"[21] present a contrarious version on the strength of what is performed in an unspeakable visceral action. Whatever notion or article is to be conveyed by the "water," and whatever person (or body part) "stands" for "the man," the effect, to cite the printer in the preface to *Tamburlaine* again, is that of "fond and frivolous gestures, digressing . . . far unmeet for the matter." Editors cautiously avoid comment on the potential physicality of these lines, but the full extent of their scandalous purpose is difficult to explain other than as a *counter*-counterfeiting, so to speak, of what, in a representation, is counterfeit about the *quid pro quo*.

One can assume that Shakespeare, even while suspending clownish digression in a largely representational frame of reference, continued to use clownage and folly deliberately in the tragedies for their countervailing effect. Significantly, this effect can be pushed to the point where sensitive memories of a rebellious battle cry would have lingered in the ears of a good many audience members. So the traditional assumption that, when Adam delved and Eve span, there were then no gentlemen, is inverted into the understanding that there were none but gentlemen.[22] This semantic game (which is another way to "moralize two meanings in one word") culminates when such "ancient gentlemen" as "gardeners, ditchers and gravemakers" are said to hold up the "profession" of Adam, as one who "was the first that ever bore arms" (5.1.33). When the Second Clown protests that Adam, being no gentleman, had no arms, the First Clown replies, "What, art a heathen? How dost thou understand the Scripture? The Scripture says Adam digged; could he dig without arms?" (35–7). For the Clown to authorize his word-play through reference to an understanding of "Scripture" is a travesty not simply of Protestant reliance on the Bible as a final location of authority, but of the validity of any truth claim based on reading and establishing too stable a meaning in scriptural sources or documents.

Conventional response to clownish confusions of language is still, to a considerable degree, marked by a bias in favor of their representational function. But it can be positively misleading to interpret the clowns' language as representing the character of who or what is performed, rather than to view it as a game or sport in performance played by the actual performer. This is the case in *Much Ado About Nothing*. Dogberry can perform a strange and hapless kind of resistance to representation and, as it were, fall victim to its self-invoked regime. Dogberry desires to be an "officer" (*Much Ado About Nothing*, 4.2.80) but forgets that the privileges of a representative (or an actor) do not extend to whoever is to be represented (or his role). As he says to Verges, "[Y]ou, constable, are to present the Prince's own person. If you meet the Prince in the night, you may stay him" (3.3.74–6). Bravely resisting the logic of numbers and precedence in the enumeration of Borachio's crimes, his signification is hilariously reductive. As Claudio notes, "there's one meaning well suited" (5.1.225) for all his accusations. Insofar as signifiers are made to float according to his own outrageous "cunning," Dogberry may echo Courage's "Will convey very clean, / And not be understood" (see above, p. 33). As Don Pedro puts it, "This learned constable is too cunning to be understood" (227–8). So it comes as no surprise that, as in the moral play, the mode of contrariety is, as a grim kind of solace, linked with the terrors of the Last Judgment. It is a verbal play of topsy-turvy meanings when Dogberry supposes that Verges's men "should suffer salvation" (3.3.2–3) and the villain "be condemn'd into everlasting redemption" (4.2.56–7). Here his confusions recall a popular tradition reaching from Mischief's language in *Mankind* (see above, pp. 34–6) to the two murderers in *Richard III* (see above, pp. 54–6), the gravediggers' game in *Hamlet*, and last but by no means least the devil-portering in *Macbeth*.

In all this clowning the frontiers of representation are very much in question. There is first of all a resolute refusal to observe the pastness and the absence of events and persons as are represented on the imaginary level of the story. The past contours of its representation are suspended in a series of anachronisms; the distance to events and their location is similarly collapsed "on this unworthy scaffold." Between the anachronism (the abuse of temporal distance) and the abuse of spatial absence in the location there is a stark type of interplay. This interplay explodes the strongest boundaries of dramatic representation; the impact on spectators is most startling and most stunning in, probably, *Macbeth*. As neighbors in the audience are led "the primrose way to th' everlasting bonfire" (2.3.19), the horrors of an ever-lasting collapse of time sequence are intertwined with an open, boundless *platea*-type of space. Undoing divisions between the here and the there, between the quivering thrill of spectators and the uncanny zest of the clowning, haunting visions of the Last Judgment set experience of the scene atingle.[23]

While, again, a topsy-turvy groundswell upsets the most basic spatial and temporal categories of representation, important frontiers of projected meaning persist. As Elaine Scarry has shown, earthly chance and cosmic order resist representation. In relation to cosmic Judgment, clowning in its grotesque forms provides us not with a picture in the mirror but with a grim sense of felt action vis-à-vis our pains in life and its hereafter. In contrast to world-ordering and world-picturing, the only sense Shakespearean clown-ing may offer about last and cosmic things is, in Scarry's phrase, an "act of world-meddling" – an earthly one, in earthy manner.[24]

Compared with the largeness of these versions, Dogberry's limitations are obvious enough. For all that, his clowning remained a tribute to the here-and-now of a performance practice unbound by any purely imaginary web of events and characters. What the occasion originally offered was plenty of fun and skill, as survived in Kemp's "Bergomask dance" (*A Midsummer Night's Dream*, 5.1.353) concluding the play within the play. Having been turned into an "ass" metaphorically (rather than through a Bottom-like masquerade), Dogberry – concluding the scene, alone on stage – speaks what may perhaps betray a trace of his own "self-resembled show": "We will spare for no wit, I warrant you. Here's that shall drive some of" them to a non-come; only get the learned writer to set down our excommunication, and meet me at the jail" (*Much Ado*, 3.5.61–4). For "the learned writer to set down our excommunication" was to take away the ground from under those "that will themselves laugh" (*Hamlet*, 3.2.40–1). A "non-come" is Dogberryese for "non-plus" – according to the *OED*, "a state in which no more can be said or done." But for the clown to be nonplussed will indeed hinder further growth of the theatre for having a "non-come" part of the audience.[25] If finally the word "examination" falls into "excommunication," the bifold order of the subtext is sober enough: what begins as an inspection becomes a rejection.

Dogberry's language, not unlike the reduced range of his comic vitality, actually points toward new limits on the clown's enfranchisement. The rights of his performance were more strictly administered. Whatever Dogberry's meaning (and Kemp's position) on this matter, there appears to be a strange complicity on either side. The writer, that is, seems to borrow the clown's authority (or the clown usurps the writer's) to make a veiled threat: the facetious interlocutor with the audience was to be excommunicated from the circulation of authority in the Elizabethan theatre. Even as its scriptural appropriation revealed how vulnerable the clown's self-assertive, self-willed type of performance practice could actually be, clowning at the frontiers of representation had a dim future.

CHAPTER 6

Cross-dressing and performance in disguise

During the past three decades, the subject of cross-dressing in Shakespeare's theatre has been greatly advanced by feminist criticism. Noting that sartorial displays both on stage and off routinely appealed to a society conscious of the power inherent in clothing (a power that rendered costumes a primary element in the theatres' montage of attractions), critics have productively explored both the boy actor's donning of female costume and female characters' strategic adoption of male garb.[1] Studies by Jean Howard, Laura Levine, Sue-Ellen Case, Lisa Jardine, Karen Newman, and Peter Stallybrass, among others, have broadened the conventional portrait of cross-dressing generated, in Stephen Orgel's words, by "three centuries of theatre historians, who have treated it as a minor point, of interest primarily for its effect on disguise plots."[2] Coinciding with the field's heightened interest in the construction and representation of gender and sexuality, recent investigations have opened up vistas on both the practice and the implications of cross-dressing, inside and outside the walls of the early modern playhouses. If a primary aim of criticism attuned to feminist interests is, as Lisa Jardine writes in the preface to her landmark study, *Still Harping on Daughters*, "to retrieve agency for the female subject in history" and to do so "at the intersection of systems of behaviour, customs, beliefs,"[3] few studies have done more to meet this goal than those which have shed light on the performance of female roles by young male actors in London's theatres.

Yet, however salutary, such criticism, as Peter Hyland argues, paradoxically "minimize[s] the very *theatricality* of disguise" by "look[ing] *through* disguise in search of cultural *meanings*."[4] Such criticism, that is, pursues important cultural meanings that are represented and conveyed on primarily an imaginary level. In doing so it unnecessarily downplays the theatrical functioning and institutional significance of cross-dressing as a mode and performance. Disguise, in our view, is a socially sustained, material practice. While remaining vitally indebted to the feminist paradigm, therefore, we will in this chapter take cross-dressing and disguise as a highly performative medium in its own right. If this medium conjoins the writings of the dramatist to peculiar, arresting productions of actors' bodies and voices, it also (as many have pointed out) advances unorthodox representations of gender positions and relations. Even so, the significance of the convention as a mixed site for the conjuncture of two media cannot be reduced to the status of representation as an imaginary and ideological form of challenge, struggle, or difference.

How did disguise achieve its impact and attractiveness on Elizabethan stages? To answer this question, we could begin by noting that nowhere did Shakespeare's theatre examine and use the media of its own operation more provocatively than in its sustained preference for the practice of disguise in performance. No other convention in his theatre more actively conjoins the disparate traditions of playing and acting, gamesomeness and mimesis. The laughter and delight derived from the staging, the showing and the watching of dramatic forms of masquerade finds articulation in Shakespeare's plays as early as 1591. Nor is the histrionic exuberance of multiple shape-changing confined to the act of disguise proper. In the Vice-like disclosure of his craftiness, for example, Richard boasts of his ability to "add colours to the chameleon" and "Change shapes with Proteus for advantages" (*3 Henry VI*, 3.2.191–2).

While Richard's words may be taken as a poignant tribute to, and deliberate foregrounding of, a strictly dramatic assimilation of the performant function, the conventions of disguise and cross-dressing go one step further. They combine the juggling of skillfully performed (and displayed) appearances with the representation of certain characters in pursuit of personally, sexually, and socially significant needs and plans. Thus disguise and cross-dressing revitalize the performant function through the display of a particular kind of performing competence. In the process the purpose of playing is not simply, not even perhaps primarily, to hold the mirror up to what attributes ("virtue," "scorn," and so forth) represented personages are given. Rather, their representation is caused to swerve from its straight course and to diverge into the game of simultaneously playing one role in/through/against the other. The purported concealment not simply of the actual agent, the actor, but of his primary role clearly enhances what is artificial about an artificial person. The alleged secrecy of such dovetailed role-playing quite disturbs what inner/outer balance any dramatic characterization can muster. As Thersites puts it, the representation of characteristic action can be reduced to a different level, with a different kind of appeal, that of "A juggling trick – to be secretly open" (*Troilus and Cressida*, 5.2.23).

Shakespearean wordplay famously juggled a thousand senses above and beyond any representational need for them. Similarly, as far as such performant functions serve strictly their own ends, all types of legerdemain like camouflage can deflect the fiction of alleged identity. On stages to graft the image of a second person onto a fictitious identity may seriously disturb the perception of character. What it yields for the player (and spectator) is a doubly intriguing delivery. Such doubly encoded masquerade has to accommodate two different images of identity and action. The promiscuous mingle-mangle of identities cannot and does not comply with Renaissance demands concerning the poetics of the self-contained play, let alone the precepts of verisimilitude. In most cases, spectators tend to accept neither the donning of a mask nor the effect of concealing a primary identity as a strategy that serves any seriously posited *imitatio vitae*. Disguise, in other words, is a dramatic convention that can scarcely be said to be in aid of lifelike resemblance.

The absence of such resemblance – and hence any sustained make-believe on the part of the audience – is significant for at least two reasons. Firstly, it points to a privileged awareness shared between player and spectator. The latter is invited to see through a convention of secrecy that, on the imaginary plane of dramatic fiction, is designed to deceive many among the *dramatis personae*. Onlookers thereby find themselves in a kind of complicity with the counterfeiting play of the player. As they look into, they also to a certain extent look *through* the ruse of role-playing, the artifice and gamesmanship in the presentation of appearances. Witnessing the entire apparatus of constructing, shedding, and reconstructing roles for a "secretly open" intercourse between acting and juggling, spectators confront the technique itself of making and unmaking identity through uses of voice, costume, and *gestus*. In fact, spectators are positively ushered into a kind of participation, whereby they understand and help facilitate, even assist by their own innocent connivance, their blinking cooperation with the working of the theatre.

Secondly, the disturbance of similitude and the porous quality of the fiction in the production and reception of a secondary guise point to an imperfect mode of representation. No doubt, there is in every staged representation a distance between the imaginary image of human action and sentiment and a mode of performance that openly, visibly displays its own symbolically rendered talent. A theatrical performance is "open" to all those who attend; what is invisible or "secret" is the act of transference or transfiguration through which the semblance of some worldly being or doing, some knowledge or experience, is artfully "translated" into a dramatic figuration. However, what balance we have in such configuration is disturbed as soon as another, second level of secrecy greatly upsets the bifold authority shared out between what is visibly and invisibly shown on stages. Positively speaking, we can say that disguise is a practice of concealment that, in theatrical performance, allows its own process to be observed. Since concealment and disclosure (once they are open to spectators) go together, the staging of disguise and, in particular, its cross-dressing variety, enter into a playful, competitive relation. On Shakespeare's stage this competition allows for, even demands, performance skill of infinite charm and fascination.

In the hands of talented actors, such visibly invisible practice proves absorbing. This is so even though the performant function, once it achieves an overwhelming thrust in the display of disguise, can scarcely assist in the act of world-picturing representation in terms of any insightful resemblance. Yet the convention is far from meaningless. While distant from most of the aims of representation, the adept delivery of artfully overlaid levels of semblance is not an end in itself. In other words, disguise does not serve only (perhaps primarily) socially or semantically significant purposes in the Elizabethan theatre. Foregrounding not only the mask but also the agent of the masquerade, disguise puts special demands on the competence, agility, and adroitness of players' bodies and voices. Their prominence, and especially the prominence of young men playing cross-dressed young women, could not but have an intriguing effect on what their words signified. The question is if (and, if so, to what degree) the signal skill and presence of the young player and the salient position in Shakespeare's text of cross-dressed characters correlated. The arresting power of performance must have served as a buoyant stimulus in the qualities of such heroines as Portia, Rosalind, Viola, and Imogen, with their refreshing sense of independence, their sprightly and vivacious bearing. Although for the acting we are thrown back on conjecture, it seems difficult not to think that the supreme quality of what these characters said and did possessed a stimulating correlative in the performed practice on stage.

Returning to our chapter's beginning, we would aver that while readings of cross-dressing as primarily a function of the construction of gender or subjectivity in the early modern playhouse have produced fascinating insights and enlarged the range of functions for disguise, they have only by implication enabled a distinctively theatrical approach to the performative dynamic of cross-dressing and masquerade. As distinct from the representational approach, the present focus is far more stringently pursued where gendered identity outside (as well as inside) the theatre is viewed as performative, and where performance is in its contingency seen as a ritual or dramatic source of unstable meanings. Along these lines, for instance, Judith Butler has redefined gender as not an expression or representation of ontologically presupposed or socially always already given bodies and attributes, but as a performative pattern of acts, gestures, conventions, and practices. In reference to these practices, she has reconceptualized gendered agency and identity as "produced or generated," in the sense that for gender to be an effect of performance "means that it is neither fatally determined nor fully artificial and arbitrary."[5] In this approach to gender, "construction is not opposed to agency; it is the necessary scene of agency, the very terms in which agency is articulated and becomes culturally intelligible."[6]

In turning to theatrical cross-dressing and disguise as socially productive modes of pleasurable sport with gamesome instability in the relations of gender and class discourses, our point is not to minimize discontinuity between theatrical and nontheatrical forms of performance. But while we recognize gaps as well as links between them, we also and perhaps primarily seek to explore a related pattern of discontinuity between imaginary representations and material practices.[7] In either case, the *tertium quid* between them is – if we follow Victor Turner and Clifford Geertz – a focus on performance as constituting, in Butler's phrase, "a stylized repetition of acts."[8] Once we link this anthropological perspective to an awareness of the historically unsanctioned character of these performative acts, gestures, and practices in their early modern dramatic and literary context, the Elizabethan stage can be said to have offered a potential site of both conflict and convergence among these different dimensions of theatrical articulation. Both were denied an exclusive place across the range of dominant discourses. While biologically determined affinities played a limited role in this conflictual convergence, boy actors, as Sue-Ellen Case puts it, "by virtue of their age, were cast in a social role similar to that of women – dependent on and inferior to the adult male. Women could be represented by boys because they shared their social attributes."[9]

Since this intersection of performative action and social dependency allowed for interaction as well as contestation, the dramatized relationship of boy actors and their female roles constituted sites of engagement, contingency, and mobility in dramaturgy. Effecting a haphazard type of playful reciprocity among agencies and images of underprivileged status, players in performance and women in representation often became complementary and interdependent in the theatrical transaction. Since conflict-torn gender relations, when staged for indiscreet publicity, could (and can) be easily turned into a game of sporting exchange and contrariety, there must have resulted a great appeal for both sexes in the display of joyful resistance to the dominant rule of win or lose. In fact, players and women must have acted in a kind of cultural collusion when, shuffling corporeal signs and symbolic meanings of femininity, they disappointed conventional expectations of power and submission. Not unlike the strange, unending fascination over the ever-present horns of cuckoldry, inversion and indeterminacy in staged exhibitions (and inhibitions) of class and patriarchal dominance must have ranked highly as assets in audience appeal. Ultimately, these games were practiced at the intersection of vastly different registers of materiality and ideology. It was along these lines that the histrionic *gestus* could disrupt "that set of relations between terms which proposes as inevitable an antithesis between masculine and feminine, men and women."[10]

However, the issue of authority in Elizabethan theatrical treatments of gender relations had yet another dimension (as well as a series of material correlatives) that could not be subsumed under either the order of representation or, for that matter, any purely linguistic system of difference. As Jean Howard has pointed out about the early modern playhouse's "contradictory nature . . . as a site of ideological production," London's commercial theatre was "an institution that can circulate recuperative fables of cross-dressing, reinscribing sexual difference and gender hierarchy, and at the same time can make visible on the level of theatrical practice the contamination of sexual kinds."[11] This contradiction, recurring throughout the theatre's multiple levels of engagement with women, is highly relevant to what the present study construes as the major division in Elizabethan theatrical authority: on the one hand, "*fables* of cross-dressing, *reinscribing* sexual difference and gender hierarchy*," conjoin with "the *text's* insistence on the return to an 'undisguised' state."[12] On the other, we have "the level of theatrical practice," the actual transaction, the performed game of disguise and masquerade, inseparable from, but ultimately irreducible to, the level of representation in the dramatist's text.

To be aware of this distinction, however, does not complete the critic's task. Since these two differing locations of authority in the Elizabethan theatre are not given or static but highly interactive, the distinction needs to be qualified further. To a certain extent, "fables of cross-dressing" (in addition to what is thereby represented as dramatic fiction) in their turn privilege a performative type of language and *gestus*. In particular and to an extent never given its due, disguise – transvestite or otherwise – entails more than the concurrence of two given types of cultural practice, one scriptural, the other corporeal.

In view of the unfixed quality of this conjuncture, it is surely not fortuitous that the convention of having boys play women has been subject to contradictory interpretations. In contemporary criticism it has been viewed either as, by and large, a neutral convention, or, alternatively, as a site marked by male homoeroticism, as in the readings of Kathleen McLuskie, Peter Stallybrass, and Mary Bly.[13] If, as we shall assume, gaps of considerable indeterminacy between the woman's textualized part and its performance occurred, and if, in this unfixed conjunction of language and play, iconic relations of signifiers and signifieds were marked by a strong degree of discontinuity, the space of theatrical transaction and audience response to such cross-dressing must have been particularly wide and open. Hence the presenter's body had the potential either to triumph over or to surrender to the female role he represented. What obtained in the former case must have been "transvestite boys in erotic situations with other boys or men."[14] These boy players, using feminine attire and voice, could, through "a kind of androgyny," kindle "homosexual love in the male members of the audience."[15]

A dramatic sequence from the beginning of Shakespeare's career in the theatre may help us explore this area of discontinuity between fictional meaning in, and actual performance of, the woman's part. In 1590–1, for instance, just before Richard's gleeful speech on the powers of theatrical change and concealment, *The Two Gentlemen of Verona* provided a nexus of disguise particularly revealing of the gap between the representation of character and the practice of role-playing. Julia, disguised as the youth Sebastian, servant to the faithless Proteus, is made the tool of her own betrayal when sent to deliver her master's amorous message to Silvia. Confronted with this commission, she complains, "[I] cannot be true servant to my master, / Unless I prove false traitor to myself" (*The Two Gentlemen of Verona*, 4.4.104–5). Julia's apprehension about betraying herself implicates a divided design according to which the disguised role (Julia's "myself") and its performing and performed persona (the agency called Sebastian) are subjected to a kind of dissociation. One catalyst of this dissociation is the unknown boy actor whose gender appears through the disguise, turning the mask itself into a vehicle of betrayal and alienation. Divisions within the representation of the disguised self come to the fore in the immediately ensuing encounter with Silvia. Asked how tall the disguised, "absent" Julia is, "Sebastian" replies with a lengthy parable of performance:

> About my stature; for at Pentecost,
> When all our pageants of delight were play'd,

> Our youth got me to play the woman's part,
> And I was trimm'd in Madam Julia's gown,
> Which served me as fit, by all men's judgments,
> As if the garment had been made for me;
> Therefore I know she is about my height.
> And at that time I made her weep agood,
> For I did play a lamentable part.
> Madam, 'twas Ariadne passioning
> For Theseus' perjury and unjust flight;
> Which I so lively acted with my tears
> That my poor mistress, moved therewithal,
> Wept bitterly; and would I might be dead,
> If I in thought felt not her very sorrow. (158–72)

Here the representation (the "tale") of Ariadne's abandonment on Naxos is mediated through role-playing Sebastian recalling an act of performance, "so lively acted with my tears." Julia, speaking through this mask of a mask, feels free to fabricate a tale of remarkably complex theatricality. Coping with the gap between impersonator and impersonated, Julia's imaginary self as well as the hidden young male agent are extraordinarily mobile. Already beside herself in her assumed role as Sebastian, she can be metamorphosed (and distanced) into a further role, that of Sebastian's "poor mistress." As such, she in her turn stages Sebastian as a boy player performing, in the disguise of a woman, a classical version of her own "lamentable part."

The construction of subjectivity here is bewildering indeed: Julia (who, to disguise her primary intent, had first undertaken to play the boy's part) now invents a specular inversion of her own persona: the boy's part (Sebastian's), which she had chosen as a form of disguise, is now transformed into the agency of his own masquerade, proceeding himself "to play the woman's part" (160). In this volatile fable of performance in disguise, the medium of the mask is, as it were, being used from both sides: the romantic heroine, once transformed into a page, is free to use her own performance metaphor to unfold herself back into a woman in and through inversion.

The agency of performance here, even when intensely interactive with a highly referential tale, retains a memory of its past status as ritual practice. The occasion invoked is Whitsun or, as the play's Arden editor notes, Whitsun-ale, a traditional context where, according to E. K. Chambers, there is evidence of a (summer) "lord" and "lady."[16] This context, in which "pageants of delight were play'd," was one where ritual disguise could still be remembered in Shakespeare's day. But, again, while this traditional element foregrounds the purely festive uses of disguise, the emphasis on performance does not preclude strong feelings of "sorrow" and empathy. The resulting "tears" are witness to a representation of pathos which is quite remote from the agent of this pathetic response – until she in turn is moved by the unperformed pathos. At the end we are left with the familiar area of discontinuity between meaning in, and performance of, "the woman's part" – here embracing both the affects of empathy in representation and the effects of game in the context of traditional cultural practices.

The irony is that Julia, seeking refuge in disguise, first sheds her "gown," then shares it, via improvised memory, with a self-invented persona. Thus the represented character, called Julia, privileges – indeed almost designates – the actor in performance, as if in stretching so far beyond her own fiction, she moves not further from but closer to the materiality of the young player.[17] Shakespeare would engage in a similarly metatheatrical instance of tethering when he has the Jailer's Daughter in *The Two Noble Kinsmen* appeal to versions of the boy actor in her self-divided madness. Singing, we are told, with the "smallness" of voice that heralds "A boy or woman," the Jailer's Daughter knowingly speculates on the hundreds of children who, "at ten years old / . . . must be all gelt for musicians, / And sing the wars of Theseus" (*The Two Noble Kinsmen*, 4.1.58–9, 132–4). Like this sequence at the end of Shakespeare's career in the theatre, Julia's cross-dressing in *The Two Gentlemen of Verona* turns in on the theatre itself – or rather, opens the theatre and theatrical process to full view, confirming what Susan Baker has noted about "representations of the processes and consequences of disguising" – the way, that is, processes and consequences "inevitably incorporate local detail and historically specific practices."[18] Insofar as its symbolic agent is Sebastian, the invention we are confronted with is a complete fiction – a fiction of a fiction, in fact. Insofar as behind Sebastian there remains the performing mind and body of a young male actor, though, the designation leads to the frontiers of representation. The existential agent behind the disguise of disguise is dramatically inscribed – earlier he had been, rather, *enacted* – in the represented fiction of Sebastian disguising himself in the female role of Ariadne. The fable of cross-dressing returns us to the cultural institution, to the boy actor's own "self-resembled" sexual and social mode of existence.

Having in mind these places of instability and indeterminacy in characterization, it should come as no surprise that, then as now, more than one cultural and political response to Shakespeare's disguised heroines was possible. This may not be quite so obvious in what we have called the complication of feminine subjectivity in *The Two Gentlemen of Verona*. On the surface the scene in question (Act 4, scene 4) may not seem innovative in relation to the betrayed woman's lot; the analogy with the "lamentable part" of Ariadne could easily be read as the attempt to evoke the pathos of an age-old tradition of female submission to suffering. But as Marjorie Curry Woods has shown us, schoolboys of this era often engaged with classical literature through exercises which asked them to empathize with narratives' tragic heroines, and Ariadne remained a potent reminder of one who would notoriously "break his faith" (*A Midsummer Night's Dream*, 2.1.80) with women.[19] Thus even as the Jailer's Daughter called into question the material relationships of the Athenian scene she fantasizes, where gelded boys "sing the wars of Theseus," Julia displays, in her improvised account of "Ariadne passioning / For Theseus' perjury," ambivalence toward the conventional allotment of power within a performative economy, an ambivalence not unrelated to the indeterminacy marking the gap between agency and representation in disguise.

This early scene illustrates how the practice of game and masquerade is entangled in a discourse of representation that is on a level entirely different from those of Vice-like stage-management or clowning. In disguise in general and in cross-dressing in particular, the issue of authority needs to be explored in a highly specific context of "performance [as] simultaneously representation and being."[20] Once disguise playfully dissociates any unitary cast of character, the closure of representation in the characterization of given standards of worthiness itself is ruptured. For instance, such figuration of worthy images of subjectivity was disturbed as soon as the donning and doffing of female disguise was conducive to the young male player's capacity for a partially self-authorized, and wholly "self-resembled," show of his own existential being. The practice of disguise, or that of any deliberately counterfeit performance, constituted the rehearsal, in the represented theatrical fiction, of what the actor's work in the real theatre was all about. His own imaginative, partially unprescribed assimilation and appropriation of the alien text of otherness was playfully turned to the uses of the dramatic action.

Shakespeare would explore the actor's grappling with cross-dressed disguise in several comedies following *The Two Gentlemen of Verona*, with *The Taming of the Shrew* providing early focus on the multiple contexts of the practice. There the Lord of the Induction instructs a servant on how best to prepare his boy page, Bartholomew, to take the "woman's part" with a drunken Sly:

> Sirrah, go you to Barthol'mew my page,
> And see him dress'd in all suits like a lady;
> That done, conduct him to the drunkard's chamber,
> And call him madam, do him obeisance.
> Tell him from me, as he will win my love,

He bear himself with honorable action,
Such as he hath observ'd in noble ladies
Unto their lords, by them accomplished;
Such duty to the drunkard let him do,
With soft low tongue and lowly courtesy,
And say, "What is't your honor will command,
Wherein your lady, and your humble wife,
May show her duty and make known her love?"
And then with kind embracements, tempting kisses,
And with declining head into his bosom,
Bid him shed tears, as being overjoyed
To see her noble lord restor'd to health. (Ind.1.105–21)

Even as a decade later Hamlet will detail (to professional actors, no less) the techniques by which persuasive performances may be brought about, the Lord catalogues the procedures and agencies that augur for a successful execution of disguise in performance. Like Hamlet, our Lord has immersed himself in the theatrical scene of his day: "This fellow I remember," he says upon the arrival of the visiting players,

Since once he play'd a farmer's eldest son.
'Twas where you woo'd the gentlewoman so well.
I have forgot your name; but sure that part
Was aptly fitted and naturally perform'd. (83–7)

But for all the models he proposes – "Such as he hath observ'd in noble ladies / Unto their lords, by them accomplished" – the Lord is fully aware that the powers of performance lie in Bartholomew himself, and, by extension, any performer. Indeed, however carefully the Lord scripts the performance, he is, in the Sly deception no less than in his earlier attendance at a production in which the unnamed actor took a part "aptly fitted and naturally perform'd," eventually no more than a spectator. Such is implied as well in his multilayered injunctions to his serving man to instruct Bartholomew to remember – for replication – his own observation of that "honorable action" which he has seen "noble ladies" perform "Unto their lords." We should note that the Lord qualifies this last statement with a potentially redundant phrase, "by them accomplished," redoubling his speech's larger emphasis upon not only the performance of disguise as performance, but also the stakes of this very performance, its function as a gamelike interlude foregrounding, in this case, the fantasy of willing service.

Just as in the Lord's ludic jest, cross-dressing would figure importantly in comedies written during the middle of Shakespeare's career as a playwright.

One could consider, for example, the various disguises of Jessica, Nerissa, and Portia in *The Merchant of Venice*, and that of Viola in *Twelfth Night*. With these transvestite performances – the range of which appears clearly in the difference between what Jessica refers to as being "transformed to a boy" (*The Merchant of Venice*, 2.6.39) and what Nerissa playfully calls "turn[ing] to men" (3.4.78) – the multiple functions no less than the diversity of disguise made themselves manifest. Along with *Twelfth Night*'s disguised Viola, *The Merchant of Venice* suggests a maturing, a rich harvest of functions in the uses of cross-dressing. No longer would his characters so freely condescend to instruct a boy page – as does *The Taming of the Shrew*'s Lord – to use an onion to stimulate stage tears (Ind.1.124–8). Indeed, one senses the playwright's growing acknowledgment of the opportunities as well as the effects of cross-dressing in some of the most intensive of Shakespeare's dramatic exercises in disguise, those in *As You Like It*. There, forced into exile in the Forest of Arden by an inconvenient turn of plot, Rosalind and Celia disguise themselves as Ganymede and Aliena. These disguises afford *As You Like It* some of the most entertaining as well as searching sequences relating to the changeful shapes of identity in the dramatic canon. Indeed, in what remains perhaps the most familiar of all Shakespeare's sequences of disguise, the boy actor disguised as Rosalind takes on the disguise of a young male, Ganymede (a name possessing, of course, its own complex significations), who, as part of a romantic plot, in turn disguises himself as "Rosalind" to instruct Orlando in the wooing of the "real" Rosalind.

This chaining of roles constitutes a set-piece of what Jan Kott has called "'theatre in the theatre'" by multiplying exponentially the arts of delivery as well as those of the representation of disguise in performance.[21] With so many facets reflecting from its gemlike surface – all of them connected, yet at slightly varied angles from the others – small wonder that the ways the performant function intersects and is enmeshed with Rosalind's role have produced varying critical responses. Juliet Dusinberre speaks for one line of interpretation in holding that the kind of cross-dressing that Rosalind, Portia, and Viola perform does not transform or deny the represented female characters beneath the roles; rather, she believes it to "extend rather than endanger their sense of self . . . A man's attire, like a man's education, allows them to be more complete and fully developed women."[22] Transvestite apparel, in this view, serves to collocate a range of experiences and powers to such characters as Rosalind, allowing them to incorporate features of life and society otherwise denied them owing to their sex. Disguise thus works as a kind of mechanism by which, perhaps not unlike theatrical spectators generally, a rounded yet curious character acquires experience of the other.

But recently this notion of a stable identity beneath Rosalind's disguise has been challenged in what remains the most extended and stimulating reading of her character vis-à-vis issues of performance. In an essay on the boy actor's performance of Rosalind in *As You Like It*, and in a section of her subsequent monograph, *Actor as Anti-Character* (which extends but does not replicate some of the arguments of her essay), Lesley Wade Soule has argued that the various disguises (and identities generated through disguise) associated with Rosalind's character essentially deconstruct the notion of a coherent, illusionistic "Rosalind" that might be thought to exist outside or above performance itself.[23] What *As You Like It* gives us, Soule maintains, is less a stable "Rosalind" who takes on disguises atop this identity than a performance of performance by a boy actor-Rosalind who spends much of the play consciously dismantling and toying with the materials of mimesis. Thus Shakespeare's comedy reveals "frequent and unmistakable signs of nonillusionistic popular theatre, including numerous indications of actors' performances – particularly that of the Rosalind role – and of their relationship to the audience."[24] In Soule's interpretation the reading of Rosalind as a represented female who tries on various identities and benefits in turn from them all – the reading offered, as we have seen, by Dusinberre – fails to apprehend the manner in which *As You Like It* depends on the material reality and implication of the boy actor and his persona, an actor who, rather than the character of Rosalind, dominates much of the play's action. Thus the drama's famous epilogue, "in which the boy actor exults in his power to create illusion at will: playing whimsically with two identities, bragging of his professional skills and flirting in two genders with the spectators," comes not at all as a rupture of what has accompanied Rosalind's disguises in *As You Like It* but rather as a continuation and merely more open celebration of the liberties of the *platea* that the boy actor has taken advantage of since at least Rosalind's exodus from the court.[25]

The strong version of Soule's argument, made in the earlier essay on *As You Like It*, offered a name for what the monograph would label simply the "boy actor-Rosalind." In her essay Soule dubbed this aggressive, boyish persona "Cocky Roscius, or Cocky Ros for short," and suggested that "Cocky Ros" possessed not only a known but a visible identity in the early modern playhouse: the talented boy actor who routinely assumed the romantic lead in Shakespeare's comedies. Soule's fascinating explication of the many engagingly nonmimetic performances associated with and emanating from this figure in *As You Like It* is qualified by a survey of the theatrical traditions that have ossified around Rosalind in the past few centuries, particularly the emphasis on an illusionistic through-line for the character that insists on her essential femininity and openness to audience appropriation. In challenging contrast to this tradition, Soule suggests that the unmistakable emphasis on the materiality of the boy player's body in *As You Like It* means that "casting a female in the role effectively destroys the character-actor relationship on which the performance and much of the meaning of the play depend."[26] And while modern theatrical casting and recent stage history are beyond the scope of our argument here, we would point out that Soule's trenchant evaluation of Rosalind agrees with our analysis of Julia's part in *The Two Gentlemen of Verona* in revealing that transvestite disguise in Shakespeare calls attention to the mechanisms and materials of the early modern playhouses, including and perhaps especially the vital agency of the boy actor and the way he delivers the performant function *par excellence*. If the frame play of *The Taming of the Shrew* saw fit to recommend homely tricks to an amateur boy actor, by the time of *The Merchant of Venice* and *As You Like It*, Shakespeare would be composing texts that not only acknowledge the boy actor's full contributions to both the fictional and performative structures of his company's productions but indeed depend on them.

Of course, these brief excursions into cross-dressing on Shakespeare's stage can suggest only some of the links and gaps between the representation of disguised characters and the actor's "self-resembl[ance]" in performance. They may nonetheless contribute a further perspective on the issue of authority in the representation of women in the playhouses of his era. As our subsequent reading of disguised figures such as Imogen, Polixenes, Autolycus, Falstaff, Edgar, and Viola will suggest, the relationship of visceral histrionic agency and representation of character in disguise and role-playing is entirely volatile. Between them, the construction of subjectivity emerges as a remarkably open project. Disguise both does and does not serve the representation of feminine dignity, initiative, sovereignty, and sentiment. As we have seen with *As You Like It*, most dramatic images of cross-dressed women are marked not simply by the absence of any given, univocal structure of meaning, but by an opening, a complication, serving as a site of negotiation that in itself has a semantic dimension.

Disguise on the Elizabethan stage privileges unprecedented richness and openness in both representation and performative interception. Taken together, these tend to entail a degree of dazzling exuberance in the production of dramatic meaning. Disguise accompanies and prompts transformations of all kinds, or at least an awareness of the vulnerability of any status quo. For example, in *King Lear* a figure in disguise can almost entirely renounce his own predisguised representation of identity hinged on social status and declare, "Edgar I nothing am" (*King Lear*, 2.3.21). After assuming "the basest and most poorest shape" (7), he can proceed to dissipate the contours of his former identity, taking on the appearance and dialect of "poor volk" (4.6.237–8). In other words, disguise achieves the stature of an institution which, in its visual impact and social association, is stronger and closer to both the actor and the spectator than the disguised persona.

Such uses of disguise are remarkable for their politics as well as their dramaturgic and aesthetic efficacy. Socially, it illustrates and takes to its radical conclusion the inversion of authority and its "great image" in an action of staged topsy-turvydom. But then it is precisely the cultural poetics of this transformation that sustains a model of contrariety which either eludes or aggressively defies any Renaissance standards of closure or verisimilitude in representation. The representation of Edgar as a dramatic image of the Earl of Gloucester's first-born is engulfed by disguise in a manner which, flatly, is as unbelievable as his downstage therapy delivered to relieve his father's despair and misery.

In Shakespeare's cross-dressed heroines, to be sure, the uses of counterfeiting are not nearly as absolute (and formally undetermined) as in the case of Edgar. Yet there is a comparable diffusion in the images and acts of characterization. Imogen, in *Cymbeline*, has hardly made her appearance in "boy's clothes" when her exile makes her speak of "poor folks" (3.6.9) that "have afflictions on them," proceeding to compare poor and "rich ones," "kings" and "beggars" (10, 12, 14). When Arviragus asks her, "Are we not brothers?," she promptly answers with an egalitarian variation on the (concealed) irony in the question: "So man and man should be, / But clay and clay differs in dignity, / Whose dust is both alike" (4.2.3–5).

In the theatre the extent to which performed "dignity" actually "differs" is at best relative, especially where the underlying sense of mobility and equality in social status connects with strong elements of liquidity in the representation of character in disguise. But most interestingly, such uses of difference in "dignity" and humanity are connected with the multiply disguised, multiply gendered figure of Imogen.

As Belarius and the princes first approach Imogen/Fidele in the cave, s/he appears, within three lines, as "a fairy," "an angel," an "earthly paragon," and "divineness" (3.6.41–3). In a later scene Imogen/Fidele is referred to as "Dishonestly afflicted, but yet honest" (4.2.40). At the intersection of two discourses of honesty and morality, s/he is perceived as "smiling with a sigh" (52):

>   as if the sigh
> Was that it was for not being such a smile;
> The smile mocking the sigh, that it would fly
> From so divine a temple to commix
> With winds that sailors rail at. (52–6)

Far from generating closure in characterization, the very attributes of behavior constitute a language of perplexing emotions that shows the vulnerability of these attributes where one attitude can mock the other. Disguise here, while it does not forgo representational functions, serves as a catalyst unfixing and disseminating the representation of any self-consistent dramatic image of character. These features are marked (literally) by volatility: the "sigh," with its stream of air from the lungs, can commingle with the elements. Both the signs of emotion and the signs of status can "commix" with what "sailors rail at"; they are revealed thereby in their transitoriness and interpermeability. There is conflict and commotion between the discourses, as between those embracing the pagan lore of fairies and the Christian firmament with its angels, as well as those between the language of "Two beggars" (3.6.8) and that of the court. Constructing an unstable kind of identity through her precarious positioning on the margins of gender, status, and discourse, Imogen is, after all, not so far removed from Edgar when, near despair, she says, "I am nothing; or if not, / Nothing to be were better" (4.2.367–8).

In view of the multiplicity of these gaps in Shakespeare's disguised *dramatis personae*, the question needs to be asked whether the issue of subjectivity in disguise can be defined in accordance with certain rules and codes that, arguably, govern the great variety of histrionic and textual practices involved. Once we assume that "matter of worthiness" in dramatic representations of women on the early modern stage could be either affirmed or intercepted by gamesome practices of histrionic license and textual indeterminacy, it is clearly not enough to say that the site of disguise could be one of both dissociation and fortification of female subjectivity. Since cross-dressed images of women resemble disguised characters at large, they can be seen as submitting to the play of contestatory forces in socially and poetically consequential patterns of dramaturgy. They are torn between the textually informed forces of representational closure, where the garb of disguise remains a meaningful extension of character, and the forces of aperture in presentation where, through the act of disguise the actor-centered art of delivery, the performed display of counterfeiting, gains the upper hand over the image of character. The former is marked by continuity with strategies of characterization, in that this type of disguise effectively helps serve and/or conceal characteristic images of a literally given, author-ially inscribed type of subjectivity. But the dramatic function and structure of disguise can equally be marked by discontinuity, as when, in the latter case, the game of masking tends to become relatively self-sufficient – at least to the degree that the counterfeiting agency can disturb the primary role's design, which then can virtually cease to shine through the disguise.

This of course cannot serve as more than a preliminary and schematic typology of the forms and functions of disguise. In Shakespeare's theatre disguise was seldom marked either by complete continuity or by its oppo-site. The convention, even when serving as meaningful extension of repre-sented character, constituted primarily a site of aperture. As our reading of Julia's disguise suggests, pregnant images of counterfeit performance could go hand in hand with performed representations, in disguise, of action in the service of characterization. These qualifications notwithstanding, an awareness of culturally significant differences among discursive patterns in the function and structure of disguise sheds light on the vast and perplexing variety in the forms of concealment.

As an example, let us look at the uses of disguise and role-playing in two plays where distinct patterns of concealment emerge. At one end of the spectrum, Polixenes's act of disguise in *The Winter's Tale* is entirely con-sonant with both the representation of his royal character and the play's emplotment at large. Polixenes, King of Bohemia, has determined to be present at the sheep-shearing feast. In his fatherly concern he conceals his identity, "not appearing what we are," in order to "have some question with the shepherd" about his son, Prince Florizel, who "is of late much retir'd from court" (*The Winter's Tale*, 4.2.47–8, 31–2). Upon arrival, Polixenes, together with his counselor, Camillo, is welcomed by Perdita, "mistress o' th' feast" (4.4.68). A change of attire shields them from recognition, yet there is continuity between the form of their concealment and the repre-sentation of their character. In their disguises they are greeted as "Reverend sirs" (73), and presented with rosemary and rue, "flow'rs of winter" which are taken to "fit our ages" (78–9). Here, clearly, the mask furthers the primary layer of characterization. Rather than constituting a gap between a character's concealed goal and his undisguised design, this type of mask actually helps project the latter, being strictly subservient to the original representation of the dramatically inscribed role.

This, indeed, is far from the residual elements of a community occasion inscribed in the sheep-shearing festivity, designed as it is "to make us better friends" (4.4.66). At one point, the scene recalls the same "Pentecost . . . pageants of delight" that Julia – as Sebastian – envisioned, as when Perdita says, "I play as I have seen them do / In Whitsun pastorals" (133–4). But Polixenes's uses of disguise are hardly affected by (and do not contribute to) the festive occasion with its elements of game and sport. By way of contrast, in *Henry V*, where another king disguises himself so as to further royal policy, the act of concealment is turned into a site of license for unpleasant truths about dying in battle. But the disguised King of Bohemia in *The Winter's Tale*, far from provoking a momentary suspension of degree and "a heavy reckoning" (*Henry V*, 4.1.135) vis-à-vis the worthiness of "so great an object" (Pro. 11), uses his concealment as a stratagem of surveillance and a means of suppressing indecorous license on the part of his royal offspring.

As against such character-centered mode of disguise, the same play contains a radically different episode of concealment, one which projects a much less volatile, more "wholesome" design of character. As an illustration, let us glance at Polixenes and compare the sustained representational function of his disguise with the strange, performed changes of garment that several times transform Autolycus. These alterations in the latter's outfit tend to dissipate, and even distract from, the idea and language of character as a represented image of action and behavior in a localized context. His first cony-catching scheme, culminating in the picking of the rustic's pocket, constitutes an inversionary type of counterfeiting, rather than a straightforward act of disguise. Presenting himself in the assumed role of an anonymous victim with "my money and apparel ta'en from me" (4.3.61–2), he identifies the culprit by his own name ("I know this man well; he hath been since an ape-bearer, . . . Some call him Autolycus" [94–5, 100]. Autolycus's Janus-faced mask of identity can be made to look at and play with the forces of both aperture and closure. Through this double-dealing mask he can represent diverse kinds of identity, all, as it were, at a distance from the site of performance. Paradoxically, through his change of garments he does not seek to disguise any particular image of character (there is none worth speaking of) but gleefully to exhibit a tricky kind of knavery, which becomes its own goal. Thus, by posing as a robbed victim with a change of clothes forced upon him, he can counterfeit through his own performing practice both the object and the agent of thievery.

The distance from his own represented action is considerable. Wanting "the blessed ease" of the self-resembled comedian (*à la* Kemp's Launce), Autolycus can nevertheless get away with "the dissolution of [his] own ends and means," to echo Hegel's phrase. Appearing as peddler and entertainer at the sheep-shearing ceremony, his disguise is so taken for granted that his only prop ("my pedlar's excrement" [4.4.713–14] – his false hair or beard) is only casually referred to at a much later stage, when about to be abandoned. But before he can return to the state he was in before this disguise, a new attire is pressed upon him: Autolycus is made accessory during the fact of Florizel's own disguising, simply by dint of having to "discase... and change garments with this gentleman" (633–5). What is thereby thrust upon him (from "out there," as it were) is in no time turned into another confidence trick. Autolycus adopts and displays the strutting and role-playing of a soldier (724) and "courtier cap-a-pe" (736) so well that the innocent rustics accept his "great authority" and let him have their gold. Again, the performed practice of disguise, the skilled act of counterfeiting, can triumph in no uncertain terms over what the disguised persona might be expected to impersonate:

Whether it like me or no, I am a courtier. Seest thou not the air of the court in these enfoldings? Hath not my gait in it the measure of the court? Receives not thy nose court-odor from me? . . .
    How blessed are we that are not simple men!
    Yet nature might have made me as these are;
    Therefore I will not disdain. (730–3, 745–7)

Here Autolycus is not so much *represented* as a courtier and gentleman as, more accurately, *self-presenting* as performer of these roles. The mask is donned not because it is "in character" but because it is superb game and entertainment, mimesis pure and simple.

Far from serving as a representation of any person or role in the play, Autolycus's willing/unwilling acts of disguise foreground, in the act of performance, the power and the travesty of the profession of playing itself. The gap between the practice of disguise and the character's meaning is such that very little coherence can result: the indexical relationship between what performs and what is represented is slight. The representation of individual character (as opposed to that of the social, or even allegorical, type) is disturbed when signifier and signified show little interaction. Autolycus *presents* the show of a courtier with a histrionic gusto that has more to do with the actor's "purpose of playing" than with any "question of the play"; the performer, celebrating the art of his own delivery, self-embodies a certain type of player playing with the shape and image of a courtier. As the Arden editor, reproducing the Folio layout as verse, suggests, this metrical use of language must be intentional. Autolycus, then, is not so much a laughable object of witty satire as a self-conscious source of it – one of those "who themselves laugh" in order to share, in providing, satirical wit.

Such disguise produces the imaginary equivalent of a theatrical space with a good deal of bifold authority: characters such as Autolycus, Falstaff, Duke Vincentio, Hamlet, Edgar, and even a borderline case like Kent more or less resist representational closure. Developing a special rapport with the audience, the language of these "plotters, schemers, disguisers, stage managers, role players – actors in a word" – to summon William Kerrigan's useful catalogue of figures central to Shakespeare's playworlds – is marked by a level of anachronism and an absence of decorum privileging the use of proverbs, puns, asides, dialect, and, of course, the play metaphor.[27] It is against this wider context of divergent uses of disguise that cross-dressing needs to be placed. Shakespeare's disguised heroines differ from most ordinary uses of disguise and role-playing in that the secondary level of role-playing – that of page or youth – is more consistently developed in interaction with their primary roles as young women and their material ground in the boy actor. In fact, it may even be said that this secondary level is fortified at the very point where it serves as both a foil to and an extension of the primary role. Even so, it is a level on which the act of performance is made to shine through the representation of character: it is here that, sexually and socially, the perception of both difference and affinity between performer and performed is inescapable. It is bifold authority at its finest and most complex.

Shakespeare's boy-heroines possess a space for an undetermined range of functions, according to which their attempts at disguise can serve either closure or aperture in the representation of female roles. In conjunction with the existential act of performance, the secondary role of page or youth can either appropriate or surrender the iconic and symbolic territory occupied by the primary female role. As far as the undoubted strength and authority of this primary representation of femininity is concerned, these boy-heroines use disguise along the lines of Polixenes to reinforce an already established character. Disguise in this case does not surrender to an awareness of the performer. So Viola in *Twelfth Night* is terrified to duel with Sir Andrew Aguecheek, revealing the prior "truth" of the woman's character beneath her male disguise as Cesario. An exception is when Kent, in his encounter with Oswald, uses the registers of wordplay, proverb, and even railing anachronism ("you base football player" [*King Lear*, 1.4.86]).

At the same time, Shakespeare's disguised heroines can construct a different type of subjectivity at the opposite end of the spectrum of role-playing, somewhat in the fashion of Falstaff. In his hands the dagger made of lead is a theatrical property and thus serves ill for a scepter. The process of secondary signification can be thrown back, even beyond the primary level of representation, so as to collapse on the impervious materiality (and triviality) of the tiring house prop. For the Prince to say, "Thy state is taken for a join'd-stool" (*1 Henry IV*, 2.4.380) is to reverse the trajectory of dramatic symbolism from signifier to signified and to expose the discourse of representation as inoperative by overextended, exacting claims. So Julia's recounting, as Sebastian, of her performance, as a boy, of a woman's part collapses all three levels of imitation there represented (Ariadne, Sebastian, Julia) onto the level of the given agency of the boy performer. So, too, does the boy actor acting in the guise of Rosalind facilitate the deconstruction of the primary character. Along with various improvised identities, the actor here works to equalize the performative and mimetic.

In view of Falstaff's extreme position – even as in *The Merry Wives of Windsor* he stretches the limits of what disguise in performance means – the analogy with cross-dressing is of course limited. But the point is that the production of dramatic meanings, wherever theatrical signs are encoded once too often, can be entirely forestalled. This holds good for both the role-playing of kingship and the disguise of femininity: both, from the common player's point of view, were conspicuously "other" in political and sexual terms. Thus, in the represented world of dramatic action, the golden crown on the monarch's head (like the sumptuous gown on the young male actor's body) must have presented the early modern player with a number of divergent responses. On the level of its primary encoding, the cheap piece of stage property called "crown" may, as in *Richard II*, assume great symbolizing force, in that it can stand for, or represent, "the worthiness of the matter itself."[28] But when the fat knight puts a cushion on his head, we no longer have the sign of the sign of royalty but something which, strictly speaking, amounts to less than the sign of the sign of the sign of royalty. The mimesis at work here functions quite contrariously. The indexical order of synecdoche is turned upside-down. The signs of throne and scepter are not, as it were, sent out into the world. They are facetiously returned to a gameworld peopled by a player playing a player king and a performance which serves brilliantly to entertain his audience.

This type of "excellent sport" with role-playing on the "unworthy scaffold" of Shakespeare's stage is at two removes from a direct symbolizing of the discourse of history. Cross-dressed role-playing can similarly be in aid of a self-reflexive display, marked by a play of contrariety, of the dominant representations of gender, patriarchy, and inequality in sexual as well as social terms. On the margins of different types of discourse there was unprecedented space for a gamesome type of resistance to "kings" and "rich ones," as well as to "lies" in the dominant discourse (*Cymbeline*,

3.6.12–14; 4.2.32). Intermingling contrarious impulses of "attraction and repulsion," appropriation and distantiation, cross-dressed performers could send out into the world images of gender and female subjectivity disrupting sexual boundaries and the discourse of male prerogative. At the same time, the act of disruption was constitutive of, and derived from, the contradiction in performance between self and otherness, existence and imitation. The fluidity of boundaries was particularly inseparable from the performed act of crossing the threshold between primary (concealed) and secondary (concealing) registers of representation. As a catalyst between them, the institution of disguise was central, engendering almost uncontrolled transformation, a superb mode of contrariety in performative practice.

It is this focus on highly diverse material and symbolic forms of cultural practice that can help us go beyond being captivated by "one set of discourses – those which form the site of a dominant ideology."[29] As we have seen, disguise in the early modern theatre constitutes a highly concentrated site of differentiation wherein the voices speaking through disguise may be understood "not as always already neutralized by the ideologies they must speak through in order to be heard, but rather as inflecting, distorting, even appropriating such ideologies, genres, values, so as to alter their configuration."[30] Once we allow for "the possibility of an other *in* discourse," the "voices 'othered' by the dominant discourse acquire a new authority, no matter how marginalized or effaced they may have been."[31] But this "authority" can best be traced where social and sexual contestation can avail itself of such material and institutionalized practices which either precede or transcend ideology in its textualized form. Shakespeare's representations of women and a male-dominated social order can be read, as Peter Erickson recommends, as "a more multifaceted and historically differentiated account," one marked by "genuine exploration and struggle rather than . . . the unfolding of doctrine."[32] Cross-dressing, disguise, and role-playing can be seen to manifest and thrive on a notable potential of discursive and corporeal conflict, a mutual contestation among diverse authorities in theatrical production, which may well be the most enthralling moment in Shakespeare's emplotment of dramatic masquerade.

CHAPTER 7

Personation and playing: "secretly open" role-playing

To reopen the question of character here is to contextualize, between page and stage, the various forms and functionings of Shakespeare's *dramatis personae*. Once we have begun, in Paul Yachnin's words, "to understand that Shakespearean characterization is an artful response to the situation of the theatre," we can better come to grips historically with the complexities of this response.[1] To do so we must examine how a distinctly literary product unfolded within a culturally innovative and socially divergent institution. Here it seems difficult to do justice to a rich variety of inter-actions between two major communicative modes of articulation without taking account of a highly varied set of effects. In view of an extremely wide and changeful range of performance practices, we propose to look at the two media in a radically contingent relationship.

In this relationship the respective weight and potency of the one inflects the workings of the other. Put simply, the making of Shakespeare's *dramatis personae* can be traced on a wide spectrum bracketed by two extreme ways of figuration. One is where writing, in shaping dramatic speech and action of imaginary agents, provides given, more or less authoritative contours for staging images of artificial persons. The other sees the strength of the perform-ative, the material act of staged counterfeiting, as pervasive enough to assert itself in its own right and to affect by its own authority the imaginary figuration of a person even before it comes to be staged. Needless to say, these exemplary positions provide entirely schematic parameters in the midst of a vibrant, mutually interdependent and interactive process of give and take among diverse forms of cultural articulation.

To bring a clearer focus upon these media we propose to divide our attention and proceed in stages, over two chapters. This chapter will examine the performative surplus in Shakespearean characterization, the indomitable part of performance able to interpenetrate the text. In the process perform-ance will strongly infuse the verbal statement of an imaginary agent. In Émile Benveniste's distinctions (to which we shall return), the staged act of the performer's *énonciation* is powerful enough not only to affect meaning in the *énoncé* but to be anticipated and, to a degree, assimilated in the writing. The following chapter, chapter 8, will proceed to define the formation of the Shakespearean character as an imaginary identity through dialogic "reflection" in other(s). In her/his act of *énonciation*, the utterance is far more strongly imbued with a characteristic, apparently self-contained *énoncé*. In other words, the *énoncé*, the enunciated statement of identity, is singular in itself; it is peculiar enough so to permeate the utterance that its medium, the enunciating actor, seems to be lost in its result.

As a point of departure, let us recall comparable uses of language and the body in the personation of Shakespeare's cross-dressed heroines. As outlined in the preceding chapter, the arts of disguise in particular (just as personation in general) sanction a performance practice that exceeds a textual given. For that reason alone, neither disguise nor personation can be reduced to the dramatic semblance of concealed or unconcealed identity in the image of a character. In several shapes of disguise, but especially in cross-dressing, the representation of concealment is blatantly punctured, or at least exposed, by a performance in pursuit of dis-closure (here used with the subtext of *dis*closure – that is, an aperture of dramatic closure). As in ordinary personation, the playhouse exposure of role-playing indicates a friction, even perhaps a potential of rupture between the imaginary figure and the very real agency on the platform stage. In a good many instances, such exposure of a fiction within the fiction of the play shows some of the inordinate energies, the sheer thrust of a performance practice that even in writing is acknowledged for its refusal quite to submit to the discipline of an alien text in the service of characterization. At the same time, this refusal allows players to foreground the art of delivery and to parade competence and skill to a degree exceeding any need for such verisimilitude as the more strictly self-contained world of the Renaissance play demanded.

Historically, then, the present emphasis on the performative element in personation addresses the most telling "mingle-mangle" within Elizabethan role-playing: the presence of the "performant function" in the mirror of representation. At the intersection of performance and representation there is a socially pregnant conjuncture of bodies and texts marked by both congruity and incongruity between two mutually contravening media. This affects the dramaturgy but also the modes of cultural communication. The dramaturgic angle asserts itself where, in Meredith Anne Skura's phrase, all theatre, but the Elizabethan theatre in particular, thrives on "the onstage tension between actor and character."[2] At the same time, the nonidentity between the two, their "onstage tension," constitutes a contingent site on which various types of social *habitus* and cultural experience engage one another in conflict, compromise, or complementarity. For a plebeian player on "this unworthy scaffold to bring forth / So great an object" (*Henry V*, Pro. 10–11) and to personate so great an institution as royalty must indeed have been, in every sense of the word, a formidable engagement. In historical retrospect, it was an act and an action raising a host of questions, not only of politics but also of epistemology and poetic theory. Critically to assimilate the double bind in this engagement is a historicizing revision of the purpose of Elizabethan personation "to attend not just to theatrical representations *qua* representations but also to the material practices and conventions of the stage."[3] On these premises, as Jean Howard notes, it is possible that "script and playhouse practice . . . ideologically reinforce one another or that, at least potentially, they can be in conflict."[4] While in the production of characters marked by closure the two media mainly reinforce one another, in personation (as we shall further define it presently) the performative thrust can be strong enough not to submit entirely to the representational poetics and politics in the purpose of playing. Here we have what David Schalkwyk calls "the power of the self-authorizing performative as a public act" being potentially strong enough to assert its relative independence.[5]

Those deliberate displays of such assertion in dramatic texts are usually comic and sometimes sarcastic. For example, the visible presence of signs and bodies on stages can be so self-sustained that a verbally conveyed symbolic mode of representation may be thwarted or otherwise affected. As we will see, an exemplary illustration comes when Falstaff, counterfeiting the king, sets out to personate "So great an object" and, in the process, has to content himself with a joint-stool for a throne or with a leaden dagger for a golden scepter (*1 Henry IV*, 2.4.376 ff.). In this playlet within the play, material objects are made to appear so massive and so distinctly fixed to a previously established (and still surrounding) environment that they tend to resist their further transfiguration into symbolic vehicles of representation. Here and in related cases, the construction of imaginary personages is comically jeopardized when the image of a fictive person jostles the material practices of staging or, for that matter, the memories of some collectively performed action. One could consider only the charivari echoes in *The Merry Wives of Windsor* which, in their peculiar mixture of the penal and the festive, draw on a wider repertory of cultural practices such as those involving an element of rejoicing at, even encouragement of, female insurrection.[6] As the traditional world of festive custom infiltrates the early modern search for individual identity, the very premises on which the representation of particularized selves is about to establish itself are challenged.[7]

The act of counterfeiting a semblance of identity in the person of an imaginary other therefore presupposes a tension, dramatically usable, between imaginary representation and staging practices. This tension can be intercepted comically, but it also and at the same time serves as a sexually and socially significant underside, especially where the performer can deliver his own, partial bit of authority. Still, conditions for a vital performative are highly contingent. As Robert Weimann has suggested elsewhere[8] there are histories in performance, and performance practices change under the impact of literacy, print, divisions in social standing and education, and, last but not least, the move from the staging of reform to reforming the stage, to use Huston Diehl's resonant phrase. It is, then, during a limited period that the world and the word of a personalized fiction could be invaded by the nonsymbolic force of actors' agencies turning personation into "A juggling trick – to be secretly open" (*Troilus and Cressida*, 5.2.24).

Here the language of *Troilus and Cressida*, saturated as it is with metaphors and allusions to a hidden dramaturgy, provides us with a phrase as revealing of the practice of personation in general as it is of the convention of Shakespearean disguise in particular. In the arts of juggling, unlike tumbling, the tricks and skills behind the show are by convention concealed, or at least partially so, in the service of a greater impact, such as the surprise effect on the audience. Even on Elizabethan theatre stages, as we have seen in the case of the Queen's Men (above, pp. 80–1), the line between the performer in person and the performer in persona was not altogether distinct. In the role-playing craft of acting under a persona, the hidden identity of a player's self, the secret of his difference from an assumed role, were inclined to leak, and not only in the case of great comedians like Richard Tarlton, Will Kemp, or Robert Armin, who in song and dance performed in person anyway. The art of counterfeiting was itself an asset that deserved to be displayed in its own right, especially where the challenge was to bridge "so great" a social distance as to embody the shape of royalty or nobility. No doubt that in almost all serious roles, acting in persona would predominate over playing in person. Here the greater challenge was to consummate the "secret" convention and for actors to subsume their own existential selves under the regime, textually available, of an imaginary otherness. In these cases, the achieved character triumphed over any "secretly open" use of a persona.

However, plenty of evidence suggests that under Elizabethan stage conditions the dramatic display of artificial persons did not invariably bring forth the illusion of a self-contained scene peopled with lifelike persons and actions. Even under the alien contours of an imaginary role, performers did not relinquish all the visible signs of their social or sexual identity. They invited onlookers to enjoy and judge their craft to the degree and in the way that this opened up for inspection not just the product of counterfeiting but the process, the mode of its production. Thereby openness, including the open witnessing of an existential relation between sender and receivers, is smuggled back into the twofold craft of acting. Hence the achieved product and the mode of its production are displayed together, constituting a frame of reference marked by what Jean Alter calls "the inherent duality of theatrical activity."[9]

An early modern usage – that of *personation* – acknowledges this double-ness. This cue comes from Thomas Heywood's well-known *Apology for Actors*, written around 1607 and published in 1612. Offering a defense of playing by stressing its legitimacy, Heywood argues that playing exceeds the art of oratory in its studied qualification of "every thing according to the nature of the person personated."[10] In a passionate reverie, Heywood makes an important distinction between "personated" and "personator":

To turne to our domesticke hystories, what English blood seeing the person of any bold English man presented and doth not hugge his fame, and hunnye at his valor, pursuing him in his enterprise with his best wishes, and as beeing wrapt in contemplation, offers to him in his hart all prosperous performance, as if the Personater were the man Personated, so bewitching a thing is liuely and well spirited action, that it hath power to new mold the harts of the spectators and fashion them to the shape of any noble and notable attempt. (B4^r)

Heywood's distinction between "personated" and "personator" reminds us that we are dealing with a perceived double bind conjoining signi-fication and being, representation and vital, material practice. Heywood is an important but also very questionable witness, for his treatise is selective as well as partisan, and saturated with the language of social bias and cultural exclusiveness.[11] Even so, the distinction offered between the "personator" and the "personated" remains immensely stimulating. While *personate* is earlier used in the Induction to *Antonio and Mellida* (published in 1602), Heywood may well be the first commentator to articulate what Edward Burns calls the "defining line between the two aspects of the performer – which is character, which is actor?"[12] Since in the twentieth century this distinction reemerged as the central concern of theories of performance, in the dramaturgies of Stanislavsky, Brecht, Artaud, Grotowski, Barba, and more recent theoreticians, students of Shakespeare's theatre may well be tempted further to explore the special significance of this twofold frame of reference in early modern dramatic performances.

In our view, it is not simply the doubleness inherent in "the two aspects of the performer" that remains at issue. Rather, the distinction between the "personator" and the "personated" furnishes us with no more than a point of departure for looking more closely at the relationship the two modes and media of cultural production – writing and performing – worked to constitute. As we have suggested, the spectrum on which this relationship unfolded was much wider and more intricate than has generally been acknowledged. In fact, no univocal style of address or delivery obtained in the wide spectrum between "dignified" excellent actors and those common players who rubbed shoulders (and could therefore easily be confounded) with dancers, minstrels, jugglers, and tumblers. Many examples could be adduced to show that role-playing in early forms of personation featured a continuing readiness to sing, dance, and tumble. Here we might recall that (as discussed in chapter 4 above) the Queen's Men, the most prominent company before the formation of the Lord Chamberlain's Men, offered the public "a Turkish rope dancer" and some of their members at Bath received a reward "given by Mr. Mayor to the queens men that were tumblers."[13] This was in the late 1580s and early 1590s. Such contiguity of dramatic and nondramatic types of performance must have been particularly pronounced in a continental context where English players played before non-English-speaking audiences.

It therefore seems hazardous to assume that the relationship "between the two aspects of the performer" (Burns's distinction between "character" and "actor") was in any way simple. Acting a role, like other forms of histrionic practice, was in the sixteenth century nearly synonymous with "playing," which is to say that, in Terence Hawkes's phrase, it could well be subsumed under "the vast, unsystemated, and often non-verbal range of communicative traffic always evident in the here-and-now immediacy that binds performer to audience." As Hawkes has persuasively argued, it was this "preliterate performative tradition" which Shakespeare "both confronts and tries to contain."[14] Small wonder, then, that the young dramatist encountered a bewildering "confusion between 'show' and 'play,' antics and actors."[15] In view of such multifarious activities, we do well to expand our notions of Elizabethan theatre and performance.

To recognize this nonliterate element in staging helps us view performative practice in its own right and not, as Michael Bristol usefully puts it, in a purely "ministerial" function of subservience to a given text.[16] Nor is it possible at this late date to account for the existing heterogeneity among performance practices in terms of the traditionally overemphasized distinction between "formal" and so-called "naturalist" styles of acting. The spectrum was certainly wide enough to encompass both the most arresting rhetoric in the recital of dramatically used poetic language and the more natural action "to the Life." As Burns has shown, in Heywood's own *Apology* the difference between these two types of delivery was quite relative when both can be understood "in the context of mainstream rhetorical theory."[17]

The emergence of verbally sustained constructions of character is inseparable from the predominant role that dramatic writing assumed even before the turn of the sixteenth century. According to Andrew Gurr, "by 1600 characterisation was the chief requisite of the successful player."[18] Without in the least underestimating the continuity of entirely unacademic, indecorous, and "indiscreet" uses of mimesis in the Elizabethan theatre, we must not minimize its literary component. Personation is, after all, role-playing, and the embodiment of a role and its representation through either dialogue or monologue is to give body and voice to something scripted. Even in the history of the concept, the scriptural connotation emerges remarkably early, as when a thoroughly literate, learned author such as Gabriel Harvey refers to one who can "featly Personise *in individuo*."[19] The combined connotation of skill and self in role-playing as a hidden, doubly layered reference for this utterance asks us to think of the Elizabethan playhouse. Its timing also evokes the environment of personal satire and other forms of personalized writing that burst forth into print culture with renewed vigor during the 1590s. Indeed, the dangerous, tremendously "embodied" writing of the 1590s – in which Harvey, Nashe, and others took open part – would of course peak by the end of a decade which witnessed the efflorescence of formal satire (nondramatic and dramatic alike). [20] It seems no accident, therefore, that another highly active writer, Joseph Hall, appears to have been the first to use the adjective *personate*, meaning "feigned, pretended, counterfeit" (*OED*) in the "Defiance to Envy" prefacing his satirical *Virgidemiarum* in 1597.

While in the following chapters we shall return to the literary and purely imaginary components of characterization, the peculiar dramaturgy of personation is incomplete unless viewed in the strength of its presentational *gestus*. To return to Patrice Pavis's definition, *gestus* "cleaves the performance into ... the shown (the said) and the showing (the saying)."[21] While the closure of representation, the purported identification of actor and character in one figuration, tends to suppress or at least domesticate the showing, the doing, the saying as an act of enunciation, the *gestus* of personation does not. On the contrary, it foregrounds the body as visible, audible medium between character and actor in its own right. Not eliminating the element of difference, such personation enters into and vitalizes what Judith Butler has called a "scandalous" conjuncture, "a relation consisting at once of incongruity and of inseparability."[22] In this "relation" the "body is the blindspot of speech," signifying "in ways that are not reducible to what such a body 'says.'" In relation to a given text, then, the actor's voice in personation "performs in ways that no convention fully governs."[23]

If for a moment we confine the agent's body to his/her voice, the reason is that the latter joins in with the *gestus* on the level of its *énonciation*. Here we use the French word for a reminder of what, in Benveniste's approach, the utterance itself is able to articulate "in ways that no convention fully governs." In a first direction, the speaker's act of enunciation is a mode of mobilizing meaning for his/her own account or reckoning. What in the original is strongly underlined is the speaker, "*qui mobilise la langue pour son compte*." Thus the act of enunciation being an "individual realization" of "*la langue*" is turned into a discursive action which can be defined as "*un procès d'appropriation*."[24] This points to a far from disinterested mode of "address," in which the "secret" viewpoint and experience of the player affected, or should we say, contaminated, even the histrionically predisposed "open" language of the dramatist.

To illustrate, let us first turn to the scene in which Thersites observes the "secretly open" practice of personation in *Troilus and Cressida*, Act 5, scene 2. What critical commentators have repeatedly noticed is the three-leveled division of the scene that allows the audience a tripartite angle of vision. First, Cressid and Diomed in front of a tent, a true *locus*, in amorous rapprochement; second, Troilus and Ulysses as behind a column, watching and commentating; and third, Thersites as sarcastic commentator in what is virtually an extra-dramatic stance. Thersites's spatial position is clearly privileged in the manner of a chorus; while he can overhear and respond to the utterances of both parties, his own speech and doing are not received on stage at all. Remaining aloof, spatially as well as acoustically, Thersites assumes the function of a presenter – though not that of a director. From this perspective, and in his coarse and scabrous manner, he is too acrid to speak for the play (even *this* play) at large. Still, he betrays an unmistakable awareness of the needs and qualities of performed action, as when he spurs, even cheers, histrionic delivery: "Now the pledge, now, now, now!" (*Troilus and Cressida*, 5.2.65). From his vantage, the representation of the lovers is viewed primarily as a show of performative achievement. In his perception of characteristic action, the line between performer and performed is poignantly addressed – the more so as he invokes a theatrical know-how of remarkable range and depth. There is his acquaintance with allegorical figures of a morality cast like "lechery" (57) and "Luxury, with his fat rump and potato finger" (55–6), as well as his reference to the juggler's craft (24), to highlight only these examples.

It is against this context that Thersites's sexually saturated interjection – "A juggling trick – to be secretly open" – needs to be read. Both in its reference to the lovers and in its self-revealing *gestus*, the phrase conveys personation to double business bound. On the one hand, it seeks to describe, even pinpoint, a fairly self-contained scene of amorous courtship, and as such borders on the order of representation. On the other, it is a presentational, almost extra-dramatic intervention. Assuming an intermediate position between the imaginary world of representation and the material world engaged in the presentation of that show, Thersites absorbs the duality of performance in both the imagery of his language and the *gestus* of his delivery.

Here the presentational element in dramaturgy is exceptionally strong. It must be quite inescapable to spectators (if not perhaps to readers) because the showing itself is as drastic as the shown. The characterization effect is provocative in the full sense of the word – calling forth responses that the localized, self-enclosed main action scarcely implicates. Still, the characterizing function of Thersites's intervention is limited and not entirely trustworthy, involving an "abuse of distance" of a sort, partially since it comes "from without," what elsewhere we have defined as *platea*. Few comparable uses of *platea* space occur in Shakespeare's plays, the most notable being in *Timon of Athens* (Act 1, scene 2).[25] Not unlike Apemantus in the later tragedy, Thersites crucially helps fashion the characteristic contours of the play's leading characters through pointed interjections. Unheard by the localized characters, these interjections evoke a captivating dialectic of concealment and disclosure, pointing far beyond disguise as material convention. Hence the fine art of sexual courtship is verbally presented as a juggling practice irresistibly inviting obscene gesturing on the part of a mimicking presenter. As Gordon Williams notes in his *Glossary of Shakespeare's Sexual Language*, there is "abundant support" for reading "juggling" in the sense of "copulating," just as "trick" may well invite a coital meaning.[26]

The same sexual innuendo informs, of course, the phrase that remains of particular interest in this presentational context: "to be secretly open" would undoubtedly, in its primary subtext, signify what Williams (and several modern editors) define as "sexually available, with anatomical overtones."[27]

Yet beyond the bawdy sarcasm, this phrase resonates vitally with the same theatrical conscience that, vibrant in the play at large, inflects the *platea* space and purpose of this speaker. In an immediate but limited sense, Thersites is hidden from both parties – the lovers and Troilus/Ulysses – in this scene, yet his "secret" position is perfectly "open" to all spectators. Even more significantly, such openness to public observance intriguingly informs the dramaturgy of his presentational practice. His presentational action, saturated with theatrical imagery, effects the aperture in person-ation: thus it will permit the performers and their practice to shine through a window in the imaginatively structured edifice of representation. While its poetics of closure is being compromised, the dramatic image of an appa-rently self-contained character is not. As a result, the stage gives us not simply a show of personal identity (however complex such a construction may be) but the ways and means by which that identity is fashioned; not simply a character or characteristic action but the making of it. Thereby the presentational mode of personation delivers less a finished product than the process of producing it. In our understanding of the concept, personation invites spectators to collaborate in what is "secretly open": it displays process as product, the characterizing process as inseparable from what is brought across as visibly, audibly the counterfeit image of an imaginary person.

Before further examining the presentational *gestus* as a defining moment in personation, let us reflect on its larger significance in the Shakespearean relationship of pages and stages. In this study it must appear striking that more or less "secretly open" spaces are inhabited by those three major groups of artificial persons marked by their configurations of presentational and representational dramaturgies. What Vice descendants, clowns, and cross-dressed boy-heroines have in common is a hybrid investment in doubly encoded forms and functions. Their double code and conscience can accommodate, if not reconcile, both the authority of dramatic language and the power of performance. As the indomitable dimension of self-exposure in a partially open betrayal of performance skills appears to suggest, their own bodies are at work, meddling with the difference in the other, the textual design.

As we consider these three groups together, a wider variety of agents of at least partial personation must not be overlooked; let us recall only the mixed gallery of personated figurations such as Berowne, Armado, Falstaff, Jacques, Lucio, Cloten, Apemantus, Enobarbus, Autolycus, or Prospero. Together, they underline the degree of divergence in whatever representa-tional shape and direction are in consistent (and not so consistent) forms of personation involved. Although criticism to this day has largely overlooked these presentational links, the time seems to be approaching when we can "take it for granted . . . that the relationship of actor to character is at the heart of the theatrical enterprise."[28] It may be too optimistic for Peter Thomson to claim that this in fact is the case now; still, attention to differences in the overall dramatic design and "purpose of playing" has, as recent work from Skura to Anthony Dawson and Lesley Wade Soule suggests, far-reaching implications for character studies in Shakespeare.

If the outcome of this "engagement between presence and representation" is neither predictable nor fully controllable, the potential discrepancy between histrionic action and textual meaning yields an important site. There this discrepancy can easily be used as source for either comic laughter or such "heteroglossia" as can especially be traced "in parodies and in various forms of verbal masquerade, 'not talking straight,' and in the more complex artistic forms for the organization of contradiction."[29]

On the early modern stage especially, the cultural horizon of the writing and the more homely sources of knowledge and experience of the actors must have involved singular tensions "between the word and the speaking subject."[30] But if the prescribed text offered for its speaker as well as for some of its listeners elements of an "alien" orientation, perception, and understanding, an important area of what we propose to call "indeterminacy" emerges. As Mikhail Bakhtin envisioned, in this context there is an unsuspected potential of the "alien word" to collide with "heteroglot social opinion."[31] On the level of enunciation, some such collision is inevitable in the personation process, especially where the personator has not ceased to identify with his own world, experience, and language.

On Elizabethan stages where players adopted an alien (for them) language, "socio-verbal intelligibility" may have been an embarrassing issue – one hard to reconceive today, when actors are academically educated. But while an understanding of the gap between "the word" and its "object" is at stake in any reading or listening to a text, in dramatic personation the crucial problem is not primarily one of signification but of enunciation. Here, again, we are content to take our cue from Benveniste who defines "enunciation" as "*cette mise en fonctionnement de la langue par un acte individuel d'utilisation*" (80). As we have just seen, it is through utterance that "*un énoncé*" is produced, in which context Benveniste uses the phrase "*la sémantisation de la langue*" as the central process of "how 'meaning' is formed."[32]

This *sémantisation* can perhaps be studied with special cogency in a play where players set out to dress and furnish a plebeian (who is of course another player) for a series of enunciations marked by a rich and grotesque collision between ordinary language and staged utterance. We see this most strikingly when Shakespeare foregrounded this collision behind staged utterance, and used it as deliberate artifice in the Induction to *The Taming of the Shrew*. As if parodying the formality of Kyd's high-classical Induction to *The Spanish Tragedy*, Shakespeare's comedy forgoes the solemnity of an allegorical chorus in favor of the boisterous plebeian Christopher Sly. Sly almost mischievously puts paid to any audience's hopes of a stately dramatic narrative with, firstly, his jocular handling of the twin sources of gravity in the Elizabethan playhouse – for "Richard Conqueror" and "Saint Jeronimy" (*The Taming of the Shrew*, Ind.1.4–5, 9) playfully demystify the genre of chronicle history and Kyd's foundational tragedy, respectively – and subsequently with his thickly demotic references to personages and places from the playwright's native Warwickshire (Ind.2.18–22).

For all Sly's gamesomeness, however, no simple dichotomy of high and low, representation and play, could be fairly mapped onto this complex opening to the play-within-the-play that we know as *The Taming of the Shrew* (that is, the play of Katherina and Petruchio). Nor does it sustain an easy or even fixed paradigm of personation and character. For when the Lord of the Induction enters and encounters the sleeping "rogue" (the first of many appellations Sly will earn [Ind.1.2]), he cycles through a series of definitions ("beast," "swine," "death," "image," "drunken man," "beggar" [34–41]) on the way to declaring his intent to "practice" on Sly. Such "practice" involves an inversionary collision of identities, a comically grafted travesty of an utterly alien personation and enunciation. The traveling players have arrived in an uncannily timely fashion to perform a play before and practice upon the duped "beggar." Although higher in its orientation, this second play bears the unmistakable traces of the lower, street theatre of the Continent in its *commedia dell'arte* subtext, from Gremio's identification as a "*pantaloon*" in the stage directions (1.1.47 S.D.) to Petruchio's and Grumio's "knock me here soundly" slapstick (1.2.5–44).

It is all the more surprising, then, for us to encounter the Lord of the Induction serving dual functions. Firstly, he acts as a representative of aristocratic, even humanistic decorum – "Grim death, how foul and loathsome is thine image!", he apostrophizes Sly in a moment of somber, *memento mori* meditation (Ind.1.35). Secondly, he stands as a figure of mischief dedicated to a temporary carnival that unleashes rather than restrains a variety of "heteroglot social opinion." A clear precursor to Hamlet in his familiarity with playing and even traveling players, the Lord has, like Hamlet, both a passion for theatre and an amateur's certainty that he can turn playing to his advantage by writing a play-within-the-play. Like Hamlet, he insists on decorum in playing; even his outlandish "practice" is to be done "kindly" (in the gloss of the *Riverside Shakespeare*: naturally, convincingly) and should "be husbanded with modesty" (Ind.1.66, 68). Indeed, even when he speaks with the visiting, professional players, the Lord insists that they maintain their "modesties" (94) in the face of a prank played on what one of the players imagines could be "the veriest antic in the world" (101). Still later, he declares the need to "counsel" his men, hoping that his "presence" will "abate the over-merry spleen, / Which otherwise would grow into extremes" (136–8).

For all his humanist-inspired endorsement of moderation and "kindly" acting, however, the Lord makes clear recourse to the "household stuff" (Ind.2.140) of the Elizabethan theatre in executing his "practice" on Sly. His high and low functions find their correlative in *Shrew*'s assemblage of dramatic materials. In some ways this comedy can be read as a virtual catalogue of the Elizabethan playhouse and of those things and elements of the world outside the play that nonetheless became a part of plays performed there. We see this in *Shrew*'s collocation of dramatic styles, including *commedia dell'arte* and Roman New Comedy; in its emphasis on multiple venues, from playing in inn yards to great houses to Italian streets; and in its play with identities, from real names such as "Marian Hacket" (Ind.2.21) and names within the dramatic fiction ("Christopher Sly," "Barthol'mew") to names of actors' roles ("Soto") mentioned within the dramatic fiction by a traveling player. Within this catalogue we find a variety of possible identities, from the apparently deep characters of Katherina and Petruchio to *commedia dell'arte* figures ("pantaloon") and such hastily personated roles as Sly's "Madam." Thus the Induction presents a sustained focus on the practice of playing itself, a practice that is not limited, in the *Shrew*, to a single mode of performance.

Indeed, when the Lord mixes, with his high-aesthetic insistence on decorum and natural-seeming, a dedication to "practice," and a desire for an ephemeral "pastime passing excellent" (Ind.1.67), he captures the vibrant hodge-podge of representation and game regularly performed on the boards of London's commercial playhouses. Thus we are permitted to feel it as a representation of Elizabethan playing itself when the Lord turns to a nearby servant and says:

> [G]o you to Barthol'mew my page,
> And see him dress'd in all suits like a lady;
> That done, conduct him to the drunkard's chamber,
> And call him madam, do him obeisance. (Ind.1.105–8)

Here the boy actor is costumed as a lady and paraded before Sly in the gamesome "practice." What remains remarkable about the boy's disguise, though, is that it is a function of costume, behavior, and such externals as the fact of other actors identifying him *as* a "lady": "call him madam, do him obeisance."

We do not have the space here to explore all the rich material this brief sequence offers, but one moment in particular bears comment for its relation to the practice of personation in the early modern theatre. In addition to instructing the boy (by proxy) to "bear himself with honorable action, / Such as he hath observ'd in noble ladies / Unto their lords, by them accomplished" (Ind.1.110–12), the Lord offers an injunction that the boy cry to show joy at the recovery of her "lord" who has, for seven years, imagined himself "No better than a poor and loathsome beggar" (123). Hamlet-like in his insistence that the body be seen revealing – unable not to reveal – its secrets, the Lord offers a homely trick for this practice:

> And if the boy have not a woman's gift
> To rain a shower of commanded tears,
> An onion will do well for such a shift,
> Which in a napkin (being close convey'd)
> Shall in despite enforce a watery eye. (124–8)

Oddly, here the common onion – proverbially a nearly worthless thing (see Tilley O66: "Not worth an Onion" [a leek]) – is recommended by an elite connoisseur of playing as a ready supplement to dramatic verisimilitude. The boy's tears, ostensibly proof of his personated identity's joy, come neither from costume (surely punned on in "all suits like a lady"), dramatic identification ("call him madam, do him obeisance"), nor even imitation ("as he hath observ'd in noble ladies"). Instead, the "secretly open" person-ation here depends on what Thersites would have called a "juggling trick": secreting an onion in a napkin to "enforce a watery eye." Far from an elevated endeavor, playing here is on a par with the common, demotic standards that Sly announces ("Richard Conqueror," "Saint Jeronimy!") before his dream. Even as the Lord communicates his "excursus on acting" (the phrase is Harold Jenkins's) to Barthol'mew, his page, by means of a proxy servant, so is the practice of playing itself to be performed by and through the "juggling trick" of holding an onion up to one's eyes.

An even more extensive focus on the role of stage properties in revealing the interdependence of game and representation occurs in *1 Henry IV* where Falstaff displays mimetic skills in personating two other characters. There the scene (2.4.373–481) is set for a hilarious presentation of histrionic game and sport in which practices vitally affect imaginary relations of leading characters. Even more than in Sly's case, a handy-dandy inversion between personator and personated is used dramatically for characteristic purposes of representation. In *1 Henry IV* there ensues a more broadly playful type of performed entertainment when Falstaff, upon the painful disclosure of his cowardice, blandly invokes "all the titles of good fellowship" and proceeds to ask, "shall we have a play extempore?" (278–80). But when, unexpectedly, threatening news from the north arrives summoning Prince Henry to court and the field of battle, Falstaff seeks to turn the tables on the heir apparent by envisioning *his* fear of the enemy and *his* plight when having to confront his father:

Falstaff. Well, thou wilt be horribly chid to-morrow when thou comest to thy father. If thou love me, practice an answer.
Prince. Do thou stand for my father and examine me upon the particulars of my life.
Falstaff. Shall I? Content. This chair shall be my state, this dagger my scepter, and this cushion my crown.
Prince. Thy state is taken for a join'd-stool, thy golden scepter for a leaden dagger, and thy precious rich crown for a pitiful bald crown!
Falstaff. Well, and the fire of grace be not quite out of thee, now shalt thou be mov'd. Give me a cup of sack to make my eyes look red, that it may be thought I have wept, for I must speak in passion, and I will do it in King Cambyses' vein.
Prince. Well, here is my leg.
Falstaff. And here is my speech. Stand aside, nobility. (4.2.373–89)

Comic personation unfolds in a context that teems self-reflexively with all those imperfections to which representation is heir. For that reason alone, the playfully spontaneous, would-be extemporal quality of playing this peculiar type of personation on stage is extremely complex. For one thing, this comically staged figuration cannot be identified simply or primarily with recycling in burlesque manner the old-fashioned bombast and rhetoric in "King Cambyses' vein." Rather, without surrendering the play's larger representational design, the entire scene comes close to being a play-within-a-play or, to be more exact, a play with playing. It is a show equally concerned with both the showing and the imaginary meaning of the shown.

Emphatically, a presentational element of game and mimesis is foregrounded and acknowledged by the onstage audience, as when the Hostess exclaims, "O Jesu, this is excellent sport, i' faith!" (390). The cue for "sport" traditionally calls for a not necessarily verbal and not strictly dramatic type of performance, and certainly one that usually precludes or antedates the uses of rhetoric in characterization. In our scene the personating practice in the showing is inspired primarily by the craft and craftiness of the imaginary personator, and only secondarily by what meaning the personated conveys. Here is a supreme case, delivered in a fiction, of the authority of the performer; in fact, the performer's self shines through the image of the personated. The personator, far from being lost in the personated, entirely dominates the performance through his presence in word and action. In particular, he accentuates, even revels in, his own display of performing as a subject of both the *énoncé* and the *énonciation*. For that, to use "a cup of sack to make my eyes look red" invokes (and unashamedly publishes) a stratagem that laughably, as in a travesty, displaces rhetorical artifice (the orator's tears and passions) in favor of a more directly material, significantly crude stimulus. With an ironic decorum of character, Falstaff's call for sack rephrases the Lord's advice about an onion in *Shrew*.

This scene is remarkable in that characters in a history play go out of their way to *personate*, and do so in a fashion explicitly identified with the histrionic practice of common players. While Falstaff's "I must speak in passion" reduces the showing of passion to some form of mimicry, the Hostess pointedly specifies the provenance of what, in Hall's formulation, is Falstaff's "self-resembled show." Overwhelmed by the sheer amount of showmanship, she notes that Falstaff "doth it as like one of these harlotry players as ever I see!" (395–6). Here the use of present tense ("doth it") is unambiguous. So is her enthusiasm, in that it praises, in the act of presenting the show, the visible doings of the presenter. Such praise is enhanced, not diminished, by the use of "harlotry," which in this sixteenth-century context must be read as "meretriciousness, illegitimate attractiveness" (*OED* 5) rather than simply profligacy or ribaldry.

These theatrically self-conscious uses of comedy in personation presuppose not a mere duality in the relationship between personator and personated but, as it were, a tripartite structure. One reason the personator as compared to the personated looms so large is the former's own duplicity. Here we have not only the corpulent vessel of wit named Falstaff but also, behind this artificial person, probably that great and well-known comedian, Will Kemp.[33] Falstaff, being himself a personated figuration, can in his turn be transfigured into a personator. As probably no other late Elizabethan comedian, Kemp possessed the authority, or should one say the mettle, of a comic performer putting his own stamp on the personated. The exuberant thrust in this transfiguration seems to draw on what publicly known doubleness the primary personator could make available on top of his Falstaffian role-playing. Thus the resulting personation richly associates a potent configuration of duplicity in both the material personator and the imaginary personator who "doth it" in this scene. As process and product come together in both the performing and the performed, Falstaff's imperfectly mediated representation can multiply the subject of comedy in a history without surrendering that massive frame of subjective reference constituting "plump Jack."

Such comic personation, once it amounts to a multiply relayed unfolding of the duplicity between personator and personated, confronts the actor with the most basic and ordinary task in his profession. To project the personated character as, simultaneously, the personator of another is, for good reason, not uncommon in Shakespeare's stage. In his theatre it can be one way of staging, without blurring, the socio-cultural difference between common player and the (for him) alien image of his subject. The comedy of such social, cultural, and gendered difference is "excellent sport i' faith." Not unlike the young male player who, playing a woman, also in his own vein plays a young male, the player behind Falstaff resorts, as in a fiction, to the reality of his own work and body. In each case, the represented character is not lost sight of, but the process of personation is, as it were, sandwiched between two types of histrionic practice: on the one hand, there is the actor's passion and his practice, the personator's existential expense of time, energy, and memory; on the other, we have the imaginary level of a representation transfiguring the actual performer's status, gender, age, and work in and through the image of the personated.

Yet, as we have seen, this provocative mode of personation, far from blurring the configuration of Falstaff, actually helps build up an unparalleled complexity in the image of his character. The latter is the more impressive in being subjected to neither finish nor closure. Instead, there prevails a hidden aperture, a juggling art of being "secretly open," which is not unlike the multilayered figuration of Autolycus, but also that of Faulconbridge, Portia, Duke Vincentio, Rosalind, Edgar, and others. In each case, their personation palters with the primary role without canceling it out. Hence the Shakespearean confluence of personating actor and personated character thrives on and artfully enhances the friction inherent in the contrariety informing the shape of an artificial person, a mere representation, himself or herself appropriating the artful player's real practice.

For the dramatist to turn the personated character itself into an agency of personation is to blur the borderline between the practice and the meaning. It is to play with the related difference between the craft of performance and the art of imaginary identity. At the same time, such comic uses of difference fall into the tradition of Elizabethan gallimaufry. In particular, they respond to those mixed purposes of playing when the player's practice moves between the poles of unabashed sport and game and of what in the language of Hamlet's advice to the actors is called "the necessary question of the play." In Falstaff's case, these two poles – one presentational, the other representational – are not contradictory: the guise and *gestus* of "one of these harlotry players" meaningfully counterpoint the themes of royal dignity and heroic action in *1 Henry IV*.

The scene extrapolates what in the context of most serious personations remains only a potentiality. Falstaff comes close to practicing a "self-resembled show" of his own professional practice. For him to ask for "a cup of sack to make my eye look red, that it may be thought that I have wept" is to provide the spectator with a comic metaphor of the labor that goes into the very means and matter of performing practice. What is at issue here is an entirely presymbolic construction of sign and delivery. Paradoxically, the presymbolic recipe for "passion" betrays (again in both senses of the word) an effect of the representation of character as it discloses the vulgar job of its delivery. The logic of representation, culminating in the image of high passion, is reduced to the logistics of the bottle.

Although the uses of props are thoroughly externalized here, the playlet in *1 Henry IV* underlines the arbitrariness in the logic of representation. The irreducible material of performance is underlined rather than reduced when we are presented with those strange and, as Hal believes, ineffective articles of signifying property. But to foreground the materiality at the cost of meaning is reminiscent of Launce's clownish tokens of resistance to symbolization in *The Two Gentlemen of Verona* or of the amateurs in *A Midsummer Night's Dream*. As in these earlier comedies, the iconic relation between the "stool" of the Boar's Head Tavern and the throne at court is so tenuous that the act of symbolization can easily be punctured, as happens in Prince Hal's answer. Comparable props of impromptu role-playing have their problems in *Dream* when, as in the Mechanicals' play, relations between signifier and signified are so outrageously "disfigure[d]" that "one must come in with a bush of thorns and a lantern, and say he comes to disfigure, or to present, the person of Moonshine" (3.1.58–61). Falstaff's own signifying practice is similarly troublesome, and less accidentally so, when it comes "to disfigure" relations between material signifiers and their imaginary signified. To reemploy an ordinary stage property (already predetermined in its codification) results in its inability to stand for anything more substantial than itself.

Still, in *1 Henry IV* the published pleasures of counterfeiting must not triumph, even when the irreducible work of performance is again highlighted in the reversal of roles between Falstaff and Hal. As soon as the Prince comes to address the failure of symbolic meaning in the uses of these tavern stage properties, he turns the table on the iconic imperfections of common performance. Flaunting the show by default of resemblance, the Prince holds up for scorn all the vulgar articles of signifying property. In doing so he points to a comic crisis in those representational premises of personation which are forfeited by a performance practice so self-willed and extemporal. Over and beyond arraigning the sheer materiality (and triviality) of the tiring-house props, the Prince rejects the order, as practiced by Falstaff, of a performance-dominated embodiment. For Hal to say "Thy state is taken for a join'd-stool" is to put first in place the imaginary signified; it is on a common scaffold to find fault with the trajectory of a dramatic personation which privileges the enunciating performance over its *énoncé*, that is, its signified. For a common "chair" to stand for a royal "state" or throne, for a "dagger" to serve as "scepter," for a "cushion" to denote a "crown" may perhaps pass muster with those "harlotry players"; according to the poetics of holding the "mirror up to nature," it is to tamper with the iconic scheme of verisimilitude.

Finally, the Prince points to a dilemma that affects many other instances of comic personation. The trouble with Falstaff playing the king and then the prince is that a primary level of symbolic meaning (that is, Falstaff's own role) is subjected to yet another, secondary level of imaginary metamorphosis. Thus the leaden dagger in Falstaff's hands is a theatrical property; because its dramatic connotations are established already, it serves ill for a scepter. Such grafting of a secondary level of symbolic meaning upon another first in place can indeed, as Prince Hal makes clear, constitute moments of great vulnerability.

However, as the analogy with other performance-dominated instances of character construction suggests, the liability in question can be turned into an asset and yield fascinating images for doubleness in certain types of figuration. Take only cross-dressing, where, as we have seen, one level of gendered role-playing is dovetailed with one or even two others. The boy-actor who plays a young woman (first level of symbolic meaning) proceeds on stage through disguise to supplant his primary role and gender by the role of a page or male youth (second level), who, as in Rosalind's case, playfully proposes to appear as female (third level). As the preceding chapter has demonstrated, the second, let alone the third, change of gender never quite seeks to displace the first of these dramatic identities. On the contrary, the *prima facie* appearance continues to shine through subsequent shapes of gendered identity, even when the "secretly open" reminder of it is comically made to appear as an accidental *lapsus*, not a deliberate move toward exposure. This is only one reason why the resulting sexual motley in the personation of Shakespeare's boy-heroines feeds into a semantically complex freedom for unorthodox representation. Ultimately, however, representational form and function, without ever being canceled, are contained, even perhaps overshadowed, by a terrific presence of performative practice. As distinct from Falstaff presenting, through the assumed voice of the Prince, an apologetic portrait of himself, the cross-dressed heroine falls back (on a second level) upon the original existential personator's own male sex. Hence it is an as yet immature gendered existence in the absent real world, not in the imaginary world of the play, which requires and plays into an intense performance function in the act and the text of personation.

Diverging from these stunning uses of a mutual engagement between symbolization and existence, there is, in other forms of personation, the sheer materiality of stage-property matter, which puts up a kind of resistance, especially when reemployed on a purely imaginary level. Here, to give just one example, Launce the clown is perhaps best equipped to trace *ad absurdum* the purported transformation of his shoes into an emblematic picture from a self-invented family album (*The Two Gentlemen of Verona*, 2.3.1–32). What results is a parody of an improper, secondary use of symbolism in the grafting upon what is already a symbolic fiction.

Not so different from Launce's facetious struggle to represent against the order of similitude, Falstaff's attempt to reuse a prop already laden with meaning ends with the prop being unable to represent anything other than what it is. But, paradoxically, by refusing to attend to the material, prerepresentational conditions of staging, Hal's condescending reversal of Falstaff's improvised sign system helps us view this entire act of comic personation in perspective. At the end of it, we are returned to both Falstaff's plight and his ironic, false triumph in the rhetoric of escaping banishment. On the doubly signifying scaffold, to plead "banish not him," and to do so through the assumed voice of the Prince, may well be a "secretly open" relapse to an actually existing comedian. If indeed it was in recourse to the prerepresentational level of the broad, plebeian performance genius of Kemp, the "banish not him" would also have to be read as an existential phrase, preceding illusions of role-playing: "banish me not."

This game of playing out both concurrence and difference between the representation and its agency culminates in personating and yet intercepting an artificial person by and through a personator's self. The impact of this sport on spectators is at two removes from both the orator's rhetoric and "the mental space" (Burns's phrase) of historiography. In this history play Falstaff's excellent game is to construct, and dance upon, a highly vulnerable bridge between the rule of kings and the sway of misrule, to appropriate the highest language of the former to the lowest purpose of the latter, and vice versa. But to use and abuse the distance between the two is not to do away with the difference between them in social status and cultural purpose. On the contrary, to establish the full measure of contrariety in staging, within the framework of a comic personation, the pleading of Falstaff and the plight of the Prince was to *use* cultural difference dramatically and theatrically. It was, in Falstaff's words, to "practice an answer" (375), but not in response to, or in the image of, a courtly occasion. It was, rather, an answer on behalf of a theatre crowded by multitudes. Fashioned in the form of an "inset," it sought to underline but also to question the "non-coherence between what the audience in the theatre sees . . . and what they listen to (about those characters long ago and somewhere)."[34] As an inset, this scene within a scene cannily addresses "the relation between the *imagined* spectacle . . . and the *actual* spectacle, presented to the eyes of the paying audience."[35] To address the gap between the seen and the unseen must have raised uncomfortable questions about the incompatibility between the rule of royalty and the sway of misrule. Such huge questions remained unanswerable elsewhere. Here finally was, as the Chorus to *Henry V* would put it, a purpose of playing informed by the attempt to "digest / Th' abuse of distance" and, in the process, "force a play" (Pro. 2.31–2).

CHAPTER 8

Character/actor: the deep matrix

As we move from personation to characterization, it is paramount to dismiss the idea of any firm boundary between these two modes of dramatic figuration. To be sure, what has come to be thought of as "deep" characterization made itself most clearly manifest in early modern drama from the late 1590s onward. Here, as is well known, such characters as Brutus, Rosalind, and Hamlet helped inaugurate fascinating displays of "that within" (*Hamlet*, 1.2.85). Such displays accompanied a linguistic and behavioral self-consciousness that would, in the ensuing years, distinguish figures such as Lear, Cleopatra, the Duchess of Malfi, and Beatrice-Joanna, to name only these. To this limited extent, then, personation and characterization may be defined in relation to their respective chronologies, according to which, for a brief period, character emerged as a more comprehending image of subjectivity in the theatre. It was a vulnerable mode of selfhood because the groping for a new depth *within* was inseparable from presenting a worldly *without*. Between the two arose a relationship that, wanting precedent as well as precept, was beset by an unexplored, untested measure of both engagement and discrepancy. In such characterization any "secret close" (*Richard III*, 1.1.158) design of passion and desire could be made interactive with a rich, imaginary set of public objects and options, challenges, and charges.

In this way characterization goes beyond personation in the dramatic fashioning of subjectivity. While the presentational type of performance tends to serve the more extrinsic purposes of role-playing, as geared to the given demands of status, office, gender, and family, the characterizing performer surrenders his own body more consistently to the symbolic process. In other words, the performance of character results in an impersonation as part of a more intrinsic, text-sustained dramaturgy. In this mode of performance, the actor tends to identify with the represented person to the degree that his or her histrionic competence becomes completely integral to the task in question. Yet rather than succeeding personation, or being irreconcilable to it, characterization must be viewed as standing in productive interplay with it. Such interplay is frequently evident not only within one and the same text, but in relation to one and the same character as well.

Understanding the difference and overlap between these various modes of dramatic figuration is difficult without recourse to changing socio-cultural circumstances in the history of the Elizabethan theatre. In our context – the relative strength of the two media – the difference in their relationship is vitally implicated in shifting modes of validating writing in a new kind of potency and performance in its own right. In the preceding chapter we defined the generic structure of personation (above, p. 143) as the mode by which a recollected notion of performance would infuse the speech of a dramatic figure even at the stage of its dramatic composition. In other words, the dimension of histrionic delivery and, with it, the act of enunciation are strong enough in "secretly open" manner to leak through the persona, to affect the enunciated statement of character, and thereby to convey awareness of the actor as an actor, the stage as a stage.

However, in our convenient formula, at about the turn of the century the prominence of actor's voice in author's pen increasingly has to cope – or exist side by side – with a marked preponderance of author's pen in actor's voice. With the advent of Ben Jonson, John Marston, and others, personation increasingly confronts a discursive shift. The self-sustained amount of "appro-priation" (Émile Benveniste's phrase) in the act of the *énonciation* tends to shrink; the "self-resembled" image of the practicing player wanes on the levels of both the writer's dramatic composition and the spectator's imagi-native transfiguration. The new strength of the *énoncé*, the self-contained statement of character, is such that it seems to hedge in the appropriative, inventive component in the process of enunciation. As the mediating prac-tice of the agent ceases to be openly acknowledged, the self-sufficient status of an imaginary identity thrives on its own. There is no need (or so it seems) for the figure to be concerned about its own mediating purpose.

Yet characters, once they are shown on stages, continue to be delivered through the "performant function."[1] As we have heard Paul Yachnin observe, it is vital "to understand that Shakespearean characterization is an artful response to the situation of the theatre, and that the dividedness of that situation is what lies behind the irreducible doubleness of charac-ter."[2] In its simplest terms, this doubleness corresponds to the two most basic aspects of acting: the "first is mimesis or role-playing; the second is performance, establishing a 'real' relation to the audience."[3] We have suggested that these two aspects or modes are rarely if ever discrete.

In Anthony Dawson's phrase, one typically encounters a "mingling of representational or mimetic acting, and 'presentational' acting whereby the actor . . . calls attention to his own skill and invites the audience to admire it."[4]

Such doubleness, as we shall see, is particularly virulent in a theatre where – as in Shakespeare's – the cultural gaps between author, actor, and character remain especially wide. Marked by deep differences in social status, habit, and bearing, these gaps can actuate a fascinating dynamic in the staging of character: they impel the fleeting but potentially enthralling relationship between who is impersonated in a fiction and who in reality is doing the impersonation. Between these there is room for an unstable play of difference and equivalence, often enough for an uncertain outcome in the relative balance between the symbolic and the real. Thus a twofold appeal, a bifold authority, operates in the staging of Shakespeare's characters. In the language of the Prologue to *Henry V*, we have, for one thing, the symbolic order in the representation of "So great an object," the "imaginary puissance" of royalty; with this, we also have the material medium of bodies and boards "On this unworthy scaffold" (Pro. 11, 10, 25).

Between them, Shakespeare's theatre used space deliberately for the lively traffic and interaction of its different media. This space allowed for playing out a wide spectrum of challenge or complementarity resulting from the difference between the symbolic order of representation and the material work of and in the theatre. While we have studied the dramaturgy of such playful "trafficking" with socio-semiotic difference elsewhere,[5] the question now is how this bifold authority helps fashion the representation of Shakespeare's characters at the crucial juncture of script and body, pages and stages. On its most elementary level, ordinary players were hard put to cope with the gap in question. For them to cross the gulf and submit to the symbolic order of an alien, often enough elevated world, stationed high up but shown right here, must have required a great deal of performative prowess. To assume a role, to capture its alien semantic and yet wrest a common understanding from it, must have taken considerable pluck and talent. Shakespeare's language at times is supple enough to acknowledge the use and abuse of the distance between the scaffold and the character in terms of an actor's stage presence. Performing "in one person many people, / And none contented" (*Richard II*, 5.5.31–2), common players had to face up to doing "nobility" with tranquility. To counterfeit "burgomasters and great oney'rs" was for the actor to bring out the distance on his own terms, according to which greatness could be made familiar. Thus difference was translated into a working relationship of a sort, whereby impersonators and impersonated submitted to a nomenclature which could state, at least in Latin, that "*homo* is a common name to all men" (*1 Henry IV*, 2.1.76, 95).

To appreciate the depth of the gap between representing actors and represented characters, we need only keep in mind that in Shakespeare's theatre different registers of performative practice were coupled with socially distinct groups. For instance, as we have seen in the mixed repertoire of the Queen's Men, activities like tumbling must have reflected the inheritance of itineracy. At the same time, the stigma of vagabondage was remembered. So was the traditional proficiency of dexterity and showmanship, together with longstanding means of audience appeal and direct address. All these socially inflected, bodily brisk modes of a strong repertoire in agile skills of delivery helped constitute a performance practice which continued to inform certain traces in staged versions of Shakespeare's characters. If the latter, as has been noted, were doubly encoded, it was nearly inevitable that players empowered by their own élan and zest were not simply content to exceed the semantic bounds of language, but had their own energies transmuted and, so to speak, transfigured into what vitally, on a preexpressive level, was conveyed to onlookers.

Being to such double business bound must have proved the source of a peculiar type of "theatrical vibrancy" (Michael Shapiro's term). Spectators were thereby urged to interact with, join in the game of, the actor/character masquerade in a spirit of "complicity."[6] As far as doubleness remained an important component in rendering and receiving an alien subjectivity, the practice marked that cultural site on which the power of performance engaged, but was also disciplined by, the superb force of a dramatic text. The actor's glance would be both ways; the interaction of page and stage, but also of language and show would by no means be limited to encounters of the contestatory kind. On the contrary, as the impact of rhetoric upon public acting witnessed, the arts of language themselves permeated the act of delivery as very much part of the show.

However, even while the signifying word of the dramatist achieved a dominating force in the symbolic order of figuration, the representation of subjectivity received an unsuspected impetus from performance practice itself. To a degree scarcely recognized, the dramatic image of selfhood thrived in strange proximity to the histrionic presence of the performer. To underline the apparent paradox is to realize that there was no dichotomy, no opposition between what was visibly, audibly real in the body and energy of the personator and what was most deeply symbolic in the personated, the "I," the particular sense of a subjective within.

To illustrate the underlying doubleness of imaginative realness and imaginary representation in some of Shakespeare's characters, let us begin by asking a seemingly paradoxical question: why is it that the grammar of personal identity finds itself most emphatically articulated in the language of "secretly open" speakers, those under the spell of a strong performative? On what grounds, that is, does the articulation of such an "I" more often than not associate a *platea* position of personalized *dis*closure, sometimes even direct address? While we shall return presently to the frequency with which the first person singular pronoun thrives precisely in the text of the most pronounced figurations of doubleness, our first example of a doubly encoded artificial person recalls the combined modes of personation and characterization which we had begun to discuss in chapter 2.

In our trajectory *Richard III* once again marks the earliest point where the mode of personation in a history play gives way to and is transformed into an early configuration of Shakespeare's tragic character. If our reading of the protagonist in that play had to be summed up in one phrase, we would say that a personation engrained in doubleness is made to unfold side by side – tends almost to jostle – with a character marked by duplicity: Richard Gloucester is designed on the cutting edge between the craft of the personator and the craftiness of the personated.

Richard, alone on stage, can entrust the audience with his "secret close intent" in wooing Lady Anne. Here, despite their constant overlapping, the two media of the theatre help inform Richard's tricky dramaturgy. In his double-dealing he *shows* (in fact betrays) himself to the audience as a "secretly open" personation; only a few moments later, in staggering dialogue with Lady Anne, his language is that of a "secret close" plotter. Starting with his opening speech, Gloucester's grand design in counterfeiting is saturated with Protean energies: he pursues both a hidden "deep intent" (*Richard III*, 1.1.149) as character within the story ("Dive, thoughts, down to my soul" [41]) and a showmanship culminating in the open betrayal of each artful stratagem. Using to the full traditional resources as vicious juggler and "director," Richard ambidextrously delivers his own embodied difference between the character and the actor. As triumphantly staged here, the former's "secret close" design and the latter's *dis*closure of it are deliberately conjoined. Together they set in motion a hodge-podge of dramaturgy, an uncanny duplicity unfixing both these codes in *mise-en-scène*.

We have here the force of closure and concealment in a character "full of deep deceit" (*2 Henry VI*, 3.1.57). Even in the early history play, the character is endowed with a plenitude of depth, in the sense that "deep" inside, invisible and unfathomed by others, there is something harboring such "intent" as the simple outward show of him conceals. The word "deep" (which we use throughout for such a character) occurs twice in five lines:

> Smooth runs the water where the brook is deep,
> And in his simple show he harbors treason.
> The fox barks not when he would steal the lamb. –
> No, no, my sovereign, Gloucester is a man
> Unsounded yet and full of deep deceit. (3.1.53–7)

Yet this same person can, especially in the later play, pierce or simply take off his persona. In doing so the disclosure is such that the entire fiction of role-playing is apparently uncovered in front of the audience. The act of aperture involves spectators with a sense of complicity ("complicity" here in its traditional sense of connivance). In opening his sinister role toward the audience, the actor does not of course cease to perform it. It is only in the plotting that his "secret close" scheme is, so to speak, publicly acknowledged. Betrayed is not simply an awesome act of dissemblance but the art it takes to devise and perform it. The audience – turned, almost, into an accessory – are invited to inspect the accomplished plot and also to witness and enjoy the plotting of it. They may even feel incited to abet, or serve as accomplice, up to a point, in the unorthodox production of a piece of villainy and disorder. We can only guess the responses of playgoers in early modern England, but even today many onlookers experience a shivering thrill in acceding to the sordid glamor of perfect knavery.[7]

To understand Richard's grandiose duplicity, we must establish the symbolic framework of his signifying language in pursuit of ambition, pride, cruelty, and treachery. Like any dramatic characterization on stage, Richard's proposes, for the question of the subject, a twofold context. We can approach this context through Benveniste's distinction between *le sujet de l'énoncé*, what we could call the enunciated subject in the dramatic statement of character, and *le sujet de l'énonciation*, the speaking subject, the agent engaged in the practice of enunciation.[8] Critical approaches to Shakespeare's characters have located the subject almost exclusively on the plane of an enunciated image in fiction. Yet the concept of an "actor-character" that exceeds the purely symbolic is in its doubleness predicated on an imaginary practice inseparable from a real, living body.

It seems impossible in performance, that is, to isolate the dramatist's text from the mode of its articulation. On stage the text is relayed through the actor's body and being, his voice, his work, his finite fund of visceral energies. While these cannot be divorced from the task of signification and representation, they exceed the bounds of the symbolic and defy what is set forth in writing. As Elaine Scarry has persuasively argued, "the body's presence in the elementary sites of artifice entails material labour"; therefore, the kind of work invested in, say, the setting up and running of scaffolds can be conceived "at once as pain's twin and as its opposite."[9] On this material level, things and doings have an "attribute of realness" which has too often been overlooked as vitally enlarging the doubly encoded practice of impersonation.[10]

These provisional remarks on the complex scene of Elizabethan "doubleness" in characterization sketch only the outlines of a wider frame of reference within which to read the following citations of subjectivity – reflective statements, that is, from numerous assertive subjects in Shakespeare's plays. We would note that these utterances transcend Shakespearean adaptations of the Vice tradition, covering as they do a similar enunciation of self from under dramatic disguise, and elsewhere:

> I am myself alone.
>
> (Richard Gloucester, *3 Henry VI*, 5.6.83)

> Richard loves Richard, that is, I am I.
> Alack, I love myself.
> I am a villain; yet I lie, I am not.
>
> (Richard Gloucester, *Richard III*, 5.3.183, 187, 191)

> And I am I, howe'er I was begot.
>
> (Bastard, *King John*, 1.1.175)

> Then think you right: I am not what I am.
>
> (Viola, *Twelfth Night*, 3.1.141)

> Simply the thing I am / Shall make me live.
>
> (Paroles, *All's Well That Ends Well*, 4.3.333–4)

> For I am nothing if not critical.   (Iago, *Othello*, 2.1.118)

> Who is it that can tell me who I am?
>
> (Lear, *King Lear*, 1.4.230)

> Edgar I nothing am.   (Edgar, *King Lear*, 2.3.21)

> I do not say I am one; but I have a hand.
>
> (Cloten, *Cymbeline*, 3.1.41)

I know myself now, and I feel within me . . .
A still and quiet conscience. (Wolsey, *Henry VIII*, 3.2.378, 380)

These, indeed, are striking articulations of selfhood. Almost all the phrases cited (as well as many of those in the preceding chapters) are engrained with that bifold authority in which the oral work of the personator and the textualized word of the personated commingle. Between these two sources, the enunciation of selfhood is grammatically as unambiguous as the order of this self-characterization appears thoroughly symbolic. Yet the resulting image of a self is deeply divided in its deliberate ambivalence. Everyone on stage can say about one's role-playing, "I am not what I am." But in secretly disclosing a silent convention, the underlying gap between the body of the actor and the language of the role (to which we will return shortly) is playfully exposed to a knowing and guessing audience.

This foray into some of the performative springs of the represented self on Shakespeare's stage does not mean to imply that the arts of language are anything secondary in the formation of dramatic character; far from it. Still, there are limits to which the first person singular pronoun can be considered as unambiguous evidence of any individual subject position. To ignore these limits (as some of the finest studies of the subject have done) is to miss out on important aspects of the dramatically represented self.[11] True enough, a linguistic concept of subjectivity is, as Lacan has taught us, vital; at the heart of the symbolic order of signifying practice, it is simply indispensable. Yet to confine ourselves to the purely verbal constituents of selfhood on Shakespeare's stage is not sufficient. If, in the linguistic sense of the word, the subject can be defined as claiming the agency (the "I" or "we") of a verb or in a sentence, the circumstances of the stage can be seen to exceed the grammar of subjectivity.

The first person singular emerges in productive tension with a plurality of cultural practices and social perspectives, not to mention the bifold appeal of two different media. The best-known exemplification offers itself in *Hamlet*, in the protagonist's intense and complex assertions of selfhood. Early in the play, in his resolve to "put an antic disposition on" (1.5.172) there first emerges the semblance of something underneath. Such masquerade invokes and, in fact, derives from socio-cultural customs and behavior that do not exclusively, not even perhaps primarily, draw on linguistic constituents. Even so, Hamlet's sense of selfhood is coupled with stark capacities, even inclinations, for the screen of an "antic" guise. As we will see, in Hamlet's just as in Edgar's case this peculiar brand of disguise is glaringly performative – one in which, next to the art of figuration, the player can ring the changes of a rich histrionic talent, from the tragic to the comic.

There are, of course, altogether different directions and degrees to which the "I" of an artificial person can actually be conjoined with a semblance of the personator's own self. In Wolsey's case, when the Cardinal (ironically) invokes his "conscience," the author's pen has little room for intimating any performer's voice. However, in view of the astonishingly wide scale of variations, there is at least one type of conjuncture, that between the scheming character and the counterfeiting actor, in which the actor's passion and profession can almost congenially be suspended in a purely imaginary subjectivity. We need take only a character like Paroles and his habit of making himself "a motley to the view" through what (in David Schalkwyk's phrase) is his "upstart profession of words, fictions, and 'borrowed flaunts.'"[12] Remarkably, the "motley" quality of his verbal identity can affirm "the thing I am" – which is indeed an "affirmation of identity and agency." Whether there is, as Schalkwyk further suggests, an analogy with the poet-player's "I am that I am" in Sonnet 121, Paroles's own partial sonnet may indeed be read as affirming a "personal independence" even in the midst of his dependence on living off a gentle thing in flattery and friendship. In our context, then, the representation of this "both-sides rogue" (*All's Well*, 4.3.221) may well claim to be fashioned according to the manner of a counterfeiting, practicing player.

However, and quite aside from all figurations of Vice and villainy, Shakespeare's "both-sides" regime in *mise-en-scène* appears to foster an altogether emphatic subject-position culminating in exceptionally dense uses of the personal pronoun. Here we have leading characters such as Rosalind, Prospero, even the King in *All's Well That Ends Well* speaking on the threshold between the world in the play and the playing in the world. At the ending of the play, each of these characters collapses her/his imaginary persona, as represented in the fiction of the story, into the physical person of the player ushering the play to its conclusion. The light-handed grace, the effortlessness by which the identity of the character is artfully made to glide into that of the player asking for applause, is highly significant. The two identities seem perfectly contiguous; closely under the skin of a private magician (to take only Prospero), there resides a master of public ceremonies in the playhouse. Could it be that the adjoining of roles is of such stuff as brings forth the dream of a larger selfhood? Rosalind in her epilogue has no less than eleven uses of the first person singular, while Prospero in the twenty lines of his epilogue uses thirteen personal pronouns, five of these in the first person, which is the same number that occur in the one sentence concluding with "I'll drown my book" (*The Tempest*, 5.1.50–7).

While such figures must remain largely suggestive, these grammatical subject positions appear more significant when seen in conjunction with the "I" mouthed by Richard, Paroles, and related figures. Between their first person pronouns and those of, say, Prospero, lies a considerable degree of difference: not only in the respective subject positions but also in the purpose and function of the "I" used. Even so, there remains a baffling affinity, at least in the overall spatial and dramaturgic contexts. None of these is, strictly speaking, extra-dramatic. Neither can they be reconciled with any dramatic conventions in aid of closure.

With the exception of Bridget Escolme's and Richard Hillman's studies, these positionings have seldom been studied for their semantic dimensions, and their spatial coordinates have never been given their due.[13] To take only a play's ending, we could point out that it offers a liminal space in which demarcations in subjectivity between characters and players are momentarily suspended. Even where such demarcations persist, they become so porous that the combined forces of the imaginary and the material achieve great "puissance" in a mutually enriched fund of performative action. Inhabiting a space betwixt and between the collapsing world in the play and the dawning contours "within the girdle of these walls" (*Henry V*, Pro. 19), character-players look both ways. Before the "expectancy" of applause is finally conveyed to the audience, actors tend to hover between dramatic fiction and semi-contractual business, between representational and presentational uses of their voices.

As things draw to a close, the concluding speech acts can be perlocutionary in that they bring about something tangible in the playhouse. The epilogue or ending thereby finds characters consummating their doubleness in a pregnant transition from the playworld to the ordinary world. The "two-sides" action in this liminal move arrives when memories of characters and stories need, so to speak, to be taken home.[14] In about a dozen plays, characters are dispatched to enjoy a post-scriptural future: as when, five lines before the play closes, "noble Timon" is invoked, "of whose memory / Hereafter more" (*Timon of Athens*, 5.80 ff.) or when in a concluding line it is resolved for home-going spectators and retiring actors "To hear the rest untold" in the story of the play just ended (*Pericles*, 5.3.84). Thus the actors, in seeking to ensure the play's afterlife, expand by making porous the frontiers of the symbolic. Aiming to make sure of a "Hereafter," they point to a hybrid temporality. With "all the particular accidents gone by" (*The Tempest*, 5.1.306), the leading character's "charms are all o'erthrown."

About to be divested of "*their stol'n apparel*" (255/6 S.D.), he and the rest have presence only to secure the play's future (and the interest of other potential spectators) for the characters they themselves have just embodied.[15]

While a play's ending can exemplify the bifold authority of the impersonating player, the actor enthralled in mid-action by a "swelling scene" (*Henry V*, Pro. 4) is captured too strongly by the regime of representation to cash in on his own doubleness. Here at least the puzzling question persists: in which ways, on what grounds, to what effect can the thrust of performance, the brazen foregrounding of a first person singular, help bring forth the semblance of identity? This question becomes even more tantalizing when we begin to realize that the first person pronoun may testify to a grammatically unambiguous subject position which does not at all indicate any particularizing image of an artificial person, let alone the configuration of a "within." As in a good many disguised characters, but also in the case of, say, Paroles, the "I" is worlds apart from serving any dimension of either roundness or inwardness.

To highlight this strictly theatrical function of the first person singular, we should throw a brief glance at the "I" in pre-Shakespearean drama. When Christopher Marlowe's Prologue to *The Jew of Malta* declares, "I am Machevil," he returns to the staged introduction of histrionic agencies flatly stating their identities in the way of a displayed label rather than that of any self-reflexivity. Such signboard betrayal of self had developed around "practicing" agents in the morality tradition during the fifteenth and sixteenth centuries. In *Mankind* Titivillus's first words to the audience are a resounding "*Ego sum dominatium dominus,* and my name is Titivillus" (475).[16] His Latin here, translating as "I am Lord of Lords," is obviously not an attribute delineating traits of a personalized arrogance in his character. Rather, it helps befuddled spectators ascertain an equivalence between name and appearance through recourse to a pointed parody of Deuteronomy 10:17 (Geneva Bible). But in what ways and to what degree could such an *ego sum* be transformed so as to adumbrate a site of emerging subjectivity? Here we may well follow Hillman's study when he suggests a countervailing, even subversive context of "self-speaking." As elsewhere in this period, a would-be personal sign of identity is mouthed by the most formidably grotesque, thoroughly theatrical agent. Almost invariably the self-speaking instance is one specially relating to onlookers. Entering with a self-introduction, his speech again and again hoists the player's presence, which further down the line is only partially transformed into a dramatic or symbolic agency enunciating some all too scary warning or some laughably thick threat of the horrible.

Here already we find the seeds of what Hillman calls "the de-subjectification of the manipulators themselves, their virtual renunciation of interiority," as thrown into relief by "the centrifugal style of their soliloquies."[17] While the "paucity" of their monologic self-speaking may indeed be another symptom of an underplayed selfhood, the authority of the first person singular is not thereby suspended. Rather, what the "I" of both the cynical and the metadramatic manipulators stands for is at least in part a real subject position of one who does things and performs actions on stage. Such a position can be inhabited by one that mediates, justifies, helps explain, and realizes the task of plotting a story in dramatic form in various modes of collusion and complicity with the audience.

The use of a first person singular subject position can therefore fill the gap between the representation of imaginary subjectivities and the presence of performing agents. In Shakespeare's time this gap persists, even when the difference itself between presentation and representation will tend to be turned into a site of play and interaction. As we have seen in relation to personation (chapter 7), these sites of difference can actually be displayed as "secretly open." But in deep characterization they more often than not collude with a "secret close intent," as in the unseen, indirectly revealed motivation of characters. In certain moments the drift toward the dramatic can (as in the 1580s and early 1590s) actually be halted when the boundary in characterization between presence and representation turns out to be more permeable than the poststructuralist reluctance over phonocentric presence once led us to believe.[18]

To reintroduce a concept of presence into the discussion of Elizabethan performance practice is in no way to minimize, in Escolme's phrase, "the contingency and constructed nature of presence itself." It is by recognizing "the life presence of the actor" that she can approach early modern "fore-grounding of actorly effort" as "integral to the meanings produced by the plays."[19] With this objective in mind, Escolme can proceed to reread the character of Shakespeare's Cressida in the process of her *mise-en-scène* which "does not appear to suggest a critical distance between performer and 'character' so much as a foregrounding of the actor's performance objective to engage the audience with his figure."[20] Even when the concept in the theatre of a "self-representing dramatic subject" unfortunately raises more questions than can be answered, this reading is significant enough in the present context for underlining not only the absence in dramatic charac- terization of any binary polarity between performative and representative strategies but also the impact on spectators of playing with the space between.

To comprehend the nonbinary difference between the representation of character and what meanings derived from the presence of the performer means differentiating the body of the Shakespearean actor. Here we can follow Erika Fischer-Lichte, who, indebted to Helmuth Plessner, observes the disjunction between "*Leib-Sein*" and "*Körper-Haben*."[21] While the former can be understood as bodily being "in flesh and blood" (or, perhaps more elegantly, *en chair et en os*), the latter denotes having and using the body as in an act of volition. Thus the former is, as in Eugenio Barba's sense of the word, "preexpressive," that is, preceding or not accessible to acts of volition and signification; in contrast, the latter can serve different levels of meaning. The difference between the two is, in Fischer-Lichte's phrase, that between the body's *Materialstatus* and its *Signifikantenstatus*, in that the visceral component of the former is without or beyond meaning, while the signifying potential of the latter connects with plenty of meaning.[22] Presence, in other words, goes with a physicality in the body that simultaneously can be both free of meaning and full of meaning.

With this differentiation in mind, one can see that the relationship between the presence of the speaking actor and the absence of the spoken character is as unstable as it is variable. Its depth and complexity are largely derived from what signifying potential is released through an interdependence, which harbors discrepancies, between present bodies and absent sayings. According to Shoshana Felman, the "speaking body is *scandalous*" in that "the relation between language and body" constitutes "a relation consisting at once of incongruity and of inseparability." The unpredictable and partially uncontrollable force of performance therefore derives from "the fact that the act cannot know what it is doing"[23] and that performative power derives precisely from the resulting breach in knowledge. Judith Butler takes up and further develops this concept of the body as "a sign of unknowingness": its "actions are never fully consciously directed or volitional."[24]

There are reasons, at which we have hinted above, to assume that Elizabethan players could be especially marked by a degree of "unknowingness." The plebeian body (or the adolescent one) must have been quite a peculiar "blindspot of speech," acting in excess of what was said, but also one that "signifies in ways that are not reducible to what such a body 'says.'"[25] In other words, images of character conveyed in language may well have had an alien tenor, an "I" not fully accessible to, or not fully assimilated by, the bodily vehicle from which it issued. The gap between the speaking body and the spoken character could therefore be turned into a site of discontinuity harboring a void filled by interaction with spectators. This, then, is the matrix of doubleness, where the representation of inwardness and the delivery of "honest" showmanship can rub shoulders.

Over and beyond the "show" of an "inky cloak," "solemn black," and "forc'd breath," Hamlet's appeal to his own "within which passes show" devalues "actions that a man might play" (*Hamlet*, 1.2.76–84) – for it is only the language of interiority that "can denote me truly" (83). But then the truth "within" remains inseparable from what difference obtains in its relation to a without. The seeming paradox is that the character's "inside" is declared incompatible with the highly performative "outside" that helps define this very "within." In other words, the show of an "antic disposition" and the knowledge of what "action" is required to play the part of the revenging Prince constitute the foil against which interiority can make sense in the first place. However, if relations between expressive knowledge and bodily performance are premised on either the "unknowingness" of the latter or the breach in the former, the scandalous connection is not simply between language and performance. Even more important for the fortunes of a character is the scandal between what thinking and feeling reign within and what the body does without, especially the unknown and unknowing part of it called *Leib*. Volition within cannot be premised on action without, or vice versa. The dynamic element in speech and action of dramatic character is inseparable from what, perhaps, is the most daunting conjunctural complication in "th'attest of eyes and ears" (*Troilus and Cressida*, 5.2.122). Between them, these organs witness to a (dis)continuity between what can be shown and what can be spoken – an ambivalent relationship central to Elizabethan relations of stages and pages. In *Hamlet* the space of such discontinuity is assimilated in two different but perfectly complementary ways. Firstly, the dumb show without language "imports the argument of the play" (3.2.139–40) for eyes to see. Secondly, the play proper – that is, *The Mousetrap* – is primarily for ears, as the prologue's appeal suggests: "We beg your hearing patiently" (3.2.151). Here the signifying medium is not that of silent bodies in dumbshow but, rather, a verbal repertoire of thoughts and symbols. As a previously entered actor in the role of an Elizabethan professional performer assumes the guise of the Player King, he reveals a far-reaching division in the representation of a dramatic character's thoughts and what results from them: "Our wills and fates do so contrary run / That our devices still are overthrown, / Our thoughts are ours, their ends none of our own" (3.2.211–13). The divorce between "wills" and "fates" is clearly depicted as the representation of a dilemma germane to what the play has to say.

Yet what is here represented as "so contrary" in worldly appropriation between "thoughts" and "ends" finds a correlative not only in the statement of the tragedy. It also may be said to adumbrate a fissure in the act of strictly verbal and purely bodily performative practice. In its subtext the player's speech comes close to addressing a fractured relationship of speaking/ thinking and doing. Such utterance is trenchant in its irony, especially when the heavy dose of humanist precept, the cognitive purpose in Hamlet's advice to the players, is kept in mind. As William West has shown, defining the idea of theatre, a humanist such as Theodor Zwinger in his *Theatrum Vitae Humanae* (1565) "connects the actor's practice... with knowledge itself" – a purpose the Prince craves for his own acting and directing, though with "ends" none of his own.[26]

The Player King is especially revealing here as a personator playing a personator with a persona from the play's prehistory. In fact, he could be called a *sujet de l'énonciation* with a threefold coding, especially when we recall that earlier in the scene, mildly protesting at Hamlet's harangue, he does venture first person pronouns both singular and plural: "I hope we have reform'd that indifferently with us, sir" (3.2.36–7). This again confirms considerable volatility in the agency of enunciation. What such redoubled figuration helps underline is the element of facility in the alternate uses of dramatic and metadramatic space in Shakespeare's theatre. The actor shown in the process of acting an actor yields the image of a juxtaposition, not to say a dovetailing, of material practice and dramatic fiction. The semblance of a presentation, especially prepared for court performance, is implanted in, assimilated by, the forceful representation at large. For those who called the stage a stage, it was a small step to show a performance *qua* performance. The First Player thereby serves as artificial person and vehicle of a staggering parallelism between the imaginary and the material.

Our point is that such rapprochement crucially animates the grammar of those different subject positions which intersect in the making of character at the crossroads of stage and page. At this angle of intersection, the production of character is vitally premised on the difference in language between the imagined subject in the statement and the voice behind the utterance. If the two are not the same, the reason is that the former, once it is made, exists as open, unfolding product. As distinct from the imaginary statement which in drama is thoroughly symbolic, the enunciation in the theatre is a discursive process demanding both an imaginary figure speaking and a real-life agent mediating that figure and his/her speeches.

Needless to say, such difference in discursive practice has been profitably studied and applied to a critical understanding of Shakespeare's dramatic characters. In an early essay, adapted from her pioneering *Critical Practice*, but also included in *The Subject of Tragedy*, Catherine Belsey has traced back to the mirror-phase "the splitting between the 'I' which is perceived and the 'I' which does the perceiving."[27] In her examination of the discourse of the subject in Elizabethan tragedy, she notes that the protagonists of Renaissance plays are often marked by a "division" which can profoundly shape their use of the first person in dramatic soliloquies. There "the occurrence of 'I' in speech is predicated on a gap between the subject of the enunciation and the subject of the utterance, the subject who is defined in the speech." This very gap "opens the possibility of glimpsing an identity behind what is said, a silent self anterior to the utterance, 'that within which passes show.'"

Thus it can plausibly be asked "Who is speaking when Hamlet castigates himself for this inaction? A rogue and peasant slave?" Belsey's answer is intriguing, as she comes to the conclusion that ultimately, "Hamlet's subjectivity is itself un-speakable since the subject of the enunciation always exceeds the subject of the utterance. Hamlet cannot be fully present to himself or to the audience in his own speeches and *this* is the heart of his mystery, his interiority." Belsey's insight is illustrated in the soliloquies of such characters as, for instance, Hieronimo, Faustus, Lady Macbeth, Heywood's Wendoll, and Macbeth. In all these, the gap in question "opens the possibility of glimpsing an identity behind what is said, a silent self anterior to the utterance."

However, rather than attempting to fill the gap and engage in character criticism, we propose to take the question further, to the point where it vitally affects material relations of page and stage in Shakespeare's theatre, which of course includes mediating bodies on stages. As dramatic vessels of subjectivity, both dialogic and monologic types of utterance have in common more than the use of the first person pronoun. Over and beyond that, both forms would be orally delivered, by a mediating agency, the voice of a staged body standing right there in flesh and blood. While of all words, the "shifters," as Roman Jakobson termed them (that is, now, then, here, there, etc.), make sense in reference to a grammatically installed subject position only, the latter has an existence in the theatre exceeding both grammar and syntax.

In the early modern theatre, the poetic formation of subjectivity in the shape of a character involves a more complex site of difference still. While the question of this other meaning is predicated on an entirely fictitious *énoncé*, the subject of the enunciation is in itself divided. This subject (that is, the ego delivering the utterance) is marked by relations between the socially inflected work of the two media. In other words, if we seek to reconcile stage-centered and page-oriented approaches to Shakespeare's characters, we must resist any unitary answer to the queries "Who is speaking?" and "Who is the speaker of the enunciation?"

Yet these questions have crucial implications for the present project. Once the subject of the enunciation in the theatre is recognized as a compound, it will not do to allot the statement or *énoncé* to the dramatist's text and to allocate the process of enunciation either to the represented person or to the representing agent, that is, the actor delivering the utterance. Such allocation oversimplifies, even obscures the admixture of fiction and realness in the oral process of enunciation. Nor does this allocation properly acknowledge that the two-leveled speaking in the dramatic utterance brings forth its own blend of an *énoncé* through both the artificial person's temper and the player's tenor, *gestus*, and body. Therefore, the person who is actually speaking is neither the actor nor the character but, rather, the actor-character on the strength of a bifold authority. The symbiotic complexity and the dynamic in the *énonciation* need strongly to be underlined, not only because the traditional critical focus was on character as an *énoncé*. Even more important is the shaping power of the doubly encoded enunciation which, apart from soliloquy, is part of a dialogic situation in both the imaginary world of the play and the playing in a material theatre addressing and responding to spectators.

Thus there is a doubleness drawing on and feeding into the subject of the enunciation. Without losing sight of the *énoncé* as an important representation that, for instance, renders the disjunction of "wills and fates," "thoughts" and their "ends," we can envision the enunciation as a site of mediation. Importantly, this site does not offer the dramatist's text pure; rather, it makes it accessible, publishes it in the process of rehearsing, adapting, and appropriating it to the communicative needs of a given theatre audience. Dictionaries agree that the verb "to enunciate" means to articulate with an audience in mind, preferably to serve their ease and the direction of their understanding. In the Elizabethan theatre, at least as long as it was a players' stage, speaking the text of a role must have been almost as important as writing it. Written words and speaking bodies came together either in an "invasion of the signifier into the real" or, more partially, in "the violent incursion of the real event into a world-picture."[28]

This, then, is one aspect of the performer's impact not simply on the production of character in the theatre but, certainly in Shakespeare's case, on the author's pen – steeped as it was in the ink of theatrical involvement, in the "working-day world" (*As You Like It*, 1.3.12) of the early modern playhouse. In view of the practical and, indeed, profoundly pragmatic job of the playwright, it may seem a little abstruse here to interfere with epistemological scruples strictly proscribed by Richard Rorty and others. Yet the present approach (dubbed "rematerializing Shakespeare" by Bryan Reynolds and William West) cannot very well ignore the differences, in his characters, between the representation of a purely imaginary person and the presence and presentation of a physically real person. To distinguish between these two on no account requires us to deny, as Philip Auslander offers, that "the actor's self is not a grounding presence that precedes the performance."[29] On the contrary, the player as ineffable medium is a mere mouthpiece, his language largely prescribed, his own voice functioning throughout within the bounds of a commercially run institution.

As such, the actor-character is a phenomenon of cultural life and in this function participates, *par excellence*, in the two dimensions of both signification and being. While we (just like the actors themselves) know nothing about what in the preexpressive *réel* remained operative in relaying a given symbolic order, we can at least be fairly certain that there *was* an impact, and that this impact was inseparable from both the signification and socialization of its mediating agents. The mode and form of this mediating were conditioned by both the corpus of its textual message and the voice and body of its dramatic enunciation. In the absence of verifiable evidence, the latter has largely been ignored, with one exception: in relation to the writing of the dramatist. Shakespeare was able to record, even to intercept in the rhythm and syntax of his language, this *gestus*. In Shakespeare's theatre, as Manfred Pfister put it, language itself was turned into a performing instance vitally assisting in the formation of character.[30]

CHAPTER 9

Character: depth, dialogue, page

During Shakespeare's lifetime, a vitalized print culture affected London's theatrical scene greatly. Making broad headway into the still strong culture of orality and storytelling, the "paper-sea" that John Florio noticed with some amazement left lasting marks on dramatic output and form.[1] That print did so even as it drew energy from the regular performances at the purpose-built playhouses testifies to the close relationship the two media shared. While we are used to thinking of stage and page in fairly linear ways – printed sources, for example, leading to theatrical narratives that in turn form the basis for printed dramatic texts – there is good reason, as Barbara Mowat has argued, for understanding the "relationships among performance, playscript, and printed text" as "more fluid, more disturbed, than scholars have tended to imagine and describe them."[2] From such examples as the complicated material life of the Pericles story, 1607, and the testimony of Sir Richard Cholmeley's Players, in 1611, that they had performed only what was available in "the printed booke," to the evidence, in the later Douai Shakespeare manuscripts, of "playtexts that have transmigrated from printed texts annotated for performance into manuscript playbooks,"[3] it is clear that the connections between stage and page were dynamic, and resist univocal pronouncements concerning the directions or duration of agency.

We have already seen how the striking physical ensemble of a clowning, "self-misformed lout" had migrated from the boards of the stage to Joseph Hall's satirical page in 1597's *Virgidemiarum* (see above, pp. 111–12). There Hall's poem, in representing the boisterous clown in all his indecorum, convincingly imagines a stage in its social environment; readers follow the "applauding audience" responding to a "goodly hotch-potch" where "vile russetings / Are matched with monarchs and with mighty kings." Yet if in this instance the popularity of a professional comedian leads Hall to portray the scene of a playing environment within his satire, the theatre would repay the favor by borrowing back from the printed page a host of cues and materials for its representations of artificial persons. In fact, some of the same cultural formations that led to the aggressive depictions of the personal within the kinds of writing that Hall's satire represents also sponsored an enlargement of dramatic character, often doing so not in opposition to but through the medium of print itself. This dialogical engagement of the newly energized domain of the printed page with the traditions of performance led, in the later 1590s and early 1600s, to an unprecedented depth of dramatic character.

If our use of the term "page" here may initially seem too forward-looking in its interest in the rapidly expanding domain of print during the late Elizabethan era, the influence of print on Shakespeare's dramatic practice – and on characterization in particular – was too strong to be ignored. At the same time, as William B. Worthen has demonstrated, all writing for the theatre in this period both enjoyed a "multiple agency" and possessed a "fungibility"; the latter asks us to see "writing changing and being changed by the circumstances of its use."[4] So while the following remarks most frequently refer to the changing status of the printed page and its effect on characterization, they nonetheless seek to convey the central and continuing influence on theatrical culture of other forms of written material – including the very roles from which players learned their parts. What will become apparent in the paragraphs that follow is that dramatic writing's "fungibility" worked two ways. That is, if the commercial playhouses constituted, as Worthen claims, "a business that insistently subjects writing to the pressure of orality," they were also a site where the pressures of writing – and, significantly, of print – made themselves felt upon the construction and performance of character.

This dialogical relationship between the media doubled a poetics of "reflection" and interaction relating to the production of character in the plays. Such engagement works not simply among the *dramatis personae* but also between the self and the social, the "I" and the other. Indeed, the conversations not only on stage but off – among, for instance, actor's voice, author's pen, and the printed pages of early modern England – were multiple and complex. It will be important to note, therefore, that by "dialogue" here we mean, in addition to back-and-forth vocalization on the stage, a full spectrum of linguistic representations of the self as it relates to the other and to society generally. As V. N. Vološinov maintained, dialogue "inevitably orients itself with respect to previous performances in the same sphere . . . it responds to something, objects to something, affirms something, anticipates possible responses and objections, seeks support, and so on."[5] In Shakespeare's plays such "dialogism," as Mikhail Bakhtin calls it, has an "internal" dimension inhabited by his "deep" characters. This "internal dialogism" is evocatively defined as "another's speech in another's language"; its dynamic, not to say dramatic, quality appears especially striking in a theatre prepared to use as well as abuse "the distance" between presence and absence, between socially high and culturally low. This results in what Bakhtin continues to call "heteroglossia" – that is, "a special type of double-voiced discourse." The latter is close to a dramatically fashioned, internalized mode of contrariety wherein, in wordplay or aside, an "alien utterance begins to sound like a socially alien language."[6]

Among such languages in the theatrical industry of early modern England we could number not only the diction of the common player in the new commercial playhouses but also the increasingly powerful rhetoric of the printed page. While our inquiry in this chapter can only touch upon the shapes of contemporary print culture, highlighting some of the more remarkable developments affecting dramatic composition during the 1590s and early 1600s, an awareness of the variety of these changes – and how they helped shape and augment the construction of artificial persons – may place us in a better position to comprehend the intensively social qualities of dramatic character on stages and pages alike.

Playwrights of the 1590s were, like authors in every other mode and genre, affected by the "structural transformation of print" in the late Elizabethan era, a veritable revolution in ways in which writer and readers related to each other, to the subjects of literary texts, and to print itself.[7] Fueled in part by unlicensed sallies of the Marprelate Controversy during the late 1580s and early 1590s, and in part by a younger generation of authors increasingly willing to put others' bodies and identities on the printed page, this pervasive transformation of the field of representation drew upon even as it affected the celebrity of authors, characters, and actors. Involving, variously, the erotic, satirical, and political handling of previously unmentioned (and, in many instances, unmentionable) persons and identities, this climate of "embodied writing" opened paths, for Shakespeare, into the deeper representation of dramatic characters. Cresting, though not ending, with the Bishop's Ban of June 1599 – a ban which gathered, under its disapproving gaze, not only erotic and satirical works but politically topical ones as well – this era of newly licentious writing led to the radical empowerment of authorial voices and a concomitant increase in the force and depth of their characterological constructs.

Indeed, at the same time that Shakespeare's name emerges on the title pages of his published works – a material testament to his growing prominence – his characters also begin to attain new levels of status within and even outside the playwright's dramatic fictions. As Lukas Erne points out, examining the "suddenness and the frequency with which Shakespeare's name appears on the title pages of printed playbooks from 1598 to 1600," we are justified in saying that "'Shakespeare,' author of dramatic texts, was born in the space of two or three years at the end of the sixteenth century."[8] In this new climate of print celebrity, the dramatist himself became a figure in others' discourses. One could compare Gullio's laud of the playwright in *The Return from Parnassus, Part I* – "O sweet Mr. Shakespeare, I'll have his picture in my study at the court" – with the Manningham jest concerning the night "William the Conqueror was before Rich[ard] the 3."[9] Both these instances come from the final years of Elizabeth's reign, and both record the remarkable notoriety of a talented theatre professional. The Manningham anecdote foregrounds, in addition, a nexus of playwright, players, and parts as they connect the Globe with an ardent admirer of its fare.

By the late 1590s, print culture in London was showing, in addition to the rise of deeply "embodied" writing and a new climate of celebrity as related to authors, characters, and actors, a new emphasis on more personal modes of expression in literature. We can see this emphasis in, for instance, the development of the essayistic voice through such publications as Montaigne's *Essays*. Published in English in 1603, Montaigne's energetically reflective pieces stood among those of Bacon and Cornwallis in their advancement of individualized meditations. This newly enlarged field of personal expressivity also appeared in the cult of "wit" in London as represented in the publications of Nicholas Ling. In addition to publishing the works of authors such as Nashe, Guilpin, and Munday, for instance, Ling would bring out such titles as *Politeuphuia: Wit's Commonwealth* (1598), *Palladis Tamia: Wit's Treasury* (1598), and *Kemp's Nine Days' Wonder* (1600). This last, as we have seen, was an attempted solidification in print of the witty genius of one of the playhouse's most notorious performers.[10] One could also note, during the 1590s, signal changes in the genre of character-writing. The publication of Theophrastus's *Characteres ethici* in Lyons in 1592, for instance, coincided with, even as it may have helped spur, the subsequent popularity of "charactery" in London's poetic circles. As its most recent chronicler attests, "by 1606 . . . the satiric character sketch was in full transition and pointing toward charactery-writing of the Overburian kind."[11]

Hand in hand with his involvement in this revolution in print culture came Shakespeare's renewed interest in a specific volume that bore particular relevance for characterization within dramatic tragedy. Here we refer to Sir Thomas North's translation of Plutarch's *Lives* (1579-). Recent commentators have seen, in Shakespeare's use of Plutarch for *Julius Caesar*, a kind of turning point in the playwright's relation to character. In an essay entitled "Shakespeare, Crossing the Rubicon," for instance, Cynthia Marshall argues that what we have in Shakespeare's transformation of Plutarch's stories "is the establishment of our culture's prevailing model of character as one that is at once intensely performative and putatively interiorized."[12] As her title suggests, Marshall sees Shakespeare's return to this resonant resource (a book he had already drawn on for such plays as *Titus Andronicus* and *A Midsummer Night's Dream*) as a watershed moment in the dramatist's career, one which "mark[ed] off the richly inventive but largely plot-driven plays of the 1590s from the deeply characterological dramas that follow."[13]

Whatever specific effect North's translation of Plutarch's *Lives* may have had on the development of Shakespeare's patterns of characterization, it is clear that many of his major characters benefited from the formal experimentation that Shakespeare had conducted throughout the 1590s. This experimentation, unfolding in the primary linguistic media of his dramas, resulted in the radical linguistic flexibility and self-consciousness of characters at the turn of the century and later. During the last decade of Elizabeth's reign, and drawing on such published prose fictions as Lyly's *Euphues* and Lodge's *Rosalind*, Shakespeare steadily increased the amount of prose in his dramas, a move which famously culminated in the Falstaff plays of the late 1590s.[14] Although this trend remains a familiar part of Shakespeare's formal development, it left an important trace on his habits of characterization that, because it is rarely mentioned, bears emphasis here: all Shakespeare's major characters after the 1590s are adept, even agile, in prose as well as verse. Prince Henry's famous boast of his proficiency – "I am so good a proficient in one quarter of an hour, that I can drink with any tinker in his own language during my life" (*1 Henry IV*, 2.4.17–20) – is not only a brag concerning slang and dialect, but also a representation in prose of Shakespeare's own mastery of a linguistic medium that found its major definition over and against verse, and in and through print.

More than a bilingualism, being "so good a proficient" in these two tongues would serve – with its own communication between these different modes and those realms of experience they represented – as a powerful basis for what we call "deep" characterization. Thus do Rosalind, Brutus, and Hamlet all display a mastery of these two media, with characters increasingly able to switch between them for dramatic and psychological effect. This mastery, common to Shakespeare's primary characters after 1600, is often taken for granted. Yet, no less than the stunning level of linguistic self-consciousness it implies, the discursive proficiency revealed in such alternation would be part of that chameleon-like flexibility we associate with actorly, "deep" characterization on the early modern stage.

From larger transformations within the field of print culture to specific genres, texts, and even representational media, the changefulness of the page during Shakespeare's career left undeniable marks upon his patterns of characterization. Clearly, with a phenomenon as complex as that of characterization, no single resource, influence, or event can be thought of as primary. At the same time, however, the role of the page had an importance to characterization never fully addressed in criticism.

Within the body of Shakespeare's plays, dialogical relationships frequently appeared in, even as they revealed the strength of, written and printed material pertaining to character. In his witty "Words, words, words" exchange with Polonius, for example, Hamlet advances an uncomfortably close approximation of the aging counselor with whom he speaks. The Prince does so by describing a satirical portrait that may appear in a book he is holding (*Hamlet*, 2.2.192, 191–204). It is to our point that this textual supplement to their dialogue becomes a contested agent in their discourse. For the Prince initially and purposely mistakes Polonius's query – "What is the matter, my lord?" – when he replies, "Between who?," pretending that "matter" has been meant agonistically, as "cause for a quarrel" (the *Riverside* gloss), rather than, as the counselor clarifies it, "the matter that you read" (195). This answer is indeed "pregnant" (209): no less than the typological summary that follows, Hamlet's quibble shows how Shakespeare often uses the page to establish that very "between" in and from which character is constructed, extended, and modified. The Q1 version of the "To be or not to be" sequence nods toward this tendency in having both Hamlet and Ophelia enter with books in their hands. If, as we have seen in the previous chapter, deep character can be detected in the echoing enunciations of leading players, and in those compelling figurations of the "inwardness *topos*" that Katherine Eisaman Maus and others have traced (figurations bolstered, as we have seen, by thick uses of the personal pronoun, soliloquies, illeism, and other forms of resonant utterance), it also comes via "matter... Between" various figures.[15] Such matter contributes to these figures' identities via the dialogical agon it encloses.

Textual "matter" of Hamlet's sort appears, for instance, at uncannily signal moments in Shakespeare's elaboration of character, from the tavern-bill itemization of what has gone into Falstaff and the latter's duplicate, disorienting *billets-doux* for Mistress Ford and Mistress Page, to Malvolio's similarly perplexing encounter with a counterfeit document and Posthumus's resonant gloss on Jupiter's tablet. Satire, reckoning, epistle, note, tablet: whether written, printed, or engraved, each of these "pages" stands in for, as *mise-en-abyme*, the textual foundations of Shakespearean character. These pages also work both to solidify and to problematize these very foundations by acknowledging the incomplete, externally determined, and dialogical nature of the dramatic self.

We can glimpse the productive tension of such "matter . . . Between" in characters' responses to these potently scripting pages:

O monstrous! but one half-penny-worth of bread to this intolerable deal of sack. (Prince Hal, *1 Henry IV*, 2.4.540–1)

. . . it makes me almost ready to wrangle with mine own honesty. I'll entertain myself like one that I am not acquainted withal . . . . (Mrs. Page, *The Merry Wives of Windsor*, 2.1.84–6)

'M.O.A.I. doth sway my life.' (Malvolio, *Twelfth Night*, 2.5.110)

The action of my life is like it. (Posthumus, *Cymbeline*, 5.4.149)

Each of these observations – uttered at moments of studied reflection in the plays – testifies to the pivotal role the page has in deepening the dynamic of character. Hal winks at the sleeping Falstaff's relation to the popular subgenre of "humours" comedy, implying, that is, that the latter is compounded entirely of what he craves and consumes. Mistress Page, Malvolio, and Posthumus equally recognize the constitutive nature of the texts they hold in their hands, texts which, through their dialogical voicing, alternately confound and confirm the identities they believe themselves to own. All these instances thereby give the lie to Peto's literalistic dismissal of what Falstaff has in his pockets: "Nothing but papers, my lord" (2.4.533).

Indeed, "pages" (a term under which we could loosely gather all the materials in question here) possess a startling ability to foreground issues of dialogical characterization in Shakespeare's plays. Significantly, the Prince's movement toward interpretation – "Let's see what they be" (*1 Henry IV*, 2.4.534) – seems to beg for a divided mode of performance when he continues, "Read them." In the midst of the laughter that follows, it is easy to forget that the parodic blazon that one hears recited – "*Item*, a capon . . . 2s. 2d" – depends for its humorous effect on a complex stage geometry that involves more than the already sizable group of Hal, Peto, a passively inactive Falstaff, and the audience (who enjoy the privilege of a discrepant awareness over the dissipated knight). For submerged within the imagined social network represented in this reckoning is also the hand responsible for penning the anonymous papers that chronicle the material ingredients of our fat and slumbering clown, as well as the institutional economy which that hand acts for. This tavern bill, then, is much more than "nothing," for it testifies to what has gone into Falstaff, both inside and outside the boundaries of the playworld proper.

For their part, these pages remain at one and the same time a representation of Falstaff's social existence (what he has committed himself to and consumed within the tavern world) and a clever token of the act of dramatic composition itself (the craft by which Falstaff has been constructed as an artificial person). If they foreground the function of the page within the economy of character on the Shakespearean stage, that is, these "papers" also open up vistas on the metadramatic thrust of dramatic composition in the plays. Structurally, this reckoning summarizes Falstaff's essence and history. It also hints at the complexity of relations among writing, performance, and characterization on the early modern stage. To cite it in full:

Item, a capon	..... 2s. 2d.
Item, sauce	...... 4d.
Item, sack, two gallons	.... 5s. 8d.
Item, anchoves and sack after supper	. 2s. 6d.
Item, bread	..... ob.

Listening closely to this list, we hear at least two "voices" behind its pendulum-like alternation between units (both generic – "*Item*" – and specific – "a capon") and their prices ("2s. 2d"). Indeed, the bill encodes a kind of double representation. Firstly, it features Falstaff's own "matter," as seen both from the outside – the material components of the character's gross physical being – and from the inside – his limited worldview, in which things are what they cost. Secondly, in recording with its back-and-forth cadence what has been bespoke by the great comedian ("sauce") and the price uttered for it by the provider ("4d"), it gives us – like an Epicurean parody of the listing tendencies of chronicle history – a record of Falstaff's lived existence in the tavern. Yet to acknowledge that we are hearing what are, in effect, lines of the comedic character's own dialogue recited over his snoring body is to recognize more than a play of personal and local history within a national history play, however powerfully this mixture figures into *1 Henry IV*. For to comprehend the dialogical structure of these "papers" and the abundantly constitutive nature of the content they convey is to perceive the form of the actor's immediate access to the Shakespearean play: the role.

It is perhaps more than a coincidence that another sleeping comedian (and perhaps one played by the same actor who performed Falstaff) awakes to invoke the dialogical nature of actors' roles in *A Midsummer Night's Dream*: "When my cue comes, call me, and I will answer. My next is, 'Most fair Pyramus'" (*A Midsummer Night's Dream*, 4.1.200–2). From their very first gathering, the Mechanicals have shown us the importance of the page to Elizabethan characterization by proceeding from mention of "scrip" (1.2.3) and "scroll" (15) – both identified, almost officiously, by Bottom – to the "parts" that Quince distributes just before they disband. As Snug has asked, "Have you the lion's part written? Pray you, if it be, give it me, for I am slow of study" (66–7). Like most Elizabethan actors, Bottom has learned his lines for Pyramus from the "side" or "role" (sometimes called a "scroll") copied out from the completed script. And like that of Falstaff, Bottom's part depends on and responds to the timely enunciations of fellow actors, enunciations that were of necessity sutured into the copied-out lines for each actor. The situated utterances of Elizabethan players – at one and the same time the product of writing and the potentially thick vocalizations of the performing agent – pointedly oriented themselves, in Vološinov's words, "with respect to previous performances in the same sphere."

Within the context of Shakespeare's theatre, then, the word "role" always possesses a double sense which includes the literal part or "side" – the strips of paper constituting the words an actor is to deliver on stage – in addition to the more familiar (because in every way less concrete) sense of what actors inhabit and convey during performance. As the *OED* reminds us, the term "role" derives from the French *rôle*, "in the same sense, properly the 'roll' containing an actor's part." To look at the part of Orlando from Robert Greene's *Orlando Furioso* is to recognize in this surviving group of papers the physical basis for an Elizabethan performance.[16] What this University Wit "set down for" an actor became a slender page in an artisanal economy that included not only the humanist-trained playwright and journeyman actor but also the scribe responsible for copying (and, perhaps, assembling) the "role" itself. Whether called parts, sides, or roles, these papers were "matter . . . Between" that – as Snug notes – remained crucial pieces of writing, informing the performance of character in the early modern theatre.

Such individualized pages encoded not only the economy of agents and agencies that influenced and participated in the construction of the role before performance, but also the intensively dialogical nature of Elizabethan acting. Each role would feature the lines an actor was to speak in performance, as well as cues connecting the utterance with its preceding one.

Inscribed on these pages, then, was a truncated version of the "colloquy of large scale" that transpired upon the early modern stage: each speech would be prefaced with the sentence, line, or phrase ending the utterance just before. As such, the individual roles saw speech as a kind of continuous thread running through the tapestry of the performance.

Yet it is worth stressing that, however much it stitched together dramatic speech, the abbreviated conversation represented on the individual strips of paper cannot have been the limit of the dialogue taken as implied or necessary for the character at hand. In an analysis of Edward Alleyn's part for Orlando, for example, David Bradley remarks on the paucity of "positional markings and scribbled annotations" in the actor's role. Observing that "there is no cue at all for Orlando's disguised, silent entry into the final scene about thirty-seven lines after it begins," the critic notes, "in order to make a correct entrance here, he must clearly have been able to *hear* the dialogue and to follow its drift." Because this surviving role both records the dialogical cues for Orlando's speech and omits many stage directions, Bradley concludes that the early modern playhouse probably "worked by well-understood convention and the intelligent co-operation of the actors with the implications of the spoken word."[17] Thus the cue provided on the scroll marks the site on which the signs of scriptural direction are transformed into acts of oral utterance.

Scripted within the actor's physical role was thus the practice of what James Siemon has called "listening around" – the necessary attention to others' voices, to voices within those voices, and to the full range of textures, cues, and gaps that inform dialogue within any communicative situation.[18] Bradley's analysis of the pages surviving for Alleyn's Orlando confirms that the Elizabethan actor's role – and by extension, character itself – was about more than enunciation. As the basis for the performance of an artificial person, the role encodes not only others' voices, but a host of practices and performative details without which the script cannot efficiently function in the theatre. Like Vološinov's printed text, the manuscript part necessarily and alternately "responds to something, objects to something, affirms something, anticipates possible responses and objections, seeks support, and so on." If the composed role speaks, in short, to the overdetermination of putative impulses behind every character, it also contains a dense range of communicative cues and exchanges that confirm a character's thoroughly social basis.

As the writer of some of his theatre's finest roles, Shakespeare was in a privileged position to understand playhouse "convention" as well as to anticipate, secure, and benefit from "the intelligent co-operation of the

actors with the implications of the spoken word." The characterological
richness of his plays – evident in the vehicles of his individual roles –
may be more explicable when one takes into account Shakespeare's
exceptional, and exceptionally multifaceted, relation to the business of
playing. Shakespeare was the only individual in early modern England
simultaneously to act in, write for, and enjoy the profits of both a
shareholder and payee from productions in the commercial playing
spaces of his era. It is not too much to suggest that, at least in part
because these relations and activities were so operative in the playwright's theatrical career, they were likely to appear in all their variety
within the individual roles he wrote for himself and his fellow actors. As
one can see in the counterfeit letter discovered and read by Malvolio, in
the written statement that Edmund pretends to have been written by
Edgar, as well as in Falstaff's "papers," performed pages can reveal an
almost dizzying proliferation of social aspects and linkages. Likewise,
Elizabethan roles exhibit a plenitude of relations from within the theatrical as well as the scriptural economy of early modern London. Peto's
commanded recitation of this reckoning is a performance which, in
ventriloquizing others' voices, touches upon the playwright's own richly
multivalent position in the institution of playing. We should be clear
here in resisting the ascription of the contours of characterization within
Shakespeare's plays solely to his biography. Yet we must insist on
recognizing how fully immersed he was – *as* playwright, actor, shareholder,
and author of printed books – within a dense network of theatrical activity
that featured, at its center, the conveyance of artificial persons through
written fictions orally delivered by actors.

As we have noted, Shakespeare puts an extreme form of this network's
energy in the service of characterization by infusing moments of personation with it. Many of Shakespeare's central characters seem to become
characters, in fact, not through dialogue itself but rather via the strongest
declarations of presence that the traditions of personation afforded. We
have an example of this declarative mode in Marlowe's "And let them know
that I am Machevil" (Pro. 7) prior to *The Jew of Malta*. However isolated
and rhetorically complete such an utterance may seem, it possesses what we
would call an internal dialogue, one conducted between the actor and his
role. For here the actor delivering the prologue surely displays, in his
performance of the role, some awareness of its artificial nature – multiply
aligned as it is, not only through its function as formal, presenting prologue,
but also through the dramatic tradition of Vice comedy and the full freight
of Machiavelli's caricatured reputation.

In just such a reverberating "I am" Shakespeare appears to have seen a nexus where two modes of dramatic figuration – one conventional and one emergent – stood in interpenetrating relation. From this nexus an explicit sense of self (the repeated "I" we have heard) emerges. Such selfhood is promoted and even mobilized in the actor-characters who retain a dialogical awareness of various performant functions, an awareness of not only the world in the play but also their own playing on a commercial scaffold. This awareness includes consciousness of their presence as real-life agents counterfeiting artificial persons. Here we could note Warwick's query:

> Why stand we like soft-hearted women here,
> Wailing our losses, whiles the foe doth rage,
> And look upon, as if the tragedy
> Were play'd in jest by counterfeiting actors? (*3 Henry VI*, 2.3.25–8)

Such highly charged theatrical imagery becomes a potent image in the actor's mouth. But in it we may well hear an awareness, too, of the actor's histrionic self-understanding, an awareness of what it means to play – whether "in jest" or in earnest.

Alongside such actorly self-understanding, we encounter the player's definition of passive inactivity likened to that of an emotionally responsive audience of "soft-hearted women" who not only "stand" and bemoan but "look upon . . . / . . . counterfeiting actors." In these marvellously compressed four lines, Shakespeare exposes us to Warwick the character through and only through the voice and body of the personating actor, an actor whose onstage experience resounds in the image of the gathered players (those who act the roles of Warwick, Edward, Clarence, and Richard) understood as opposite-gendered audience members beholding four such "counterfeiting actors." In composing such a theatrical speech, Shakespeare is, if not its "only begetter," undeniably the controlling intelligence behind its many glinting facets. But what remains equally apparent is that the speech itself depends on an intelligence, communicated dialogically, of the multiple varieties of theatrical labor and experience. This intelligence comprehends the very construction of a role as well as the actor's own sense, within and behind that role, of what it means to be a physical body "counterfeiting" an action in the presence, and with the cooperation, of an audience that has an equal potential to act and even shape the performative event.

While we shall return to the social and economic dynamic informing Shakespearean characterization, let us here pursue further the point where the interaction of characters in and through dialogue objectifies, and is indebted to, that other utterance, which takes place in the theatre. This question addresses a crucial nexus, where the literary composition of imaginary selves – that is, "identity construction in its fictional interactions" (William Dodd's phrase) – confronts and is intercepted by live actors involved in a communication situation which they visibly, physically realize and materialize.[19] The conjuncture in question is of exceptional interest because two different types of situated utterances, one imaginary, the other material, come together to shape a "scandalous" relationship of a sort: one marked by textual invention, the other by bodies actually speaking, actually conversing through a persona. The *gestus* of material bodies is, again, in excess of what the dramatic text says, while that text in its own turn exceeds any one embodiment of it offered on stage.

Such areas of interpellation between the characterization of a strictly enclosed, scroll-inscribed role and the orally delivered actor's performative act deserve to be studied more closely. Let us begin by looking at how, in *Troilus and Cressida*, Ulysses, in pursuing his well-devised strategy of "strangeness" and "pride" toward Achilles, is made to remark, "That no man is the lord of any thing, / Though in and of him there be much consisting, / Till he communicate his parts to others" (*Troilus and Cressida*, 3.3.115–17). We will set aside here the potential pun on "parts" that inhabits the passage, though it seems plausible to suppose that this pun was active – perhaps undeniably so – not only to the playwright himself but to any and all connected with the repertorial system of Elizabethan playing. The weight of the passage, over and beyond the immediate scheme of the Greek general, is underlined by Ulysses himself in his earlier reference to that "strange fellow" who

> Writes me that man, how dearly ever parted,
> How much in having, or without or in,
> Cannot make boast to have that which he hath,
> Nor feels not what he owes, but by reflection;
> As when his virtues, aiming upon others,
> Heat them, and they retort that heat again
> To the first giver. (3.3.96–102)

At the center of these utterances we see a discourse that represents character as processed, even as brought forth, by a certain *gestus* of communication. The main direction of the argument is that represented character and the discursive relations of that "artificial person" are interconnected, and that it is through an awareness of this interconnection that each must help define the other. True enough, in this passage discourse and identity do not appear to preclude one another. The imaginary subject in this text (the third person singular who "feels" and/or "owes") is assumed to bring forth signs and meanings (he/she has "that which he hath") of his/her own self. But whatever figuration of self or character obtains, it draws its authority not from positing an autonomous unified subject but, on the contrary, from relations of the individual as implicated in a communicative and performative mode of exchange and "reflection."

Thus the envisioned pattern of characterization is not one of self-sustained inherence: Shakespeare's dramatic "character" is a figuration that defies an intrinsic type of closure, even when continuity between what represents and what is represented strongly predominates. What appears is how something "owe[d]," some "parts," constitute themselves "but by reflection." "Reflection" here signifies the returning back of that which is projected. Dramatic character comes to be representable precisely at the point of intersection between the representation of these "parts" and the performative act of their communication. But since this text concerns character as well as characterization, the image of subjectivity is here redefined as object as well as agent of representations. Characters "having, or without or in," a stake in the performance of their own selves are capable, communicatively, of shining "upon others."

This language of characterization thrives on the performative energy of communication within/without the world of the play. As here dramatized, the context is three-dimensional; it is one in which (1) an artificial person is substantially allowed "to have that which he hath," but in which such notion of self-possessed "parts," of property and identity, is (2) both borne out and made relative "by reflection." Even more puzzling, such "reflection," as we shall see, does not so much involve a given point of reference for what, characteristically, is represented; on the contrary, "reflection" seems to implicate (3) communicative exchange as an appropriate category of "consistency" itself. In other words, whatever identity can be derived from "much consisting" "in and of" such represented figures presupposes a contingent process of performance and exchange with others who in their own turn "Heat," enhance and return the "first giver['s]" parts.[20]

No matter how consistent in themselves, the attributes of character are caught up in the circumstances and relations of cultural productions, exchange, and reception. They are caught up in, but not entirely lost to, those coordinates of political power within which Elizabethan representations could not but position themselves. There was, as Louis Montrose has noted acutely, "a mode of contestation at work within the Elizabethan subject's very gesture of submission to the official fictions. We might call this mode *appropriative*, for it does not repudiate the given fictions of power but rather works within and through them . . . as the fictions of the speaking or writing subject."[21] Playing in general and characterization in particular was unthinkable without an appropriative energy that richly informed performative action on a verbal and gestural level.

As we have argued, whatever fascination continues to be derived from the sparkling histrionic energy in the presumed link between character and action does not – once it is relocated in modern production – have to be sacrificed in favor of any nonrepresentable difference between saying and showing (to recall Wittgenstein's distinction, when it is so relevant to the developing relations between poetic representation and theatrical performance).[22] Thus the specter of romantic ideas of character, that is, the notion "that the calamities and catastrophe follow inevitably from the deeds of men, and that the main source of these deeds is character"[23] may definitely be laid to rest. Henceforth, the representation of Shakespeare's characters can be reopened beyond any positioning of the particularity of self and the generality of society. As the passage from *Troilus and Cressida* suggests, there is not necessarily a sense of opposition between them when consistency (and "identity") in a fiction are referred to the instability of "reflection" as part of the signifying (and socializing) potential of the dramatic uses of language.

To illustrate such an approach to Shakespeare's dramatic representations of character, we will suggest some ways in which the inscribed terms of characterization may be read in their historical context. There is, to begin with, very little doubt that the language of "reflection" as well as that of "consisting" and "having, or without or in" needs to be reassociated with late sixteenth-century faculty psychology,[24] and with the *sententia* tradition such as that of the *Nosce Teipsum* topos, reaching from Plato's Alcibiades and Cicero to Montaigne and, finally, John Davies.[25] Although less apparent in the present text, contemporary religious and philosophical concepts such as "*una*" or "oneness," according to which the "little brief authority" of "man, proud man" tended to be viewed in his "glassy essence" (*Measure for Measure*, 2.2.117–20), have relevance as well.[26]

The passage quoted appears particularly indebted to the faculty psychology of Shakespeare's day – as is, even more so, Achilles's reply with his reference to "the eye itself, / That most pure spirit of sense" (*Troilus and Cressida*, 3.3.105–6) together with the whole terminology of "reflection" (99) and "speculation" (109). At the same time, the language of Elizabethan psychology is here used metaphorically, as a poetic vehicle for indirectness and differentiation achieved not at all against but rather through the imagery of contemporary psychological thought. For to say that "man . . . / Cannot make boast to have that which he hath, / Nor feels not what he owes, but by reflection" is to suffuse a traditional topos with a vision of the social and communicative dimension that is part of a character's dramatic meaning. The word "reflection" should be read in the context of the preceding statement, "That no man is the lord of any thing, . . . / Till he communicate his parts to others." Note the use of the verb "communicate" which here, we would suggest, has a complex meaning, drawing at least partly on the traditional sense of what the *OED* defines as "To give to another as a partaker, to give a share of, impart." It is worth noting that Shakespeare uses this traditional sense, though intransitively, in *The Comedy of Errors*: "Thou art an elm, my husband, I a vine, / Whose weakness, married to thy stronger state, / Makes me with thy strength to communicate" (2.2.174–6).

At the same time, and this is the seeming paradox in question, Shakespeare links the traditional concept of "communication" with a distinctively modern idea of individuality as an act of worldly (though not necessarily material) appropriation. According to this, man potentially can feel "what he owes," that is, what he or she possesses. As it appears, one can be "lord of any thing," one can at least claim "to have that which he hath." The link between the traditional and the individualizing perspectives on artificial persons in the drama may still be metaphorically drawn from Elizabethan faculty psychology. Even so, the tension involved between the two reflects an awareness (no longer psychological) of a new type of contradiction. The image of the individual, while viewed as part of socio-cultural and discursive relations, is also and at the same time conceived as more stringently apart from these. For whereas the traditional content of "communication" and "reflection" stipulates a view of humans in their relatedness and their relationships, the other (opposing) assumption seems to grant at least the possibility for a person "to have that which he hath"; in other words, to possess and control himself/herself alone, in terms of some potential autonomy or identity.

In Shakespeare's discursive practice these two differing perspectives on subjectivity – one as socially shared, the other as personally autonomous – are quite contradictory but also profoundly interrelated. In fact, the degree of a character's relatedness or "reflection," the extent to which he can "communicate his parts to others" is viewed as a measure of his identity. To be "lord of any thing" *presupposes* the communication of one's parts to others. The awareness of "what he owes" is gained "but by reflection" – "reflection" in the sense that a character's qualities, when "aiming upon others, / Heat them, and they retort that heat again / To the first giver." Self-possession through the appropriation of one's "belongings" presupposes discursive practice. For a dramatic person to be "author of himself"

(*Coriolanus*, 5.3.36) is impossible without verbally and through performance relating himself to others. In other words, the fiction of dramatic identity and the poetic mode of the appropriation of socio-linguistic relations coalesce.

This is the barest of generalizations which, in an approach to Shakespeare's plays, can be useful only to the extent that differentiations are made between the various registers (typifying or particularizing) of representation. But whatever degree of generality or individuality is represented, the basic formula as summarized here appears to apply to most levels of characterization. As Thomas F. van Laan has shown in an analysis of *The Comedy of Errors*, "all the characters are properly iden-tified ... only in terms of their links with one another, that is as husbands, wives, fathers, sons, mothers, masters, servants." But if this is so, then "a focus on character reveals ... that identity consists of the various functions a character acquires through participating in a number of social relationships."[27] On that level the "overwhelming importance of external relationships in the composition of identity"[28] in an early comedy must obviously be differentiated from a more highly specified representation of subjectivity through, say, a nexus in performance of several layers of role-playing.

Only when these two points of reference – the self and the social – are seen as entering into a dynamic and unpredictable kind of discursive relationship can the most original and far-reaching dimension in Shakespeare's conception of character – the dimension of growth and change – be adequately under-stood. This is not the place to discuss the practical amount of change and/or development that some of his characters are subject to. But from within the premises of Shakespeare's representation itself it seems possible to say that the very process of a character's "reflection" can contribute to the fiction of his dramatic particularity. If "reflection" in the context of theatrical repre-sentation is comprehended as embracing both verbal and nonverbal modes of communicating with and to others, if indeed "reflection" is based on the giving and receiving of that "heat" (a metaphor transgressing purely rational exchange), then the representation of dramatic subjectivity through the appropriation of relationships must be a process in time and of the times. In the words of the Duke speaking to Angelo:

> There is a kind of character in thy life,
> That to th' observer doth thy history
> Fully unfold. Thyself and thy belongings
> Are not thine own so proper as to waste
> Thyself upon thy virtues, they on thee. (*Measure for Measure*, 1.1.27–31)

A "kind of character" in Angelo's life unfolds his "history." If "character" takes our attention to the inscribed letter upon a page, the word "history," in connection with an artificial person's life, should come as no surprise either: in *2 Henry IV* Shakespeare had related the individual's fate and "progress" (3.1.54) to the "revolution of the times" (46) and "the main chance of things" (83) by envisioning those many "changes" (52) and "necessities" which the individual is faced with. "Are these things then necessities? / Then let us meet them like necessities" (92–3) is King Henry's response to Warwick's words "There is a history in all men's lives" (80) – a history by which "the hatch and brood of time" (86) can be assumed to be a process of great personal consequence to the individual.

Thus a person's "history," like Angelo's, is related to and indeed can be unfolded by "a kind of character." Such "character," even when it is like an engraving on the image of a person, is nothing external. In fact, it is inseparable from what the Duke calls "Thyself and thy belongings." "Belongings," in the language of the Duke, must not be read in the feudal sense, as referring to properties. For it was the tendency of the early modern playhouse to insist on the performative, social basis of things, identities, and processes. Even Falstaff's "items," we will recall, needed to be activated through a performed "recital" before they could be acknowledged as owned. Thus does the editor of the Arden edition of the play cite the *OED* for "belongings" here as "qualities pertaining to" and notes that the dictionary gives this as the only use of the word as substantive before the nineteenth century. This parallels, and almost astonishingly so, the highly personalized use of "lord" in the phrase "to be lord of any thing," in the sense that a character "without or in" can be said "to have that which he hath." We could adduce, in support here, Sonnet 94's "lords and owners of their faces" (l. 7). To recognize a person's belongings, that is to say his qualities, is one way of acknowledging his particularity – what he or she is. In the words of Mercutio, "Now art thou sociable, now art thou Romeo; now art thou what thou art, by art as well as by nature" (*Romeo and Juliet*, 2.4.89–91).

Here, again, we have a character referring to personal qualities as individually significant precisely because they are socially achieved or reflected. But this social dimension of personality is unthinkable in a world where "Time" is denied "his customary rights" and where the element of change is not made part of "a continuing order with expectations and rewards."[29] To obstruct the flow of time, to upset this "unknown order" (Philip Sidney) by refusing to allow, even in "the revolution of the times," the sequence of the years, the generations, and the bearers of the office is to destroy identity:

take from Time
His charters and his customary rights;
Let not to-morrow then ensue to-day;
Be not thyself; (*Richard II*, 2.1.195–8)

It is through discursive practice itself that "Time" is conveyed into whatever
movement constitutes the new representational quality in characterization.
Such representation involves an unfixed order of signs whose very instability
provides a source of controlled energy for both the correlation of signifier
and signified and for the space of variation in particularizing identity. Hence
it is impossible for a man as an individual to grow (or decay) and be himself
unless he relates to the laws of "Time," the change, the "sequence and
succession" (199). But if the office of the king is traditional and its ceremonies are predictable, the sense of personal apartness is not. Rather, it
results from the expectations and rewards, the relating and the doings of
contingencies, not from any preordained status, such as degree, inherited
possession, or birth. The resonant line, "and I am I, howe'er I was begot,"
reflects a new form of self-knowledge and a new kind of pride that comes
from the Bastard's personally achieved sense of identity (*King John*, 1.1.175).
What finally counts is not a person's belongings but the use to which they
are put in "the hatch and brood of time." For such "belongings / Are not
thine own so proper as to waste / Thyself upon thy virtues." A dramatic
personality is wasted until his private qualities are successfully (or otherwise)
tested in public. The testing itself (as a process in time), not the qualities as
such (as given conditions or heritage), is the dramatic source of what
authority an artificial person as "character" can achieve.

The parallels between the Duke's speech and that of Ulysses seem all the
more significant since, with one exception, the contexts of the two are
dramatically so very different. The exception is that in both *Measure for
Measure* and in *Troilus and Cressida* these poetic statements on character
seem to be ironically counterpointed by what actually happens on the stage.
The poetically stated concepts of communication and "reflection" are as far
removed from the scheme-practising egotism of the Greek generals as is the
theoretical purity of Angelo's virtues from his actual practice during his
"deputation" (*Measure for Measure*, 1.1.20). If the context in each case is
darkly ironic, in its impact the irony is iridescent in bringing to light some
unsuspected "deep" quality of characterization.

Such irony invalidates neither the values in any ethical position nor the
impressions of practical experience but makes their connection precarious as
well as ambivalent. In that sense, the irony of the context itself is, for
Shakespeare, a means to explore the possible and the impossible areas of

interaction between idea and experience. The irony, then, is one way of emphasizing the strenuous quality of any attempt at coming to terms with the contradiction between what seems to constitute personal character and the images of an outside world of society. The contradiction is there, but even in the process of exploring it the imaginary juxtaposition of character and society fails to satisfy Shakespeare's immense sense of "how this world goes." Hence merely to confront the idea of personal selfhood with the experience of social relations is not good enough as a definition of character. For Shakespeare, the outside world of society is inseparable from, already implicated in, what a person's character unfolds as his "belongings."

It is here that Shakespeare's achievement in the concept and the representation of character most significantly departs from the traditional premises of characterization in the literary history of the Middle Ages and the earlier Renaissance. This is not the place to discuss the prehistory of the social dimension of Shakespeare's characterization. But in order to see characterization in historical perspective, let us in conclusion throw a brief glance at the larger background of early modern configurations in various sixteenth-century prose narratives – clearly a comparative "page" in the genealogy of modern characterization.

From a bird's-eye view, the most salient difference between these Renaissance representations and the medieval traditions of, say, allegory or romance is that the latter provided an altogether different way of relating images of the individual to the social or the general. The poet of allegory started out from a previously established notion of the general and the social: his subject was, say, the meaning of virtue or vice, youth or sin. The figuring forth of these abstractions in the form of sensuous images of experience precluded that peculiar mediation between individuality and generality which is so marked an element in Shakespeare's mature mode of characterization. But in dramatic allegory the form of personation or the particular image of human activity was subsumed under a given medium of the general. And even when the richness and splendor of allegorical form refused to be so functionalized, it was virtue, not the virtuous, youth, not the young, which normally were represented. Consequently, the achieved figuration in action (no matter how elaborate) stood in no interactive relation to the transcendent meaning of the allegory through which a view of the world was related in poetry or drama.[30]

This is not to deny that allegory brought forth an impressive conglomerate of evolving discourses projecting socially and morally significant specifications of human attitudes, actions, and behavior. These abstractions (Mercy, Charity, Pride, Riot, and so forth) can engage in "a conflict of self-definition," as when "an allegorical personification is to challenge/destroy the uttered being of a rival."[31] Whatever self-rendering occurred, the aggressive energy in figuration came from, and thereby shaped and was shaped by, that "chasm between image and significance" of which Walter Benjamin has written so suggestively.[32] This chasm between sensuous form and general notion was symptomatic of the fact that both the writer and the spectator or reader of allegory had accepted some firmly given, ulterior standard of *éthé* governing form and function in characterization.

In contrast to that, Renaissance writing brings forth a new form of figuration at the interface of the general and the particular. As long as in allegory and, even, in medieval romance, characterization was based not on the exploration of an imaginary identity through his or her relations in nature and society, the quality of experience and the nature of selfhood do not consistently affect each other. This is why the character of the romance hero may be said to resemble rather "a rehearsed interior monologue than a meaningful and unpredictable dialogue" with particular images of the outside world.[33]

It is only in Shakespearean drama that these two aspects (a character's imaginary relations and his or her own sense of identity) no longer form any opposition or alternative. On the contrary, Shakespeare's most striking characters, much like contemporary narrative characters such as Panurge, Lazarillo, Jack Wilton, or Don Quixote, have meaningful and, sometimes, unpredictable dialogues with all sorts of configurations of the outside world.[34] The way Shakespeare's characters come to terms with the representation of "life" interacts with their discursive potential. This potential is inseparable from theatrical performance which, in its verbal form, is inherently dialogic.

CHAPTER 10

King Lear: *representations on stage and page*

King Lear sets into motion before us a dynamic compendium of modes of playing in the early modern theatre. These modes range from Lear's madness, Edgar's excessive role-playing, Kent's threadbare disguise, and the "all-licensed Fool" to the lower, more earthy "new pranks" (Goneril's phrases [*King Lear*, 1.4.201, 238]) that recur so frequently in the tragedy. To an unsurpassed, even staggering extent, a thick performative mingles, but only partially coalesces, with a representation of Albion's division. Between them, and over a residual gap, the play is saturated with insights as unsanctioned as its wild assemblage of performance tricks and practices. The rendering of characters alone includes a full, bewildering assortment of acting styles and affects of the personal, from allegorical figuration and iconographic portraiture to the improvised personation and "deep" characterization we have examined in the preceding chapters. Far from narrowing the cultural scope that certain historicist readings have discerned in it, *King Lear*'s astonishing array of dramaturgies enhances that scope. When "the realm of Albion" is "Come to great confusion" (3.2.85–6), for instance, it is the body-centered, diversionary practices of the mad Lear, the lawless Edgar, the proverbial fool, which seek to set it right. In its turn, the topsy-turvy thrust in bodies and discourses is itself subjected to a kind of reversal: "contrariety" is used to heal and to reveal, to turn a false order of things crossways, upside-down or inside-out. In the end, it is these performance-centered practices and discourses that advance the play's meaning in terms of an unprecedented insight into "how this world goes" (4.6.147–8).[1]

In this breathtaking admixture *King Lear* stages a lively picture of all the interrelations and bifurcations of page and stage, script and performance that characterized playing in London during the first decade of the seventeenth century. The audacity in the commingling of the two media is such that it helps explain certain difficulties that critics of the stature of Charles Lamb and Leo Tolstoy have had with the play. In particular, the apprehensive dismissal of its ability to be performed derived from the refusal (or was it inability?) to accommodate the representation of unbearable pain and suffering with outrageous antics, lewd and strange pranks. Surely these were part of those "turbulent scenes" dismissed between Nahum Tate and, as late as 1783, Thomas Davies; they were offensive when marked by "resentment, violence, disobedience, ingratitude, and rage."[2] The play clearly harbors a host of performance shows not necessarily sustained by any textual rationale, such as psychology or consistency. These range from the delivery of songs, riddles, show trials, and jests to almost gymnastic "new pranks" such as the notorious "trick" which Edgar plays upon Gloucester when trifling "thus with his despair" (4.6.33). In particular, the middle scenes of *King Lear* offer not only the tragically comic portrait of suffering in a malign green world – a world fraught with painful poverty and home-lessness – but also, in its assembly of various styles and modes of perform-ance, a display of what we could anachronistically think of as the early modern playhouse's green room.[3]

Yet, in the face of its teeming performatives, this tragedy boldly vindi-cates its own authority in representation. *King Lear* asserts the freedom of a popular play to reveal how royal power is both solemnized and lost in a stately act of division, whereupon political rule is beset by oppression, infested by corruption, and overrun by criminal acts of self-interest. In terms of early modern Latin terminology, forceful *potestas* is in its repre-sentation defied by an *auctoritas* validated in the recent institution of two widely accessible media. Through these it is possible for large audiences to hear and to see that the presumed mandate for dominion, "the great image of authority" (158), is found wanting. Serving a savage rule of privilege, "justice" (166) can "change places" (153) with the practice of thievery. Thus the represented order of *potestas* is challenged by an early modern author-ship, a dramatic use of language in which thinking and writing, knowledge and language achieve an unprecedented authority in their public conjunc-ture with a nonrational, nonpsychological, visceral repertoire of bodily-centered performance practices. Together they turn a bare stage into a site of awesome discoveries about what is "contrary" to and between the "wills and fates" of a great feudal inheritance.

Dramatically to face the gap between volition and destiny demands representation, a *quid pro quo* between the world as willed within and as perceived without. As long as something would stand for something else, the register of what is representative makes representation tick. In Gayatri Spivak's phrase, the "portrait" in representation is inseparable from func-tions of a "proxy."[4] But in *King Lear* the decline and corruption of feudal rule accompanies the waning representativity of all forms, moods, and shapes of outward show: former signs of authority cease to be honored. Since they no longer serve in the function of a proxy, they can hypocritically be abused, even abolished (as with Goneril and Regan) or die away in speechless silence (as with Cordelia). In George Hartley's words, there yawns an "abyss of representation" between an intensely personal "within" and the reluctance to accept, as signs of authority, such outsides as "robes and furr'd gowns."[5]

A disturbing, complicit element of interdependence bridges the rendering of inwardness and the suspicion of appearances. Between them, as Katherine Eisaman Maus suggests, we have those "profound and fascinating crises of authenticity" which enwrap "theatrical representation" at the very point of what is displayed in performance.[6] In *King Lear* in particular it is the opening scene where "a radical, unprincipled estrangement of internal truth from external manifestation" heralds the disturbing contours of a representation tragic in its own workings, in dire need of closing the gap between word and show.[7] As Goneril and Regan demonstrate, the gap between private within and public without is rife with unforeseeable consequences. Later, we learn that a "scurvy politician" (171) can project an invisible show of things unseen by himself. As precious outsides "hide all," the entrapping claims of counterfeiting lead the aging Lear to despair of his grand vision to embrace and control both love within and the show of it outside.

As against some such overall reading of the play, let us turn first to the abundant, highly volatile uses of performance in *King Lear*. Questioned in earlier criticism, rediscovered in the twentieth century, the strange and dazzling medley of performance practices in the play serves several altogether variable purposes. It can be shown to actuate the plot, to impress deceit and plotting, to invite and direct audience appeal, and to elicit response. As outlined by Bertrand Evans in his *Shakespeare's Tragic Practice*, the play advances a particularly dense series of theatrical situations on stage and off stage, involving the audience in "a serviceable awareness-unawareness gap that . . . could work across, back and forth, touching off showers of varied effects at will."[8] Evans had earlier shown how such gaps produced "discrepant awareness" in the comedies (discrepancy, that is, between what the audience knows about things and events in the playworld and what most of its own characters know or do not know). But in the tragedies the difference in proportioning out discrepant degrees of recognition propels much of the insight and impact that these plays possess. In *King Lear* especially there appears to be an unsuspected link between performative prowess, such as the aptitude for disguise or playful trickery, and a penchant for being in the know, through either innate acumen or "openly secret" familiarity with the game. The most performatively saturated characters, the Fool and Edgar, partially even Edmund and Kent, enjoy the greatest degree of awareness. They are brought to life upon, and confirm, the link in question. We need to ask, then, whether the player, as far as he does not get lost in the purely ministerial function of a fully scripted role, is perhaps closer in awareness or even social *gestus* to the audience than otherwise.

Here as elsewhere, the respective gradations in the allotment of awareness are crucially borne out by different types of actor-sustained performance, which by and large exceed, or even unsettle, representational meaning. Among these, counterfeiting "practices" (in the sense of deluding ruses, misleading maneuvers, double-dealing stratagems) are as numerous as they are conspicuous. Among the best-known double-dealing characters in Shakespeare, we have Edmund in *King Lear*, Aaron in *Titus Andronicus*, and Iago in *Othello*. We have identified the thick performatives of these characters with the legacy of the Vice in Shakespeare's theatre. They offer only the most familiar of the several other instances of such "practicing" in the tragedies.

At the same time, there are entirely different vehicles of privileged awareness – those who, free from wiles and related trickery, often enough tend to advance and share with the audience a "secretly open" perspective. Among these is not only Thersites in *Troilus and Cressida* (who gives us this phrase), but also Horatio at the end of *Hamlet*, the Porter in *Macbeth*, Enobarbus in *Antony and Cleopatra*, Apemantus in *Timon of Athens*, and, again, the Fool and, partially, the disguised Kent, in *King Lear*. What remains remarkable about *King Lear*, in fact, is the sheer prevalence of a "practicing" which ensues from or accompanies modes of performance excluding an awareness derived from ordinary forms of tragic representation. If we follow Evans, "the active practisers of *King Lear* number five – Regan, Goneril, Kent, Edmund, and Edgar." If such quantification can pass muster, *King Lear* is unique; in Evans's counting, no other Shakespearean play approximates such a total of performed contrivances. Since the tragedy is of practices "all compact," their sheer frequency is conducive to an unusual degree of discrepancy in awareness: "twenty-two of the twenty-six scenes involve persons who are unaware of some aspect or aspects of situations, and at one time or another we hold advantage over every participant except Cordelia."

Yet *King Lear* is exceptional not only in the number but also, and more significantly, in the uses of these practices. Surprisingly, the multiple machinations in *King Lear* fail, and fail remarkably, to meet what deception and tricky plotting add up to in some of Shakespeare's other plays. Examined in isolation, such practices as Kent's disguise or Edgar's Poor Tom persona – even Edmund's ambitious plans – are not stringently connected to the crucial action of the protagonist. As so many commentators have pointed out, the scene of Gloucester's attempted suicide at Dover Cliff has elements of a gimmick and is uncomfortably strange. In the final analysis, then, the performed deceptions of *King Lear* may appear, in Evans's phrase, "not germane"; they are "more diversionary than integral."[9]

Yet before we proceed to the critical question – "not germane" to what? – let us look more closely at the play's most radical "practicers," Edmund and Edgar. We are in debt to the former for some of the most glaring, bravura lines of practice within Shakespeare's tragedy, articulated with entrancing glee in his prayerlike apostrophe to his controlling "goddess" (1.2.1–22). We may feel with increasing conviction that Thespis rather than Natura functions as his central deity, but the erotic aspects of his attraction to mischief (evident in this laughing soliloquy) remain (as with Richard Gloucester before him) a powerful component of his strategy. As he later remarks,

> To both these sisters have I sworn my love;
> Each jealous of the other, as the stung
> Are of the adder. Which of them shall I take?
> Both? one? or neither? Neither can be enjoy'd
> If both remain alive . . . (5.1.55–9)

Almost in parody of the triangular psychomachia in the morality tradition – a fallen "everyman" standing not between good and bad impulses but betwen two equally fallen angels – Edmund can imagine himself alternately choosing one of the sisters and salaciously enjoying them both.

The most confident of the play's major practisers, Edmund channels his erotic attraction to possessive choice in two directions: into his dramatic "secret close intent" in pursuit of both Goneril's and Regan's affections and into his extra-dramatic, "secretly open" understanding with the audience. As these phrases from *Richard III* and *Troilus and Cressida* recall (see above, pp. 46, 142), Edmund embraces and characteristically combines strategies of personation and those of a plotting character. In personation, we will remember, an actor not only declines to submerge his own social self within the contours of a fictional role but, maintaining an openly displayed relation to his competence in performance, invites the audience to appreciate the very process of counterfeiting in the theatre. In the service of just such personation, Edmund introduces himself as a devotee of "Nature,"

promising to "top th' legitimate" (1.2.1, 21) with the complicity or connivance of spectators. It is this absence of closure and decorum which (in the
very presence of Gloucester) he describes with such terms and phrases as
"cunning" (60) and "a great gap in your own honor" (84). In each of these
phrases we hear the open play with meaning in the punning, sexualized
register ("cunning," "gap") that marks Edmund's raw relation to the world.
Following this opening practice upon Gloucester, he sarcastically mocks his
father's faith in "a divine thrusting on" (126), and instead defers the agency
for how he has been "compounded" (128) to his own first person singular
selfhood that we have traced throughout Shakespeare's works (see chapter 8):
"I should have been that I am, had the maidenl'est star in the firmament
twinkled on my bastardizing" (131–3; cf. above, pp. 166 ff.).

The complex syntactical and grammatical modality of this declaration – "I
should have been that I am" – only partly obscures its membership in the
string of subject assertions that Shakespeare may have modeled on the biblical
"I am." Yet this subject position is far from a rounded or deep kind of
character space. Edmund, for instance, almost gymnastically readies a personation for the audience from the comparatively free area of the *platea*. Noticing
Edgar, he interjects, "Pat! he comes like the catastrophe of the old comedy.
My cue is villainous melancholy, with a sigh like Tom o' Bedlam. – O, these
eclipses do portend these divsions! *fa, sol, la, mi*" (134–7). As a double-coded
personator, Edmund has his "cue" always "pat." The word in its utterance
has, like "sigh," an almost tangible physicality, from the excited exclamation
with which the remarks begin ("Pat!") to the obnoxiously counterfeited notes
of the scale he hums or sings at their close ("*fa, sol, la, mi*"). Such awareness is
linked to both a dramatic past ("like the catastrophe of the old comedy") and
the near future ("Tom o' Bedlam" – Edgar's impending and powerful
persona). The links between these moments are borne out by a shared
performative constructed for and with the audience's consent. What elsewhere is "secretly open" is here readily put: "My cue is villainous melancholy." Shakespeare would give us few clearer instances of conjunctions of a
strong personator and his awareness, with Edmund's malign practice
sketched in a "secretly open" way both before and as it unfolds.

The same conjunction is established more strongly still in Edgar's adoption of the "Tom o' Bedlam" persona. Midway through Act 2 Edgar bursts
onto a stage already occupied by a sleeping Kent restrained in the stocks and
declares his own practice of disguise:

> Whiles I may scape
> I will preserve myself, and am bethought
> To take the basest and most poorest shape

> That ever penury, in contempt of man,
> Brought near to beast. My face I'll grime with filth,
> Blanket my loins, elf all my hairs in knots,
> And with presented nakedness outface
> The winds and persecutions of the sky. (2.3.5–12)

As the details of Edgar's disguise suggest, the Poor Tom persona itself allows for an astonishing degree of theatrical masquerade. The near-nakedness that other figures will comment on in subsequent scenes not only prefigures the comprehensive dismantling of humanity that Shakespeare will attempt in *Timon of Athens* but also the importance of costume, even in its absence. Yet in closing his prefatory soliloquy, Edgar, eye to eye with his audience, rehearses the remarkable scenario of a merciless world that images of "Poor Tom" will involve. When he ends with "Poor Turlygod! poor Tom! / That's something yet: Edgar I nothing am" (20–1), Edgar moves in and out of the persona he will enact, giving certainly the sound of Poor Tom and also, it seems likely, a crass specimen of what posture and gesture his version of the Bedlam beggar will feature.

As personator, Edgar wears his costumed fictions so lightly that he can renounce the illusion of any role, including his primary one as Edgar, son to the Earl of Gloucester. What matters here is not cogency and consistency in the representation of character but the almost inexhaustible skill and stamina of the player's counterfeiting. As far as the latter is inscribed by the dramatist, it is clearly a case of actor's voice in author's pen.

Edgar's personae are as easily put aside and modified as they are adopted. We see this changefulness clearly when Edgar sets aside his new vocal repertoire for formal couplets (3.6.102–13), then blank verse (4.1.1–9). He is in these moments again Edgar; then Poor Tom; then, when he "cannot daub it further" (4.1.52), a "better spoken" figure whom Gloucester rightly describes as speaking "In better phrase and matter than" he did previously (4.6.9, 7); then an unidentified "friend" (46) who claims to have seen Gloucester's fall and increasingly refers to him as "father" (219, 255, 286); and finally, and almost inexplicably, just before his appearance as a chivalric "champion" (5.1.43) seemingly out of Sidney's *Arcadia*, a "bold peasant" (4.6.231) who scourges Oswald in a Somerset dialect: "Chill not let go, zir, without vurther cagion" (235). Here he may have taken his cue from a disguised Kent – whose "occupation to be plain" (2.2.92) means adopting a brisk dialect of insult. The latter includes an anachronism like "base football player" (1.4.86), a reference to the lower-class sport – in telling contrast to Lear's metaphor "bandy" (84), taken from upper-class tennis – that Sir Thomas Elyot had warned "al noble men" against.[10]

Edgar, however, goes further, cycling his speech through an extensive variety of genres and modes even as he practices upon his father. Leading Gloucester through one of the "new pranks" that Goneril detests, he painfully dupes the sightless man into performing a pratfall whose comedic form rides upon the shoulders of the tragedy in the same way that his son's dialect performance piggybacks on his customary speech. Again, practice in performance and language in representation engage one another. At issue, in Catherine Belsey's phrase, "is not a binary opposition: meaning and practice inevitably inform and, indeed, invade each other."[11] If Edgar performed anything like an Elizabethan equivalent of what the Brechtian *gestus* aimed at, then his delivery combined knowledge and physicality, awareness in and of his counterfeiting body.

King Lear ends with this pair of its most energetic and vital practicers observing the paired bodies of their dead monarch and his plain-spoken daughter. A small group of characters assembles as though inviting post-dramatic witnesses to the heartbreaking spectacle before them. A benediction of sorts stoically summarizes their situation. The now familiar comment achieves a poignant and lapidary status in part through its tandem of rhymes, in part through the gravity of its sentiment, and in part from its position here at the conclusion of Shakespeare's tragedy:

> The weight of this sad time we must obey,
> Speak what we feel, not what we ought to say:
> The oldest hath borne most; we that are young
> Shall never see so much, nor live so long. (5.3.324–7)

These haunting lines offer up a resonant and pathetic reading of the stage situation, a dramatic show invoking an entirely nonceremonial, postscriptural hereafter, the time after the play is ended.[12] Significantly, these lines pertain less to the painful evidence of mortality and accident that the apparently lifeless bodies of Lear and Cordelia represent than to the prosaic future which both the player and spectators face.

As is well known, precisely who delivers this speech varies in the earliest texts of *King Lear*. Perhaps owing in part to a textual effect of the drama's own uncertainty regarding its practicers, the Quartos of 1608 and 1619 give the speech to Albany ("Duke") in distinction to the Folio's assignment of it to Edgar. If we return to the uncertainty that Evans expressed over Edgar's almost heroic reentry into the social world of *King Lear*, we may see the play's early Quartos as conveying, in their assignment of the speech to Albany, a reluctance already in the play. As Evans asks, rhetorically,

But who and what is the Edgar behind the visor? When the visor is raised and Edgar's voice emerges – 'My name is Edgar, and thy father's son' – we should, perhaps, respond with such a thrill as we experience when Hamlet leaps into Ophelia's grave with Laertes, crying 'This is I, Hamlet the Dane.' But we cannot do so, for while we know Hamlet and care about him, we know Edgar not at all; Edgar is a non-entity, whose original dim image has been obliterated by his successive roles.[13]

Indeed, character remains here as elusive as reference, with Edgar, not unlike Kent, continuing in disguise long after its purposes have been achieved. Disguise provides a platform for doubly encoding imaginary identities, as when Kent, at Lear's question, "What dost thou profess?", replies, "I do profess to be no less than I seem" (1.4.11–13). It is the same threefold incongruity among primary role, disguised role, and the actual player as personator that Edgar multiplies. If not quite a "non-entity," he is a chameleonlike figure whose "successive roles" sacrifice any specific, any perdurable image of subjectivity in favor of a very broad spectrum, if not a whirligig, of powerful deliveries and "contraries" (Kent's word at 2.2.87).

As far as Edgar's mad, antic metamorphoses are at loggerheads with the formation of an imaginary identity, the representation of this is already seriously in question. Such representation, as the preceding chapter has shown, obtains when, in Ulysses's phrase, a "having, or without or in" results "but by reflection" (*Troilus and Cressida*, 3.3.97, 99). Along these lines, discursive practice and the fashioning of a character's identity constitute a very close circuit. Lynne Magnusson in her reading of *King Lear* also quotes the passage from *Troilus and Cressida* to show "how the self is constituted through the recognition of the other."[14] However, when in this tragedy such recognition is either withheld or reduced to a deceitful formality, speech as the most vital medium of this recognition fails in the representation of what sense of identity can be derived from dialogic uses of language. It is in the teeth of their failure that "*King Lear* puts on display the normal, everyday mechanisms" by which, in successful interaction, people normally "maintain one another's identities."

The question we are tempted to ask in this context is whether the prominence of madness, disguise, role-changing, prank, and "impertinency" does not perhaps serve as witness to difficulties in representation which arise when discursive practice, as in the Fool's topsy-turvy "prophecy," ceases either to signify dramatically or to bring forth a dialogic effect of signification as clue to identity. As we shall see, when the "proxy," the regime of the representative, and the "portrait," the authority of the representational, part company, we are left with what Magnusson (in a somewhat different context) calls "circumstances of breakdown or dysfunction."

Indeed, this friction in *King Lear*'s language of social interaction works, as William Dodd has demonstrated in his reading of the tragedy's opening scene, less to chart the status of feudalism in the play's historical imaginary than to produce a choice for the audience regarding the dramatic persons they see before them in the commercial playhouse.[15] Dodd argues that "Cordelia's clash with Lear is sparked by her fidelity to the personal as a sphere distinct from the political"[16], a position replicated in part (and certainly extended) by those aspects of *King Lear* which allow for an audience to choose among the kinds of competence and attraction offered by a performance. Acknowledging that Kent, for instance, "embodies class-conscious feudal nostalgia," Dodd avers that "paradoxically," Kent's "relationship with the audience . . .voices a newer, more pragmatic and egalitarian social outlook that for the moment finds more space in the interlocutive liberties of the commercial theater than in contemporary social or political formations."[17]

As Dodd's reading confirms, to return from the ending of *King Lear* to its beginning is to confront with more than hindsight the semiotic energy that inhabits this self-aware tragedy. We witness in this opening scene, for example, the political abdication and the personal defeat of a royal ruler who, almost like a failing playwright, attempts to demarcate the space of his realm and the parts for his heirs. The grand design is to "set down for them" by plotting out what lands to have and what roles to play. However, what little power remains after the loss of his representative station squares ill with the portrait of his personal demands and dignities. Having relinquished, with his royal office, powerful *potestas* on almost all material levels, the personal "Authority," which Kent perceives at an early stage of Lear's throneless progress (1.4.30), cannot abide and outlast the trials to come. On stage the most devastating of these trials upsets the symbolic order of dramatic language when its dialogic purpose fails to function under the burden of a partially self-sustained, semi-independent performative, especially in recourse to a topsy-turvy, apparently nonsensical patter.

In *King Lear* dramatic representation is most conspicuously jeopardized in the Fool's prophecy and the delivery of madness in the performance of both Lear and Edgar. Shakespeare introduced madness as a major figure in this tragedy, associating concealment, desperation, and privation. Madness's full meaning is more than ordinarily negotiated between stage and page, especially where the preeminent verbal representation is bound to reach an impasse. To underline this impasse is not to neglect the significance of Shakespeare's sources. Here it must be sufficient to recall that by 1581 there was important classical precedence scripturally available in Seneca's *Tenne Tragedies*, where "madness" was rendered in terms of some ecstasy Englished as "frenzy," "prophecy," "fury," "folly," and related words.[18] These words by themselves indicate how difficult it is to represent insanity in and by a dramatic context determined by the order of Western *logos*. As Michel Foucault has graphically shown in his *Madness and Civilization*, in its acoustic manifestations insanity affords us the "evidence of a broken dialogue," with "all these stammered, imperfect words without meaning."[19] In other words, even while the show or appearance of madness can to a certain degree be mimed, the thing itself resists the symbolic order of any adequate linguistic circumscription. As far as madness is, like pain or death, an emanation of the *Leib* – that is, the visceral – it is not accessible to any actualization through language.

At this point, the fiction of Lear's insanity, just as the masked version of it embodied by Edgar, is a *topos* that, ironically, must be staged by a personation of someone acting *as if beside oneself*. Shakespeare was deeply aware of how such being beside oneself entailed a split in the identity of a represented character. The most graphic rendering is found in Hamlet's words when, moments before the duel with Laertes begins, he deplores his "sore distraction":

> What I have done
> . . . I here proclaim was madness.
> Was't Hamlet wrong'd Laertes? Never Hamlet!
> If Hamlet from himself be ta'en away,
> And when he's not himself does wrong Laertes,
> Then Hamlet does it not, Hamlet denies it.
> Who does it then? His madness. (5.2.230–7)

Here we have a protagonist addressing what in popular parlance might be glossed as his own schizophrenia. Throughout the play, we have a deep split as well as a mingle-mangle between the humanistic Prince under the discursive spell of the *logos* and a highly performative "John-a-dreams" who, under the mantle of an "antic disposition," wilfully "puts on this confusion" (3.1.2). In the end, the angle of enunciation is that of the Prince who regrets that "Hamlet from himself" was taken away. Thus his wildest performing self is declared a hostile other: "His madness is poor Hamlet's enemy" (239).

In this comparison the earlier tragedy is miles away from *King Lear*, where *logos*, the language of reason and, here, mercy do not so part company with madness. Yet Lear's brief reunion with Cordelia as well as Edgar's reentry into the official world of the play may at least hint at a related dilemma. In Jacques Derrida's reading, any "speaking subject . . . must evoke madness from the *interior* of thought (and not only from within the body or some other extrinsic agency)."[20] The irony, crucial to our understanding of the play, is that the dramatist in his construction of insanity must "evoke madness from the interior of thought," even while the player in the enactment of it is unthinkable without a "raving" body, the delirious gesture, the frenzy in his voice. When Shakespeare first envisioned madness in the comic context of a festive wedding, not without previous reference to "The rite of May" (*A Midsummer Night's Dream*, 4.1.133), he was inclined to embrace in happy unity "The lunatic, the lover and the poet" (5.1.7). For perfectly cogent reasons, there was no mention of the player, even though in the same scene the lay actors opened their performance madly, "like a tangled chain . . . all disorder'd," with less a sense than "a sound, but not in government" (124–6).

Again on the level of delivery, contrariety defies representation in its two major functions: it can "disfigure" (Quince's lapse, 3.1.60 ff.) rather than figure any adequate *portrait*; and it refuses to serve as *proxy*, that is, as representative of any social station, purpose, idea. Even more important in our context, madness inhabits a fissure in the confederation of pages and stages. While in writing the fiction of insanity is accessible to the poet whose "imagination bodies forth / The forms of things unknown" (5.1.14–15), its material embodiment on stage is an altogether different matter. Whereas the imaginative intellect behind poetic writing is of such shaping fantasy as can body forth "minds transfigur'd" (24), the Elizabethan player, minding his professional business, is likely to have foregrounded the outward show, the bodily appearance, as preferable to the interior confusion of lunacy.

It is precisely at this point that, in Eisaman Maus's phrase, "the authenticity of representation" is in question; we would like to add, from within its own staging. The dilemma is one of incongruity, where the transfiguring faculty of the dramatist in his imaginative vision "More witnesseth than fancy's images" (25), while the actor seeks to bring forth an image, and nothing but an image, of the other. When, in this situation, the two cultural modes of production are conjoined, the symbolic order of literary representation becomes extremely vulnerable. As distinct from the latter, the material medium of the raving body, on the strength of its sensuous, visual immediacy, achieves from its sheer outside an overpowering impress, even while the "interior of thought" in the writing can deflect attention away from mere "seems" in favor of the deep character's "within."

Here the uses of madness in *King Lear* point to a larger pattern of difficult relations between theatrical production and dramatic script, which on the early modern stage would culminate in the conflicts between Inigo Jones and Ben Jonson. In Shakespeare's case, these relations attest to a bifurcation of stage and page adumbrated fairly early in his oeuvre. However, as *King Lear* suggests, the entire pattern of contrariety between material perform-ance and imaginary representation can constitute a productive relationship as soon as the former is made to share vitally in the privilege of securing and sharing out knowledge and awareness of and in the play. This is the case wherever "secretly open" dramaturgy is instrumental in conveying among characters and toward audience a discrepancy of awareness.

As we have seen throughout this study, some privileged insight into the course of events and the motivations of characters is, paradoxically, often enough tied to a strong, partially self-sustained practice of performance. Here we can only recall in passing the rich awareness of the clown, begin-ning with the early Launce who can betray truth in the play when he ("I am but a fool") "yet" has "the wit to think my master is a kind of a knave" (*The Two Gentlemen of Verona*, 3.1.263–4). But clowning is only one version of comic contrariety and shares a privileged perception with a tragic pro-tagonist's "antic disposition" as a device through which Hamlet seeks to conceal rather than blunt a character's perspicacity.

It should come as no surprise, then, that "the interplay between the actor as character ... and the actor as actor" affects and helps qualify tragic representations in *King Lear* as well as in *Hamlet*.[21] The Prince of Denmark and Edgar, and partially Lear himself, witness to comparable degrees of entanglement in relations of page and stage: a highly articulate author's pen prescribes players' voices while the latter strongly, with all the playhouse's traditional contrariety, resonate in author's pen. The quality of their mutual engagements is such that a certain imbalance ensues: while "some necessary question of the play" (Hamlet's hortatory phrase, *Hamlet*, 3.2.42–3) is lost sight of, "the word" tends to be suited to "the action" rather than, in the humanist Prince's postulate, vice versa.

In other words, the semiotics of performative delivery can clash with what elsewhere the dramatic text of representation is made to signify. One could recall the resulting dilemma in *Hamlet*. In the protagonist's first grand courtly appearance, he introduces himself as a "deep" character, postulating for himself a pronounced "within," as in his rejection of "the trappings and the suits" (1.1.85–6) of mourning as mere "seems." However, this emphatic and quite unambiguous representation of a leading character's identity suffers a rift, when the Prince only a few hundred lines later decides – for questionably effective reasons – to slip into "the trappings and the suits" of a highly performative guise. His resolve "To put an antic disposition on" (1.5.172) is precisely what Hamlet on his return from post-Reformation Wittenberg rejects as "actions that a man might play": "These indeed seem" (1.1.83–4). As it turns out, the histrionic delivery of these antic "actions" so entangles "The courtier's, soldier's, scholar's ... tongue" that the Renaissance "mould of form," the text of "sovereign reason," is "Blasted with ecstasy" (3.1.151–60), thereby delaying his coming to terms with "the necessary question of the play."[22]

The performance-derived "antic" impacts not only upon the "mould of form" but also the function of representation is obvious enough. Even when on the level of characterization the mad role-playing may seem acceptable as enriching a multifaceted identity, Hamlet as self-styled "rogue and peasant slave" (2.2.550) and "John-a-dreams" (568) raises questions of function and meaning. For one thing, this scenario breaks up the link between the dramatic "portrait" of the Prince of Denmark and his representative role of "proxy," as one next to the throne. Here again, the issue of *quid pro quo*, i.e., of representativity – so crucial in *King Lear* – surfaces in the wake of a prolonged and extensive endeavor of the playwright to come to grips with the proxy function of symbolic signs and ceremonies. Reaching at least from *Richard II* via *Henry IV*, *Henry V*, and *Julius Caesar* through *Measure for Measure* to *Coriolanus*, this question is not primarily one of power but one of authorization and choice between the two media. Fully articulated in the culture of literacy and print, the question, even while almost always overrun by political concerns, branches out into jurisprudence, poetics, church administration, and modern government, not to forget theatre management, where the question of "Who stands for which role?" is always germane.[23] As deeply ingrained in literary, especially (post-)Reformation discursive practices, the question of what is representative has an intellectual and political dynamic which ill assorts with the player's physical presence as an openly entertaining business. That is precisely where creatures of the stage, even when sufficiently disciplined to stand for textually inscribed figurations, must have had difficulties coming to terms with the wider symbolic ramifications of *quid pro quo*.

Here we have room for only the barest of illustrations. In *Richard II* the Gardener hints at the larger basis on which the unfixing in early modern representation unfolds. "Why should we," he questions, "Keep law and form and due proportion, / Showing as in a model our firm estate" (3.4.40–2) when, as the play suggests, any person's station in the world is part of an endless whirligig? The mold and order of a garden are taken to be representative of the state of the realm. The mold of "form" in the latter can thus inflect conflicts and contingencies in the mode of representation. The use of language is semiotically insecure where authorization itself is in question, "intermix'd / With scruples." Even the "better sort" in church and state would "set the word itself / Against the word" (5.5.11–14). It is, again, a post-Reformation dilemma that so affects hierarchical degree and status that any role is given for those bold enough to take it. The well-known words of the imprisoned Richard II, "Thus play I in one person many people" (5.5.31), might as well be pronounced in *Henry IV* by the Prince of Wales, in Eastcheap, with as unsettling a spectrum not of given, but of purely personal, choices in mind. We could take, for example, only Hal's speech, recalling "small beer" and an "appetite . . . not princely got," as he ironically discloses "humble" concerns which "make me out of love with my greatness" (*2 Henry IV*, 2.2.9–14) – and jeopardize his right to succession. Still, there was a need for the actor-character to perform in the wake of his boon companion, thereby fracturing the mirror of what is representative in princely behavior.

A similar chord is poignantly rung in *Henry V*. Again, a strong performative is loosening the clutches of verisimilitude: in disguise, royalty in the camp allows unheard of liberties. So Henry, too, can in one person play with (and play out) against a broad spectrum of socially loaded signs and emblems. In his speech on "ceremony" (*Henry V*, 4.1.238–84) we have a deep gap between the dominant politics of self-display and its momentary inversion on the popular Renaissance stage – a gap that at least partially foreshadows a comparable gulf between the awesome claims of Lear and what becomes of them in his "madness of discourse." Although perfectly unaware of the depth of that tragic abyss, Henry probes the distance between what, politically, late sixteenth-century "ceremony" would stand for and what, vitally, in terms of ordinary use value it was good for:

> And what art thou, thou idol Ceremony? . . .
> What are thy rents? What are thy comings-in?
> O Ceremony, show me but thy worth!

This culminates in an ambivalent invocation of "thrice-gorgeous ceremony" which cannot cure "the fiery fever" or "command" a beggar's "health" and which, "laid in bed majestical," cannot "sleep so soundly as the wretched slave" (4.1.240, 253, 257, 266–8).

While the speech almost certainly harbors an element of demagogy or at least rationalization, in its entirety it cannot be reduced to that. What in the first instance has to be taken into account is the gap between the signs of *potestas* as officially practiced and the representing of the signs of these signs in the theatre. Listed almost in catalogue fashion ("balm," "sceptre," "ball," "sword," "mace," "crown imperial," "robe," "gold and pearl," and "throne"), all this formidable "tide of pomp," no matter how dazzling in courtly and processional spectacle, is finally found wanting on "this unworthy scaffold." Even while representative of sovereign power, these majestic signs of worthiness do not satisfy the more immediate question of what people share as their most basic need. However, what sounds superficially like a universalizing subtext in this speech is, on closer reading, far from wanting a socially, even economically, specific angle. As the speaker views it, the trouble with ceremony is that, ultimately, it does not *pay*. Indeed, a monetary metaphor is best able to suggest that, over and beyond the demagogic note, the ultimate challenge of "ceremony" derives from images of lived experience in early modern England sustained by unformulated notions of both exchange and use values. Ceremony is an unprofitable investment when exposed to a market economy.

As against the proxy-function in this representation of "ceremony," even the most persuasive and historicist readings need to be qualified. Take, for instance, Stephen Greenblatt's landmark argument about court ceremonials in the Tudor monarchy, wherein their "power depends on its privileged visibility"; or Thomas Cartelli's thoughtful response to this "Ceremony" speech, in which he argues that Henry seeks to recuperate his prerogative by saying that it is nothing but a burden.[24] While to this day these approaches remain perceptive, their problem is that, to a certain extent, they do not go far enough. This at least needs to be said when "ceremony" in *Henry V* is examined from the point of view of what in this speech it is representative of, especially in terms of its authority and its interests – questions that will be raised on a tragic scale in *King Lear*. As a historicizing answer, there is no reason to belittle the extent to which Tudor courtly ceremony was designed to be without compare and, in its incomparable splendor, not to be equaled by any other noble show of dazzling self-display. Still, the new monarchy's politics, including its royal pomp and circumstance, were marked by a new title not only to local but also to nationwide representativity. While this far-reaching claim begins positively to be invoked in the time of Henry VII, it is vitally strengthened by Reformation policies. In Shakespeare's later years Parliament humbly but at least occasionally begins to represent not only county but, over and beyond that, country affairs as, unnoticeably at first, distinct from royal concerns.[25]

However, as far as a broader national appeal in political discourses is inflected, advanced, or interrogated in Shakespeare's plays, different social practices and interests are bound to jostle in dramatic utterances. It is not only that conflicting interests come to be comprehended under one wider representational frame of reference. Rather, there emerges a potential of conflict within the mode of representation itself. Even in the present set speech, there is at work a dynamic diversion in gesture, positioning, and preference which "sets up with and against itself" (Troilus's phrase, *Troilus and Cressida*, 5.2.143). For Henry, the larger, conflicting range of discourses gives rise to searching questions. For him, these are not, as for Troilus and Lear, confusing to the effect that there results an unfathomable "madness of discourse" (*Troilus and Cressida*, 142). It is only that the answer to the question of what is and what is not representative of a diverging ensemble of social, cultural, and regional standards would hopelessly overdetermine any traditional allegorical, emblematic, or pastoral mode of dramatic representation and open up an unexplored space of what in more than one way serves as a catalyst.

As we shall see, it is a space in which "ceremony" can occupy an exemplary site, not only because it socially appeals to or calls for a wide spectrum of highly diverse needs, expectations, and responses. What is more, it constitutes an object of representation which in Shakespeare's plays can actuate a sense of difference between inside and outside, between what one feels "within" and what false "trappings" (*Hamlet*, 1.2.85–6) are, mere "lendings" which replace genuine sentiment by "what we ought to say" (*King Lear*, 3.4.108; 5.3.325). Again, "ceremony" can serve as a catalyst as far as the dramatist's *inventio* projects its rather different uses, as either in the service of *potestas* ("Creating awe and fear in other men," *Henry V*, 1.247) or as a perfectly congenial, authentic part of civilized sociability.

Shakespeare's achievement and interests in other plays show us more than those highly variegated versions of both conflict and concurrence between the signs of *potestas* as represented and what *auctoritas* the representing signs themselves can claim. For here we also find a host of Shakespearean rulers evincing concern with the manipulation and effects of what we heard Henry, in his great soliloquy, call "thrice gorgeous ceremony" (*Henry V*, 4.1.230–84, 266). Whether the scripted action consists of a hypocritical Richard Gloucester displaying himself "*aloft, between two* BISHOPS" (*Richard III*, 3.7.94 S.D.) – that parodic, morality-play triangulation that Edmund proposes with Goneril and Regan – Prospero's sequence of the alternately malign ("*ARIEL, like a harpy*" [*The Tempest*, 3.3.52 S.D.]) and beneficent ("*Juno descends*" [4.1.74]), or even Duke Vincentio's studied reluctance to "stage" himself to his people's "eyes" (*Measure for Measure*, 1.1.67–8), Shakespeare's ruling aristocrats commonly define their power in strong relation to the ceremonial staging of a scripted show.

In *Julius Caesar*, for example, such signs of authority are addressed as part of a political semiotics of rule either administered or intercepted from conflicting angles. While Caesar demands a veritable plenitude in display ("Set on, and leave no ceremony out," *Julius Caesar*, 1.2.11), the tribunes Flavius and Murellus seek to "Disrobe the images, / If you do find them deck'd with ceremonies" (1.1.64–5). Obviously, the signs of power and warlike glory can serve diametrically opposed purposes; their perceived functions vary according to what political impulse inspires their communicative affect and effect. The question of what a representation stands for, what is representative in representation, can be a divisive one. In *Julius Caesar* the difference between the signs of ceremony and what they stand for profoundly divides the issue of any one given authority in representation.[26] It also reminds us of what remains at stake in the economies of power within an institution – whether state or repertory – taking its cues from a figure who, with whatever success, seeks to dominate the reach and working of scripted ceremony.

The opening scene of *King Lear* takes the issues of script, ceremony, and performance to an even greater level of tension than its Roman predecessor. The division of the kingdom among Lear's daughters is inseparably bound up with the representation of how an inheritance, marked by the possession of land and power, is being handed on or delegated to a younger generation. This act of delegation is predicated on the assumption that he who authorizes the transfer of authority does not in the process himself lose his own. Taken, even acknowledged, by others as an innate attribute, the giver expects the receivers to honor the former's royal and paternal status as representative of an indivisible legitimacy independent of the relinquished office.

While most criticism of the play tends to emphasize the act and the consequences of dividing the kingdom, the underlying politics and poetics of authority in representation have received considerably less notice. In our context, this issue appears especially pregnant where the political and the paternal angles of representation and the more strictly theatrical dimensions are being intertwined in the scene. Such linkage among the dimensions first emerges upon Lear's assumption that the endowment of authority in the world of political power ensues upon, can even be tied to, the dramatically crucial portrayal of filial affection. The vivid, competitive rendering of the latter ("Which of you shall we say doth love us most?" [*King Lear*, 1.1.51]) conditions and provides reassuring grounds of the former. What Lear, prepared to "divest" himself "of rule," expects his daughters to deliver are imaginary and theatrically potent representations of their love. The plenitude of such representation must be such (and so representative of purely personal attachment) that, presumably, it can be taken to promise further inclination on the part of the younger generation to respect their father's expectation of enduring gratitude.

It may be said that ceremony inhabits a tragic space in that it demonstrates an abyss of representation in its irreducible gap between the composition of character (itself with an unfathomed depth) and the dazzling but delusive surface of what is performed as outside appearance. In this tragedy "the trappings and the suits" of love do not in truth "denote" a self; they are indeed "actions that a man might play" (*Hamlet*, 1.2.83–6). So are the "trappings" of filial love and affection, especially when uttered from under courtly "robes and furr'd gowns" and linked to the well-dowered bestowal of landed power. As the receipt of such vast *potestas* is being traded for the language, the mere signs of filial love, there results a knotty conjuncture among different issues: the conflict-ridden uses of legitimation harboring notions of what is representative of and in authority, and a radical diversity in the reading of a highly ceremonial occasion and context. These issues are briefly foreshadowed in the opening scene, not only in Gloucester's somewhat frivolous distinction between having both "a son, sir, by order of law" and a "whoreson" that "must be acknowledg'd" (1.1.19–24) but also through those would-be royal "equalities" between Albany and Cornwall who, though differently valued by Lear on a personal level, leave "choice of either's moi'ty" (6–7) undetermined.

Along these lines, the first scene offers a staggering array of potential dramatic conflicts. In their midst the proxy function of representation itself is brewing wherever words, deeds, and bodies serve as agents standing for something/someone else. This function is tested most vitally, and is of greatest consequence, when intertwined with a divisive, socially significant divergence in the representation of affections. While all three daughters articulate their devotion and their "love" (as does Cordelia, too, in her "Obey you, love you, and most honor you" [98]), the symbolic order of representation in her language is worlds apart from that in Goneril's and Regan's protestations. The latter in their uses of language establish a deliberate gap between what nicely signifies and what ultimately or strategically may be signified in their utterances. Once we recall a similar abyss between what represents and what is represented in the words of Prince Hal, Henry V or, for that matter, Hector and Duke Vincentio, we should not content ourselves simply or exclusively with our initial reading of the speeches of Lear's elder daughters as only insincere or so much cunning. Although these attributes cannot finally be disputed, both Goneril and

Regan pursue a political semiotics fully in accordance with the ceremonial *gestus*, the emblematic tenor, and the great courtly occasion of the play's opening. What they deliver in response to these formal circumstances is perfectly congenial with that celebration of royal idols (which Henry in his speech on ceremony weighs and finds wanting). Theirs, precisely, is a tribute, again in Henry's words, to a "soul of adoration," observing "place, degree, and form" on a stately stage of "great greatness" (*Henry V*, 4.1.245–6, 251).

Small wonder then that Lear in his royal show of abdication is quite content with what they have to say. With all the pomp and circumstance before his eyes, he seems to have no such problem (as Henry has) in reconciling "thrice gorgeous ceremony" with what in emotional, rational, and economic terms amounts to its "worth." Even more important, behind Lear's refusal to doubt the language of his elder daughters we have so much more than the blind indulgence of an aging patriarch. Rather, there is an element of the Renaissance *uomo universale* in his determination simultaneously to enjoy and command both the world of politics and power and, equally, the world of feeling, thinking, loving.

In an early modern perspective, where the grounds of authority encompassing both these worlds become more and more tenuous, this claim may well seem audacious. In Shakespeare's tragedies, but especially in *Coriolanus* and *Antony and Cleopatra*, the yawning abyss between the dictates of material power and the demands of personal attachment is such that it seems only to wait for the hero's downfall. In *Hamlet* a different but comparable gulf between the conflicting demands of family revenge and individual conscience provokes, or coincides with, an antic dilemma culminating in a self-concealing "madness of discourse." However, it is only in *King Lear* that this madness engulfs the tragic hero when, in the midst of an unhealable rupture, he continues to insist that, in Troilus's words, "there be rule in unity itself" (*Troilus and Cressida*, 5.2.141). Such unity among diverse locations of authority surrenders to the inroads of contingency and desire; "bifold authority," with a divisive impact all its own, can drive a wedge between politically powerful and psychologically affect-driven shapes of validity and authority in the theatre as elsewhere in early modern civilization.[27]

Since Lear stubbornly persists in wanting to reconcile the stately "idol ceremony" to the private image of true feelings, Cordelia's rejection of any such reconciliation must come as a brusque surprise. For him, it is both an outrageous violation of a crowning moment in public dignity and decorum *and* a staggering personal blow from someone most beloved of all.

Cordelia's uncompromising stance, her proud unyielding resolve not to "heave / My heart into my mouth" (*King Lear*, 1.1.91–2) may well appear to us as stern and inappropriately austere in the face of a generous, bountiful endowment to follow. On the unique threshold between receiving love and sharing land, her father, with his inflammable temper, must feel provoked by what he perceives as an unpardonable rebuff on both the political and the personal side. Fully to appreciate the reckless *fortissimo* of Lear's response, we need to recall a residual feudal conscience in this postfeudal monarch, which inflects the standards of rigorous loyalty and a sense of "personal dependence" that Marx again and again associated with prebourgeois society.

At this moment the carefully staged triumph in combining his resolve of relinquishing office with his intent to maintain some sort of "rule in unity itself" is irretrievably thwarted by Cordelia's anticeremonial invocation of her own "heart" within. Lear's failure to reap, in one all-encompassing act of rule, the landed, the ceremonial, and the fondest kinship fruits of his authority goes hand in hand with a controlled crisis in representational form. Representation, as has often been noted, has a way of healing difference – even where, as in *King Lear*, the healing tragically reveals its impossibility. This *leitmotif* unfolds, in the opening scene, with a kind of wood-cut directness. Here is royalty in its ultimate delivery of and from rule in unity. Appearing almost larger than life, Lear ostentatiously seeks one more time to indulge in "thrice gorgeous ceremony." But even while the represented show of courtly pomp and politics holds sway, the supreme token of love is slipping. What was anxiously craved, the performed self-representation of filial fondness, is not forthcoming. Defying her father, Cordelia fails to deliver – though not because she lacks love. On the contrary, her loving attachment is too intensely felt to allow the public display of what within her "passes show." Upon command, no power could "heave" her love into representational shape by impulsion from without. Authority, paternal or political, cannot coerce the avidly desired token from her "heart." Neither huge promise nor threatening curse can induce Cordelia to represent through performance what in truth she feels.

The resulting impasse between father and daughter is one of representational form itself. When Cordelia determines to "Love, and be silent" (1.1.62), she does so because "my love's / More ponderous than my tongue" (77–8). In other words, her inward sentiment is too deep, and too deeply ingrained, to be translated into language, least of all into the fixed, set speeches of her unloving sisters that, as Kent implies, in their glibness "Reverb . . . hollowness" (154). Remarkably, Cordelia's love is the more "real" or too deeply saturated in the unnamable bonds of blood and kinship to be expressed in words. Or, in a late modern phrase, we might say that her love is more authentic for being nonrepresentable. The sheer determination to be "silent" and her distrust of representational language (at least vis-à-vis the material promise of rule and possession) provide an important clue to the tragic course of events in the play.

What in its more general direction this crisis anticipates is Lear's own dilemma. Unable to perceive behind Cordelia's silence the felt inadequacy of signs, their inability to point beyond the prescribed order of ceremonial power, Lear resolves to do something fatal. He turns to Goneril and Regan and entrusts their husbands with his "power" (1.1.130) while himself still trusting in something purely representational, the "name . . . to a king" (136). This is arguably the play's most consequential act: Lear's division of the kingdom accompanies his relinquishing of an all-embracing court of appeal and validity.

The "name" he insists upon is, like the title and land it designates (Kent, Cornwall, France, Burgundy, etc.), a highly representative signifier. The royal title in particular stands for what King Henry refers to as this "tide of pomp," signifying "balm," "sceptre," "mace," and so forth. In *King Lear*, where so much land is lost and won, the proxy function of the name has an extraordinary instability. Elsewhere, in Shakespeare's tragic vision of things, "name" and "show," like other "ceremonies" such as we have in *Julius Caesar*, are vulnerable articles in representation, especially where the generality of the proxy function confronts the particularity of a self with an assumed inwardness. While they can all be undermined through their self-conscious theatricality, they can also be challenged as hallowed signs of petrified custom, questioned privilege, and family lineage bolstered by external *potestas*. Here we can only recall Juliet's all-important resolve not to respect "What's in a name" (*Romeo and Juliet*, 2.2.38–48). Her first impulse is to greet and ask "Romeo, Romeo . . . refuse thy name" (33–4), simply because "Thou art thyself" (39).

What Juliet's love and Hamlet's nonceremonial "within" which "passes" the "show" of silence have in common with Cordelia's silence is that in each case signs (name, show, or word) fail to convey what is more "ponderous" on a level deeper than the symbolic order of representation. The dramatic language of inwardness comes up against the frontiers of representation – especially when and where signs are supposed to stand for what is ineffable in the passion or disposition of an individual character. Such images of alleged singularity defy impulsion on behalf of rank or title or any ceremonial show. Again, there is within Romeo "that dear perfection which he owes / Without that title" (2.2.46–7). In *King Lear* it takes the discourse of madness, a passionate disturbance within, to pass the show of ceremony and, even more important, the scenario of politically or socially enforceable authority. Such "within" claims an imaginary identity (Romeo's "thyself") constituting its own valid frame of reference – be it the authority residing in a deeper "truth" (Cordelia), the authority in an impassioned love (Juliet), or the authority in the unfathomable conscience of mournful *ressentiment* (Hamlet).

However, Lear's way of coping with the boundaries of representation takes a different, more eccentric, and therefore more catastrophic point of departure. In his imposing, elevated manner, the aging king, confidently conjoining the sovereign authority of powerful office and the plentiful representation of filial love, embarks on a most vulnerable project. While he will divest himself of regal power (together with the "sway, revenue, execution" of his former office), his belief in the "tongue," the "show," and the "name" of things continues unbroken. We could say that for him, both portrait and proxy in representation, even in the face of Cordelia's exceptionable difficulties with it, appear undiminished – until madness overwhelms but also liberates his speech. He continues to trust the authority in and of representation, even in his own "countenance" embodying "authority" (*King Lear*, 1.3.27–30), up to the point at which he is divested of both the chivalrous "tide of pomp" and the filial respect and attention of his elder daughters. Until that happens, representation for him remains an unquestioned tool for accommodating all kinds of difference and rupture. Only when his confidence in both the wholesome representation and the fulsome authority of royalty is shattered can he, descending to the "poor naked wretches," shed his unthinking trust in closing the gap between words and what they stand for.

Shakespeare pursues the passage of his protagonist from blind arrogance to humbling awareness through the impasse, in the play itself, of the figure of representation. What earlier we have noted as "discrepant awareness" (Evans's term) now unfolds as staged insight into the rupture between socially significant attributes, ceremonies, accords, tokens of social standing, and what is concealed behind them. As Hobbes will show a few decades later, authority in and authorization of a representative postulates a contractual relationship; its acknowledgment helps reconcile differences.

But the massive force of performative turns and halts, noted above, deflects and defuses the progress of representation, the rapprochement between the world and the mirror of language in *King Lear*. Hence the protagonist's passage from royalty to the world of the beggar confronts the absolute limits of what is contractual in a civil *quid pro quo*. On the heath, with no shelter from the "terrors of the earth," the king learns what it takes "To keep base life afoot" (2.4.282, 215). With the barest "art of our necessities" (3.2.70) absent, he is exposed to something elementary – a world predating representation and authorization. Poor Tom, the "bare, fork'd animal" (3.4.107–8) seeks refuge in the topsyturvydom of disguise, thereby obliterating any representation of his former identity. With all civilization behind, Lear now turns to the poorest naked wretch, for him the image of "unaccommodated man," and his response is to tear off his own clothes: "Off, off, you lendings! Come, unbutton here" (3.4.108–9).

To understand Lear's gesture, we need to recall that – in a manner and to a degree difficult to grasp – early modern apparel was overloaded with symbolic connotations of social status. Up to this scene, Lear needs to be envisioned as attired according to his station. For the protagonist to propose to disrobe, to divest himself of his royal array, attests an urge to cancel or crucially qualify the functions, in his role, of both proxy and portrait in representation. In seeking to efface the outward signs of royal authority, Lear sets out to nullify the representation of social difference, to invalidate what validity and authority the former had in fact claimed. His quandary resembles but is not identical with that of Edgar, who takes "the basest and most poorest shape" so as to escape his plight by deliberately changing his identity: "Edgar I nothing am" (2.3.7, 21).

Impulsively discarding the signs of authority, Lear in his language is even more revealing about contingency in the uses of both representation and identity. When he refers to his royal garments as "you lendings," he does so as something almost apart from himself. In his view, they do not quite belong to him. As property of a royal role he has abdicated (and as owned by the theatrical company for which he labors), they are not really his clothes. Thus the notion of his attire is that of an alien, acquired article. As a material matter not so much performed as in fact performing, the dramatic garment serves as the tenor of important meaning: Lear had borrowed, even in his countenance, an "addition" of authority. What they represent is not, or not any longer, felt as constitutive of his self. Now his hubris gives way and public office and personal being so part company that, out of their division, new questions about what is representative arise.

Notice the shifting perspectives on what authority there is between privileged costume and elevated station. The superfluity of the late monarch's "lendings" already invalidates the cultural semiotics correlating privileged signs and their distinctive meanings. Once the authority of these signs is discharged or reaches a state of crisis, the character's sense of identity gives way and the all-encompassing cast of his self-fashioned claim begins to crumble. Now that the combined "marks of sovereignty, knowledge, and reason" are of no avail, the contours of self need to be redrawn. Almost echoing the configuration behind "Edgar I nothing am," Lear cries out the incipient crisis in his representation: "Who is it that can tell me who I am?" (1.4.230).

Such a reading can best be tested against Shakespeare's ex-centric uses of the language of madness, here and throughout the canon. Suffice it to say that, at the height of Lear's madness, the semiotic gap in representation and the crisis of "authority" become inextricably intertwined. Indeed, both these aspects come together at that crucial moment in the play when Lear in his mad, infuriating, visionary passion encounters the blinded Gloucester, and the latter is given an unprecedented answer to what may well be the play's most momentous question, "how this world goes."

Notes

INTRODUCTION

1. Unless otherwise noted, all references to Shakespeare's text in this study draw on *The Riverside Shakespeare*, 2nd edn, ed. G. Blakemore Evans et al. (Boston: Houghton Mifflin, 1997).
2. William B. Worthen, *Shakespeare and the Authority of Performance* (Cambridge: Cambridge University Press, 1997), 27.
3. Michael D. Bristol, *Shakespeare's America, America's Shakespeare* (London and New York: Routledge, 1989), 105.
4. Simon Palfrey and Tiffany Stern, *Shakespeare in Parts* (Oxford: Oxford University Press, 2007), 2, 3. The authors are grateful to Palfrey and Stern for sharing this work with them before its publication.
5. Michael Goldman, *The Actor's Freedom: Toward a Theory of Drama* (Princeton: Princeton University Press, 1972), 7, and Bernard Beckerman in Gloria Brim Beckerman and William Coco, eds., *Theatrical Presentation: Performer, Audience, and Act* (New York: Routledge, 1990), 6–7 (italics in original).
6. Here we have in mind the path-breaking theatre historiography of scholars such as John H. Astington, David Bradley, William Ingram, Janet S. Loengard, Paul W. White, and others. Their contributions are documented and in some of their implications discussed by Robert Weimann, *Author's Pen and Actor's Voice* (Cambridge: Cambridge University Press, 2000), 8–10, 110–16.
7. Philip Butterworth, *Magic on the Early English Stage* (Cambridge: Cambridge University Press, 2005).
8. In Shakespeare studies these "two aspects to acting" have been persuasively addressed by Meredith Anne Skura, *Shakespeare the Actor and the Purpose of Playing* (Chicago and London: University of Chicago Press, 1993), esp. 9–11, 57–63. In theatre and performance studies, we have found most helpful Goldman, *The Actor's Freedom;* William B. Worthen, *The Idea of the Actor: Drama and the Ethics of Performance* (Princeton: Princeton University Press, 1984); and especially Jean Alter, *A Sociosemiotic Theory of Theatre* (Philadelphia: University of Pennsylvania Press, 1990), where the two dimensions are defined in terms of "an inherent duality of theatrical activity" (29).
9. See, for a culmination of Rudolf Stamm's earlier work, *Shakespeare's Theatrical Notation: The Early Tragedies* (Bern: Francke, 1989); this complements David

Bevington's important study, *Action Is Eloquence: Shakespeare's Language of Gesture* (Cambridge, MA: Harvard University Press, 1984).

10. We call this question timely because a reconsideration of representation is overdue in view of the shifting paradigm in the humanities. Today's discontent with the state of critical theory hardly needs to be documented; for just one influential voice, see Toril Moi's outcry: the present "paradigm is now exhausted"; theorists "need to rethink their most fundamental assumptions about language and meaning." This concludes a forum on "Theories and Methodologies" in *PMLA* 121 (October 2006), 1735. In Shakespeare studies new directions have emerged between the appearance of, say, David Kastan's *Shakespeare After Theory* (1999) and Catherine Belsey's *Why Shakespeare?* (2007), with Bryan Reynolds's and William West's collection *Rematerializing Shakespeare* (2005), as one potentially path-pointing trajectory. Against this backcloth, we have, in the body of our introduction here, made recourse to various positions on representation that in the present context appear fruitful and stimulating. To these should be added a recent exquisitely nuanced essay by John Drakakis, welcoming the renewed probing into "the nature of the interplay between... world and word," in a move "beyond the heady rhetoric of an irreducible textuality" characteristic of the early poststructuralism. See his Afterword to Jonathan Holmes and Adrian Streete, eds., *Refiguring Mimesis: Representation in Early Modern Literature* (Hatfield: University of Hertfordshire Press, 2005), 208–16. At the same time, we fall back on what may be seen as preparatory work for the present study, such as Robert Weimann's *Authority and Representation in Early Modern Discourse* (Baltimore and London: Johns Hopkins University Press, 1996), including the counterproposals therein to Michel Foucault's position, together with Douglas Bruster's and Robert Weimann's *Prologues to Shakespeare's Theatre: Performance and Liminality in Early Modern Drama* (London and New York: Routledge, 2004), as well as Weimann's debate with promising perspectives in recent critical approaches to mimesis and representation (such as those by Jacques Derrida, George Hartley, Wolfgang Iser, Louis Marin, Gayatri Chakravorty Spivak, and others), in the yearbook *Symbolism* 6 (2006), 3–36.

11. For evidence of such conflict-ridden interplay between worldly *potestas* and intellectual or imaginary *auctoritas*, see Weimann, *Authority and Representation in Early Modern Discourse*. Remarkably, Janette Dillon has pointed to a tradition of self-representation, reaching from the players of *Mankind* to the Chamberlain's Men: "What they are negotiating, in a sense, is their awareness of the contradictions of their own position." See Dillon, *Language and Stage in Medieval and Renaissance England* (Cambridge: Cambridge University Press, 1998), 217, 57–63.

12. David Schalkwyk, *Literature and the Touch of the Real* (Newark: University of Delaware Press, 2004), 71.

13. Louis Montrose, "New Historicisms," in Stephen Greenblatt and Giles Gunn, eds., *Redrawing the Boundaries* (New York: MLA, 1982), 396.

14. Catherine Belsey, *Shakespeare and the Loss of Eden: The Construction of Family Values in Early Modern Culture* (London: Macmillan, 1999), 7.

15. Pauline Kiernan, *Shakespeare's Theory of Drama* (Cambridge: Cambridge University Press, 1996), 9–10.
16. M. M. Bakhtin, *The Dialogic Imagination: Four Essays*, ed. Michael Holquist, trans. Caryl Emerson and Holquist (Austin: University of Texas Press, 1981), 296, 293, 324.
17. Lukas Erne, *Shakespeare as Literary Dramatist* (Cambridge and New York: Cambridge University Press, 2003), 92, 20.
18. Patrick Cheney, *Shakespeare, National Poet-Playwright* (Cambridge: Cambridge University Press, 2004).
19. See Douglas A. Brooks, *From Playhouse to Printing House: Drama and Authorship in Early Modern England* (Cambridge: Cambridge University Press, 2000), and Alan B. Farmer and Zachary Lesser, "The Popularity of Playbooks Revisited," *Shakespeare Quarterly* 56.1 (2005), 1–32, and "Structures of Popularity in the Early Modern Book Trade," *Shakespeare Quarterly* 56.2 (2005), 206–13.
20. Frank Kermode, *Shakespeare's Language* (London and New York: Allen Lane, 2000), 17.
21. Richard Howard, review of *Shakespeare's Language* in *The American Scholar* 69.3 (2000), 146–8 (quotation at 147–8).
22. Julie Stone Peters, *The Theatre of the Book, 1480–1880: Print, Text, and Performance in Europe* (Oxford and New York: Oxford University Press, 2000), 7.
23. Graham Holderness, *Textual Shakespeare: Writing and the Word* (Hatfield: University of Hertfordshire Press, 2003), xi.
24. Stanley Wells, ed., *William Shakespeare: The Complete Works* (Oxford: Oxford University Press, 1986), xxxviii.
25. David Scott Kastan, *Shakespeare and the Book* (Cambridge and New York: Cambridge University Press, 2001), 6.
26. Ibid., 7.
27. See, for example, Goldman, *The Actor's Freedom*; Inga-Stina Ewbank, "The Word in the Theater," in Kenneth Muir et al., eds., *Shakespeare, Man of the Theater* (Newark: University of Delaware Press, 1983), 55–76; and Robert Hapgood, *Shakespeare the Theatre-Poet* (Oxford: Clarendon Press, 1988).
28. For these phrases, see Ewbank, "The Word in the Theater," 72.
29. See Michael Goldman, "Acting Values and Shakespearean Meaning: Some Suggestions," in David Bevington and Jay Halio, eds., *Shakespeare: Pattern of Excelling Nature* (Newark: University of Delaware Press, 1978), 190–7 (quotation at 190).
30. Ewbank, "The Word in the Theater," 72, 64.
31. Hapgood, *Shakespeare the Theatre-Poet*, 216.
32. Erika Fischer-Lichte, "Reversing the Hierarchy between Text and Performance," *European Review* 9 (2001), 244–91, esp. 280–1. See the unyielding critical contest: R. A. Foakes, "Performance Theory and Textual Theory: A Retort Courteous," *Shakespeare* 2.1 (2006), 47–58, and W. B. Worthen, "Texts, Tools, and Technologies: A Quip Modest," *Shakespeare* 2.2 (2006), 208–19.

33. Eugenio Barba, *Beyond the Floating Islands* (New York: Performing Arts Journal Publications, 1968), 57.
34. Kastan, *Shakespeare and the Book*, 8.
35. Here we would like to acknowledge our abiding debt to Wolfgang Iser's studies in literary anthropology and, especially, Ludwig Pfeiffer's *The Protoliterary: Steps Toward an Anthropology of Culture* (Stanford: Stanford University Press, 2002), together with recent work such as Eugenio Barba and Nicola Savorese, *A Dictionary of Theatre Anthropology* (London: Routledge, 2005), and Sally Banes and André Lepecka, eds., *The Senses of Performance* (London: Routledge, 2006).
36. Simon Shepherd, *Theatre, Body and Pleasure* (New York and London: Routledge, 2006), 35. As in Manfred Pfister's work, "the inscription of body and the bodiliness of text" (ibid., 18) are viewed as interdependent. See below, ch. 8.
37. R. J. E. Tiddy, *The Mummers' Play* (Oxford: Clarendon Press, 1923), 84 ff., 117. For this and the following, see Robert Weimann, *Shakespeare and the Popular Tradition in the Theater: Studies in the Social Dimension of Dramatic Form and Function* (Baltimore: Johns Hopkins University Press, 1978), 80, 86, 146–8, 151–3.
38. Against the "one-dimensional" reading of "body," noticed by Anthony Dawson in Dawson and Paul Yachnin, *The Culture of Playgoing in Shakespeare's England: A Collaborative Debate* (Cambridge and New York: Cambridge University Press, 2001), 15, we differentiate the term between the body as signifying in symbolic action (*Körper*) and its nonrepresentable, nonsymbolic materiality (*Leib*). See chs. 5, pp. 108–09, and 8, pp. 172–3, in this volume.
39. Butterworth, *Magic on the Early English Stage*. The recorded dates are 1588 and 1589 (33); for further evidence, see 216 n48.
40. Samuel Johnson, in *Johnson on Shakespeare*, ed. Walter Raleigh (Oxford: Oxford University Press, 1965), 25.
41. See her recent study *Le Vagabond dans l'Angleterre de Shakespeare, ou l'art de contrefaire à la ville et à la scène* (Paris: L'Harmattan, 2003), 206–78.
42. William Dodd, "Destined Livery? Character and Person in Shakespeare," *Shakespeare Survey* 51 (1998), 147–58, 154n (italics in original).
43. Ibid., 151–2.
44. Alter, *A Sociosemiotic Theory of Theatre*, 29. See, in this connection, note 8 above.
45. Marvin Carlson, *Theatre Semiotics: Signs of Life* (Bloomington: Indiana University Press, 1990), 82.
46. The socio-cultural context of the "duality" in question has been extensively studied in Weimann's *Shakespeare and the Popular Tradition in the Theater*, and the dramaturgic circumstances of "bifold authority" were surveyed in his article in *Shakespeare Quarterly* 39 (1988), 401–18. For contextualizing this "duality" in theatre history and theory, see Alter and Carlson. The most balanced integration of the communicative circumstances in a large view of

Shakespeare's stage we owe to Franco Marenco, *La Parola in Scena: La communicazione teatrale nell'età di Shakespeare* (Turin: UTET, 2004).

47. Michael Shapiro, *Gender in Play on the Shakespearean Stage: Boy Heroines and Female Pages* (Ann Arbor: University of Michigan Press, 1994), 62.

48. See Dawson in *The Culture of Playgoing*, 32, 20. See also Dawson's searching note on staging "the conflict between body and meaning," together with his brief definition of "impersonation" (35, 35 n52).

49. Lesley Wade Soule, *Actor as Anti-Character: Dionysus, the Devil, and the Boy Rosalind* (Westport, CT: Greenwood Press, 2000), 3.

50. For the underlying dialectic of signified *potestas* and signifying *auctoritas*, see below, ch. 10; for its political ubiquity in the Renaissance, see Weimann's *Authority and Representation in Early Modern Discourse*.

51. See the collection edited by Hugh Grady and Terence Hawkes, *Presentist Shakespeares* (London and New York: Routledge, 2007), esp. 247, 233. For an admirable exploration of "the entanglement between 'past' and 'present,'" see John Drakakis, "Present Text," in ibid., esp. 82–5.

52. See Terence Hawkes, *Shakespeare in the Present* (London and New York: Routledge, 2002).

53. Barbara Hodgdon and W. B. Worthen, eds., *A Companion to Shakespeare and Performance* (Oxford: Blackwell, 2006), 6 ff.

54. William N. West, *Theatres and Encyclopedias in Early Modern Europe* (Cambridge and New York: Cambridge University Press, 2002), 129; cf. the evidence for a profound impact of knowledge in its print form upon *Hamlet* and Heywood alike (122–32, 141–2).

55. Leo Salingar, "Jacobean Playwrights and 'Judicious' Spectators," in E. A. J. Honigmann, ed., *British Academy Lectures, 1980–1989* (Oxford: Oxford University Press, 1993), 231–53.

56. Peter Burke, in *Popular Culture in Early Modern Europe* (rev. edn, Aldershot: Scolar Press, 1994), views these changes as part of a European "split between learned and popular culture" (274), a "reform" movement in which traditional "recreation . . . bore the brunt of the attack" (208). Keith Wrightson, in *English Society, 1580–1680* (London: Hutchinson, 1982), sees the century in question as marked by "a growing cultural differentiation" (184), especially in moving from "illiteracy" as "character-istic of the vast majority" in 1580 to illiteracy as "a special characteristic of the poor" in 1680 (220). For the spread of a "censoriously negative view of sports and pastimes," see Patrick Collinson, *The Birthpangs of Protestant England* (London: Macmillan, 1988), 108; for a "moral and cultural water-shed" in "1580, or thereabouts," see his *From Iconoclasm to Iconophobia: The Cultural Impact of the Second English Reformation* (Reading: University of Reading Press, 1986), 8. The rise of a new type of dramatic representation in these years coincided with the incipient decline, especially among the better sort, of nonliterate sports and pastimes. As Mervyn James suggests, the growing interpenetration of the local and the national brought forth the demand for generalized, even universalized, standards of value and

behavior, with new ties and differences among landed interests and court politics. These trends informed and enabled the expression of individual beliefs and convictions through, ironically, the ideological use of "generalized constitutional, religious or philosophical terms." See Mervyn James, *Family, Lineage, and Civil Society: A Study of Society, Politics and Mentality in the Durham Region* (Oxford: Clarendon Press, 1974), 98, 104–5.

57. For further materials and perspectives on this much-neglected matrix of Elizabethan performance practice and theatre history, see Weimann, *Author's Pen and Actor's Voice*, 121–50.

58. Huston Diehl, *Staging Reform, Reforming the Stage: Protestantism and Popular Theatre in Early Modern England* (Ithaca: Cornell University Press, 1997).

59. Barbara A. Mowat, "The Theatre and Literary Culture," in John D. Cox and David Scott Kastan, eds., *A New History of Early English Drama* (New York: Columbia University Press, 1997), 213–15, 218.

60. Ibid., 216.

61. Ibid., 220.

62. Margreta de Grazia, "World Pictures, Modern Periods, and the Early Stage," in ibid., 19 (italics in original).

1. "MORALIZE TWO MEANINGS" IN ONE PLAY: CONTRARIETY ON THE TUDOR STAGE

1. Our approach to the Vice is revisionist, in that it challenges the homiletic bias in what is still the most influential study on the subject: Bernard Spivack, *Shakespeare and the Allegory of Evil* (New York: Columbia University Press, 1958). Setting out "to read the play as a metaphor" (122), the author emphasizes the homiletic uses of farcical evil throughout his learned and – to this day – pathbreaking study. Hence we have "the homiletic stage" (307) on which the Vice performs "homiletic intimacy" (119) and "homiletic showmanship" (303, 339), all "by natural extension of his homiletic energy" (186) and, even, his "homiletic zeal" (178). For criticism and scholarship dealing with the Renaissance Vice in the wake of Spivack's study, see David Klausner, "The Improvising Vice in Renaissance England," in T. J. McGee, ed., *Improvisation in the Arts of the Middle Ages and Renaissance* (Kalamazoo: Western Michigan University Press, 2003), 273–85. See also Robert C. Jones, "Dangerous Sport: The Audience's Engagement with Vice in the Moral Interlude," *Renaissance Drama* 6 (1973), 45–64, as well as Jones, *Engagement with Knavery: Point of View in "Richard III," "The Jew of Malta," "Volpone," and "The Revenger's Tragedy"* (Durham: Duke University Press, 1986). As Ruth Lunney notes, such "engagement," far from limited to either identification or transgression, entails "an awareness, even a sharing" and is inseparable from an achieved theatrical experience. See Lunney, *Marlowe and the Popular Tradition: Innovation in the English Drama before 1595* (Manchester: Manchester University Press, 2002), 102.

2. On the figure of the metadramatic "maker" within Renaissance plays, see Douglas Bruster, *Quoting Shakespeare: Form and Culture in Early Modern*

Drama (Lincoln: University of Nebraska Press, 2000), ch. 3, "The Agency of Quotation in Shakespearean Comedy," 88–116.

3. Patrice Pavis, *Languages of the Stage: Essays in the Semiology of the Theatre* (New York: Performing Arts Journal Publications, 1982), 45. We would note again that the present concept of *gestus* is not to be understood as, in Peter Brooker's phrase, an alienating "analysis" within a "progressive and educative narrative" (*Bertolt Brecht: Dialectics, Poetry, Politics* [London: Croom Helm, 1988], 51–2), but as derived from the fusion of two different media, two contrarious modes of epistemology, cultural production, and social living.

4. Robert Grudin, *Mighty Opposites: Shakespeare and Renaissance Contrariety* (Berkeley: University of California Press, 1979).

5. Ibid., 3.

6. We owe this reference to Marion Trousdale, "Reading the Early Modern Text," *Shakespeare Survey* 50 (1997), 135–45 (at 139).

7. John Hoskins, *Directions for Speech and Style*, ed. Hoyt H. Hudson (Princeton: Princeton University Press, 1935), 21.

8. Thomas Wilson, *The Arte of Rhetorique* (1533; Gainesville: Scholars' Facsimiles, 1962), 214.

9. See Rosalie L. Colie, *Paradoxia Epidemica: The Renaissance Tradition of Paradox* (Princeton: Princeton University Press, 1966); Joel Altman, *The Tudor Play of Mind* (Berkeley: University of California Press, 1978); and Steven Mullaney, "Lying Like Truth: Riddle, Representation, and Treason in Renaissance England," *ELH* 47 (1980), 32–47.

10. Debora Kuller Shuger, *Habits of Thought in the English Renaissance: Religion, Politics, and the Dominant Culture* (Berkeley: University of California Press, 1990).

11. Michael Neill, "The Defence of Contraries: Skeptical Paradox in *A King and No King*," *SEL* 21 (1981), 319–32 (quotation at 320–1).

12. See A. P. Rossiter, *English Drama From Early Times to the Elizabethans* (London: Hutchinson, 1962), who addresses himself to this "disturbing doubleness of tone and point of view" (69). See also the important work of V. A. Kolve, who, in *The Play Called Corpus Christi* (Stanford: Stanford University Press, 1966) argued that "the generic 'self-awareness'" (11) of this drama derived from a deliberate use, within a framework of theological narrative, of "play" and "game" (11–32). But Kolve did not pursue the theatrical implications of this major insight; instead, the emphasis is on the plays' "special gift . . . to imitate life" (233). Although justifiably criticizing "Rossiter's shadowy antinomies" (138), Kolve's groundbreaking study, as far as it failed to follow up its own point of departure, cannot present a fully convincing alternative reading of what "disturbing doubleness" we have in the medieval theatre.

13. Thomas Lupton, *All For Money*, ed. M. E. P. Concolato (Napoli: Liguori Editore, 1985), ll. 92–8. We have collated this edition with the Tudor Facsimile Text, ed. John S. Farmer (1910; rpt. New York: AMS Press, 1970).

14. For these interconnections, see Robert Weimann, "Representation and Performance: The Uses of Authority in Shakespeare's Theater," *PMLA* 107 (May 1992), 497–510.

15. Sir Philip Sidney, *The Defence of Poesy*, in *Sir Philip Sidney: Selected Prose and Poetry*, 2nd edn, ed. Robert Kimbrough (Madison: University of Wisconsin Press, 1983), 150.

16. From John Lyly's prologue to *Midas* (1589), in *The Complete Works of John Lyly*, ed. R. Warwick Bond, 3 vols. (Oxford: Clarendon Press, 1902), 3:115.

17. See M. M. Bakhtin, *The Dialogic Imagination: Four Essays*, ed. Michael Holquist, trans. Caryl Emerson and Holquist (Austin: University of Texas Press, 1981). Independently of Benveniste (see p. 146 in this volume), Bakhtin draws on "distinctive links and interrelationships between utterances and languages" (263).

18. Richard Hillman, *Self-Speaking in Medieval and Early Modern English Drama: Subjectivity, Discourse and the Stage* (New York: St. Martin's Press, 1997), 46.

19. Citations and line numbering given in our text follow George Wapull, *The Tide Tarrieth No Man*, ed. Ernst Rühl, *Shakespeare-Jahrbuch* 43 (1907), 1–52 ll. 45–8.

20. Hillman, *Self-Speaking*, 1. See also ch. 3, "Tudor Transitions and Ramifications," 68–106.

21. From G. A. Lester, ed., *Three Late Medieval Morality Plays* (London: A & C Black, 1990), ll. 30–71.

22. Mischief's "big head, little wit" is another case of "convey[ing] very cleane, / And not be[ing] understood." This literally echoes the most ubiquitous traditional formula, which Robert Weimann has counted no less than nineteen times in the thirty-three folk plays printed in R. J. E. Tiddy's *The Mummers' Play* (Oxford: Clarendon Press, 1923); cf. Robert Weimann, *Shakespeare and the Popular Tradition in the Theater: Studies in the Social Dimension of Dramatic Form and Function* (Baltimore: Johns Hopkins University Press, 1978), 112–53.

23. Angus Fletcher, *Allegory: The Theory of a Symbolic Mode* (Ithaca: Cornell University Press, 1970), 332.

24. Stephen Greenblatt, Preface to Greenblatt, ed., *Allegory and Representation: Selected Papers from the English Institute, 1979–80* (Baltimore: Johns Hopkins University Press, 1981), viii.

25. David Bevington, *From "Mankind" to Marlowe: Growth of Structure in the Popular Drama of Tudor England* (Cambridge, MA: Harvard University Press, 1962), 80–3.

26. For evidence, including a detailed reading of *Mankind* and moral wordplay, see Weimann, *Shakespeare and the Popular Tradition*, 112–51.

27. *A Select Collection of Old English Plays* (Dodsley), ed. W. Carew Hazlitt, 4th edn (repr. New York: Benjamin Blom, 1964), 3:268. Here we identify the volume using the original numbering scheme; in this republication volumes 3–5 are gathered in a new volume 2.

28. Ibid., 3:299.

29. Although Richard Southern in *The Medieval Theatre in the Round* (London: Faber and Faber, 1958) had developed the concept of "place" in reference to an early morality play – *The Castle of Perseverence* – there is compelling evidence that *platea*-like space was constitutive of important conventions of speech and dramaturgy in the mystery plays, where we have, in Hans-Jürgen Diller's phrase, an "offene Spielsphäre." See Diller's magisterial *Redeformen des englischen Misterienspiels* (Munich: Fink, 1973), 148–216, translated into English as *The Middle English Mystery Play: A Study in Dramatic Speech and Form*, trans. Frances Wessels (Cambridge and New York: Cambridge University Press, 1992).

30. On the distinction between (and interplay among) *locus* and *platea* on the early stage, see Robert Weimann, *Author's Pen and Actor's Voice* (Cambridge: Cambridge University Press, 2000), ch. 7, "Space (In)dividable: *Locus* and *Platea* Revisited," 180–215.

31. Dodsley, *Select Collection* 3:344; preceding citations, in order: 3:315, 332.

32. Ibid., 1:161. Such geographical promiscuity resonates, of course, in the better-known line from Marlowe's *The Jew of Malta*: "Fornication? / But that was in another country, / And besides, the wench is dead" (4.1.43–5).

2. PERFORMANCE, GAME, AND REPRESENTATION IN *RICHARD III*

1. The phrase is that of John H. Astington, in "The London Stage in the 1580s," *The Elizabethan Theatre* 11 (1990), 1–18 (quotation at 1).

2. William Ingram, *The Business of Playing: The Beginnings of the Adult Professional Theater in Elizabethan London* (Ithaca: Cornell University Press, 1992), 241.

3. David Bradley, *From Text to Performance in the Elizabethan Theatre: Preparing the Play for the Stage* (Cambridge and New York: Cambridge University Press, 1992), 58.

4. For some of the evidence, see Robert Weimann's *Drama und Wirklichkeit in der Shakespearezeit* (Halle: Niemeyer, 1958), 147–59. The beggar/actor nexus has, since William Carroll's pioneering *Fat King, Lean Beggar* (1996) and Linda Woodbridge's *Vagrancy, Homelessness, and English Renaissance Literature* (2001), found its closest focus in Pascale Drouet's study (see above, p. 227, note 41) and Paola Pugliatti, *Beggary and the Theatre in Early Modern England* (2003).

5. See David Wiles, *Shakespeare's Clown: Actor and Text in the Elizabethan Playhouse* (Cambridge: Cambridge University Press, 1987).

6. See Cornelius Castoriadis, *The Imaginary Institution of Society*, trans. Kathleen Blamey (Cambridge, MA: MIT Press, 1998), 238.

7. Ruth Lunney, *Marlowe and the Popular Tradition: Innovation in the English Drama before 1595* (Manchester: Manchester University Press, 2002), 102–4, 183–4, and *passim*.

8. On the "performant function," see Jean Alter, *A Sociosemiotic Theory of Theatre* (Philadelphia: University of Pennsylvania Press, 1990), 31–2. In view

of "an inherent duality of theatrical activity" (29), Alter elsewhere notes that "performance cannot, and must not, be reduced to its referential function alone," that is, to a "function, which relies on signs to produce meaning." As distinct from a representational kind of "reference," the "performant function" also serves in response to the "need to witness special achievements: physical, aesthetic, technical, and so on" (Michael Issacharoff and Robin F. Jones, eds., *Performing Texts* [Philadelphia: University of Pennsylvania Press, 1988], 32). Andrew Parker and Eve K. Sedgwick refer to this function as "the non-reference of the performative," in Parker and Sedgwick, eds., "Introduction," *Performativity and Performance* (New York: Routledge, 1995), 3.

9. On this privileged position, see Bertrand Evans's description of "discrepant awareness" in *Shakespeare's Comedies* (Oxford: Clarendon Press, 1960), esp. 14, 34, 188–208. As Evans has it, the divisions in awareness are inseparable from comic sport (clowns "are commonly immune to the condition of unawareness" [10]) and masquerade ("Rosalind . . . overpeered all and was never overpeered" [122]). See chs. 4 and 10 of this volume. For early modern performances sharing gamesome play and authority with the audience, see Robert Weimann, *Author's Pen and Actor's Voice* (Cambridge: Cambridge University Press, 2000), esp. 137–9, 223–6.

10. For Marlowe's *Tamburlaine* and Richard Jones's epistle, we use the Revels edition of *Tamburlaine the Great*, ed. J. S. Cunningham (Manchester: Manchester University Press, 1981). For the Epistle, see Douglas Bruster and Robert Weimann, *Prologues to Shakespeare's Theatre: Performance and Liminality in Early Modern Drama* (London and New York: Routledge, 2004), 82, 172 n13; and pp. 53 and 57–8 in this volume.

11. For the subversive potential of Cade and his companions, see Michael D. Bristol, *Carnival and Theater: Plebeian Culture and the Structure of Authority in Renaissance England* (New York: Methuen, 1985), 88–90. See also Richard Wilson's essay, "'A Mingled Yarn': Shakespeare and the Cloth Workers," *Literature and History* 12 (1986), 164–80.

12. For criticism dealing with the Renaissance Vice, see p. 229, note 1, above. Recent criticism dealing specifically with the legacy of the Vice in *Richard III* includes Marie-Hélène Besnault and Michel Bitot, "Historical Legacy and Fiction: The Poetical Reinvention of King Richard III" in Michael Hattaway, ed., *The Cambridge Companion to Shakespeare's History Plays* (Cambridge: Cambridge University Press, 2002), 106–25, esp. 112–16; Pauline Blanc, "Richard III, personnage-Vice protéiforme," in Francis Guinle and Jacques Ramel, eds., *William Shakespeare, Richard III: Nouvelles perspectives critiques* (Montpellier: Centre d'Études et de Recherches sur la Renaissance Anglaise, Université Paul-Valéry–Montpellier III, 2000), 133–59; Jean-Paul Debax, "'The formal vice, iniquity': Traditions dramatiques dans *Richard III*," in Henri Suhamy, ed., *Richard III* (Paris: Ellipses, 1999), 41–51; and Rory Duckles, "*Richard III*: The Transformation of Antecedents," *Johannesburg Shakespeare Quarterly* 1.1 (1993), 6–18. Powerful

characters who attempt to control plays from the inside out are a hallmark of Shakespeare's dramatic practice. Such characters have been identified with a number of terms, from "practicer" and "plotter" to "antic" and "trickster." For a discussion of this central character type and function, see Douglas Bruster, "The Agency of Shakespearean Quotation," ch. 3 in his *Quoting Shakespeare: Form and Culture in Early Modern Drama* (Lincoln: University of Nebraska Press, 2000), 88–116.

13. On the *platea* area of the stage, see "Space (In)dividable: *Locus* and *Platea* Revisited," ch. 7 in Weimann, *Author's Pen and Actor's Voice*, 180–215. Of course, one aspect of Richard's "apartness" surfaces in relation to what Linda Charnes calls his "notorious identity." See Linda Charnes, *Notorious Identity: Materializing the Subject in Shakespeare* (Cambridge, MA: Harvard University Press, 1993), 20–69.

14. Here as elsewhere we are indebted to David Bevington's foundational study, *From "Mankind" to Marlowe* (Cambridge, MA: Harvard University Press, 1962). On the question of Elizabethan direction, see Meredith Anne Skura, *Shakespeare the Actor and the Purpose of Playing* (Chicago: University of Chicago Press, 1993), 46–9, 250–1 nn103–9; Mike Wilcock, *Hamlet: The Shakespearean Director* (Dublin: Carysfort, 2002); and Fran Helphinstine, "Peter Quince as Director," *Shakespeare* 3.2 (Georgetown University, 1999), 14.

15. On the political "game" of the play, and Richard's manipulation of symbols of power for his own ends, see Bridget Gellert Lyons, "'Kings Games': Stage Imagery and Political Symbolism in *Richard III*," *Criticism* 20 (1978), 17–30.

16. According to the *OED*, "post" was only "[f]rom the beginning of the 16th c. applied to . . . [o]ne who travels express with letters, messages, etc., esp. on a fixed route" (s.v. "post," n.2).

17. On *sermo humilis*, see Erich Auerbach, *Literary Language and Its Public in Latin Antiquity and in the Middle Ages*, trans. Ralph Manheim (1958; New York: Pantheon Books, 1965), 25–81.

18. See C. L. Barber, "The Saturnalian Pattern in Shakespeare's Comedy," *The Sewanee Review* 59 (1951), 593–611 (quotation at 595).

19. For the peculiar dramaturgy involved, see Bruster and Weimann, *Prologues to Shakespeare's Theatre*, 139–42, 151.

20. For this position, see Stephen Marche, "Mocking Dead Bones: Historical Memory and the Theater of the Dead in *Richard III*," *Comparative Drama* 37.1 (2003), 37–57 (at 40). On the interrelation of Marlowe's and Shakespeare's works, see, among other studies, James Shapiro, *Rival Playwrights: Marlowe, Jonson, Shakespeare* (New York: Columbia University Press, 1991), and Marjorie Garber, "Marlovian Vision/Shakespearean Revision," *Research Opportunities in Renaissance Drama* 22 (1979), 3–9.

21. On the real and potential contrariety in the writing of history in one of Shakespeare's central resources, see Annabel Patterson, *Reading Holinshed's "Chronicles"* (Chicago: University of Chicago Press, 1994).

22. Ritchie D. Kendall, *The Drama of Dissent: The Radical Poetics of Nonconformity, 1380–1590* (Chapel Hill: University of North Carolina Press, 1985), 127.

23. E. K. Chambers, *The Elizabethan Stage*, 4 vols. (Oxford: Clarendon Press, 1923), 4:267.

24. Such profanation would be the target of the well-known 1606 "Acte to Restraine Abuses of Players," which aimed at "the preventing and avoiding of the greate Abuse of the Holy Name of God in Stageplayes, Interludes, Maygames, Shewes, and such like." See Chambers, vol. 4, Appendix D, 338–9.

25. For a compelling study of the Book of Common Prayer as a central resource for imaginative writers of the era, see Ramie Targoff, *Common Prayer: The Language of Religious Devotion in Early Modern England* (Chicago: University of Chicago Press, 2001).

3. MINGLING VICE AND "WORTHINESS" IN *KING JOHN*

1. Christopher Marlowe, *Tamburlaine the Great*, ed. J. S. Cunningham (Manchester: Manchester University Press, 1981). This is the text from which we continue to cite Marlowe's prologues and Richard Jones's preface.

2. J. Leeds Barroll, *Politics, Plague and Shakespeare's Theater: The Stuart Years* (Ithaca: Cornell University Press, 1991), 8.

3. The date of *King John* is clearly important for the status of *The Troublesome Reign* – possibly a text independently adapted for performance, even a politically motivated "propaganda piece," though "not exactly a bad quarto" (L. A. Beaurline). In the most recent examination of the chronology of Shakespeare's plays, MacDonald P. Jackson dates *King John* to 1595. See Jackson, "Pause Patterns in Shakespeare's Verse: Canon and Chronology," *Literary and Linguistic Computing* 17.1 (2002), 37–45 (at 41). Admitting that "This play is pivotal in the dating of the whole early Shakespeare dramatic canon," Jackson argues that internal evidence (including pause patterns and the use of hendiadys) places it "later than the first ten Shakespeare plays" (43). Jackson assigns it to the mid-1590s cluster of *A Midsummer Night's Dream*, *Romeo and Juliet*, *Love's Labour's Lost*, *The Comedy of Errors*, and *Richard II* (41), noting that "The theory that *King John* influenced *The Troublesome Reign* might conceivably be reconciled with acceptance of the conventional dating of other early Shakespeare plays by postulating the original existence of *King John* in an earlier form than that preserved in the First Folio" (41). For arguments offering the earlier date, see *King John*, ed. E. A. J. Honigmann, The Arden Shakespeare (London: Methuen, 1954), esp. xviii–xxv, liii–lviii; and *King John*, ed. L. A. Beaurline, The New Cambridge Shakespeare (Cambridge: Cambridge University Press, 1990), 194–210 (especially at 206). For further debate as to whether *The Troublesome Reign* preceded *King John*, see Sidney Thomas in *Shakespeare Quarterly* 37 (1986), 98–100, and the exchange between Honigmann, Paul Werstine, and Thomas in *Shakespeare Quarterly* 38 (1987), 125–30, on the interpretation of "documentary links" – mainly a stage direction – in establishing precedence. See also Guy Hamel, "*King John* and *The Troublesome Raigne*: A Reexamination," in Deborah T. Curren-Aquino, ed., "*King John*": *New Perspectives* (Newark: University of Delaware Press, 1989),

esp. 41, 58 n2, and Brian Boyd, "*King John* and *The Troublesome Raigne*: Sources, Structure, Sequence," in *Philological Quarterly* 74 (1995), 37–56. On the question of sequence, A. R. Braunmuller's consideration that the better stylistic, metrical, critical, and historical circumstantial evidence is in favor of *King John* postdating *The Troublesome Reign* seems to us, if not the last word, the most persuasive answer we have. See Braunmuller, ed., *The Life and Death of King John* (Oxford: Clarendon Press, 1989), 15.

4. *The Macro Plays*, ed. Mark Eccles, EETS 262 (London: Oxford University Press, 1969), 155, l. 54.

5. Our text is *The Troublesome Raigne of King John*, ed. Geoffrey Bullough, in his *Narrative and Dramatic Sources of Shakespeare*, 7 vols. (London: Routledge; New York: Columbia University Press, 1962), 4:72–151.

6. On the role of status and service in these two plays, see Edward Gieskes, "'He is But a Bastard to the Time': Status and Service in *The Troublesome Raigne of King John* and Shakespeare's *King John*," *ELH* 65 (1998), 779–98.

7. Braunmuller, ed., *The Life and Death of King John*, 69, 71.

8. For the links between Hamlet and diverse Vice figurations, see Robert Weimann, *Shakespeare and the Popular Tradition in the Theater: Studies in the Social Dimension of Dramatic Form and Function* (Baltimore: Johns Hopkins University Press, 1978), 125–33, 150 ff.

9. See Alan C. Dessen, *Shakespeare and the Late Moral Plays* (Lincoln: University of Nebraska Press, 1986), 18–23, 137–8, 162–3, who lists "a wealth of allusions to the Vice" (21). Recently David N. Klausner has examined improvisation as it relates to the Vice figure during this period, concluding that one can divide improvisation into "two types": "improvisation intended by the playwright, which I have called planned improvisation, and improvisation not intended by the playwright, or unplanned improvisation." See Klausner, "The Improvising Vice in Renaissance England," in Timothy J. McGee, ed., *Improvisation in the Arts of the Middle Ages and Renaissance* (Kalamazoo, MI: Western Michigan University Press, 2003), 273–85 (quotation at 283).

10. On the "performant function," see Jean Alter, *A Sociosemiotic Theory of Theatre* (Philadelphia: University of Pennsylvania Press, 1990), 31–2.

11. Ben Jonson, *The Staple of News*, ed. Anthony Parr (Manchester: Manchester University Press, 1988), 2, Interlude, 14–15.

12. For a cogent reading of "instrumental reason" as it functions in characters like Iago in Shakespeare's plays, see Hugh Grady, *Shakespeare's Universal Wolf: Postmodernist Studies in Early Modern Reification* (Oxford: Oxford University Press, 1996).

13. On the genealogy of the Bastard, see *King John*, ed. John Dover Wilson (Cambridge: Cambridge University Press, 1936), xxxix–xli, and *King John*, ed. Honigmann, xxii–xxv, as well as other editors. See, further, Richard Levin, "*King John's* Bastard," *The Upstart Crow* 3 (Fall 1980), 29–41. What especially deserves to be underlined is the multivocal nature of the Bastard's presence in the play, as discussed by Michael Manheim in "The Four Voices of the Bastard" (*"King John": New Perspectives*, ed. Curren-Aquino, 126–35). But in

the present context, the most consequential division in his "purpose of playing" is between his presentational and representational cast – conveniently summed up by Alexander Leggatt as "an unmistakable amalgam of participant and commentator." See Leggatt, "Dramatic Perspective in *King John*," *English Studies in Canada* 3 (1977), 15–16. On the seminal dimension of the Bastard, see Emrys Jones, *Scenic Form in Shakespeare* (Oxford: Clarendon Press, 1971), esp. 99–101, 185–6, 239–42.

14. Annabel Patterson, *Reading Holinshed's "Chronicles"* (Chicago: University of Chicago Press, 1994), xv. On persisting images of movement in the play, see James E. May, "Imagery in Disorderly Motion in *King John*: A Thematic Gloss," *Essays in Literature* 10 (1983), 17–28.

15. Here we use L. A. Beaurline's paraphrase, *King John*, 98 (l. 574).

16. Christopher Z. Hobson, "Bastard Speech: The Rhetoric of 'Commodity' in *King John*," *Shakespeare Yearbook* 2 (1991), 95–114.

17. See Appendix C, *King John*, ed. Braunmuller, 286–9.

18. *Hyckescorner*, in *Specimens of the Pre-Shakespearean Drama*, ed. J. M. Manly, 2 vols. (1925; Boston: Athenaeum Press, 1987), 1:396 (cf. ll. 309–25). On the combined geographical and social mobility found in many of the Vice's descendants in early modern drama, see Douglas Bruster, *Quoting Shakespeare: Form and Culture in Early Modern Drama* (Lincoln: University of Nebraska Press, 2000), 109–16.

19. Francis Bacon, *The New Organon*, ed. Fulton H. Anderson (New York: Liberal Arts Press, 1960), 81.

20. *King John*, ed. Honigmann, 15.

21. *King John*, ed. Braunmuller, 132.

22. Walter Benjamin, *Gesammelte Schriften*, ed. Rolf Tiedemann and Hermann Schweppenhauser (Frankfurt: Suhrkamp, 1974), 1.1.342; in the German original the "abyss between figurate being and meaning" (Robert Weimann's translation) is, literally, an *Abgrund*.

23. Robert Weimann, *Authority and Representation in Early Modern Discourse* (Baltimore and London: Johns Hopkins University Press, 1996), 133–59.

24. Stephen Gosson, *The Ephemerides of Phialo* (London, 1579), 10.

4. CLOWNING: AGENCIES BETWEEN VOICE AND PEN

1. Thomas Nashe, Dedication in *An Almond for a Parrot* (1589), in *The Works of Thomas Nashe*, ed. R. B. McKerrow, 5 vols. (London: A. H. Bullen, 1904–10), 3:331.

2. *The Book of Sir Thomas More*, ed. Vittorio Gabrieli and Giorgio Melchiori, The Revels Plays (Manchester and New York: Manchester University Press), 3.2.349, 354 (159).

3. David Wiles, *Shakespeare's Clown: Actor and Text in the Elizabethan Playhouse* (Cambridge: Cambridge University Press, 1987), 1.

4. Ibid., 33, 111.

5. John H. Astington, "The London Stage in the 1580s," *The Elizabethan Theatre* 11 (1990), 1–18 (at 1).

6. Ibid., 13.
7. Andrew Gurr, *The Shakespearian Playing Companies* (Oxford: Clarendon Press; New York: Oxford University Press, 1996), 41.
8. Ibid., 36, 189.
9. Ibid., 189.
10. Kemp had been paid an extra ten shillings at Leicester House in May of 1585. See Sally-Beth MacLean, "The Politics of Patronage: Dramatic Records in Robert Dudley's Household Books," *Shakespeare Quarterly* 44.2 (1993), 175–82, 180.
11. Gurr, *Shakespearian Playing Companies*, 192. We would note that the few titles Gurr lists contrast significantly with hundreds of recorded provincial performances.
12. Scott McMillin and Sally-Beth MacLean, *The Queen's Men and Their Plays* (Cambridge and New York: Cambridge University Press, 1998), 85.
13. Ibid., 122, 85.
14. Ibid., 166.
15. *Henslowe's Diary*, ed. R. A. Foakes and R. T. Rickert (Cambridge: Cambridge University Press, 1961), 7.
16. David Bradley, *From Text to Performance in the Elizabethan Theatre: Preparing the Play for the Stage* (Cambridge and New York: Cambridge University Press, 1992), 253 n19, 65.
17. Terence Hawkes, *Shakespeare in the Present* (New York: Routledge, 2002), 87. See also the more recent anthology edited by Hugh Grady and Hawkes, *Presentist Shakespeares* (London: Routledge, 2006).
18. Hawkes, *Shakespeare in the Present*, 93.
19. See the New Arden *Hamlet*, ed. Harold Jenkins (London: Methuen, 1982), longer note, 547 ff.
20. See Hawkes, *Shakespeare in the Present*, 93, 94, 97. Hawkes adds, "we can call it making meaning."
21. Meredith Anne Skura, *Shakespeare the Actor and the Purpose of Playing* (Chicago: University of Chicago Press, 1993), 161.
22. Ibid., 237 n5.
23. Nora Johnson, *The Actor as Playwright in Early Modern Drama* (Cambridge and New York: Cambridge University Press, 2003), 21.
24. See Robert Weimann, *Shakespeare and the Popular Tradition in the Theater: Studies in the Social Dimension of Dramatic Form and Function* (Baltimore: Johns Hopkins University Press, 1978), esp. 256–9; and pp. 104–10 in this volume.
25. Here we follow the dating suggested by McMillin and MacLean, *The Queen's Men*, 90, 94.
26. Our text of *The Famous Victories* is that provided in Geoffrey Bullough's *Narrative and Dramatic Sources of Shakespeare* (London: Routledge and Kegan Paul; New York: Columbia University Press, 1961–), 4:299 ff., 123; cf. also 127–9.
27. For a similar confusion of clownish agency and dramatic role, see ll. 407–13, 420. Unaccountably, Bullough prints Dericke's speech in verse. Following

Joseph Quincy Adams's edition in *Chief Pre-Shakespearean Dramas* (Boston: Houghton Mifflin, 1924), ll. 178–84, we here revert to prose.

28. Andrew Gurr, *Playgoing in Shakespeare's London* (Cambridge and New York: Cambridge University Press, 1997), 125.

29. Ibid., 35.

30. *The Works of Thomas Nashe*, ed. McKerrow, 1:286–7.

31. Wiles, *Shakespeare's Clown*, 74.

32. Ibid., 33.

33. William Shakespeare, *The Two Gentlemen of Verona*, ed. Clifford Leech, The New Arden Shakespeare (London and New York: Methuen, 1969), xxxvi.

34. See *The Book of Sir Thomas More*, ed. Gabrieli and Melchiori, 27, and Eric Rasmussen, "Setting Down What the Clown Spoke: Improvisation, Hand B, and *The Book of Sir Thomas More*," *The Library* (1990), 126–36.

35. Rasmussen, "Setting Down What the Clown Spoke," 128.

36. Ibid., 130.

37. Scott McMillin, *The Elizabethan Theatre and "The Book of Sir Thomas More,"* (Ithaca: Cornell University Press, 1987), 45. Gabrieli and Melchiori in their edition confirm the date, 46 (cf. 12).

38. G. E. Bentley, *The Professions of Dramatist and Player in Shakespeare's Time, 1590–1642*, 1 vol. paperback edn (Princeton: Princeton University Press, 1984), 87, 79.

39. See Richard Helgerson, *Forms of Nationhood: The Elizabethan Writing of England* (Chicago: University of Chicago Press, 1992), 199–204 (at 204).

40. Alexander Leggatt, "The Companies and Actors," in *The Revels History of Drama in English*, 8 vols. (London: Methuen, 1975), 3:107.

41. Johnson, *The Actor as Playwright*, 14, 10.

42. Ibid., 26.

43. Ibid., 25.

44. For well-nuanced differences among Field, Heywood, and Munday, however, see ibid., *passim*.

45. For their social function and cultural valence, see Robert Weimann, *Author's Pen and Actor's Voice* (Cambridge: Cambridge University Press, 2000), *passim*.

46. Lukas Erne, *Shakespeare as Literary Dramatist* (Cambridge and New York: Cambridge University Press, 2003), 220, 92.

47. M. M. Bakhtin, *The Dialogic Imagination: Four Essays*, ed. Michael Holquist, trans. Caryl Emerson and Holquist (Austin: University of Texas Press, 1981), 163.

48. Ibid., 324 (italics in original).

49. Desiderius Erasmus, *The Praise of Folly*, trans. Clarence H. Miller (New Haven: Yale University Press, 1979), 139. For a more detailed study of "Allegory and the Authorization of Folly" in Erasmus, see Robert Weimann, *Authority and Representation in Early Modern Discourse* (Baltimore and London: Johns Hopkins University Press, 1996), 133–46.

50. Erasmus, *The Praise of Folly*, ed. Miller, 12, 10.

51. Charles Estienne, *The Defence of Contraries. Paradoxes against Common Opinion*, trans. A.[nthony] M.[unday] (London: 1593), 4. As Donna B. Hamilton points

out in her recent study, *Anthony Munday and the Catholics, 1560–1633* (Aldershot, Hants, and Burlington, VT: Ashgate Publishing, 2005), Estienne's treatise is itself an imitation of Ortensio Landi's *Paradossi* (124–5).

52. Estienne, *The Defence of Contraries*, 25.

53. Ibid., 30.

54. Its history is well documented, from Wilhelm Reich to Allardyce Nicoll. See Weimann, *Shakespeare and Popular Tradition*, 50, 269 n2.

55. See Kenneth Muir, *Shakespeare's Sources* (London: Methuen, 1961), 177, 188, 261, 16, and Stuart Gillespie, *Shakespeare's Books: A Dictionary of Shakespeare's Sources* (London and New York: Continuum, 2004), 152–60. On Shakespeare's debt to Erasmus for Bottom's speech and elements of his characterization, see D. J. Palmer, "Bottom, St. Paul, and Erasmus' *Praise of Folly*," in Philip Edwards et al., eds., *KM 80: A Birthday Album for Kenneth Muir* (Liverpool: Liverpool University Press, 1987), 112–13, and Thelma N. Greenfield, "*A Midsummer Night's Dream* and *The Praise of Folly*," *Comparative Literature* 20 (1968), 236–44.

56. See Erasmus, *The Praise of Folly*, ed. Miller, 27, 43, and esp. 159.

57. *The Adages of Erasmus*, trans. Margaret Mann Phillips (Cambridge: Cambridge University Press, 1964), 270, 269.

58. Erasmus, *The Praise of Folly*, ed. Miller, 43.

59. Ibid., 43–4.

60. Johnson, personal communication to authors.

61. Erving Goffman, *The Presentation of Self in Everyday Life* (New York: Doubleday, 1959), 252, 254.

62. Johnson, *The Actor as Playwright*, 23.

63. See, for example, our remarks on Richard Gloucester and Bastard Faulconbridge, pp. 48–56 and 59–76 in this volume.

64. David Schalkwyk, *Speech and Performance in Shakespeare's Sonnets and Plays* (Cambridge: Cambridge University Press, 2002).

65. See, for the evidence, D. F. Sutton, "Father Silenus: Actor or Coryphaeus?" *Classical Quarterly* 24 (1974), 19–23.

66. We use the standard text of François Rabelais, *Œuvres complètes*, ed. Pierre Jourda, 2 vols. (Paris: Garnier Frères, 1962), 1:5. The English is our translation and paraphrase.

67. In the original: "*car en icelle bien aultre goust trouverez, et doctrine plus absconse, laquelle vous revelera de très haultz sacremens et mysteres horrificques, tant en ce que concerne nostre religion que aussi l'estat politicq et vie oeconomicque.*" Rabelais, *Œuvres complètes*, ed. Jourda, 1:8.

68. Here we draw on the translation in *The Histories of Gargantua and Pantagruel*, ed. and trans. J. M. Cohen (Harmondsworth and New York: Penguin, 1955), 692; the French passage comes from Rabelais, *Œuvres complètes*, ed. Jourda, 2:433. For a much closer look at "the word of the bottle" and Rabelais's symbolic counterproposals to the allegory of emblems and colours, see Weimann, *Authority and Representation in Early Modern Discourse*, 147–59.

69. Ibid., 37.

70. Ibid., 705.

71. From the Prologue, *The Histories of Gargantua and Pantagruel*, ed. and trans. Cohen, 38.

5. CLOWNING AT THE FRONTIERS OF REPRESENTATION

1. Here we must content ourselves with a thoroughly pragmatic concept of representation; for some definitions, see the respective contributions of Catherine Belsey, Pauline Kiernan, Louis Montrose, David Schalkwyk, and Robert Weimann, cited in the Introduction, notes 10 and 12–15.

2. *The Works of Thomas Nashe*, ed. R. B. McKerrow, 5 vols. (London: A. H. Bullen, 1904–10), 3:279–80.

3. On the role of *disputatio* in the early modern classroom and playhouse, see the classic study by Joel B. Altman, *The Tudor Play of Mind: Rhetorical Inquiry and the Development of Elizabethan Drama* (Berkeley: University of California Press, 1978).

4. William Shakespeare, *The Two Gentlemen of Verona*, ed. Kurt Schlueter (Cambridge: Cambridge University Press, 1980), 15.

5. *Tarltons iests Drawne into these three parts. 1 His court-wittie iests 2 His sound cittie iests. 3 His country prettie iests. Full of delight, wit, and honest myrth* (London: Printed [by Thomas Snodham] for Iohn Budge, and are to be sold at his shop, at the great South doore of Paules, 1613), C2v.

6. See Stephen Greenblatt, "Filthy Rites," *Daedalus* 111 (1983), 1–16, on the "management," not the representation, "of the body's products" (2); Elaine Scarry, *The Body in Pain* (New York and Oxford: Oxford University Press, 1985): "to be intensely embodied is the equivalent of being unrepresentative" (207), at least in religious belief, where "animal representation" (229) has its own particular problems; and Gail Kern Paster, *The Body Embarrassed: Drama and the Discipline of Shame in Early Modern England* (Ithaca: Cornell University Press, 1993), and her essay on "Nervous Tension" in David Hillman and Carla Mazzio, eds., *The Body in Parts: Fantasies of Corporeality in Early Modern Europe* (London and New York: Routledge, 1997), 107–28, to name just a few.

7. Paster, "Nervous Tension," 120, 112.

8. David Hillman, "Visceral Knowledge," in Hillman and Mazzio, eds., *The Body in Parts*, 104 n53.

9. According to the *OED*, *Leib* in its etymology is cognate with "loaf," and resonates in "loafing" – not to employ the body properly, either in work or sport or pleasure. See Helmuth Plessner, "Zur Anthropologie des Schauspielers," in Günter Dux, Odo Marquard, and Elisabeth Ströker, eds., *Gesammelte Schriften* (Frankfurt am Main: Suhrkamp, 1982), 399–418, as well as his eye-opening studies of *Lachen und Weinen* (München: Francke, 1961) and *Die Stufen des Organischen und der Mensch* (Frankfurt am Main: Suhrkamp, 1981); the former of these has been translated as *Laughing and Crying: A Study of the Limits of Human Behavior* (Evanston, IL: Northwestern

University Press, 1970). For a more recent survey of the phenomenological and sociological directions in the field, see Robert Gugutzer, *Leib, Körper und Identität* (Wiesbaden: Westdeutscher Verlag, 2002), whose frame of reference is enriched by drawing on Merleau-Ponty and Pierre Bourdieu's concept of "habitus" as an embodied site of social memory and history (esp. 112–16). For a persuasive introduction of the *Leib/Körper* distinction into contemporary performance theory, see Erika Fischer-Lichte, *Ästhetik des Performativen* (Frankfurt am Main: Suhrkamp, 2004), esp. 52–7 and 129–75; note the remarks there on the "indisposability" (*Unverfügbarkeit*) of the staged animal body in and after Joseph Beuys's spectacular three-day co-performance with a coyote in New York City, May 1974.

10. Terence Hawkes, *Shakespeare in the Present* (London and New York: Routledge, 2002), 93. For a fascinating probe into staging the species boundary, see Andreas Höfele, "Humanity at Stake: Man and Animal in Shakespeare's Theatre," *Shakespeare Survey* 60 (2007), 118–29.

11. Mary Thomas Crane, *Shakespeare's Brain: Reading with Cognitive Theory* (Princeton: Princeton University Press, 2001), 71.

12. Ibid., 75.

13. See Lukas Erne, *Shakespeare as Literary Dramatist* (Cambridge: Cambridge University Press, 2003).

14. See Richard Helgerson, *Forms of Nationhood: The Elizabethan Writing of England* (Chicago: University of Chicago Press, 1992), 199.

15. Joseph Hall, *Virgidemiarum* (1597), 1.1.31–44, in Joseph Hall, *The Works*, ed. Philip Wynter, 10 vols. (Oxford, 1863; New York: AMS Press rpt. 1969), 9:58.

16. Although of course pejorative, the use of "puppets" harbors an irony in its reference to early modern culture; cf. Scott Cutler Shershow, *Puppets and "Popular" Culture* (Ithaca: Cornell University Press, 1995).

17. David Mann, *The Elizabethan Player: Contemporary Stage Representation* (London: Routledge, 1991), 178.

18. Richard Brome, *Antipodes*, ed. A. Haaker (Lincoln: University of Nebraska Press, 1966), 40; cited in David Wiles, *Shakespeare's Clown: Actor and Text in the Elizabethan Playhouse* (Cambridge: Cambridge University Press, 1987), 35.

19. See Douglas Bruster, *Quoting Shakespeare: Form and Culture in Early Modern Drama* (Lincoln: University of Nebraska Press, 2000), ch. 4, esp. 132–9.

20. See Jenkins's Long Note, in *Hamlet*, The Arden Shakespeare (London: Methuen, 1982), 547. For a sensitive reading of the play's relationship to this case, and to legal discourse generally, see Luke Wilson, *Theaters of Intention: Drama and the Law in Early Modern England* (Stanford: Stanford University Press, 2000), 25–67.

21. The phrase is from the 1610 Quarto of *Histrio-mastix, or The Player Whipped* (1599), arguably the play most trenchant in disparaging common players. See Robert Weimann, *Author's Pen and Actor's Voice* (Cambridge: Cambridge University Press, 2000), 124–5; Mann, *The Elizabethan Player*, 148; and James Bednarz, "Representing Jonson: *Histriomastix* and the Origin of the Poets' War," *Huntington Library Quarterly* 54.1 (1991), 1–30.

22. For a reading of this scene that stresses the gravediggers' "perception of a world defined by concrete experience," see Michael D. Bristol, *Carnival and Theater: Plebeian Culture and the Structure of Authority in Renaissance England* (New York and London: Routledge, 1985), 185–93 (quotation at 191).

23. For a more detailed reading of the Porter's scene, see Weimann, *Author's Pen and Actor's Voice*, 196–208.

24. Elaine Scarry, *Resisting Representation* (New York and Oxford: Oxford University Press, 1994), 10, 149, 166.

25. According to Alfred Harbage's estimate, attendance at London playhouses had reached its peak by 1605; cf. Harbage, *Shakespeare's Audience* (New York/London: Columbia University Press, 1964), 41.

6. CROSS-DRESSING AND PERFORMANCE IN DISGUISE

1. On the role of clothing in the early modern entertainment industry, see Jean MacIntyre and Garrett P. J. Epp, "'Clothes Worth All the Rest': Costumes and Properties," in John D. Cox and David Kastan, eds., *A New History of Early English Drama* (New York: Columbia University Press, 1997), 269–85, and Ann Rosalind Jones and Peter Stallybrass, "The Circulation of Clothes and the Making of the English Theatre," ch. 7 in Jones and Stallybrass, *Renaissance Clothing and the Materials of Memory* (Cambridge: Cambridge University Press, 2001), 175–206.

2. Stephen Orgel, *Impersonations: The Performance of Gender in Shakespeare's England* (Cambridge: Cambridge University Press, 1996), 1. See also Jean Howard, "Cross-Dressing, the Theatre, and Gender Struggle in Early Modern England," *Shakespeare Quarterly* 39.4 (1988), 418–40; Laura Levine, *Men in Women's Clothing: Anti-Theatricality and Effeminization 1579–1642* (Cambridge: Cambridge University Press, 1994); and Peter Stallybrass, "Transvestism and the 'Body Beneath': Speculating on the Boy Actor," in Susan Zimmerman, ed., *Erotic Politics: Desire on the Renaissance Stage* (New York: Routledge, 1992), 64–83. More recently, James C. Bulman has addressed the role of male sexuality in modern, all-male productions of Shakespeare; see his "Queering the Audience: All-Male Casts in Recent Productions of Shakespeare," in Barbara Hodgdon and W. B. Worthen, eds., *A Companion to Shakespeare and Performance* (Oxford: Blackwell Publishing, 2005), 564–87. See also Cécile Jordi, who has explored the implications of cross-dressing for the *theatrum mundi* trope; see "Réflexion sur l'art de l'acteur à travers le travesti dans *Comme il vous plaira* de William Shakespeare," *Revue d'histoire du théâtre* 58 (2006), 325–32.

3. Lisa Jardine, *Still Harping on Daughters: Women and Drama in the Age of Shakespeare* (New York: Columbia University Press, 1989), viii–ix.

4. See Peter Hyland, "The Performance of Disguise," *Early Theatre* 5.1 (2002), 77–83 (at 78). We have added emphasis on "meanings" here. For an early but still useful survey of disguise in Renaissance plays, see Victor O. Freeburg, *Disguise Plots in Elizabethan Drama: A Study in Stage Tradition*

(New York: Columbia University Press, 1915; rpt. New York: Benjamin Blom, 1965). See also M. C. Bradbrook, "Shakespeare and the Use of Disguise in Elizabethan Drama," *Essays in Criticism* 2 (1952), 159–68; Thomas Van Laan, *Role-Playing in Shakespeare* (Toronto: University of Toronto Press, 1978); Joan Lord Hall, *The Dynamics of Role-Playing in Jacobean Tragedy* (New York: St. Martin's Press, 1991); and Anthony B. Dawson, *Indirections: Shakespeare and the Art of Illusion* (Toronto: University of Toronto Press, 1978). See also the significant debate on "personation" and "masquerade" in Dawson and Paul Yachnin's *The Culture of Playgoing in Shakespeare's England: A Collaborative Debate* (Cambridge: Cambridge University Press, 2001), 1–65.

5. Judith Butler, *Gender Trouble: Feminism and the Subversion of Identity* (London: Routledge, 1990), 147.

6. Ibid., 147.

7. For an important critique of Derridean ("unsocial") textuality, see Judith Butler, *Excitable Speech: A Politics of the Performative* (New York: Routledge, 1997), 145–50.

8. Butler, *Gender Trouble*, 140.

9. Sue-Ellen Case, *Feminism and Theatre* (London: Macmillan, 1988), 22.

10. Catherine Belsey, "Disrupting Sexual Difference: Meaning and Gender in the Comedies," in John Drakakis, ed., *Alternative Shakespeares* (London and New York: Methuen, 1985), 167.

11. Howard, "Cross-dressing, the Theater, and Gender Struggle," 435.

12. Ibid., 431 n39 (our italics).

13. As Kathleen McLuskie suggests in "The Act, the Role, and the Actor: Boy Actresses on the Elizabethan Stage," *New Theatre Quarterly* 3 (1987), 120–30.

14. Case, *Feminism and Theatre*, 22.

15. Jardine, *Still Harping on Daughters*, 17.

16. E. K. Chambers, *The Medieval Stage*, 2 vols. (Oxford: Oxford University Press, 1903), 1:179; cited by Clifford Leech in William Shakespeare, *The Two Gentlemen of Verona*, The Arden Shakespeare, ed. Leech (London: Methuen, 1969), 102.

17. On this sequence in *The Two Noble Kinsmen*, see Douglas Bruster, *Quoting Shakespeare: Form and Culture in Early Modern Drama* (Lincoln: University of Nebraska Press, 2000), 163–5.

18. Susan Baker, "Personating Persons: Rethinking Shakespearean Disguises," *Shakespeare Quarterly* 43.3 (1992), 303–16 (at 304). Baker provides a four-part taxonomy of disguise in Shakespeare, in which characters may (1) "hide their own identities without asserting any other"; (2) "substitute another, already existing identity for their own"; (3) "invent a specific role or persona for a specific and limited purpose"; and (4) "adopt a role – personate an invented, particular identity – to be played in multiple circumstances and for multiple audiences" (305). Our argument here is that many sequences involving disguise overlay one or more of Baker's actions atop another.

19. For schoolboys' engagement with the heroines of classical literature, see Marjorie Curry Woods, "Boys Will Be Women: Musings on Classroom

Nostalgia and the Chaucerian Audience(s)," in R. F. Yeager and Charlotte C. Morse, eds., *Speaking Images: Essays in Honor of V. A. Kolve* (Asheville, NC: Pegasus Press, 2000), 143–66.

20. Julian Hilton, *Performance* (London: Macmillan, 1991), 152.

21. Jan Kott, "The Gender of Rosalind," *New Theatre Quarterly* 7 (1991), 113–25 (at 113).

22. Juliet Dusinberre, *Shakespeare and the Nature of Women* (London: Macmillan, 1975), 264–5.

23. See Lesley Anne Soule, "Subverting Rosalind: Cocky Ros in the Forest of Arden," *New Theatre Quarterly* 7 (1991), 126–36, and Lesley Wade Soule, *Actor as Anti-Character: Dionysus, the Devil, and the Boy Rosalind* (Westport, CT: Greenwood Press, 2000). We believe that it is important to consult both forms of Soule's argument, for while her thinking on Rosalind clearly undergoes some changes from essay to book, not all her remarks in *Actor as Anti-Character* fully reflect her essay's compressed and provocative argument.

24. Soule, "Subverting Rosalind," 127.

25. Soule, *Actor as Anti-Character*, 158.

26. Soule, "Subverting Rosalind," 127.

27. See William Kerrigan, "The Personal Shakespeare: Three Clues," in Norman N. Holland, Sidney Homan, and Bernard J. Paris, eds., *Shakespeare's Personality* (Berkeley: University of California Press, 1989), 175–90, 175.

28. The concept of "worthiness" used here (and throughout this study) is introduced by Richard Jones in his prefatory epistle to *Tamburlaine*. See "To the Gentlemen Readers and Others that Take Pleasure in Reading Histories," in Christopher Marlowe, *Tamburlaine the Great, Parts I and II*, ed. John D. Jump, 3–4, 3 ll. 19–20. For the underlying poetics and sociology of this phrase and concept, see Robert Weimann, *Author's Pen and Actor's Voice* (Cambridge: Cambridge University Press, 2000), 59–60.

29. Michael Goldman, *The Actor's Freedom: Toward a Theory of Drama* (New York: Viking Press, 1975), 12 ff., 8.

30. Peter Stallybrass, "The World Turned Upside Down," in Valerie Wayne, ed., *The Matter of Difference: Materialist Feminist Criticism of Shakespeare* (Ithaca: Cornell University Press, 1991), 217, 204. The concept of "hegemony" here is of course Antonio Gramsci's.

31. Carolyn Porter, "History and Literature: 'After the New Historicism,'" *New Literary History* 21.2 (Winter 1990), 253–72, 268.

32. Peter Erickson, *Rewriting Shakespeare, Rewriting Ourselves* (Berkeley: University of California Press, 1991), 1, 24.

7. PERSONATION AND PLAYING: "SECRETLY OPEN" ROLE-PLAYING

1. See Paul Yachnin in Anthony Dawson and Yachnin, *The Culture of Playgoing in Shakespeare's England* (Cambridge and New York: Cambridge University Press, 2001), 58.

2. Meredith Anne Skura, *Shakespeare the Actor and the Purpose of Playing* (Chicago and London: University of Chicago Press, 1993), 29.

3. Jean E. Howard, "Scripts and/versus Playhouses: Ideological Production and the Renaissance Public Stage," in Valerie Wayne, ed., *The Matter of Difference: Materialist Feminist Criticism of Shakespeare* (Ithaca: Cornell University Press, 1991), 221–36 (at 228).

4. Ibid.

5. David Schalkwyk, *Speech and Performance in Shakespeare's Sonnets and Plays* (Cambridge: Cambridge University Press, 2002), 38.

6. See Martin Ingram, "Ridings, Rough Music and the Reform of Popular Culture in Early Modern England," *Past and Present* 105 (November 1984), 79–113, 96–7. For the insurrectionary aspect, vitally relevant in cross-dressing but also a good many other personations of women, see Natalie Zemon Davis, *Society and Culture in Early Modern France* (London: Duckworth, 1975), 140.

7. On the festive strain in early modern culture, we continue to owe a great and lasting debt to C. L. Barber even when he tended to play down the frictions we here underline. See Barber, *Shakespeare's Festive Comedy: A Study of Dramatic Form and Its Relation to Social Custom* (Princeton: Princeton University Press, 1959). See also François Laroque, *Shakespeare's Festive World: Elizabethan Seasonal Entertainment and the Professional Stage*, trans. Janet Lloyd (Cambridge: Cambridge University Press, 1991).

8. See the chapter "Histories in Elizabethan Performance," in Robert Weimann, *Author's Pen and Actor's Voice* (Cambridge: Cambridge University Press, 2000), 109–50.

9. Jean Alter, *A Sociosemiotic Theory of Theatre* (Philadelphia: University of Pennsylvania Press, 1990), 29.

10. Thomas Heywood, *An Apology for Actors*, facsimile edn (New York: Garland Publishing, 1973), C4r.

11. See Weimann, *Author's Pen and Actor's Voice*, esp. 128–31, 133–4, and 154–8.

12. Edward Burns, *Character: Acting and Being on the Pre-modern Stage* (New York: St. Martin's Press, 1990), 13.

13. As given in *Henslowe's Diary*, ed. R. A. Foakes and R. T. Rickert (Cambridge: Cambridge University Press, 1961), 7. See also E. K. Chambers, *The Elizabethan Stage*, 4 vols. (Oxford: Clarendon Press, 1923), 2:98.

14. Terence Hawkes, *Shakespeare in the Present* (London and New York: Routledge, 2002), 110. For the full weight and reach of Hawkes's argument, see his early study, *Shakespeare's Talking Animals*, in which "the resonant world" of orality is brilliantly shown to engage "the silent world of writing" (*Shakespeare's Talking Animals: Language in Drama and Society* [London: Edward Arnold, 1973], 53 ff).

15. M. C. Bradbrook, *The Rise of the Common Player: A Study of Actor and Society in Shakespeare's England* (London: Chatto & Windus, 1962), 123.

16. Michael D. Bristol, *Shakespeare's America/America's Shakespeare* (London: Routledge, 1990), 105.

17. Burns, *Character: Acting and Being*, 70; cf. 66, 128.

18. Andrew Gurr, *The Shakespearean Stage 1574–1642*, 3rd edn (Cambridge: Cambridge University Press, 1992), 100.

19. Gabriel Harvey, *Pierces Supererogation or A new Prayse of the Old Asse A Preparatiue to Certaine Larger Discourses, Intituled Nashes S. Fame* (London: John Wolfe, 1593), 197 (Bb4).

20. On "embodied" writing, see Douglas Bruster, "The Structural Transformation of Print in Late Elizabethan England," ch. 3 in Bruster, *Shakespeare and the Question of Culture: Early Modern Literature and the Cultural Turn* (New York: Palgrave Macmillan, 2003), 65–93.

21. Patrice Pavis, *Languages of the Stage: Essays in the Semiology of the Theatre* (New York: Performing Arts Journal Publications, 1982), 45.

22. Judith Butler, *Excitable Speech: A Politics of the Performative* (New York: Routledge, 1997), 10. Butler here cites Shoshana Felman's study, *The Literary Speech Act* (Ithaca: Cornell University Press, 1983), 94.

23. Butler, *Excitable Speech*, 10 f., 166 n8.

24. Émile Benveniste, *Problèmes de linguistique générale*, 2 Parts (Paris: Gallimard, 1974), 2:80, 82 (italics in original).

25. As an illustration of a characterizing, specifically presentational use of the *platea*, we refer the reader to Weimann, *Author's Pen and Actor's Voice*, 208–12.

26. Gordon Williams, *A Glossary of Shakespeare's Sexual Language* (London: Athlone Press, 1997), 175, 313.

27. Ibid., 222.

28. Peter Thomson, "The Elizabethan Actor: A Matter of Temperament," *Studies in Theatre and Performance* 20.1 (2000), 4–13; 5.

29. M. M. Bakhtin, *The Dialogic Imagination: Four Essays*, ed. Michael Holquist, trans. Caryl Emerson and Holquist (Austin: University of Texas Press, 1981), 274 ff.

30. Ibid., 276.

31. Ibid., 279. For a discussion of Bakhtin's skepticism concerning the polyphony of early modern drama in England, see Douglas Bruster, "'Come To the Tent Again': The Passionate Shepherd, Dramatic Rape, and Lyric Time," *Criticism* 33.1 (1991), 49–72.

32. Benveniste, *Problèmes de linguistique générale*, Part II, 80, 81.

33. On the likelihood of Kemp playing Falstaff, see Martin Holmes, *Shakespeare and His Players* (New York: Charles Scribner's Sons, 1972), 47–50, and John Dover Wilson, *The Fortunes of Falstaff* (Cambridge and New York: Cambridge University Press, 1943/4). Wilson takes note of the "Enter Will" stage direction in the Quarto of *2 Henry IV*, and suggests, partly on the basis of its similarity to the "Enter Will Kemp" stage direction in the second Quarto of *Romeo and Juliet*, that such "is best explained, I think, as a Falstaff entry for the same player" (124). David Wiles supports the Kemp-Falstaff linkage in *Shakespeare's Clown: Actor and Text in the Elizabethan Playhouse* (Cambridge: Cambridge University Press, 1987), but a dissenting opinion was registered in a review of his book by T. J. King, who holds that "It ... seems likely that Burbage, the

leading actor of the Chamberlain's Men, played Falstaff, the largest role in *1 Henry IV*." See King in *Shakespeare Quarterly* 39.4 (1988), 518–19, 519.

34. Francis Berry, *The Shakespearean Inset: Word and Picture* (London: Routledge and Kegan Paul, 1965), 147.
35. Ibid., 3.

8. CHARACTER/ACTOR: THE DEEP MATRIX

1. For Alter's distinction, see pp. 20–1 and p. 224, note 8, in this volume.
2. Paul Yachnin, in Anthony Dawson and Paul Yachnin, *The Culture of Playgoing in Shakespeare's England* (Cambridge and New York: Cambridge University Press, 2001), 58.
3. Meredith Anne Skura, *Shakespeare the Actor and the Purpose of Playing* (Chicago: University of Chicago Press, 1993), 9.
4. Dawson and Yachnin, *The Culture of Playgoing*, 32. Dawson is here responding to Michael Shapiro's *Gender in Play on the Shakespearean Stage: Boy Heroines and Female Pages* (Ann Arbor: University of Michigan Press, 1994), 62. See also our references to Shapiro's foundational analysis in the Introduction to this volume.
5. See, for instance, Douglas Bruster and Robert Weimann, *Prologues to Shakespeare's Theatre: Performance and Liminality in Early Modern Drama* (London and New York: Routledge, 2004), esp. 117–34, and Robert Weimann, "Playing with a Difference: Revisiting 'Pen' and 'Voice' in Shakespeare's Theater," *Shakespeare Quarterly* 50.4 (1999), 415–32.
6. Shapiro, *Gender in Play*, 62. The phrase is similarly used and developed in John Gillies's unpublished paper on "Personation and Complicity"; we are grateful to the author for permission to cite it.
7. For an important analysis of the available evidence concerning early playgoers' responses to early modern drama, see Charles Whitney, *Early Responses to Renaissance Drama* (Cambridge: Cambridge University Press, 2006).
8. Benveniste points to the general interaction between *parole* or discourse and subjectivity: the "'I' refers to the act of individual discourse in which it is pronounced" and "so it is literally true that the basis of subjectivity is in the exercise of language." See Émile Benveniste, *Problems in General Linguistics*, trans. Mary Elizabeth Meek (Coral Gables: University of Miami Press, 1971), 226.
9. Elaine Scarry, *The Body in Pain* (New York and Oxford: Oxford University Press, 1985), 249, 169.
10. Ibid., 220. At this point, we recall Helmuth Plessner's anthropological distinction between *being* in the form of a *Leib*, as visceral, nonrepresentable part of corporeality, and *having* as disposable and representable a *Körper*. This distinction appears indispensable in any attempt, as in Bryan Reynolds's and William West's collection, *Rematerializing Shakespeare* (New York: Palgrave, 2005). See the Introduction to this volume.
11. Here we would mention, for example, Edward Burns, *Character: Acting and Being on the Pre-modern Stage* (New York: St. Martin's Press, 1990), and

Christy Desmet, *Reading Shakespeare's Characters* (Amherst: University of Massachusetts Press, 1992).

12. David Schalkwyk, *Speech and Performance in Shakespeare's Sonnets and Plays* (Cambridge: Cambridge University Press, 2002), 200 (following quotation at 208).

13. See Bridget Escolme, *Talking to the Audience: Shakespeare, Performance, Self* (Abingdon and New York: Routledge, 2005), and Richard Hillman, *Self-speaking in Medieval and Early Modern English Drama: Subjectivity, Discourse, and the Stage* (New York: St. Martin's Press, 1997).

14. On liminality in the playgoing experience, see Bruster and Weimann, *Prologues to Shakespeare's Theatre*, esp. viii–ix, 2, 31–40, 130–1, and Robert Weimann, "Thresholds to Memory and Commodity in Shakespeare's Endings," *Representations* 53 (1996), 1–20.

15. For a more detailed reading of Shakespeare's endings, see Robert Weimann, *Author's Pen and Actor's Voice* (Cambridge: Cambridge University Press, 2000), 216–45.

16. *Mankind* in *Three Late Medieval Morality Plays*, ed. G. A. Lester (London: A. & C. Black, 1999).

17. Hillman, *Self-speaking*, 86.

18. See in this context Richard Paul Knowles, *Reading the Material Theatre* (Cambridge: Cambridge University Press, 2004), with the emphasis on the realness of this material medium. We have also benefited from Hans Ulrich Gumbrecht, *Production of Presence: What Meaning Cannot Convey* (Stanford: Stanford University Press, 2004), and the distinguished work in German by Erika Fischer-Lichte, including *Ästhetik des Performativen* (Frankfurt: Suhrkamp, 2004). See also Dieter Mersch, *Ereignis und Aura: Untersuchungen zu einer Ästhetik des Performativen* (Frankfurt: Suhrkamp, 2002), and the collection edited by Joseph Früchtl and Jörg Zimmermann, *Ästhetik der Inszenierung: Dimensionen eines künstlerischen, kulturellen und gesellschaftlichen Phänomens* (Frankfurt: Suhrkamp, 2001). In English we have the important studies of Philip Auslander, including *Presence and Resistance: Postmodernism and Cultural Politics in Contemporary American Performance* (Ann Arbor: University of Michigan Press, 1992) and *From Acting to Performance: Essays in Modernism and Postmodernism* (London and New York: Routledge, 1997). In the way of a good seismograph, Simon Shepherd and Mick Wallis in *Drama/Theatre/Performance* (London and New York: Routledge, 2004) use their discussion of "Representation and Presence" (225–35) to look back on the "use of the word presence in the theory decade"; as against "Derrida's overstatement of the case with respect to a 'theological theatre,'" they proceed, in reference to Eugenio Barba, to emphasize the "physical . . . learnt muscular disciplines" of the actor as a "pre-expressive" real; together with "the way the performer stands, occupies space, physically 'is'" (234).

19. Escolme, *Talking to the Audience*, 148–9.

20. Ibid., 45.

21. Fischer-Lichte, *Ästhetik des Performativen*, 139.

22. Ibid., 29.
23. Shoshana Felman, *The Literary Speech Act: Don Juan with J. L. Austin, or Seduction in Two Languages*, trans. Catherine Porter (Ithaca: Cornell University Press, 1983), 96.
24. Judith Butler, *Excitable Speech: A Politics of the Performative* (New York: Routledge, 1997), 10.
25. Ibid., 10 ff.
26. William West, *Theatres and Encyclopedias in Early Modern Europe* (Cambridge and New York: Cambridge University Press, 2002), 63. For Theodor Zwinger's encyclopedic treatise, see the incisive analysis of how the humanist's "timeless space of print replaces the imaginary space of the world, not only ekphrastically," 52.
27. Catherine Belsey, "Constructing the Subject: Deconstructing the Text," in Judith Newton and Deborah Rosenfelt, eds., *Feminist Criticism and Social Change* (London: Methuen, 1985), esp. 48–51; the following quotations are from, respectively, 48–49, 50, 49.
28. Belsey, ibid., 63.
29. Auslander, *From Acting to Performance*, 36.
30. Manfred Pfister, "Reading the Body: The Corporeality of Shakespeare's Text," in Hanna Scolnicov and Peter Holland, eds., *Reading Plays: Interpretation and Reception* (Cambridge and New York: Cambridge University Press, 1992), 110–22.

9. CHARACTER: DEPTH, DIALOGUE, PAGE

1. For discussion of print's effects upon the drama, see Julie Stone Peters, *The Theatre of the Book, 1480–1880: Print, Text, and Performance in Europe* (Oxford and New York: Oxford University Press, 2000); Douglas A. Brooks, *From Playhouse to Printing House: Drama and Authorship in Early Modern England* (Cambridge and New York: Cambridge University Press, 2000); and David Scott Kastan, *Shakespeare and the Book* (Cambridge and New York: Cambridge University Press, 2001).
2. Barbara Mowat, "The Theater and Literary Culture," in John D. Cox and David Scott Kastan, eds., *A New History of Early English Drama* (New York: Columbia University Press, 1997), 213–30 (at 216). The following instances come from Mowat's chapter.
3. Ibid., 213, 218–22, 216.
4. William B. Worthen, *Print and the Poetics of Modern Drama* (Cambridge: Cambridge University Press, 2005), 23.
5. V. N. Vološinov, *Marxism and the Philosophy of Language*, trans. Ladislav Matejka and I. R. Titunik (Cambridge, MA: Harvard University Press, 1986), 95 (italics in original).
6. M. M. Bakhtin, *The Dialogic Imagination: Four Essays*, ed. Michael Holquist, trans. Caryl Emerson and Holquist (Austin: University of Texas Press, 1981), 324, 283; cf. esp. 279–96.

7. See Douglas Bruster, "The Structural Transformation of Print in Late Elizabethan England," ch. 3 in Bruster, *Shakespeare and the Question of Culture: Early Modern Literature and the Cultural Turn* (New York: Palgrave Macmillan, 2003), 65–93.

8. Lukas Erne, *Shakespeare as Literary Dramatist* (Cambridge: Cambridge University Press, 2003), 63.

9. For record of (and further citations for) these two passages, see the Appendix to *The Riverside Shakespeare*, 1836, 1837.

10. On the burgeoning scope of "wit" in early modern London, see Ian Munro, "Shakespeare's Jestbook: Wit, Print, Performance," *ELH* 71.1 (Spring 2004), 89–113. For Ling's central role in advancing this new genre of publication, we have benefited from Steven Mentz's "The Age of Ling: Publishing and Early Modern English Literary Culture," a paper presented at the 2006 meeting of the Modern Language Association.

11. Donald Beecher, ed., *Characters, Together with Poems, News, Edicts, and Paradoxes (Based on the Eleventh Edition of "A Wife Now the Widow of Sir Thomas Overbury")* (Ottawa: Dovehouse Editions, 2003), 48. For a much-needed qualification of arguments concerning Theophrastus and character-writing in the Renaissance, see John Considine, "The Humanist Antecedents of the First English Character-Books," unpublished PhD Diss., Oxford University, 1994.

12. Cynthia Marshall, "Shakespeare, Crossing the Rubicon," *Shakespeare Survey* 53 (2000), 73–88. Marshall's intriguing reading extends foundational work by such scholars as M. W. MacCallum and J. A. K. Thomson, the latter of whom suggested that Plutarch virtually taught Shakespeare how to write his great tragedies – especially in the apprentice work of *Julius Caesar*.

13. Ibid., 73, 80.

14. On the verse/prose dynamic within the world-picturing system of early modern drama, see Douglas Bruster, "The Politics of Shakespeare's Prose," in Bryan Reynolds and William West, eds., *Rematerializing Shakespeare* (New York: Palgrave Macmillan, 2005), 95–114.

15. See Katherine Eisaman Maus, *Inwardness and Theater in the English Renaissance* (Chicago: University of Chicago Press, 1995), especially concerning the "inwardness topos" and its "very widespread circulation" (15).

16. See the facsimile and transcription of these pages in W. W. Greg, ed., *Dramatic Documents from the Elizabethan Playhouses* (Oxford: Clarendon Press, 1931).

17. David Bradley, *From Text to Performance in the Elizabethan Theatre: Preparing the Play for the Stage* (Cambridge: Cambridge University Press, 1992), 25.

18. James R. Siemon, *Word Against Word: Shakespearean Utterance* (Amherst, MA: University of Massachusetts Press, 2002), 2.

19. See William Dodd, "Destined Livery? Character and Person in Shakespeare," *Shakespeare Survey* 51 (1998), 147–58.

20. We would point out that when John Weever chose to flatter Shakespeare's abilities in characterization, he chose just such a firing topos. Although

Shakespeare's characters initially seem to be the offspring of "*Apollo* . . . and none other," Weever eventually understands them as the writer's own offspring: "They burn in love thy children *Shakespeare* het them, / Go, woo thy Muse more Nymphish brood beget them." "[H]et" here means "heated." See Weever's poem in E. A. J. Honigmann, *John Weever: A Biography of a Literary Associate of Shakespeare and Jonson, Together with a Photographic Facsimile of Weever's "Epigrammes" (1599)* (Manchester: Manchester University Press, 1987), 27.

21. Louis Montrose, "The Elizabethan Subject and the Spenserian Text," in Patricia Parker and David Quint, eds., *Literary Theory/Renaissance Texts* (Baltimore and London: Johns Hopkins University Press, 1986), 303–40 (quotation at 331 [italics in original]).

22. See, for example, Ludwig Wittgenstein, *Philosophical Investigations: The English Text of the Third Edition*, trans. G. E. M. Anscombe (New York: Macmillan, 1958), 2–21 and *passim*. On "saying and showing" in Derrida, see also David Schalkwyk, *Literature and the Touch of the Real* (Newark: University of Delaware Press, 2004), 82–4.

23. A. C. Bradley, *Shakespearean Tragedy: Lectures on "Hamlet," "Othello," "King Lear," "Macbeth"* (London: Macmillan, 1907), 13.

24. Cf. William Shakespeare, *Troilus and Cressida*, New Variorum, ed. Harold H. Hillebrand (Philadelphia and London: Lippincott, 1953), 416–18, 411–15.

25. On John Davies's influential treatise and some of the governing conventions it unfolds, see the comparative essay by Ruby Nemser, "*Nosce Teipsum* and the *Essais* of Montaigne," *SEL* 16.1 (1976), 95–103.

26. As J. Leeds Barroll, *Artificial Persons: The Formation of Character in the Tragedies of Shakespeare* (New York: Columbia University Press, 1974), notes, "any human's claim to his own 'identity' was conditional upon his merging in some measure with a 'hyper-personality', involving some 'identification' with God, Being, Essence, or Beauty" (70).

27. Thomas F. van Laan, *Role-Playing in Shakespeare* (Toronto: University of Toronto Press, 1978), 25. For a visual demonstration of what van Laan describes, see the illustration from a 1568 edition of Terence's *Woman of Andros* as reproduced in Peters, *The Theatre of the Book, 1480–1880*, 182 (fig. 38). As described by Peters, the image not only shows various scenes as transpiring simultaneously (not unusual in Renaissance representation), but adds "a series of criss-crossing vectors, identifying a complex set of familial, social, and narrative relations among the characters" (181).

28. Van Laan, *Role-Playing*, 25.

29. Ricardo J. Quinones, *The Renaissance Discovery of Time* (Cambridge, MA: Harvard University Press, 1972), 313.

30. See M. C. Bradbrook, *Shakespeare and Elizabethan Poetry* (Harmondsworth: Penguin, 1964), 48.

31. Edward Burns, *Character: Acting and Being on the Pre-Modern Stage* (New York: St. Martin's Press, 1990), 59, 50 ff.

32. See Walter Benjamin, *Gesammelte Schriften*, ed. Rolf Tiedemann and Hermann Schweppenhäuser (Frankfurt am Main: Suhrkamp, 1974), 1.1.342.

33. John Stevens, *Medieval Romance: Themes and Approaches* (New York: W. W. Norton, 1974), 170.

34. See Robert Weimann, *Authority and Representation in Early Modern Discourse* (Baltimore and London: Johns Hopkins University Press, 1996), 147–89.

10. *KING LEAR*: REPRESENTATIONS ON STAGE AND PAGE

1. Throughout, our reading of *King Lear* as an open, theatrically self-aware text is indebted to, even as it seeks to augment, various historicist readings of the tragedy. Among the more influential of these has been Richard Halpern's chapter "*Historica Passio*: *King Lear*'s Fall into Feudalism" in his study *The Poetics of Primitive Accumulation: English Renaissance Culture and the Genealogy of Capital* (Ithaca: Cornell University Press, 1991), 215–69. More recently, a critic aware of "*King Lear*'s metatheatrical commentary on its own thematic obsession with darkness and discovery" holds that such discovery redounds primarily upon "the fundamental contingency of sovereign power." See Dan Brayton, "Angling in the Lake of Darkness: Possession, Dispossession, and the Politics of Discovery in *King Lear*," *ELH* 70 (2003), 399–426, 420, 421. For an influential account of theatricality in this play, see Stephen Greenblatt's reading in "Shakespeare and the Exorcists," in Patricia Parker and Geoffrey Hartman, eds., *Shakespeare and the Question of Theory* (New York: Methuen, 1985), 163–87; later revised in his *Shakespearean Negotiations: The Circulation of Social Energy in Renaissance England* (Berkeley: University of California Press, 1988), 94–128.

2. Thomas Davies, *Dramatic Miscellanies*, 3 vols. (London, 1875), 2:262–8; cited in William Shakespeare, *King Lear*, ed. Jay L. Halio (Cambridge: Cambridge University Press, 1992), 37.

3. For the relation of *King Lear* to those issues of poverty and vagabondage that haunted the early seventeenth century, see William C. Carroll, *Fat King, Lean Beggar: Representations of Poverty in the Age of Shakespeare* (Ithaca: Cornell University Press, 1996), 108–207.

4. Gayatri Chakravorty Spivak, "Can the Subaltern Speak?," in Cary Nelson and Lawrence Grossberg, eds., *Marxism and the Interpretation of Culture* (Urbana: University of Illinois Press, 1988), 271–313, esp. 276–9.

5. See George Hartley, *The Abyss of Representation: Marxism and the Postmodern Sublime* (Durham: Duke University Press, 2003). What is at stake here are "relations" which "assign rank and influence to others" (183). For the concept of what is "representative," see the somewhat limited definition of the "typical register" in Susan Wells, *The Dialectics of Representation* (Baltimore: Johns Hopkins University Press, 1985).

6. Katherine Eisaman Maus, *Inwardness and Theater in the English Renaissance* (Chicago: University of Chicago Press, 1995), 32.

7. Ibid., 35. For the rather troubling "continuities" of inwardness, its past significance and present meaning, see Maus's helpful suggestions (210–15).

8. Bertrand Evans, *Shakespeare's Tragic Practice* (Oxford: Clarendon Press, 1979), 148.

9. Ibid., 149, 148.

10. A reference first noted in the *New Shakespeare* edition of the play by George Ian Duthie and John Dover Wilson (Cambridge: Cambridge University Press, 1960); we owe the "foot-ball"/tennis connection to George K. Hunter's Penguin edition, 207. Note that Lear also uses "bandy" at 2.4.175, assuring Regan that it is not in her "To bandy hasty words."

11. Catherine Belsey, *Shakespeare and the Loss of Eden* (London: Macmillan, 1999), 7.

12. See Robert Weimann, *Author's Pen and Actor's Voice* (Cambridge: Cambridge University Press, 2000), 227–33.

13. Evans, *Shakespeare's Tragic Practice*, 179–80.

14. Lynne Magnusson, *Shakespeare and Social Dialogue: Dramatic Language and Elizabethan Letters* (Cambridge: Cambridge University Press, 1999), 143. For "communication," in Ulysses's words, as a key to the formation and identity of a dramatic character, see Robert Weimann's essay, "Society and the Individual in Shakespeare's Conception of Character," *Shakespeare Survey* 34 (1981), 23–31.

15. William Dodd, "Impossible Worlds: What Happens in *King Lear*, Act 1, Scene 1?," *Shakespeare Quarterly* 50.4 (1999), 477–507.

16. Ibid., 501.

17. Ibid., 506.

18. Here and in what follows we are indebted to Duncan Salkeld's remarkable study, *Madness and Drama in the Age of Shakespeare* (Manchester: Manchester University Press, 1993).

19. Michel Foucault, *Madness and Civilization: A History of Insanity in the Age of Reason* (New York: Random House, 1965), x. See also Shoshana Felman, *Writing and Madness*, trans. M. N. Evans et al. (Ithaca: Cornell University Press, 1984), esp. 37–54, where she discusses Jacques Derrida's critical position.

20. Jacques Derrida, "Cogito and the History of Madness," in Derrida, *Writing and Difference*, trans. Alan Bass (Chicago: University of Chicago Press, 1978), 54 (italics in original). By implication this emphasis contradicts Descartes's and, largely, Foucault's concepts of madness as "only a sensory and corporeal fault" (51) and helps underline "the irreducible role" of silence, "outside and *against* which alone language can emerge" (54; italics in original).

21. Michael Shapiro, *Gender in Play on the Shakespearean Stage: Boy Heroines and Female Pages* (Ann Arbor: University of Michigan Press, 1994), 11.

22. For evidence demonstrating the antic scenario as madly digressive challenge of the play's world-picture, see Weimann's reading of the "antic disposition" in *Author's Pen and Actor's Voice*, 161–79.

23. For a classic study of these ramifications of "representation," see Hanna Fenichel Pitkin, *The Concept of Representation* (Berkeley: University of California Press, 1967); "attending not merely to 'representation' itself, but to the entire family of words . . . including 'representative'" (6), she thereby "links representation with activity . . . political, juridical and symbolic" (12).

24. See Stephen Greenblatt, "Invisible Bullets," in Jonathan Dollimore and Alan Sinfield, eds., *Political Shakespeare* (Manchester: Manchester University Press, 1985), 44, and Thomas Cartelli, "Ideology and Subversion in the Shakespearean Set Speech," *ELH* 53.1 (1986), 1–25.

25. Obviously, these arguments are immeasurably indebted to the work of social and political historians, who can here be consulted only in passing. The intriguing element in sixteenth-century social history is that centralization and diversification advanced simultaneously. As we noted elsewhere, the "centralization of government and the emergence of nascent forms of nation-wide administration went hand in hand with the gradual formation, and even polarization, of distinct classes, interests, lifestyles." See Robert Weimann, *Authority and Representation in Early Modern Discourse* (Baltimore and London: Johns Hopkins University Press, 1996), 193. Thus we have a whole series of socio-cultural differentiations in "speech, dress, manners, living conditions, leisure pursuits and literary interests," most of them resulting from "a process of withdrawal by the gentry and middling groups from a common heritage of assumptions." The quotation here is from Anthony Fletcher and John Stevenson, eds., *Order and Disorder in Early Modern England* (Cambridge: Cambridge University Press, 1985), 10.

26. See John Drakakis on this problem in "'Fashion It Thus': *Julius Caesar* and the Politics of Theatrical Representation," *Shakespeare Survey* 44 (1992), 65–73.

27. It is more than fortuitous, then, that the most distinguished Lacanian view of *King Lear* that we have offers a striking element of concurrence with the present reading. See Catherine Belsey, "*King Lear* and the Missing Salt," ch. 3 in her recent study *Why Shakespeare?* (London and New York: Palgrave Macmillan, 2007), 42–64.

Index

acting 18, 51, 163, 174, 187
  awareness of 63–4
  and character 20, 21, 163, 164, 165, 168, 169, 170,
      171, 172, 176, 177, 185, 187, 188, 189, 190,
      211, 213
  and disguise 120
  divided 7–8
  as inversion 18
  and performance 45–6, 54, 144, 174, 177, 189
  practice of 144, 152, 156
  presence of 171
  and representation 8–9, 54, 156
  as transformation 19–20
acting companies
  Admiral's Men 17
  Leicester's Men 80
  Lord Chamberlain's Men 4, 43, 58, 110, 112,
      144, 248
  Lord Strange's Men 17, 79, 85, 86
  Queen's Men 80–1, 142, 144, 163
  Sir Richard Cholmeley's Men 24, 178
Adams, John 81
Alleyn, Edward 187
Alter, Jean 20, 21, 46, 66, 80, 143, 224, 227, 232,
      236, 246, 248
Altman, Joel 28, 230, 241
amphibology 28, 32
anachronism 69–70, 82, 113, 115, 136, 205
Archer, William 21
argumentum ab utramque partem 28
Armin, Robert 78, 83, 86, 87–8, 89, 95,
      99, 142
Artaud, Antonin 143
Astington, John 79, 224, 232, 237, 238
Attewell, George 81
auctoritas 11, 200, 215, 225, 228
  see also authority
audience
  awareness of 119, 201, 211
    and performance 201–2
    and personation 204

and representation 202
  and representational meaning 202
participation of 165
relationship with 208
Auerbach, Eric 234
Auslander, Philip 177, 249, 250
Austin, J. L. 6
authority 54–5, 72, 73, 122, 208, 218,
      219, 221
  and bifold structure 72
  in clowning 84, 89
  as derived from forceful uses of language 9, 57,
      94, 101, 110, 112, 116
  as derived from skillful bodily show and
      performance 50, 52, 53, 57
  in disguise 126, 131, 136, 138
  and identity 190–1, 222–3
  inversion of 131
  and religion 53
  and representation 50, 52, 126, 136, 200, 210,
      216, 217, 220, 221, 222, 223
  and Vice 37
  see also auctoritas; *gestus*: and authority;
      performance: and authority; *potestas*

Bacon, Francis 72, 73, 181, 237
Baker, Susan 244
Bakhtin, Mikhail 12, 30, 40, 89, 90, 149, 179, 180,
      226, 231, 239, 247, 250
Barba, Eugenio 14, 143, 172, 227, 249
Barber, C. L. 50, 234, 246
Barker, Granville 13
Barroll, Leeds 58, 235, 252
Beaurline, L. A. 235, 237
Beckerman, Bernard 7, 24, 27, 224
Bednarz, James 242
Beecher, David 251
Belsey, Catherine 11, 175, 206, 225, 241, 244, 250,
      254, 255
Benjamin, Walter 73, 198, 237, 252
Bentley, G. E. 86, 239

Lightning Source UK Ltd.
Milton Keynes UK
UKOW04f1811071113

220646UK00001B/65/P